# DAVE BRUBECK

*a life in time*

## PHILIP CLARK

Da Capo Press

Hachette Books
Hachette Book Group
1290 Avenue of the Americas
New York, NY 10104
HachetteBooks.com
@HachetteBooks
Twitter.com/HachetteBooks
Instagram.com/HachetteBooks

First Edition: February 2020

Hachette Books is a division of Hachette Book Group, Inc.

The Hachette Books name and logo are trademarks of Hachette Book Group,
Inc.

The publisher is not responsible for websites (or their content) that are not
owned by the publisher.

The Hachette Speakers Bureau provides a wide range of authors for speaking
events. To find out more, go to www.hachettespeakersbureau.com or call
(866) 376-6591.

Print book interior design by Jeff Williams.

Library of Congress Cataloging-in-Publication Data has been applied for.

ISBNs: 978-0-306-92164-3 (hardcover); 978-0-306-92165-0 (e-book)

Printed in the United States of America

LSC-C

10 9 8 7 6 5 4 3 2 1

*For Olivia, Humphrey, and Lovell.*
*And Monk and Willow.*

# CONTENTS

# FOREWORD

Classical, jazz, rock, country, blues, rhythm and blues, bluegrass, avant-garde, hip-hop, contemporary classical, modern classical, modern jazz, free jazz, fusion, electric jazz, freeform country, world music, island music, standards, film music, alternative rock, indie rock, folk rock, grunge, punk rock, psychedelic rock, post-rock, garage rock, math rock, progressive rock, pop, electropop, electro swing, Europop, Britpop, power pop, Latin jazz, bebop, EDM, trap, dubstep, house, lo-fi, alternative R&B, rap, mumble rap, soul, funk, folk, reggae, metal, heavy metal.

On and on (and on), as the years advance, the music changes, cultures change, all things change while we continually attempt to describe the music and art we make. We need to talk about it. It's an essential part of life—a basic and native sense to be artistic, create something beautiful, have art in our lives.

We try to explain to others what music is; encourage them to understand. As musicians and artists, we want them to get it—to participate. We inherently know that tuning up to the wavelength of art and creativity will bring benefits, will make life more enjoyable, lift the spirits.

The talk and discussion about music and art comes in all forms—but basically two: friendly with a high interest and critical. Mostly, the artists and public converse with friendly high interest—whereas you'll find the critical approach in the media and in schools and universities.

Personally, I have found the only way to understand and appreciate music and art is to touch the artists making it. To listen, to look, to experience, and, best of all, to do.

Dave and Iola were an amazing couple. My sweet wife, Gayle, and I had the pleasure of visiting them in their Connecticut home one time. They had an ideal relationship as man and wife and as artistic collaborators. Very similar to Gayle's and my life together. They were a big inspiration to us.

As the years and decades rolled on, my appreciation for Dave and for his compositions, bands, and piano playing increased as I listened and experienced his dedication and commitment to creating his music. In the 1970s, when the term "fusion" was invented to negatively describe Return to Forever, the Mahavishnu Orchestra, and Weather Report, I realized that Dave's music was an early breakthrough well before the 70s. That combination of composed and improvised music forms was well under way in his creative hands. The musicians and artists were combining more influences from other parts of the world and other cultures. The artists were sharing their ideas more quickly. Dave was a pioneer and an innovator.

My memory of playing "Strange Meadowlark" at Dave's memorial, with Iola in the front row with the whole Brubeck family, is a beautiful spiritual moment I won't ever forget for the love that we shared in that great cathedral for Dave.

Words are simply inadequate to describe music and art—or Dave Brubeck—unless you are a poet.

I and the music world are forever thankful for Dave's reverence for creativity and irreverence for categories.

CHICK COREA
*November, 2019*

# INTRODUCTION

Once I had my title, *not* writing became more of a problem than sitting down to begin.

*A Life in Time* was a title that encapsulated the classic biographical model of "the life and times," but it also opened up the terrain. The project was not to write a book that marched through Dave Brubeck's life chronologically—casually observing, perhaps as an aside, that shortly after his quartet recorded "Take Five" in 1959, Vice President Richard Nixon flew on a trade mission to Moscow and Billie Holiday died. The plan instead was to thread his life back through the times that formed it. Brubeck saw active service as a solider during the Second World War; he led a commercially successful, racially mixed jazz group during some of the ugliest days of American segregation; and in the late 1960s and early 1970s he created a series of large-scale compositions that reflected variously on issues of race, religion, and the messy politics of an uncertain era. Threading his life back through these times was both a musical and a social concern—I wanted to shine a light on how Brubeck, thoughtful and sensitive as he was, had been changed as a musician and as a man by the troubled times through which he lived and during which he produced such optimistic, life-enhancing art.

As a biographer in search of a title, I was handed a gift by Brubeck, even if it took me a while to realize it. He was a man obsessed with time. From the moment he founded the Dave Brubeck Quartet in 1951 to only eighteen months before his death at the end of 2012, Brubeck spent much of his life touring the world, which adds up to sixty years of playing concerts in every continent of the world, including some countries that today would be too dangerous to contemplate visiting.

He was also a man impatient with time. Finding time to play jazz, time to compose, and time to devote to his wife Iola and their six children were all important to Brubeck, and with only so many hours in the day, one solution was to overlap those activities. Compositions originally written for his extended sacred pieces were adapted for his jazz groups; and, if you want to spend more time with your teenage children, one sure way to know where they are every night is to play jazz with them. Beginning in 1973, Brubeck toured with three of his sons—Darius, Chris, and Dan—as Two Generations of Brubeck and the New Brubeck Quartet, his initial reluctance to embrace their newfangled cultural reference points—which included rock, funk, and soul music—quickly forgotten.

But that word, *time*, also had another meaning altogether. Whenever I interviewed Brubeck, it never took long for two key terms to emerge: *polytonality* and *polyrhythm*. Polytonality—music sounding in two or more keys simultaneously—and polyrhythm—overlays of different rhythmic pulses and grooves—were, like the attitude he took toward life, techniques that allowed obsessions and tics to coexist. Brubeck plied his music with overlaps: between musical cultures in "Blue Rondo à la Turk," which combined an indigenous Turkish rhythm with the blues, and in "Three to Get Ready," which squared the circle of a waltz by inserting bars of 4/4; between different time signatures, like his version of "Someday My Prince Will Come," which managed to be in 4/4 and 3/4 at the same time; between the radically diverse range of musical styles through which he waded in his improvised solos—no sweat as Liszt flowed into James P. Johnson.

And *time* also meant time signatures. "Take Five" in 5/4 time, "Blue Rondo à la Turk" in an asymmetrically arranged 9/8, "Unsquare Dance" in 7/4—before Brubeck, no jazz musician had worked so consistently, or so successfully, with extending metric possibilities. For all their bold innovations and harmonic daring, Charlie Parker, Dizzy Gillespie, and Thelonious Monk, the occasional waltz aside, kept to 4/4 time, but Brubeck's experiments with time signatures became his calling card. In the US, May 4—5/4—has become an unofficial Dave Brubeck Day and Twitter meme; and Tchaikovsky might have composed a famous waltz in 5/4 time in his *Pathétique* Symphony, but Brubeck came to own the idea of 5/4 time in the way that Van Gogh owned the sunflower and Philip Glass the arpeggio—which meant he owned nothing at all. Anyone can paint a sunflower or play music in any time signature they like; but Brubeck's 5/4 time stuck in the public imagination, to the point that he and it became inseparable.

Even before he had recorded a note of music in 5/4 or 7/4, Columbia Records bosses sniffed something in the air and decided to call his first studio album for the company *Brubeck Time*; and after the soar-away triumph of *Time Out*, Brubeck followed up with *Time Further Out, Time Changes, Countdown—Time in Outer Space*, and *Time In*. His gift to any prospective biographer, especially one searching for a title, was that word, *time*, which needed to feature as part of my title—but in a more meaningful way than a mere wisecracking play on words. Reconciling all those connotations of time, from the broadly historical to the directly musical, became my way forward. A structure pieced itself together as I took time to think through all these various meanings of *time*.

"Go back to the music if in doubt" became my mantra as I wrote, and the structural inner workings of Brubeck's music led the way from the get-go. The story within a story of the blues and Turkish music in "Blue Rondo à la Turk" and of 3/4 versus 4/4 in "Three to Get Ready," and Brubeck's knack for nesting one time signature inside another, freed up time: no need to slavishly adhere to the chronology. I was interested in investigating how one aspect of his life illuminated another against the panorama of American history; and if you're wondering why the first chapter begins in 2003 and then flips back to 1953—when the Dave Brubeck Quartet was touring in a package with Charlie Parker—that is why. Opening the book by explaining where Brubeck's music stood in relation to Parker's—who was then considered to be the very embodiment of modern jazz—journey straight to the heart of the music.

And another reason to cut direct to the chase, leaving Brubeck's birth until later, was that I didn't want to wait for the chronological narrative to catch up with my own role as an embedded reporter. In 2003, I shadowed the Dave Brubeck Quartet (then featuring Bobby Militello, Michael Moore, and Randy Jones) during a ten-day tour of the UK. I couldn't make every gig, but as the quartet traveled between their rented apartment in Maida Vale, West London, and Brighton, Southend, Manchester, and Birmingham, I had the privilege of sitting next to Dave on the bus and we talked and talked, sometimes late into the night; I also spent time with Brubeck and his wife Iola in their Maida Vale flat. Ostensibly this extended interview was for a feature commissioned by the British jazz magazine *Jazz Review*—published as "Adventures in the Sound of Modernist Swing" in July 2003—but Dave gave me hours' worth of material, many more words and memories than could be stuffed into a 3,500-word article. I always worried that my original article, rushed out in a couple of days to satisfy press deadlines, was not the finessed, definitive piece I'd hoped for. The origins of this book go back to the realization that I owed it to myself and, more importantly, to Brubeck to write something more permanent and fitting.

Most of the interview material was collected on the road in 2003, but this book also draws on face-to-face interviews recorded after that date, and occasional e-mail supplements routed through Iola's AOL account. Brubeck was, typically, very generous with his time and willing to talk, but at the age of eighty-two, his memory was fallible, especially regarding dates and names. Some things he reported as fact were directly contradicted by my subsequent research, and all such occasions are highlighted in the text. Brubeck also had a tendency—like many musicians I've interviewed—to repeat a settled account of a story that, as he told it yet again, wandered further and further from reality. I learned quickly to nudge him in another direction when I'd heard the answers before. Sometimes he held back information to protect former associates and sidemen who were still living in 2003—in one such case, I was only able to piece together the full story of why his bass player and drummer both quit suddenly at the end of 1953 by reading through his later correspondence. But almost everything he told me about the making of *Time Out* was undermined by one troubling inconsistency that, with access to other sources and the rehearsal tapes, I have done my best to iron out.

One sure way I found to keep Brubeck's interest engaged was to pose questions about less-often-discussed areas of his career, and that strategy threw up some remarkable details about his friendship with Charlie Parker. Brubeck was born in California in 1920; I was born in the north of England in 1972, and that Brubeck had so much to tell me about a time and place so far outside of my own experience became intoxicating. As he talked in 2003 about segregation in the mid-1960s— and especially about how the quartet defied the Ku Klux Klan during a now-notorious concert in Alabama in 1964—the thought that such an event had taken place only eight years before I was born haunted me. As I wrote all these years later, that Brubeck's accounts of his country's gravest shame should

have such damning relevance to Trump's America felt unbearably poignant and tragic—time overlaps, but it is also cyclic.

The origins of this book are traceable to 2003, but the origins of my relationship with Brubeck's music stretch back much
further. At Newcastle City Hall, in the early 1960s, had Brubeck
turned around to look at the seats that were arranged onstage
to accommodate a capacity crowd, he might have looked
directly into the eyes of his future biographer's father. Later my
father, who is a painter, worked on his canvases every night with
*Time Out* on his turntable. I can remember, at the age of six or
seven, keeping myself awake to hear "Blue Rondo à la Turk,"
the sound of which enthralled me; family mythology insists that
I would run into his studio cheering whenever it was played. In
the summer of 1986, during a family holiday to Spain, I found
a cassette of Brubeck's 1973 album *We're All Together Again for
the First Time* in a record shop in Figueres following a visit to the
Dalí Theatre-Museum. As we drove out of the city in the scorch-
ing Mediterranean sun, with the tape pumping through the
rental car, threatening to blow the doors off, my mother shifted
uncomfortably in the backseat next to my younger sister as the
opening track, "Truth," unfolded. This was Brubeck at his wild-
est, vaulting free-form clusters around the keyboard before
entering into a gladiatorial dialogue with drummer Alan Dawson. Once again, I was captivated.

Everything I have achieved in my life as a musician and
as a writer began with those two experiences. "Blue Rondo à
la Turk" led me to more Brubeck, then to Miles Davis, Duke
Ellington, Thelonious Monk, Charles Mingus, Ornette Coleman, and John Coltrane (and back in history to Louis Armstrong and Jelly Roll Morton). And after I played it for my
music teacher, John Hastie, "Truth" spun me in a whole other
direction. If you like this, he suggested, you might well appreciate Béla Bartók's Sonata for Two Pianos and Percussion. A trip
to the local library unearthed a long-unborrowed boxed set
in which the Bartók piece was paired with music by Karlheinz

Stockhausen. I was immediately hooked, and I returned a few days later to borrow LPs of music by Pierre Boulez, Charles Ives, and Krzysztof Penderecki.

I met Brubeck for the first time in October 1992, when I was a music student and, following a quartet concert in Manchester, he graciously agreed to look through a piano composition I'd written called *Thelonious Dreaming*. Iola took me backstage and Dave played some of my harmonies through on the piano, and then he suggested we ought to keep in touch. The next time I had some music ready, I sent it to his address in Wilton, Connecticut, and was amazed when, only a week later, a reply arrived. When I was looking for employment in 1998, I pitched an interview with Brubeck to the editor of the now-defunct *Classic CD* magazine; the Brubeck Quartet was touring the UK, and to this day, I remain convinced that the editor muddled my name with some proper journalist who knew what they were doing. But no matter. The article, my first paid piece of journalism, was duly published in the February 1999 issue, and from that point every magazine and newspaper I've written for—*Jazz Review*, the *Wire, Gramophone, Classic FM, International Piano, Choir and Organ, Jazzwise, The Guardian*, and the *Financial Times*—seemingly had cause to commission a Brubeck article. Not writing a Brubeck book was becoming a big problem for me, and after writing the program booklet for Brubeck's eighty-fifth birthday concerts with the London Symphony Orchestra at the Barbican Centre in 2005, I intimated to Dave, in the greenroom, that I ought to write a book. "Well . . . we'll talk." He smiled. Two or three attempts to write a Brubeck biography then went nowhere, and it was only after the title *A Life in Time* popped into my head—in a supermarket in East Finchley, North London—that everything fell into place.

A long personal digression, I know, but one that I hope helps explain the book that *A Life in Time* has ultimately become. Having gone to so much effort to place Brubeck's life within his time, lifting him *out* of his time became important as I was nearing the end of the book. There was nothing to be gained by abandoning Brubeck in the 1950s and '60s. Too many critical perspectives on Brubeck's work, I felt, lacked credibility and were ill informed because they tapered off post-1967, when the classic quartet, featuring alto saxophonist Paul Desmond, disbanded. Another critical cliché—the crazy number of records Brubeck sold was directly out of proportion to his influence—also struck me as suspect. True enough, the lineage of influence that led from Art Tatum to Matthew Shipp, via Thelonious Monk and Cecil Taylor—or from Miles Davis to Wadada Leo Smith, Wallace Roney, and every other trumpeter who followed him—did not apply to Brubeck. In that sense, the naysayers were right: there was/is no school of Brubeck. But being the sort of music fan who had discovered the joys of both Benny Goodman *and* Iannis Xenakis through Brubeck, I couldn't buy in to the notion that the shadow he cast began and ended with *Time Out* and "Take Five." The pianist who recorded "Truth" was clearly not the commercial smooth jazz pianist of myth.

A knottier web of influence was at play, a view confirmed by the other music journalism I was writing. When I wrote about the British post-punk band the Stranglers in 2013, I couldn't help but notice how deeply indebted their hit record "Golden Brown" was to "Take Five"; when I interviewed Ray Davies of the Kinks, he mentioned in passing how much he had loved the Brubeck Quartet in the 1960s; then the American composer John Adams told me something similar. When I heard Australian rock band AC/DC's "Whole Lotta Rosie" during a taxi ride, the fuzzy guitar riff sounded oddly familiar—then I realized it was based on the title track of Brubeck's 1962 album *Countdown—Time in Outer Space.*

These experiences, and similar ones, sent me to trace Brubeck's influence outside jazz. Musicians as varied as Anthony Braxton, Herbie Hancock, Cecil Taylor, Chick Corea, and Keith Jarrett had gone on the record to express how important Brubeck had been at different points during their careers. But

I wasn't prepared for the much-feted pianist Andrew Hill—who recorded a strikingly radical series of albums for Blue Note, beginning in 1963 with *Black Fire* and *Smoke Stack*, with progressive thinkers like Eric Dolphy, Joe Henderson, and Sam Rivers at his side—to tell me how deeply he admired Brubeck's pianism. And so, with my title in place, I began to write a book that threw chronology to the wind, a biography that told Brubeck's story and investigated, as rigorously as I could, the aftermath.

Flip this page and you'll find yourself in 2003: at the age of eighty-two, Brubeck still felt like such a vital creative force that I thought the dust of history could wait a while. For Brubeck, jazz was never a done deal or marooned in history. He always played music in the present tense—which is where *A Life in Time* begins.

PHILIP CLARK
*Oxford, July 3, 2019*

*Chapter One*

# ON THE ROAD

"This is the story of America. Everybody's doing
what they think they're supposed to do."

JACK KEROUAC, *On the Road*, 1957

An opulently upholstered private bus which twenty-four hours
earlier was ferrying the England cricket team somewhere
between disaster and triumph, turns the corner onto Park
Lane in central London, as Dave Brubeck, the jazz pianist and
composer, eighty-two years old, rests on a cushioned sofa in an
alcove at the rear of the vehicle. Wearing a burgundy shirt and
cream linen suit, those signature horn-rimmed glasses of the
1950s long since traded in for chunkier light-reactive spectacles,
he has entered a heightened state of anecdotal nirvana. Brubeck
is leading his quartet toward their next gig and reminiscing
about Charlie Parker, Leonard Bernstein . . . and gangsters.

"When Al Capone kidnapped Caesar Petrillo," Brubeck
muses, referring to the occasion when the mob snatched the

1

omnipotent, all-seeing head honcho of the American Federation of Musicians and held him for ransom, "it was Joe Glaser who arranged his release."[1] And Dave, naturally, knew Joe Glaser, the dollar-fixated jazz and entertainment impresario whom even Louis Armstrong would reverentially greet as "Mr. Glaser."

At the very mention of Glaser's name, an agog wolf whistle cuts across the four-square rhythmic plod of the bus as it powers through South London, a melodic fanfare that implies, *Wow, Dave, now you're talking.* After twenty years of killing time on the Brubeck band bus—a lifestyle guaranteed to test anyone's tolerance for hearing that same story once too often—Bobby Militello, Brubeck's long-serving saxophonist, is a lucky man. His boss is a memory bank who keeps on withdrawing nuggets of jazz history, and, with a thirsty smile, he leans in to eavesdrop.

It's April 23, 2003. Tonight the latest incarnation of the Dave Brubeck Quartet will be performing in Brighton, the East Sussex coastal town affectionately nicknamed by its locals "London-by-the-Sea." That the Dave Brubeck Quartet is still performing anywhere is, let's be honest, nothing short of miraculous. The revolutions in sound brokered during the 1950s and '60s by the Miles Davis Quintet, the Thelonious Monk Quartet, Art Blakey's Jazz Messengers and the Ornette Coleman Quartet, the Modern Jazz Quartet, the Charles Mingus Jazz Workshop, and the John Coltrane Quartet endure as defining moments in jazz history, and Brubeck's quartet is the last surviving "name" band from that golden age still going about its business. The earliest version of his quartet carved its own first grooves into history in August 1951, when the pianist and his musicians, including alto saxophonist Paul Desmond, the player with whom Brubeck would become most associated, walked into a San Francisco recording studio and cut four tracks: George Gershwin's

---

1. Interview with the author, April 23, 2003.

"A Foggy Day" and "Somebody Loves Me" and two original Brubeck compositions, "Crazy Chris" and "Lyons Busy."[2]

Those experiments with what Brubeck invariably referred to as "odd time signatures"—the work that defined him and which came to fruition on his 1959 album *Time Out*—were a whole eight years into the future. But already, in 1951, we hear the Brubeck Quartet refashioning the fundamentals of jazz around the leader's own ideas about rhythm and harmony—and about how improvisation could flourish inside a music that also placed a premium on inventive composition. *Time Out*, which spurned the hit single "Take Five," was released at the end of 1959 and appeared in record stores alongside Miles Davis's *Kind of Blue*, John Coltrane's *Giant Steps*, Charles Mingus's *Mingus Ah Um*, and Ornette Coleman's *The Shape of Jazz to Come*, which were all recorded within an implausibly fertile few months during 1959.

Miles recorded Brubeck's song "In Your Own Sweet Way" in 1957, but then he became embroiled in a spat with Mingus, fought in the letters page of *DownBeat* magazine, regarding Brubeck's effectiveness as a pianist—Mingus for, Davis against.[3] Brubeck was embedded deep inside the heat of ongoing debates about modern jazz. The general critical mood sensed him standing outside its prevailing directions; his classicism, that fixation with odd time signatures, his ear for improvisational flow and rhythm feel, they said, were allied to some other musical project altogether; Brubeck was a shameless popularist, a one-hit wonder, the only thing wrong with his own quartet—but then the modernist heavyweights Cecil Taylor and Anthony Braxton testified that his idea of composition and the contours of his hands against piano keys seeded ideas about jazz that influenced their own early work. Keep calm and carry on, and

2. Fantasy Records 51BX, 517X.

3. Charles Mingus, "An Open Letter to Miles Davis," *DownBeat*, November 30, 1955.

explain where necessary, was how he rode these controversies, until he emerged—exactly when is arguable—as an elder statesman in charge of a significant and unique legacy. The creative relationship between Brubeck and Desmond became venerated and adored; yet something about their chemistry continues to be unfathomable and therefore endlessly alluring. And whenever Brubeck comes to town, this web of association, reaching back into the birth pangs of modern jazz, casts an irresistible spell.

The Brubeck band bus, circa 2003, is a haven of contentment. A quartet of musicians (Brubeck and Militello joined by bassist Michael Moore and drummer Randy Jones), one musician's spouse (Dave and Iola have been married since 1942), one agent-manager (Russell Gloyd, who joined Brubeck in 1976), and a crack squad of roadies and technicians—when Dave arrives, Dave just wants to play—are settling down for the journey ahead. The Nissens, a semiretired couple from Hamburg, Germany, whom Brubeck noticed attending at every port of call during previous European tours, now travel on the band bus: as officially endorsed groupies, they streamline their working lives and plan their holidays around the Brubeck concert schedule. As Iola makes herself comfortable, Dave worries about her motion sickness, but then he marvels at the magnitude and unknowable scale of London.

Tonight's concert will represent a return visit that few had thought likely. The Brighton Dome's faux-Gothic splendor was on the schedule when Brubeck toured the UK five years before, in 1998, in order to celebrate the fortieth anniversary of his quartet's first British tour. Then Brighton hung out the Brubeck bunting and the seaside air felt discernibly different—to the jazz fan at least. In a favorite café, piped Brubeck usurped the customary anesthetizing spew of Classic FM baroque jangle. Recordland, Brighton's secondhand vinyl and CD wonderland—"We specialise in jazz—records bought, sold and exchanged"—had decked out its front display window with a wall of gig-specific merchandise—*Jazz at Oberlin, Jazz at the College of the Pacific, Southern Scene, Time Out, Blues Roots, The Last Set at Newport, Paper Moon, Late Night Brubeck*—like an altarpiece venerating Brubeck's sixty-year career on record.

Midway through that 1998 Brighton concert, Brubeck casually informed the audience that they had just heard his next record, and true to his word, when that next album duly appeared a year later, under the title *The 40th Anniversary Tour of the UK*, a crop of freshly composed material flowered alongside a selection of jazz standards that included "I Got Rhythm," "Someday My Prince Will Come," and "All of Me." "Oh You Can Run (But You Can't Hide)" was a reimagining of the classic blues form; "The Time of Our Madness" was underpinned by a hobbling tango rhythm, a reminder of Jelly Roll Morton's insistence on the importance of what he termed the "Spanish tinge" in jazz; while "The Salmon Strikes" was Brubeck at what Paul Desmond once called his most "wiggy," sculpting musical form out of a leapfrogging twelve-tone row that ricocheted against the regulated plod of an orderly bass line.

Whether by accident or design, this set of new pieces laid bare two seemingly contradictory sides of Dave Brubeck's musical makeup, a tension in which he had long rejoiced. Brubeck always had plenty to say about the blues. "Blue Rondo à la Turk," the opening track of *Time Out*, spliced improvised twelve-bar blues choruses inside the structure of his most ingenious composition, while Brubeck called "Travelin' Blues" and "Blues for Newport" whenever he wanted his musicians to preach some fundamental jazz truths.

"The Salmon Strikes," though, was teased out from that other side of his musician brain—Brubeck the compositional thinker who, having found the great Austrian twelve-tone pioneer Arnold Schoenberg unwilling to entertain his idea of putting notes on manuscript paper simply because he liked how they sounded, found an entirely simpatico sounding board in the French composer and pedagogue Darius Milhaud, who encouraged him to make use of jazz forms in his compositions. These three pieces tell us about Brubeck's starting point as a pianist who was immersed in the blues and in the 1920s swing piano styles of Art Tatum, Earl Hines, and Fats Waller; but they also tell us how far he advanced into what, during the latter half of the 1940s, was considered the very apex of modernism and music that you probably ought not to trust.

Despite his abortive lessons with Schoenberg in 1942, Brubeck never forgot how twelve-tone technique could be used to scatter familiar melodic patterns to the harmonic margins or move notes around like pawns in an inscrutable game of chess.[4] But it was Milhaud's grounding in polytonality—in prying open conventional harmonic thinking by operating in two or three keys simultaneously—that gave Brubeck food for thought for the rest of his career. Everything he achieved in music grew from allowing the underlying principles of jazz to coexist—and fuse—with musical concepts imported from modern composition. And, now in his eighties, that irresistible spell is all the more potent because fresh ideas about how raw swing and "wiggy" modernist compositional techniques might meet each other halfway guards Brubeck's legacy from solidifying into repertory music or escapist nostalgia.

"I often wonder," Brubeck reflects in a quiet moment, "how much time in my life I've spent on coaches like this—all those hours. And there's not much else you can do apart from getting ideas down on manuscript paper. Cities go past, new tunes stack up, and then you can take them right onstage—and play. Sometimes, on the road, the music and my surroundings kind of come together. The last orchestral piece I wrote, which I called Millennium Intervals,[5] was written in the back seat of a

---

4. By arranging all twelve notes of the octave into a sequence or "row" as the basis for a composition, Schoenberg neutered the hierarchies between notes through which the tonal system expressed itself.

5. Premiered by the Stockton Symphony Orchestra, conducted by Peter Jaffe, February 8, 2001.

car as we traveled around Europe a few years ago. You know that the augmented fourth is the most important melodic interval in twentieth-century music, right?[6] Well, I'm writing this piece that's full of augmented fourths. Now we're in this new millennium, I thought, what can you do with the augmented fourth that's still gonna surprise people and make them think? My mind was *full* of augmented fourths. Then we arrive at a town in Switzerland and I hear a siren blaring away. At an augmented fourth! So I wrote exactly the sound I was hearing and put it in the piece."

But what about Joe Glaser taking up Caesar Petrillo's cause with Al Capone, a different life and time altogether? Glaser put the dampers on something big, and Brubeck winces at the memory. Dave, with Iola writing the lyrics, had tailor-made his only musical, *The Real Ambassadors*, for Louis Armstrong. And for "one nite only" in 1962, Armstrong and his All Stars, musicians from Brubeck's quartet, the vocalese supergroup Lambert, Hendricks & Bavan, and the jazz singer Carmen McRae clustered together onstage at the Monterey Jazz Festival to perform the premiere.[7] A dream ticket, you would imagine, for an extended run on Broadway. But Glaser, wily enough to make sure he had signed the bankable Armstrong *and* Brubeck, balked at the prospect. "Joe didn't want Louis and me to be tied up every night because he'd lose too much money," Brubeck explains, the injustice still clearly rankling. And then a grinning punch line to the Petrillo story arrives unannounced: "I asked Joe if he was afraid [of] negotiating, you know, *with*

---

6. The melodic interval of the augmented fourth will have an important role in this book. It was termed the *diabolus in musica* ("the devil in music") during the eighteenth century because its arrangement of notes fell in the cracks where normally harmony could resolve, and Brubeck viewed it as a portal into allowing different key centers to coexist. Known alternatively as the *tritone* or *flattened fifth*, it was also the signature melodic interval of bebop.

7. The studio version, recorded in December 1961, had involved Lambert, Hendricks & Ross; Annie Ross left the group soon after the recording and was replaced by Yolande Bavan.

*gangsters*, and he just shrugged like this was a perfectly normal thing to be doing." Much laughter. Marble Arch, a tourist spot that Brubeck celebrated with a postcard composition on his 1958 album *Jazz Impressions of Eurasia*, looms into view, and then the approach toward Buckingham Palace provokes an improbable discussion about the dimensions of the queen's walled-off garden.[8] Those sepia flashbacks to the world of Al Capone and organized crime register as the comedy of pure incongruity as this luxury bus heads from the most famous postcode in England into suburban London.

Through the window of the Brubeck band bus, Michael Moore, recruited two years ago as the quartet's new bassist, spots an elderly gentleman stooped against the lashing rain, a vision of pure L. S. Lowry[9] pathos transformed by Moore's improviser's wit throwing in a local jazz link—"Look at that guy! He used to play with Humphrey Lyttelton!"[10] he roars. Brubeck has always aroused profound loyalty from his musicians, and Moore's status as a player parachuted in from outside the pianist's go-to pool of long-trusted musical associates—with his CV ranging from Benny Goodman to Gil Evans—is a source of understandable intrigue to Brubeck fans. As the bus breaks for the London borders, with the motorway to Brighton stretching ahead, Moore falls into earnest conversation with Iola Brubeck. Heads nod remorsefully, then Moore's grotesque caricature of President George W. Bush's nervy Texas drawl hits a manic crescendo reminiscent of an operatic mad scene.

Sitting at the next table, opposite Militello, is the man who has become Brubeck's longest-serving sideman. Randy Jones—

---

8. Forty-two acres, in case you were wondering.

9. British artist (1887–1976) noted for his paintings of working-class Britons in bleak northern settings.

10. British trumpeter (1921–2008) known for leading traditional and mainstream jazz bands. Moore's gag is predicated on the long-standing joke in British jazz circles that trad jazz is only of interest to old fogeys who view the modern world with suspicion.

whom Brubeck introduces during British tours as being "from Slough, England," which guarantees a laugh because this drab commuter town in Greater London is about the last place you'd go looking for a jazz drummer—made his first appearance on a Dave Brubeck Quartet album in 1980. On *Tritonis,* one tune required Jones to give the kiss of rhythmic life to a tentative sketch from Dave's notebook, retrofitting Brubeck's salty eight-to-the-bar boogie-woogie patterns with a funk backbeat and choked hi-hat stabs—a tune that became known as "Mr. Fats" (Waller, not Domino). The title track was a spry Brubeck composition in 5/4 time, originally conceived for flute and guitar,[11] which Jones nudged forward with a chamber musician's sensibility in this reworking for the quartet. Dave Brubeck's new drummer made a decisive, dynamic start.

Militello and Jones share history pre-Brubeck. Both men came to the Brubeck Quartet via the big band led by the Canadian trumpeter, singer, and swing-era veteran Maynard Ferguson. Ferguson spent much of the 1960s on an LSD high as a member of Timothy Leary's druggy commune, and Jones worked with him when the trumpeter relocated to Britain in 1969. Militello's tenure began in 1975, after Ferguson returned to the US. And although Militello and Jones never played the same Ferguson gig, they now feel the kinship. As Jones recounts the traumas of being in a car driven by Ferguson—who never quite reconciled himself to driving on the left side of the road in the UK—Militello concurs: "Although to be fair, Randy, he couldn't drive in the US either." Rooted in the swing principles of Count Basie, Ferguson later flirted with pseudo-Stravinskian "progressive" harmonies and, eventually, glitter-ball disco beats—a fertile boot camp for Militello and Jones before Brubeck came calling.

As Brighton heaves into view, Russell Gloyd phones ahead to make sure everything is prepared at the venue, and Dave's alert

---

11. For flutist Andrew Bolotowsky and guitarist Joe Karpenia.

eyes suddenly look heavy—time for a restorative nap. The bus skirts around Brighton Palace Pier and docks outside another Victorian building of note: the Grand Brighton hotel, where Team Brubeck will be spending the night. Barely an hour later the Dave Brubeck Quartet is onstage at the Brighton Dome for a sound check. Ordinarily sound checks function as the word would imply: an opportunity to ascertain whether a venue's PA system is relaying a faithful balance of an ensemble's dynamic levels and tonal colors to the audience. Gloyd sits behind his mixing desk and adjusts the levels, but Brubeck, having been cooped up in the bus, is itching to play, and the sound check evolves into a rehearsal and blowing session.

He begins by punching out "Limehouse Blues" with a ferocity that lets everybody know that he is already warmed up. A fan has written in asking to hear "For All We Know," a jazz standard and a regular standby during the earliest days of the Dave Brubeck Quartet; its first appearance on a Brubeck album was in 1953 on *Jazz at the College of the Pacific*. Paul Desmond loved the tune as a vehicle for improvisation, but this quartet has played it only rarely, and they painstakingly loop its melodic and harmonic patterns, ensuring the nuts and bolts of the notes are sitting under their fingers so that they can properly play the music. Then something wholly unexpected happens. Militello segues into "Strange Meadow Lark," the tune that separated "Blue Rondo à la Turk" and "Take Five" on *Time Out*. Inexplicably, this group has never played it, and Brubeck patiently shepherds his quartet around its harmonic trip wires. "I've been trying to get Dave to play that tune for years," Militello reveals afterward, "and perhaps, finally, he's taken the hint."

A roadie arrives with another, hopefully more comfortable, piano stool, and as one stool is exchanged for the other, Militello launches into "Donna Lee," Charlie Parker's bebop paraphrase of the jazz standard "Indiana." Militello's fluid bop phrasing is pure Parker—but Brubeck, who in his enthusiasm to rise to his saxophonist's challenge very nearly sends the roadie sprawling, causes a clash of styles by shadowing him with "Indiana" itself, his left hand outlining a rolling, barrelhouse eight-to-a-bar.

Following dinner at the hotel, Brubeck arrives back at the Brighton Dome at seven forty—twenty minutes before curtain up—to be greeted by a posse of fans waving secondhand LPs, concert programs, and CD sleeves. The stage door catapults open and a doorman, magnificent in his indignant fury, screams, "Give this man some space, let him take his coat off at least!" But Brubeck signs patiently, satisfying the demand for autographs, until Russell Gloyd gently apologizes to those destined to be left disappointed and ushers Dave inside. "In Europe guys—and it's always guys—do queue for autographs," Michael Moore explains to the doorman, "but in Britain they'll arrive hours before and camp outside until Dave arrives. You just don't see it the same way anywhere else." The doorman, unimpressed, indicates that his Dave of choice is actually Beckham, not Brubeck. He's going to be watching soccer on television tonight—"But I might pop upstairs when he plays a few of the old favorites."

Otherwise, the audience waiting patiently in the elegant round of the Brighton Dome is giddy with anticipation. Gloyd is perched behind his mixing desk, and the sight of Iola Brubeck making her way into the auditorium signals that the main event is about to commence. When Brubeck arrives on stage from the wings, appearing with his characteristically deliberate gait behind Jones, Militello, and Moore, a roar of approval circles the round. Then Jones's tintinnabulous cymbals unleash an ecstatic Latin sizzle. It's showtime.

E♭

Another time, another continent, another road trip. The Dave Brubeck Quartet was touring the West Coast of the United States in a ten-date package with the Charlie Parker Quintet, under the auspices of jazz promoter Gene Norman[12] and his Just Jazz concert series. It was November 1953. Both bandleaders were thirty-two. That March, Brubeck had recorded live at the Finney Chapel at Oberlin College, Ohio, music that, when released as *Jazz at Oberlin*, represented his first career-defining album. In May, Parker had traveled to Toronto to perform with a bebop supergroup—Dizzy Gillespie (trumpet), Bud Powell (piano), Charles Mingus (bass), and Max Roach (drums)—at Massey Hall, a concert that assumed the mantle of a jazz must-listen when Mingus released a recording via his own Debut label. Parker was considered to be the very embodiment of New York bebop and modernism in jazz, the sped-up majesty of his improvisational brilliance and his lifestyle excesses helping build a mythomaniac image around him. Brubeck was, by comparison, a hick from the West Coast sticks playing an idea of jazz without any recognizable label, which, they said, was dragged down by concepts imported from the classical conservatoire. Within two years Parker would be dead, but in 1953 he was playing an extended lap of honor—Brubeck, though, still had it all to prove.

The program book issued by Gene Norman's organization to accompany the tour made no bones about the relative status of the two musicians. Parker was the "undisputed lord and master of the Modern Sounds . . . the great originator that has set the pattern for all others to follow," while Brubeck was "the newest meteor to streak across the jazz horizon . . . represent[ing] in a great measure the developing maturity of the Modern Sounds." Norman's copywriter—or Norman himself—highlighted the stark cultural divide between how Parker and Brubeck had developed their music: "Falling in league with

12. New York–born club owner, disc jockey, and concert promoter, 1922–2015. Norman (born Eugene Nabatoff) founded the GNP Crescendo label in 1954 (which still endures) and, during the same year, opened the Crescendo Club in Los Angeles (which closed in 1964).

a group of restless and inquisitive musicians who were looking for something fresh and new to say in jazz—musicians like the legendary Theolonious [*sic*] Monk and Dizzy Gillespie—Parker spearheaded a series of revolutionary innovations." There are those, the notes accepted, who would likely resist progressive tendencies in jazz, but Parker's deployment of the "flattened fifth and other more advanced harmonic patterns and the use of the poly-rhythmic beat" had elevated him to the new jazz's "true Messiah."

Brubeck hadn't fallen in league with anybody—he was Ivy League. The notes told of "a young composer with an impressive academic background; he has studied personally both with Darius Milhaud and Arnold Schoenberg. Combine a trained musical mind steeped in the approach of extended serious composition with a natural knack for jazz improvisation, and you have a remarkably fresh and valid result—you have the unique and exciting music of Dave Brubeck." We read how his initial musical experiments were undertaken with an octet and then a trio—but "feeling the need [for] a singing voice with[in] the group, Paul Desmond was added on alto. Paul himself has developed into one of the leading lights of the alto saxophone, following in the soft-spoken, ethereal tradition of Lee Konitz.[13] The Brubeck Quartet features Ron Crotty on bass and Lloyd Davis on drums." Parker performed the tour with a pickup group of the finest musicians West Coast jazz had to offer. Trumpeter Chet Baker and drummer Shelly Manne were well established in their own right and on the cusp of making their debuts on record as leaders; bassist Carson Smith was

---

13. Alto saxophonist (b. 1927) initially associated with pianist Lennie Tristano and later with Miles Davis's *Birth of the Cool* sessions, and who later performed with the British free improviser Derek Bailey. Konitz's sound and approach to improvisation were considered radical departures from the dominant influence of Charlie Parker.

identified as a member of baritone saxophonist Gerry Mulligan's[14] quartet, while pianist Jimmy Rowles had played with clarinetist Woody Herman's orchestra.

There was nothing unusual about a star soloist touring with local musicians, and Brubeck of course had the geographic advantage of the West Coast being his home turf, but the symbolism of Brubeck's meticulously rehearsed quartet sharing a bill with Parker's pickup band belied the chaos that had become the bebop star's everyday reality. And, despite Gene Norman's careful billing, not everybody understood the boundaries between the two groups. "Featured in Brubeck's band are Paul Desmond, alto sax player who was named the 'best newcomer to jazz' by *DownBeat* magazine, and Charlie Parker, who is one of the instigators of bop. The entire band has been on tour of the major clubs and night spots of the country," reported the University of Oregon's *Daily Emerald* with chirpy confidence on October 30, 1953; when the paper followed up on their promotional article a few weeks later, Parker was still "Brubeck's alto saxophone player" and Shelly Manne— "formerly with Stan Kenton and Woody Herman . . . and one of the top drummers in the field of jazz today"—was also tagged erroneously as a Brubeck Quartet member. The assumption that Parker was a Brubeck sideman might raise a laugh if it weren't for the nagging suspicion that this category error might be down to unthinking prejudice. But Parker was *the* omnipotent presence in modern jazz, and nobody's sideman.

By November 5, 1953, the Brubeck and Parker groups had reached Eugene, Oregon. Chet Baker sat in with Brubeck for a dulcet reading of "Lover, Come Back to Me," and Parker's quintet delivered high-velocity bop evergreens, including "How High the Moon," the bebop movement's unofficial

---

14. Baritone saxophonist and arranger (1927–1996) initially associated with Miles Davis in New York, although most famous for his West Coast quartet with Chet Baker. In 1968 Brubeck would form a group with Mulligan, which toured and recorded as the "Dave Brubeck Trio featuring Gerry Mulligan."

theme song.[15] Captured from the wings of the stage, in Eugene or another town, a vivid action shot shows Parker's hunched frame squashed inside an immaculate white suit; Carson Smith is hugging his bass while Shelly Manne is holding his mouth wide open in amazement, perhaps at Parker's outrageously pacey tempo or some miraculous thing dancing out of his horn. Paul Desmond had cultivated an interest in capturing everyday life on the road with his camera, and watching Parker would have given him the perfect opportunity to photograph the preeminent influence on his own instrument—could he have taken this uncredited image? The other photograph, annotated in Brubeck's own handwriting on the reverse side of the print, shows Ron Crotty and Shelly Manne standing by the tour bus. Bizarrely, nobody thought to take a picture of Brubeck with Bird, and no firm evidence exists to suggest that the pair played together—we can't know whether, had Parker called "Donna Lee," Brubeck's instinct would have been to slip "Indiana" underneath him.

One piece of evidence, though, does point to this tour being a happy one, despite Parker's habit of disappearing into the night until just before he was due to play. When he played a weeklong residency at the Hi-Hat Club in Boston in January 1954, the city's local radio station, WHDH, broadcast an interview with Parker structured around his own key recordings, about which his comments were sought—in conversation with Desmond. Given that the two men were recently on the road together, the obvious warmth and ease of their personal relationship is touching. Parker never pulls rank on Desmond, who, although palpably starstruck, is not afraid to aim some searching questions at Parker about the nature of his art. ("That is very reassuring to hear," he says as Parker details the

---

15. Some of the music Parker's group played that night is documented on *Charlie Parker and Chet Baker Complete Jam Sessions* (Definitive Records DRCD 11231).

history of his exacting practice regime, "because somehow I got the idea that you were just born with that technique and never had to worry too much about it, about keeping it working.")

As they discuss his innovations and career, Parker tells of the pleasure he takes in discovering younger musicians. "I enjoy working with them when I have the pleasure to [and] if I might say you, yourself, Paul." Desmond swells with pride and thanks him for the tribute, and then Parker continues, "I've had lots of fun working you, that's a pleasure in a million. David, Dave Brubeck, David Brubeck—lots of other fellows have come along since that particular era [1942, when Parker and Gillespie recorded "Groovin' High," the record under discussion]. It makes you feel that everything you do wasn't for naught."

With the conversation turning toward his own future, Parker tells Desmond about meeting the composer Edgard Varèse[16] in New York City: "He's a classical composer from Europe, he's a Frenchman, very nice fellow, and he wants to teach me." And far from dismissing the Brubeck Quartet on the grounds that they were failing to conform to bebop orthodoxies, therein, you feel, lay the attraction for Parker. The cult of Parker was such that he was surrounded by paler imitations of his own innovations, and Desmond embodied an all-too-rare example of a saxophonist prepared to chance a whole other sound and method of improvisation. Inside Brubeck's compositional approach to jazz, had Parker heard traces of those modern composers he admired—Stravinsky, Ravel, Debussy, Bartók, all of whom had inspired Varèse—and recognized a hinterland between composition and improvisation that he, too, wanted to explore and inhabit? During an earlier interview on WHDH, recorded in June 1953,[17] Parker was asked about Brubeck and

---

16. French composer (1883–1965) who relocated to New York City in 1916 and began a series of visionary modernist works, including the orchestral *Amériques* (1921) and *Arcana* (1927) and the tape piece *Poème électronique* (1958).

17. Interview by John McLellan, WHDH, Boston, June 13, 1953, transcript, www.plosin.com/milesahead/BirdInterviews.aspx#530600.

Gerry Mulligan, and he said he found plenty to satisfy head and heart in what he had heard: "Well, the two men you mentioned [are] extremely good friends of mine, [but] even if they weren't friends of mine I'd find their music very, very interesting, not only from an intellectual standpoint—it's very intelligent music, and it's very well played, it's got a lot of feeling and it isn't missing anything. It's definitely music, one hundred percent."

The music Parker and Brubeck played on tour may largely be lost today, but the ghosts of those evenings on the road can be resurrected, together with an image of what those West Coast audiences likely heard, by investigating the records that they made immediately before and, in Brubeck's case, after the tour. "No modern musician has ever had more things of special interest to say than Dave Brubeck. He's here to say them tonight!" Gene Norman's program notes gushed—and, as Brubeck said them, no one could doubt how far his vision of jazz stood from the emotional temperament and technical conventions of bebop.

When Mingus decided to issue *Jazz at Massey Hall* on his Debut label, two practical problems needed to be addressed: his own bass lines were inaudible in the mix, and Charlie Parker was already signed to jazz impresario Norman Granz's Verve Records but Mingus was not minded to pay Granz a fee to borrow Parker. The first difficulty was overcome by Mingus's overdubbing a fresh set of bass lines, together with a completely new solo on "All the Things You Are," and the second by listing Parker on the record sleeve as "Charlie Chan"; "Chan" was Parker's wife's name, although you didn't need to be Sherlock Holmes to work out the true identity of "Charlie Chan." This one-off meeting of five bebop pioneers marked the last time that Parker and Gillespie were captured together on record, and the billing Mingus gave his record—"the Quintet"—reflected its historical consequence. This was a summit meeting; there was no—could be no—leader.

As the group stampeded through "Wee," "Salt Peanuts," "Hot House," and "A Night in Tunisia" (and the standards "Perdido" and "All the Things You Are"), their rhythmic Russian roulette cracked the foundations open again—this was restless, open-ended music. The urgent dispatch of the melody line and the rhythmic abandon of Parker's improvised solo on "Wee" looked forward to how Ornette Coleman's elasticity of rhythm would give the structure of a piece infinite stretch. Parker wholly inhabited the idiom of the music, his concrete certainty about what bebop was unearthing new freedoms. Had Parker played with anything like that degree of raw energy during the Gene Norman tour, Brubeck and Desmond could only have looked on from the wings in slack-jawed wonder.

The year 1953 also happened to be a vintage year for the Dave Brubeck Quartet on record. It began with *Jazz at Oberlin* in March and ended, a month after the Parker tour, with another live on-campus recording, issued as *Jazz at the College of the Pacific*. The lesser-known *Dave Brubeck & Paul Desmond at Wilshire-Ebell*,[18] which Brubeck considered below par and which he actively blocked from being reissued during his lifetime, was recorded in July '53; and *Jazz at the Black Hawk* pulled together eight tracks captured during various West Coast engagements during 1952 and '53. By anybody's reckoning this was a prolific outpouring of material. *Jazz at Oberlin*'s "Perdido" and "How High the Moon" dealt in off-the-leash swing; "Stardust" and, from *Jazz at the College of the Pacific*, "For All We Know" presented early examples of the group's idyllic approach to balladry; while "Let's Fall in Love" and "All the Things You Are" from *At Wilshire-Ebell* rained down dazzling, luminous counterpoint. In contrast to

---

18. The historic theater in Los Angeles, near Windsor Square, dating back to 1894.

Charlie Parker in 1953, the Brubeck Quartet in the same year feels like an exploratory work in progress, with multiple avenues of investigation opening up, waiting to be pursued. What the music *could* become is as intriguing as what it already is.

Anybody arriving at these early records with the dapper vamps and smart metric chess moves of *Time Out* as their only point of reference might recognize a distant cousin of something familiar. Brubeck and Desmond's telepathic understanding; Brubeck's knack of scooping up an ostensibly innocent turn of phrase from the closing moments of a Desmond solo to re-present it as a loaded question; and the sense that, together, the two men made a sum greater and deeper than their individual parts—all were already fully formed.

But at this stage the Dave Brubeck Quartet was, in reality, Dave Brubeck and Paul Desmond supported and accompanied by a bassist and a drummer—only rarely did the dialogue cut four ways. The vanguard of modern jazz drumming reverberated somewhere between the hands, sticks, and feet of Max Roach, whose lashing impetus and nests of cross-rhythms powered the Massey Hall concert forward. Lloyd Davis was, in comparison, a capable enough practitioner, but his playing showed only a negligible awareness of Roach's state-of-the-art percussion theories. On *Jazz at Oberlin* and *At Wilshire-Ebell,* he proved most effective on the up-tempo numbers, where he bedded down inside the groove and faithfully maintained time, but ballads exposed his imaginative and technical limitations. Both albums feature "Stardust," and on each occasion Davis's tickling pulse lets the side down. And with Brubeck's solo gathering momentum on "These Foolish Things (Remind Me of You)" on *Oberlin,* Davis is perversely noninterventionist and aloof, doing little to help shape the music, preferring instead to stay resolutely out of harm's way.

The evolution of thought that occurred within the Dave Brubeck Quartet between 1953 and 1959—the ideas that would lead Brubeck toward *Time Out*—involved a reevaluation of how bass and drums might contribute something more meaningful than just the outline of a song's harmonic and rhythmic grid. Ron Crotty, on bass, retained his place in the quartet while, immediately after the Parker tour, Davis bowed to the inevitable. When the quartet reconvened on December 14 to record *Jazz at the College of the Pacific* a new drummer was in place, and Joe Dodge's rhythmic assertiveness raised the tone of the percussion discussion. But, as he confessed during a 1992 interview, his technique would have struggled to keep account of Brubeck's increasing predilection for "odd," asymmetrical time signatures.[19] And if even Dodge balked at the prospect of navigating his way around those odd time signatures, the sort of composer that Brubeck would become—basing compositions like "Blue Rondo à la Turk," "Three to Get Ready," and "Unsquare Dance" around asymmetrical meter—could never have been served by the cautious, plodding Lloyd Davis.

Missing conspicuously from Brubeck Quartet albums of the early 1950s was the leader's contributions as composer. "How High the Moon," "Crazy Rhythm," and "All the Things You Are" were, as it happened, also staples of the bebop repertoire. Benny Goodman's "Lullaby in Rhythm," Jerome Kern's "Why Do I Love You?," and Harold Arlen's "Let's Fall in Love" were more personal enthusiasms. His early-1950s set lists were drawn overwhelmingly from Tin Pan Alley standards, the go-to source for most jazz musicians. But the group's musical evolution would prove inseparable from changing ideas about repertoire.

At the end of 1956, Dodge's exit led Brubeck toward Joe Morello, the most gifted drummer Brubeck had hitherto engaged: an exemplary technician who also delivered style, imagination, and prodigious swing. In 1958, when Brubeck hired Eugene Wright, a bass player from Chicago who was

---

19. Gordon Jack, *Fifties Jazz Talk: An Oral Retrospective* (Lanham, Md., Scarecrow Press, 2004), 76.

proudly rooted in the swing traditions of Count Basie (in whose orchestra he had played for two years), the final ingredient that made the classic Dave Brubeck Quartet cook fell into place. Brubeck had acquired an intriguing blend of musical personalities and all the tools he could need to fully develop his quartet's potential, and this fresh-look quartet would inch toward a new collective identity by uniting around the leader's compositions.

But Brubeck's knack of having that composerly part of his brain transform material co-opted from popular songs was already, in the early 1950s, drawing clear lines of differentiation between his jazz and Parker's bebop.

By 1953, "Perdido" was woven into the fabric of popular music as a jazz standard. It was recorded for the first time by Duke Ellington and His Orchestra on December 3, 1941,[20] and written by his Puerto Rican–born trombonist Juan Tizol, and the Duke clothed Tizol's composition in the instrumental splendor of his orchestra so convincingly that many people assumed Ellington was the composer: "Perdido" became a piece of Ellingtonia by proxy. The seductive glide of the melody line allied to a Latin groove had obvious attractions for Ellington—and Parker and Brubeck obviously concurred. They both recorded the piece in 1953—Parker, masquerading as Charlie Chan, as a member of the Quintet on *Jazz at Massey Hall*, and Brubeck on *Jazz at Oberlin*—recordings that are musically poles apart.

The Quintet's rethink, faithful to the principles of bebop, emphasized their prowess as superhero improvisers over the intricacies of Tizol's composition. Max Roach basted the heat with a roasting Latin rhythm. Parker set the scene with

---

20. However, the version that Ellington made six weeks later, on January 21, 1942, is considered the classic recording.

a radiantly executed précis of Tizol's theme; the rationale instead was to illuminate the melodic and harmonic tics of "Perdido" through improvisation. Parker, Gillespie, and then Bud Powell soloed before the performance climaxed with a more developed reading of Tizol's composed line that incorporated aspects of the original Ellington orchestration.

Brubeck and Desmond, too, wanted to flex their improviser muscles, but sprinting through Tizol's theme as a launchpad for improvisation was not Brubeck's style. He needed to figure out how "Perdido" could be brought inside the sound world of his quartet, which meant imprinting Tizol's melody line with his own compositional fingerprints. To that end, Brubeck turned the flow of strong and weak beats around—not only making the weak beats strong but accenting them with a ferocity that was pure *Rite of Spring*—which created a distorted mirror image. Those weak beats, now obliged to carry a heavier rhythmic load, kick-started the quartet's version. Relief from the rhythmic tension came in the middle section of the tune, which restored the natural order of strong and weak beats with a straight-ahead swing feel. But whenever the opening strain of Tizol's theme returned, so did Brubeck's rhythmic hiccups: "In my version," his arrangement told listeners, "the division between composition and improvisation is finely balanced; both elements are simultaneously in play." Brubeck was discovering that manipulating time and meter could open up line, form, and rhythm in a multitude of unexpected ways.

Following their improvised solos, rather than head back to the "Perdido" theme directly or via the same linking passage commandeered by Parker and Gillespie, Brubeck and Desmond dealt a quartet calling card: piano and alto saxophone improvised spontaneously overlapping lines, the contrapuntal principles of J. S. Bach made an ongoing concern in modern jazz. Elsewhere on the album, Brubeck's ingenious arrangement of Jerome Kern's "The Way You Look Tonight"—from the 1936 Fred Astaire and Ginger Rogers film *Swing Time*—wrapped the principle theme around its own linking bridge. Brubeck and Desmond played these contrapuntal lines with liquid speed, making Kern's tune dance once again.

As early as February 1950, in an article entitled "Jazz's Evolvement as an Art Form," published over two editions of *DownBeat* magazine under the byline "David Brubeck," Brubeck talked up the allure of jazz's emotional heat as being inseparable from improvisation. "I will not go as far as to say that jazz ceases to be jazz once it is written," he argued. "But I do say that improvisation is the criterion by which all jazz, written or unwritten, is judged." Brubeck opened part two of his article by equating the process of improvisation to a mountain climber treading with care to avoid the plunging rock face below: "He is protected on one side by the mountain of tradition and exposed on the other to the abyss of the unknown. Progress is possible only by the use of a strong rope which anchors the climber to the mountain, while at the same time it gives him a greater freedom of movement than if he had no security."

This smart analogy was, unfortunately for Brubeck, undermined by what the magazine published directly opposite the first installment of his article: a dismissive review of a recent Brubeck appearance at the Burma Lounge jazz club in Oakland. "Dave's bunch, extremely competent musicians," wrote the uncredited reviewer, "play a type of thing which must be heard rather than seen, to be appreciated. They are extremely popular right now with the crewcut set from California, who can get down there for 11 cents on the bus. The group does not swing and is, frankly, entirely too earnest for these ears, but a difference of opinion is what makes horse races and jazz scraps. To those who like him, Brubeck is God and [club promoter Jimmy] Lyons[21] is his prophet."

---

21. Founder of the Monterey Jazz Festival (1916–1994) and radio disc-jockey, Lyons was also a regular at the Burma Lounge jazz club in Oakland, where he enthusiastically promoted the Dave Brubeck Trio. (Not to be confused with Jimmy Lyons, alto saxophonist, who played with Cecil Taylor.)

As his philosophy of what he wanted jazz to be glanced across the page at words that expressed another view altogether, Brubeck received an early taste of the phraseology, and the general puzzlement, of the many critical lashings he would endure over the next thirty years. Brubeck was introduced to *DownBeat* readers as "a twenty-nine-year-old Californian [who] has been causing considerable comment in recent months for his efforts in behalf of modern music," but you can't help wonder how many readers were troubled by one perplexing inconsistency in his article.

His claim that jazz had emulated European harmony to the extent that it had "unfortunately lost a great deal of the rhythmic drive which African music offers" ignored the reality that Mother Africa was embedded deep inside bebop, in both the notes themselves and as a point of proud cultural reference. The multilayered rhythmic finery of hard-core bop drummers like Max Roach and Kenny Clarke had left far behind the European marching band tradition in which drummers of the previous generation, typified by Gene Krupa and Buddy Rich, had been versed. In 1947, Gillespie had met the Cuban percussionist Chano Pozo, who revolutionized the trumpeter's thinking about rhythm and introduced him to a string of new kinks in the beat. Gillespie's 1942 composition "A Night in Tunisia" demonstrated that his ears were open already to Africa, but his creative partnership with Pozo—which blossomed before the percussionist was murdered in New York City at the end of 1948—pushed his interest to the next level. Together they wrote pieces like "Tin Tin Deo" and "Manteca," and the term *Afro-Cuban jazz* was born.

Brubeck's oversight was unfortunate and might well have landed him in hot water had the rest of his article not been so diligently argued. Any white musician taking the wider jazz community to task for neglecting Africa, while overhauling standards with rhythmic sleights of hand developed out of his interest in Milhaud and Stravinsky, was opening himself up to accusations of racial insensitivity. In his *DownBeat* article, Brubeck wrote, "The jammed-to-the-exploding-point thirty-two-bar chorus," a typical jazz form, needed to expand and become structurally more pliant—which, he added, would be done "naturally and logically by the composers of the future."

But, just as fears were raised that Brubeck was stumbling into that unpardonable sin of cultural misappropriation by implying that only classically trained composers were equipped to develop jazz, a stunning and unexpected twist: "Since jazz is not provincial, regional, nor chauvinistic, but as much an expression of our people as our language, it is the natural idiom for the American composer," he stated. "I firmly believe that the composer who will most successfully typify America will have been born into jazz, will have absorbed it in his early years unconsciously, and will probably be an active participant in shaping its future course." For Brubeck, jazz had rendered contemporary definitions of the word *composer* useless. If musicians trained in the techniques of jazz and classical music were prepared to step into each other's worlds—if symphony orchestra musicians would equip themselves to feel the rhythms and phrasing of jazz, and jazz musicians could learn to read complex musical notation—only then might an authentic "new" American music emerge.

Being a twenty-nine-year-old Californian, the jazz hub of New York City, the milieu of East Coast bebop, and developments like Afro-Cuban jazz were not part of Brubeck's daily experience. But he had been imbibing African music through other sources. Issued on the Commodore label in 1950, *The Belgian Congo Records of the Denis-Roosevelt Expedition*[22] anthologized field recordings collected between 1934 and '35 in the Belgian Congo by the documentary makers (and husband-and-wife team) Armand Denis and Leila Roosevelt. The forty-minute album was a collection of ritualistic dances, songs, and chants,

---

22. Commodore DL 30005.

precisely the sort of record to which the innately musically curious, and especially a young musician with an appetite for off-kilter rhythms, was liable to be drawn.

Brubeck listened avidly. One of the pieces, "Royal Watusi Drums," threw up a ribbon of melody that later he would fashion into a drum feature for Joe Morello, which, given the title "Watusi Drums,"[23] would act as a climactic concert set piece before "Take Five" had been recorded. And as he listened, Brubeck experienced a whole new way of calculating rhythm: he was hearing rhythmic motifs building into larger structures by spontaneously dividing, multiplying, and combining like blood cells on the move, creating rhythmic twists and eddies through the process of performance.[24] Strong beats collided with weak beats, and they overlapped in ways not likely to add up to neatly countable patterns of four or two. In *DownBeat*, had Brubeck managed to link this discovery back to the innovations of bebop drumming, his argument would have undoubtedly been strengthened. But the basic point stood—as jazz musicians were stretching the harmonic and melodic basis of their music, could there be more to rhythm than 4/4 time?

When he told *DownBeat* readers that "since the jazzman plays the double role of creator and interpreter, there is no disparity between conception and performance," he was speaking of his belief in treating improvisation and composition with the same seriousness of purpose, one bleeding through into the other. "Within one generation," he concluded, "the jazzman's harmonic comprehension has expanded to the point where he is now capable of understanding the choice that is offered to the serious composer. Two great musical minds of the century, Milhaud and Schoenberg, have already blazed separate paths.

---

23. Recorded on *The Dave Brubeck Quartet in Europe* (1958).

24. Spontaneous in the sense that there was no guiding score and the musicians developed their material aurally; as Steve Reich would later point out, the fascination of such music was in following the *process* rather than worrying too much about the end result.

True to his tradition, the jazz musician has attempted to follow these new trials and is at this moment exploring in his improvised choruses the realms of polytonality and atonality at least to the limits of his understanding."

*Jazz at Oberlin* offered the tastiest demonstration yet of how these theories sounded when put into practice. The first piece on the record was an action-packed six-and-a-half-minute excursion around "These Foolish Things" that, with unmistakable clarity, laid out how the dialogue between composition and improvisation operated on Brubeck's senses. Following on the heels of such a devastatingly astute solo as Desmond's, which ended with torrents of notes double-timing the pulse, presented Brubeck with a challenge. Now was not the time for routine patterns, and Brubeck painted the canvas with a giddy assortment of impetuous mood swings, pianistic colors and styles. Multiple key centers built grinding tension. Brubeck's left hand challenged his right with a niggling harmonic question that bubbled over into an eloquent two-part discussion. Densely compacted brutalist chords, pecked at with stabbing clusters, were answered in the next chorus by cascading, Romantic arpeggios. Brubeck's lessons from Milhaud and Schoenberg spilled over into the improvisation.

Elsewhere the striking dynamism of the harmony prevented the arranged elements of "Perdido" or "The Way You Look Tonight" from feeling overly schooled; written ideas vaulted off the manuscript paper with a freshness that was entirely authentic to the spirit of jazz, and those fortunate enough to experience the Dave Brubeck Quartet on the road with the Charlie Parker Quintet in November 1953 heard two musicians passionately engaged in improvisation but otherwise taking a radically different perspective on jazz. Multiple meanings of *compose* were at play in Brubeck's music. Composed music had altered his perspective on the art of improvisation. His "These Foolish Things" solo at Oberlin was composed of a multitude of materials and approaches, elegant melodic shapes wrenched apart by the joyous physicality of bulky block chords, unpredictable in their direction and defining possible points of resolution. Teasing incompatibility, the prospect that not all loose ends in a solo would, or could, be resolved, would prove a source of endless fascination for Brubeck.

But improvisation for Parker was intimately tied to the raw physics and Romantic heritage of his horn: he heard— and experienced to the point of self-destruction—the world through his alto saxophone. He had been alerted to the potency of the saxophone during a well-spent misspent youth in Kansas City, a place that, unlike Brubeck's Californian hometown of Concord, where surely everyone went to bed on time, had a thriving and distinctive jazz scene all of its own. When the Count Basie Orchestra was in residency at Club Kay-cee, an underage Parker would sneak into the balcony above the bandstand to hear his favorite musicians; and it was Lester Young,[25] Basie's tenor saxophonist, who captured the young boy's imagination.[26]

And everything Parker intuited from Young about freeing up rhythm and harmony instilled within him a sense of purpose. As Parker unpicked complex relationships between chords, creative possibilities accumulated exponentially. He channeled what he had learned back through his instrument, and the more he played and improvised and scrutinized the patterns of his own playing, the more liberated his ears, technique, and imagination became, as his solos darted forward with the force of an arrowhead.

---

25. Tenor saxophonist (1909–1959) famed for his soft, spongy tone and use of an extended harmonic palette; for his close personal and musical relationship with Billie Holiday; and for anticipating the harmonic and rhythmic advances of bebop.

26. For a vivid account of Parker sneaking into the balcony, see Ross Russell, *Bird Lives! The High Life and Hard Times of Charlie (Yardbird) Parker* (Boston: Da Capo Press, 1996).

Brubeck's compositional approach to improvisation—and his interest in making distinct types of material coexist, or contradict each other—counted against that inexorable forward motion at which Parker excelled. Where Parker's close, idiomatic bond with his instrument had helped form his view of bebop, Brubeck reversed that loop. His absorption in composition, the various ways in which composed music intersected with his unassailable belief in the urgency of improvisation, formed his approach to the piano—and the instrument became a laboratory in sound for this composer who improvised and improviser who composed.

*Chapter Two*

# WELCOME TO HARD TIMES

"I always had the feeling somebody had certified
Hard Times as a place in the world and that's why
it was happening."

E. L. DOCTOROW, *Welcome to Hard Times*, 1960

The morning after the night before in Brighton, Brubeck
considers himself a very happy man. "You guys played *great* last
night," he beams as everybody is reassembling in the bus for
the journey back to London. "I couldn't believe what you did
on 'Take Five,' Dave!" Michael Moore says before unleashing
an uncanny impersonation of the pianist in full block-chord
splendor, utilizing the table in front of him as a dummy
keyboard—mannerisms and fingerwork all precisely observed.
And last night's "Take Five" was indeed noteworthy and unique,
a prime example of how Brubeck can mold even his signature
piece around the consequences of time, place, and mood.

At the start of the concert, Randy Jones set pulses jan-
gling with his Latin groove, which established a fast, furious,
and funky pace. This opening piece turned out to be "Broadway Bossa Nova," the standout tune from the quartet's 1964
album *Jazz Impressions of New York*. During Brubeck's solo, ragged block chords lunged provocatively against the neat harmonic foundations spelled out by Moore's bass; then a twisting
melodic curve wormed its way toward the keyboard, and the
remainder of Brubeck's solo was spent reconciling what he had
unleashed: his melodic line variously spliced up, turned on its
head, crammed into any corner where it might fit, and, finally,
made to balance precariously above increasingly insistent block
chords. Then "Margie," by the Original Dixieland Jazz Band's
pianist J. Russel Robinson,[1] showcased Brubeck's flair for stride
piano, authentic stride struts giving way to his left hand cruis-
ing at twice the speed of the groove, an illusion of sound fast-
forwarding in double time.

Moore's soulful bowed bass was featured on "These Foolish
Things," and the eggshell delicacy of the chorale-like "Elegy,"
a recent Brubeck composition dedicated to the memory of
his friend the Norwegian artist and jazz writer Randi Hultin,
coaxed out the lyrical heart of Bobby Militello's flute playing. Despite these moments of cathartic balladry, though, the
coiled-up energy released earlier refused to disperse, and the
concert hit a powerful dramatic peak with an epic "Travelin'
Blues," Brubeck's barely audible tremolos, framed by hectic
pockets of silence, voyaging toward churchy gospel shouts and
hollering left-hand clusters. Thunderous approval from the
crowd. But instead of capitalizing on the moment by triggering
the "Take Five" vamp, Brubeck decided to turn down the heat.
The familiar melody found itself recast as a tender, lilting waltz

---

1. The group's 1917 record "Livery Stable Blues," recorded three years before
Brubeck's birth, is often cited as the first jazz record—although some would
argue that depends on what you mean by "jazz."

on solo piano. And even once he segued into the vamp—cue enthusiastic applause—this "Take Five" was noticeably light on its feet.

For which don't read "lightweight." Militello's solo strayed from a regular 5/4 pulse and the groove fizzled out, usurped by a free-associating slipstream of sound. Brubeck took the unusual liberty of dovetailing the opening of his solo over the wind-down of Militello's. Mindful of the alien waters into which his hit tune had sailed, Brubeck kept the audience on his side by throwing a skeleton of the theme, outlined in naked octaves, against bass and drums, which were dicing up time into dislocated rhythmic units, before gradually adding layers of harmony to flesh out the texture. Melody, rhythm, and harmony were in gleeful flux. To the delectation of a sold-out house in an English seaside town, the Dave Brubeck Quartet was playing free jazz.

As the bus retraces yesterday's route, posters advertising a comedy show at the Brighton Dome turn the conversation briefly from jazz to stand-up. "Lenny Bruce[2] used to babysit Darius!" Brubeck grins and explains how the last person anyone would have expected to babysit came to look after his eldest son. "Lenny and I used to be on the same bill at a club in Hollywood and we became good friends. I didn't expect Lenny and Darius to get close, but they kind of gravitated toward each other and we thought, well, okay, it's fine with us if someone wants to take the kids off our hands for the afternoon. And Lenny took it very seriously and was completely responsible, I have to say."[3]

The club in question was the Crescendo, at 8572 Sunset Boulevard, where proprietor Gene Norman—who had paired

---

2. Comedian (1925–1966) whose free-form style of stand-up had an improvisational feel that was regularly compared to free jazz.

3. Interview with the author, April 24, 2003.

the Dave Brubeck Quartet with the Charlie Parker Quintet in 1953—also owned a smaller club, one floor up, called the Interlude. Customers could hear sets by Duke Ellington, Ella Fitzgerald, George Shearing, or Chico Hamilton at the Crescendo and then head upstairs to see emerging comedians like Woody Allen, Bob Newhart, Mort Sahl, Bill Cosby, and Tom Lehrer. Lenny Bruce began a series of residencies at the Interlude in July 1957, when the Brubeck Quartet was in town, playing the Crescendo at night and, by day, completing their album *Dave Digs Disney* at the Radio Recorders studio on Santa Monica Boulevard.

"My idea—always—was to get the quartet working steady and then think about re-forming as an octet," Brubeck says, all this talk of 1950s California reconnecting him to the past.

"Not by 1957, though, Dave," Iola interjects. "By then, the quartet could have been working every night of the year—and sometimes felt like it was—and getting the octet back together was no longer a—"

"True," Brubeck interrupts, "but earlier . . . early 1950s, when the quartet was doing 'The Way You Look Tonight' and 'How High the Moon,' the way we played those tunes came out of the octet. And back in 1952, '53, my dream was to get the octet going as a regular group."

All ideas about Dave Brubeck rightly begin with the Dave Brubeck Octet, which was formed in 1946, and not only because this group presented Brubeck's music to a paying public for the first time. Familiar names in the Brubeck saga begin to emerge. On alto saxophone was Paul Desmond. Octet drummer Cal Tjader and, later, bassist Ron Crotty would become the rhythm section of the Dave Brubeck Trio, and Crotty would remain as bass player in the Dave Brubeck Quartet. On clarinet (and occasional baritone saxophone) was William O. Smith, who would be actively associated with Brubeck for a whole six decades. As Brubeck was fine-tuning the material eventually released as *Time Out*, Smith recorded *The Riddle*, the first in a sequence of albums in which he effectively replaced Desmond inside the classic Dave Brubeck Quartet lineup, with Eugene Wright and Joe Morello. Smith re-re-emerged as a full-time quartet member in time for the 1982 album *Concord on a Summer Night* and made his final appearance on a Brubeck record in 1993 (though he continued to put in occasional guest appearances in concert right up to the end of Brubeck's life). Other octet regulars—including trumpeter Dick Collins, bassist Jack Weeks, and tenor saxophonist David Van Kriedt—would largely fade away from Brubeck's circle once the rise and rise of the quartet kicked the prospect of an octet recall into the long grass. But the importance of the group to Brubeck was absolute.

For the first time Brubeck was surrounded by inquiring musicians, all determined to carve out a musical language to call their own. The octet's prime concern was reconciling jazz and popular song form with the techniques and the sounds of modern composition inherited from Darius Milhaud, a composer with his own roots in Stravinsky, Satie, and Debussy. The instrumental makeup—trumpet, trombone, clarinet, alto saxophone, tenor saxophone, piano, bass, drums—allowed the ensemble to operate like a small, aerodynamic big band when required, stabbing chords punctuating under solos in the style of big bands from Fletcher Henderson to Duke Ellington. But hat tips toward big-band tradition were the exception—otherwise the octet boasted a strikingly fresh palette of sounds, textures, and instrumental combinations.

Today the group's legacy is preserved on eighteen officially released tracks, recorded over four sessions between 1946 and 1950 and issued originally by Fantasy Records under the titles *Old Sounds from San Francisco* and *Dave Brubeck Octet: Distinctive Rhythm Instrumentals.*[4] When, in 1956, Fantasy released an

---

4. *Old Sounds from San Francisco* documented the octet from 1946 to 1949; *Distinctive Rhythm Instrumentals* was recorded in a single session in July 1950. Both were released on ten-inch vinyl (and, confusingly, the title *Distinctive Rhythm Instrumentals* was also given to a Dave Brubeck Trio album).

anthology of all eighteen tracks, Brubeck chose not to reissue them in chronological order, and between the end of Brubeck's composition "Rondo" and the start of David Van Kriedt's arrangement of "I Hear a Rhapsody," the group's stylistic breadth became apparent. "Rondo" (not to be confused with the later "Blue Rondo à la Turk") set in motion a bustling, bumptious fanfare in the spirit of Satie's 1917 absurdist ballet score *Parade*, with Cal Tjader's snare drum, cymbals, and bass drum supporting the marchlike precision of the ensemble: an orchestral concept of percussion rather than anything to do with jazz time. Meanwhile, Brubeck's composition "Playland-at-the-Beach" and Smith's "Schizophrenic Scherzo" could easily have been mistaken for offcuts of Stravinsky's *The Soldier's Tale*, Octet, or his big-band jazz composition, *Ebony Concerto*.[5]

But then, in place of the regal pomp of "Rondo," the brutalist clang of the drill-bit chords with which Brubeck introduced "I Hear a Rhapsody" told anyone who cared to listen that the Dave Brubeck Octet could also be a red-hot jazz band. Van Kriedt's arrangements of "I Hear a Rhapsody," "Love Walked In," and "September in the Rain," and Brubeck's versions of "The Way You Look Tonight" and "Laura," were also bona fide jazz arrangements, the arranged material establishing a mood out of which improvised solos grew. Van Kriedt also contributed a composition he called "Fugue on Bop Themes," which was much admired by Milhaud and used by Igor Stravinsky, no less, to demonstrate flawless counterpoint when he taught at UCLA in 1951, and the octet, throughout its existence, managed to sashay with ease between jazz and composed music.

The foundations of their world were defined, in the beginning, by Milhaud. Brubeck's elder brother, Howard, had also studied with Milhaud, alongside Pete Rugolo, who would eventually become an arranger in Stan Kenton's band. While still an undergraduate at the College of the Pacific in Stockton,

5. Premiered by Woody Herman's orchestra at Carnegie Hall in 1946.

Brubeck hitchhiked to Mills for an introductory meeting with Milhaud. Once in Milhaud's class, "I'd hear Milhaud talk about how strict other composers could be in their teaching," Brubeck says. "He'd talk about Paul Hindemith,[6] who at that time was teaching at Yale, and you could see from his eyes that he was telling us, 'Boy, you're lucky to be with me—Hindemith is so strict you got to feel sorry for his students.'"

> Milhaud wanted to give you enough technique so that you could truly be free to make the music you wanted to make. He made those comments about Hindemith because, I think, he felt that Hindemith was using teaching as a way to impose his ideas about music onto his students. Milhaud never did that. He was certainly rigorous about counterpoint and fugue—as far as he was concerned, you couldn't understand Bach deeply enough. But when it came to composition, taking the techniques he had taught and using them to make our own pieces, he never tried to tell anybody what to do. He was interested in how the harmony worked and whether the counterpoint was really happening—he didn't like lazy counterpoint that just held the melody in place. But if you were being creative, he was happy; his students were then completely free to write what they wanted.
>
> Every week I had a private lesson and normally I'd take along a little piano piece; later in the week there would be lessons in orchestration and counterpoint. When David Van Kriedt, Bill Smith, Dick Collins, Bob Collins, and Jack Weeks came into the class, Milhaud knew that if we composed for our jazz instruments—and even played our counterpoint lessons on them—he would likely get the best out of us. And that is how the octet was born.

---

6. Prolific composer (1895–1963) known for his distinctive neoclassical style; his Concert Music for Brass and Strings, Op. 50 (1930) includes a section heavily influenced by big-band jazz.

Darius Milhaud arrived at Mills College in Oakland, California, in the summer of 1940. He had docked in New York on July 15, and as he recalled in his autobiography *My Happy Life*,[7] the Milhauds took a leisurely drive to the West Coast: buying a car was cheaper than paying for train tickets for himself, his wife Madeleine, and their son, Daniel. Milhaud had been recommended to Mills College by a panel of eminent names, including the conductor Pierre Monteux, who had premiered *The Rite of Spring* in 1913, and members of the Pro Arte Quartet, celebrated for their recordings of Haydn, Bartók, and Ravel. Securing Milhaud was a coup for the college, and the authorities built him a house on campus, where Brubeck would later take his weekly composition lesson. In his autobiography, Milhaud painted an idyllic image of a blissful, balmy day-to-day existence: the house "stands on a little height from which we can catch a glimpse of the [San Francisco] bay . . . surrounded by all kinds of trees, mimosas, palms, camellias, magnolias, and all the varieties of plants that grow in the warm temperate zone."

Alongside the composers Georges Auric, Arthur Honegger, Francis Poulenc, Germaine Tailleferre, and Louis Durey, Milhaud had gained notoriety as a member of Les Six, a composer collective resolute in its determination to create a musical language relevant to the street buzz and creative energy of 1920s Paris, where James Joyce held court in cafés, where Picasso, Man Ray, and Serge Diaghilev rewrote the rule book with each new work. With Erik Satie acting as their guiding spirit, membership of Les Six presupposed a distrust of the stern-browed Romanticism of Richard Wagner and Richard Strauss, whom they considered overly ripe and emotionally manipulative; even the florid chromaticism and perfumed orchestration of Claude Debussy were deemed ideologically suspect. The composers

---

7. Originally published as *Ma vie heureuse* (Paris: Éditions Belfond, 1987); English translation *My Happy Life*, trans. Donald Evans, George Hall and Christopher Palmer (London: Marion Boyars Publishers, 1995).

of Les Six instead took their lead from cubism and from the whimsical surrealist films of Jean Cocteau and René Clair. Les Six scores—like *L'Album des Six* (1920) and *Les Mariés de la Tour Eiffel* (1921)—were cut-and-pasted together from short, brusque pieces, with each member contributing a movement. The cult of personality that surrounded Wagner had no place in this new French music—pieces by Les Six had an air of affected self-importance that would usually implode as you listened.

Jazz, too, was essential to the mix. During the 1921 grand opening of Le Boeuf sur le Toit, a bar in the eighth arrondissement of Paris that would become the unofficial headquarters of Les Six, Milhaud and Cocteau played drums and percussion as the pianist Jean Wiéner entertained a gathering that included Picasso and Maurice Chevalier with Tin Pan Alley standards. The following year in New York, Milhaud guessed that a concert he had attended by the Paul Whiteman Orchestra[8] might not be the real jazz: the orchestra "had the precision of an elegant, well-oiled machine, a sort of Rolls Royce of dance music, but . . . remained entirely of this world and without inspiration," he wrote.

Milhaud was keen to visit some jazz clubs in Harlem and was not disappointed by what he heard: "Harlem had not yet been discovered by the snobs and aesthetes: we were the only white folk there. The music I heard was absolutely different from anything I had heard before, and was a revelation to me. Against the beat of the drums, the melodic lines crisscrossed in a breathless pattern of broken and twisted rhythms." Milhaud described how affected he had been by a black female singer whose refrain was set against the "kaleidoscopic background" of the orchestra's "constantly changing melodic pattern." He returned to Paris with a bundle of records on the Black Swan

---

8. Paul Whiteman (1890–1967), nicknamed "the King of Jazz," led a large orchestra that, despite including star jazz soloists like Bix Beiderbecke, Eddie Lang, and Jack Teagarden in its ranks, played stiff arrangements . . . stiffly.

label—a Harlem-based company with a black proprietor who recorded black music, usually to be sold to black customers—and a resolve to, he said, "use jazz for a chamber-music work."

These records were the real deal: Black Swan released an exhaustive catalog of three-minute masterpieces from the likes of Fletcher Henderson, James P. Johnson, Bessie Smith, and Ethel Waters, and Milhaud's resulting chamber music work was *La création du monde*, a sixteen-minute ballet scored for a small ensemble that, a century after it was composed, still packs a potent punch.[9] Milhaud accommodated those moments where the energy spills incorrigibly over the bar lines by letting his structure buckle in sympathy. His overlaid melody lines and his "patterns of broken and twisted rhythms" generated spontaneous heat and excitement through abrupt and unruly structural disjoints. The questing spirit of improvisation had infiltrated his attitude toward composition: his sounds live and breathe. Regularly cited as the work that triggered the classical world's embrace of jazz, George Gershwin's 1924 *Rhapsody in Blue* feels stiff and regimented in comparison. If Brubeck ever wondered why Milhaud was so insistent that true creative freedom could be expressed only through robust technique, he need have looked no further than his teacher's most famous work.

Both Milhaud and Brubeck came to Mills College as a direct consequence of World War II. Like the migrations of Stravinsky and Schoenberg (who ended up living as near neighbors in Los Angeles) before him, Milhaud's relocation to the US had been precipitated by the escalating chaos in Europe: in May 1940, with the German army within striking distance of Paris, the Milhauds fled to Lisbon and from there sought sanctuary in America. Brubeck arrived at Mills College in 1946 on the

---

9. Commissioned by Ballets Suédois and premiered in October 1923 at the Théâtre des Champs-Élysées, where Stravinsky's *Rite of Spring* had premiered ten years earlier. Leonard Bernstein, with the Orchestre National de France, made a benchmark recording in 1976.

GI Bill, an enlightened piece of legislation from the Roosevelt administration that handed war veterans financial assistance and other benefits, including the funds to pursue vocational or academic education. Under the GI Bill, male students could be admitted to the advanced master's-level courses at Mills, ordinarily an institution devoted to the education of girls—and as that extraordinary group of young musicians gathered in Milhaud's house, they found the essentials of their art lay somewhere between European and American ideals about music.

Today, heading back to London, is not the moment Brubeck chooses to talk about his experiences in the US Army, mobilized to Europe in 1944 as a GI. Those memories will come—for now he wants to stay focused on the music. After the war Milhaud negotiated a deal that allowed him to alternate his teaching duties between Mills College and the Conservatoire de Paris, and in 1948, Collins, Weeks, and Van Kriedt accepted his invitation to continue their studies in Paris. The invitation was also extended to Brubeck, who had already graduated from Mills, but as he remembered in 2000, "I had intended to go to Paris with him, but we had a newborn child and Milhaud wrote back to me that Paris was still in a state of deprivation and he thought it unwise to bring an infant."[10] A pity perhaps. A 2010 interview with Dick Collins abounds with fond memories of the year he spent in Paris, studying with Milhaud during the day, then disappearing into club land in the company of the local bebop fraternity, which included the expat drum great Kenny Clarke,[11] the onetime rhythmic motor of Dizzy Gillespie's big band.

---

10. Dave Brubeck to Gerry Collatz, June 22, 2000, Personal Correspondence, Brubeck Collection.

11. Drummer (1914–1985) who organized the house band at Minton's Playhouse in Harlem, where musicians later associated with bebop, like Parker, Gillespie, and Monk, played. Later Clarke played in Dizzy Gillespie's big band, out of which grew the first incarnation of the Modern Jazz Quartet, in which Clarke also played. He moved to Paris permanently in 1956.

But the unfinished business of the octet would pull them back to California. Collins and Kenny Clarke had become firm friends, and the microsubtleties of the drummer's approach to time and subdividing the beat left him endlessly fascinated, but Collins felt that he "wasn't really a bebop player . . . I could play it, but my style wasn't that way."[12] More significantly, Collins thought that David Van Kriedt's attempts to reconcile bop with his existing style "broke his back in a way. . . . You grow up and have your own style and go straight ahead with that. But all of a sudden, when bop came in, everyone was playing it. You had to if you wanted to keep working. But Dave [Van Kriedt] couldn't fit into that at all. He was more melodic."

William O. Smith had already tested his fortunes on the East Coast, enrolling at the Juilliard School of Music in New York City in 1945 to study clarinet and composition. Smith picked up a regular gig playing tenor saxophone at Kelly's Stables, a jazz club on Fifty-Second Street, in a trio led by the pianist Vicki Zimmer. This job helped pay his way and brought other benefits: after his own gig had finished he could wander along to other Fifty-Second Street clubs, where, on any given night, he might hear Charlie Parker, Billie Holiday, or Coleman Hawkins. But Smith felt his studies at Juilliard—with an old-school clarinet tutor and an unsympathetic composition department—were leading nowhere, and a chance encounter with Milhaud's music made him reassess everything. Smith's piano teacher handed him a suite of Milhaud piano pieces entitled *The Household Muse*,[13] and, immediately entranced, Smith realized that scraping together a living in New York was not for him. He decided to return home to California in the hope that Milhaud would accept him as a composition student at Mills.

---

12. Marc Meyers, "Interview: Dick Collins (Part 1)," JazzWax, June 7, 2010, www.jazzwax.com/2010/06/interview-dick-collins-part-1.html.

13. Milhaud's Opus 245, written in 1943.

And a few months later, following his discharge from the army in January 1946, Brubeck slipped through the city en route back to California. By January 24 he had reached Camp Kilmer, the US Army base in New Jersey. He was officially discharged on January 31 at Fort MacArthur in Los Angeles and the next day returned to the family home in Ione, California, and then headed for a long-awaited reunion with Iola.

E𝄞

"Milhaud was important to me, and everyone in the octet, in so many ways," Brubeck reflects, the tread of wheel against motorway establishing a steady groove that concentrates his mind. "Little, practical things became important, which I would understand just by being around him. I lived in a house opposite Milhaud's place at Mills, and every morning, while I was still waking up, I'd look through the window and see his lights come on at six in the morning. Writing music is hard work—you gotta get up early!

In his class, one of his favorite words was "continue"—if he said that word you knew it was going well. He was happy that I, and Bill Smith and Kriedt, were writing jazz, and by "continue" he meant that he did not need the music to be something else; he did not want it to sound like his music, certainly not like an academic fugue. The suggestions he made about how we could improve our compositions came from his understanding of our individual approaches as composers. In terms of the octet, the most important thing Milhaud taught us all—and you can hear it in the records—was about counterpoint, which helped us create our own sound. If you think back to what had been happening in the swing era, especially in big bands—Duke Ellington, Basie, Benny Goodman— counterpoint was never really important. Blocks of harmony passing between the brass and the saxophones, that was how arrangers tended to think, and I loved those arrangements.

And Milhaud never said [that] what jazz lacks these days is counterpoint. But because counterpoint was so important to the way he thought, we all latched on to that, and it became important to us.

The reason, Milhaud said, he never wrote—or cared for—twelve-tone music is that in a twelve-tone piece you are nowhere in particular [harmonically], therefore you can't go anywhere.[14] You think of Beethoven, or Stravinsky, he'd say, they are always leading you somewhere new, and for that to happen you need to move between keys. This, for Milhaud, was the basis of architecture in music. I remember bringing him a piano piece, which he played through, and he said, "This is very good, but look at your second theme; if you put a flat in front of every note, your piece will have modulated when the first theme comes back." He was right—the whole piece was transformed because the harmony moved somewhere. And when you learn to modulate between keys, then you can get into a whole load of stuff, putting keys on top of each other, using two, or more, keys at once. Polytonality was central to the music we all wrote for the octet; and in the quartet, then in the choral and orchestral pieces I wrote after the quartet split up.

We'd bring records to play for Milhaud. I remember Bill Smith coming along with Boyd Raeburn,[15] who he loved, and I was very keen on Stan Kenton.[16] Stan, along with Benny Goodman and Ellington, had played in Stockton when I was young, and I could tell even then Kenton was playing something different from standard big-band charts. By the time I was with Milhaud, I could hear that Kenton was putting different keys

---

14. Disciples of twelve-tone and serial composition would refute this analysis.

15. Big-band leader (1913–1966) whose staff arranger George Handy was captivated by Stravinsky. "Dalvatore Sally," "Boyd Meets Stravinsky," and "March of the Boyds" explicitly recalled the orchestration and the harmonic and rhythmic bite of *The Rite of Spring* and *Les Noces*.

16. Big-band leader (1911–1979) whose self-termed "progressive jazz" eagerly embraced dissonance and polyrhythms.

together and he was adventurous with rhythm—he'd obviously been studying Stravinsky. And he was from Los Angeles,
and I liked that he was from California. Kenton opened things
up, for me and for how people thought about using a big
band, and Milhaud liked what he heard.

Brubeck, in his sleeve note for the 1956 octet anthology,
expressed gratitude that somebody—although he doesn't spec-
ify who—had had the forethought to bring along a portable
acetate recorder to the group's earliest meetings in 1946; otherwise these early experiments with rhythm and tonality would
have been lost. Tonality, conventionally configured, takes listeners on a journey through and around a spectrum of different
keys. Composers might take digressive swerves, stretching melody and harmony so wide and far that you wonder where the
music is leading you—and indeed, for some composers, tonal
ambiguity is the very point. But even the most ambiguous tonal
music is usually anchored around one fundamental key—the
tonic, or home. Brubeck's "Rondo" and his thirty-second "Curtain Music,"[17] along with Jack Weeks's arrangement of "Prisoner's Song," were fully scored pieces designed to show off the
group's absorption in polytonality—and in "Curtain Music,"
polytonal thinking kept deferring any return to "home."
    Just as the first witheringly dry, slammed block chord that
announced "Curtain Music" declared A major as a possibility, it also contradicted A major. Brubeck's opening chord
was a polytonal hybrid—A major in the right hand stacked
against G major in his left. When the end of his first phrase
cadences at the stretched limits of what would normally be
allowed in A major, our ears become accepting of what might
otherwise sound harmonically inconsistent because Brubeck
had set up a context in which more than one tonality was in

17. Originally called "Closing Theme," Brubeck's theme was subsequently
used to open and close concerts and retitled "Curtain Music."

play. Quick-moving ensemble figurations answered Brubeck's inquisitive piano with chains of melody that flitted between different keys; only in the final bar did the music rest on an unambiguous chord of pure A major.

Layering one raw tonality against a different tonality has a complex psychoacoustic effect. Chords retain their basic identities while spawning a spectrum of notes, now forced into unlikely alliances, that blend and clash unpredictably. The brain, hopefully, grasps increasingly complex interrelationships between unrelated chords as our ears acquire a taste for a tarter and more aromatic harmonic palette. Brubeck was also interested in rhythm, and in stoking the rhythmic intensity. True enough, interrupting bars of 6/4 with sudden breakouts of 4/4 was a modest innovation compared to the rhythmic math of Stravinsky's *Rite of Spring*, composed three decades earlier. But Brubeck, now twenty-six, was beginning to recognize where these experiments with polytonality and upsetting rhythmic regularity might lead him.

Within the context of the octet, standards served the purpose of allowing audiences to measure the group's innovations against the yardstick of songs they already knew. Jack Weeks's version of "Prisoner's Song" (a country ballad recorded in 1924 by Vernon Dalhart and later covered by Hank Snow and Johnny Cash) pinned all its dramatic impetus on the expectation that the music was heading toward one key, before a polytonal sleight of hand propelled the music toward a wholly unexpected chord. A wheezy wind-band sound allied with brittle, square rhythms became reminiscent of Kurt Weill's famously arid style of orchestration, and Weeks's piece amounted to a wholesale recomposition of the original song, with chords compressed into each other until they smudged and Brubeck's role reduced to oscillating around the essential notes of the final chord.

Van Kriedt's arrangement of "I Hear a Rhapsody" was the octet at its most routine. His solo work justified Dick Collins's description of the Van Kriedt style as "melodic" and harmonically adventurous—but independently so of bebop. The luminescence of his tone and the rarefied melodic curve he traced as his solo licked the upper register of his tenor saxophone were logical extensions of Lester Young rather than anything to do with Charlie Parker. But the different moving parts of his arrangement didn't quite make a satisfying whole. The sweet-toothed ensemble accompaniment was noticeably at odds with the testosterone of Brubeck's comping—and the stuttering polytonal thud skidding across the glide of bass and drums, with which he began the piece—and you wonder why, when Van Kriedt's solo sails away from Parker, his written backdrop hinted strongly at bebop harmony.

Bill Smith's arrangement of "You Go to My Head" began with stacked-up polytonal chords that lurked like ominous clouds of acrid smoke which eventually parted and allowed the sunshine of his clarinet to glow. Smith's knack of marginally sharpening notes toward the peak of a phrase warmed the music from the inside, contrasting with swirls of harmony noir from the ensemble. A nonchalant gear change suddenly tripped the music into a double-time swing section, during which Smith invoked Benny Goodman (while Brubeck's flirtatious keyboard tickle provided a decent approximation of Teddy Wilson, Goodman's pianist of choice). And then something entirely unexpected. By remapping the tread of weak and strong beats—the last beat of a 4/4 bar becoming the first beat of a 3/4 bar—Smith sewed a brief waltz into the texture of the music, around which he floated arpeggios reminiscent of Mozartian passagework.

Brubeck's take on "Laura" also opened with bleak, troubling chords, as he injected something of the night into those sumptuous string chords with which the composer David Raksin scored Otto Preminger's 1944 film *Laura*.[18] This side contained

---

18. Preminger's 1959 film *Anatomy of a Murder* was scored by Duke Ellington, and Brubeck was mentioned in the script.

Brubeck's fully fledged solo on record and a powerful snap-shot of the future. His solo climaxed with six hammered clus-ters, perched somewhere on the border between harmony and noise, irregularly placed within the bar. Instead of following the logic of the song, Brubeck followed his intuition and, after his pummeling of the piano smashed the fourth wall of the tune so convincingly, he then slipped back with ease inside the flow of Raksin's melody. But those fatalistic clusters spooked the remainder of his solo.

In 1947, the octet recorded two fully scored Stravinskian com-positions—Van Kriedt's "Serenade Suite" and Smith's "Schizo-phrenic Scherzo"—featuring the wind players alone. Brubeck had no reason to be at these sessions, and perhaps wasn't, but in later interviews he would cite "Schizophrenic Scherzo" as an important staging post on the way to what the group was collec-tively attempting to achieve. Smith's keenly sculpted polytonal harmonies and sections that slipped into 7/4 time were the very essence of octet thinking.

When the Paris contingent returned in 1949, the group recorded two pieces—Brubeck's "Playland-at-the-Beach" and a hokum take on "How High the Moon"—as an audition for NBC Radio in San Francisco. "Playland-at-the-Beach" had originally been written for Milhaud's composition class in a version for solo piano, and Brubeck's treatment for the ensem-ble—without piano—avoided sounding too obviously like orchestrated piano music. Brubeck made the instruments talk to each other, and Bill Smith's trick of hitting and then rap-idly sliding away from a note helped implant an illusion of the ensemble tottering gracefully, as if the sounds were dan-gling from a puppeteer's strings. The opening section darted agitatedly between three distinct keys, with jolts and collisions in the orchestration—like a trumpet line being snatched and sucked inside the texture like a Venus flytrap—matching the non sequitur upsets of Brubeck's harmony. This vision of Cal-ifornian beach life, a hubbub of uncorked energy, had none of the surfer chill with which Brian Wilson's Beach Boys would breeze up two decades later.

Anticipating "Blue Rondo à la Turk" and "Three to Get Ready" ten years in advance, "Playland-at-the-Beach" functioned like an intricately constructed timepiece mosaic. In 1959, "Blue Rondo"'s 9/8 time—counted 2+2+2+3—would part to reveal inserts of the blues in 4/4 time. In 1949, Brubeck grounded "Playland-at-the-Beach" in 6/8 time, with each four-bar 6/8 phrase coming to rest on a bar in 3/8, which had the effect of gliding the last chord of one phrase into the first chord of the next. A caustic march in 2/4 time suddenly elbowed its way to the foreground, like a flashback to Stravinsky's *Soldier's Tale*; but Brubeck hadn't finished his grand rhythmic tease. Another episode reaccented the 3+3 of 6/8 to become the 2+2+2 of 3/4, a neat rhythmic pun to chew on as Brubeck's harmony feasted on another, more existential ambiguity: Was this music in the major or the minor? Brightly lit major chords fell toward the minor, and the harmonically open-ended bass part purposely left that question hanging—and the uncertainty was delightful. Polytonal chords riding over a fixed bass line would become a staple Brubeck gesture, and Milhaud, we can presume, looked at this section and contentedly advised Dave to "continue."

Their other NBC audition piece was designed to show off the stylistic range of the octet. Over six minutes—and with Burma Lounge owner and radio host Jimmy Lyons providing a droll hipster narration—"How High the Moon" was taken on a kaleidoscopic journey through jazz history, from Dixieland to bebop. Dick Collins demonstrated a mastery of 1920s trumpet—with a tone nearer to Bix Beiderbecke's than to Louis Armstrong's—and later turned in a neat takeoff of Dizzy Gillespie. Bill Smith revived his immaculate Benny Goodman impression in a section depicting the swing era as Brubeck rolled out snatches of ragtime and boogie-woogie. The tonality-busting chordal density of "Laura" had showed one way forward, but, equally, Brubeck was rooted in the elementals of 1920s jazz piano styles.

· "How High the Moon" ended with, in the words of Jimmy Lyons's narration, "our young modernists negotiating a fugue." The rules for creating a fugue are strict and watertight. Academia sets great store by any student's ability to follow these rules by the book. As different lines weave together, the harmony must be organized so that the same note *never* appears in different parts at the same time, which would dilute the richness of the harmony. For Brubeck, fugue was a more formal technique than the "Playland-at-the-Beach" model of a mosaic—but it was another way in which overlapping strands of musical activity could be made to coexist.

A final eight pieces, recorded in July 1950, drew a line under the octet's history on record by pushing their fixation on counterpoint to the max. "Love Walked In," "IPCA," "What Is This Thing Called Love?," "The Way You Look Tonight," "September in the Rain," "Prelude," "Fugue on Bop Themes," and "Let's Fall in Love" parked the Stravinsky-meets-Milhaud side of the group to one side and were all dispatched with effortless, blithe swing. Compared to that first session at Mills College four years previously, the well-drilled and assured playing had noticeably matured.

Brubeck told *DownBeat* readers in 1953 that his arrangement of Jerome Kern's "The Way You Look Tonight" had been written to rebut one critic's description of what he had termed a "typical" jazz arrangement.[19] The critic wrote, Brubeck said, that "most jazz arrangements start with a huge introduction that sounds like Prokofiev and then goes into some terrible melody for three minutes; then it goes out with a Prokofiev ending . . . and that's an arrangement." Having the good grace not to name this hapless critic, who clearly hadn't heard

---

19. "The Jazz Scene Today," *DownBeat,* June 3, 1953 (an edited transcription of an undated Q and A session involving Brubeck at Boston University).

any Fletcher Henderson, Duke Ellington, or Don Redman (nor much Prokofiev), Brubeck said he had become inspired "to write an arrangement that would hold together"—not by including big introductions or endings but by delicately rethreading the song's different parts.

"To make [the arrangement] have more unity, I put the first eight bars and the bridge together," he told *DownBeat*. Brubeck's composer's brain had stripped out its constituent parts to investigate how Kern had put his song together—and how it might be reassembled. His remake opened with the melody played in two-part counterpoint, ping-ponging between Dick Collins's trumpet and Paul Desmond's alto saxophone, as further lines were gradually added in. At the end, the bridge yearned to link back to the song's opening strain, and this superimposition of the opening eight bars of Kern's melody with the bridge left the arrangement hanging off a question mark. The role of a commercial arranger was to wrap a song up in elaborate instrumental colors while remaining largely faithful to its original structure. But Brubeck reassembled the different pieces and tantalized listeners' ears with the possibility that his arrangement had an imaginary afterlife beyond the final bar line.

David Van Kriedt prefaced his "Fugue on Bop Themes" with an elegant Ellingtonian "Prelude," on which Paul Desmond had an opportunity to display his honeyed tone and empyreal phrasing for the first time on record in a solo, while the "Fugue" itself, crisply introduced by Brubeck and Smith, was a joyous affair. Elsewhere, on tunes like "Love Walked In" and "September in the Rain," octet members delivered swinging, melodic solos, and its members dared to hope that they were perched on the brink of commercial success.

But popular success for Brubeck was not to be, not yet. Fantasy's anthology of the complete octet music was issued in the summer of 1956, and Brubeck hoped that the publicity campaign Columbia Records had mounted to promote *Brubeck Plays Brubeck*, his first solo piano album, released that July, might rub off on these old sounds from San Francisco.

His sleeve note put optimum spin on the octet's checkered fortunes. "Within the past ten years I can think of very few released recordings with more musical importance than the work of the Octet," he wrote, before adding the bold assertion that he had "heard more and more of the Octet innovations being used and accepted in the 'mainstream' of jazz." Octet colleagues, he reasoned, had enjoyed thriving careers since. William O. Smith and Jack Weeks had studied with the twelve-tone composer Roger Sessions at the University of California, Berkeley, and they had both received the Prix de Paris. Dick Collins had been working with Woody Herman's orchestra. Cal Tjader, after drumming for pianist George Shearing's quintet, had spearheaded a revival of Afro-Cuban jazz; while the ascent of Paul Desmond as a member of the Dave Brubeck Quartet and winner of the "best alto saxophone" category in polls conducted by *DownBeat* and *Metronome* magazines spoke for itself.[20]

The achievements of the octet had gone largely unacknowledged, according to Brubeck, because of an imbalance in the way jazz was reported and disseminated: "The jazz-conscious public, the agents, the recording companies, the jazz journals, the reporters, all had their eyes and ears focused on the East Coast," he claimed. Both Shearing and Duke Ellington, he continued, had helped spread the word, and while the octet had been an essential part of helping to establish their "individual successes . . . the economic struggle of keeping so large a group together was too great. After three years without work we disbanded." But talk of disbanding and of mere economic "struggle," understandable given that the purpose of Brubeck's words was to help sell records, belied a harsher reality. After the

---

20. Desmond won "best alto" in the *DownBeat* readers' poll from 1955 to 1960, and again in 1962, and in *Metronome* magazine from 1955 to 1960.

joy of their year at Mills College, the Brubecks—who by now included four-month-old Darius, born June 14, 1947—moved to San Francisco in the fall of 1947 with no prospect of regular employment. Welcome, indeed, to hard times.

But Brubeck's sleeve note, no doubt unwittingly, also managed to implant into the history of the octet a series of misunderstandings, both large and small. Why did Brubeck assiduously avoid referring to the group in his notes as "my" octet, preferring "the" octet? He made it clear that they had operated as a "co-operative group, each man conducting and rehearsing the band in his own work." But William O. Smith, speaking in 2018, stressed that the eighteen surviving tracks have unfortunately skewed the totality of the group's ambitions and achievements.[21] "We were an *experimental* group," Smith said.

> Someone like Paul [Desmond], although certainly very interested in composers like Stravinsky and Bartók, had already decided he wanted to have a career playing jazz; but for me, and I think for Jack Weeks, jazz was only a part of what we wanted to be as musicians. My piece "Schizophrenic Scherzo" had a jazz setting, but I used a tone row when I composed it. David Van Kriedt's "Fugue on Bop Themes" brought fugue into jazz, but there was also a side of the octet's activities that had nothing to do with jazz. I wrote some little pieces based on [poems by] E. E. Cummings, and also made arrangements of Milhaud's Clarinet Concerto,[22] and some things by Bartók and [Ernst] Krenek,[23] for the group that were never recorded.

(The David Van Kriedt papers, housed at the University of the Pacific, includes a long and tantalizing list of unrecorded

---

21. Interview with the author, February 21, 2018.

22. Opus 230 (1941).

23. Austrian composer (1900–1991) who was married to Gustav Mahler's daughter Anna and who embraced twelve-tone composition and the influence of jazz in his opera *Jonny spielt auf* (1926).

octet pieces, including Van Kriedt originals with intriguing titles like "In My Craft" and "Kon Tiki" and his arrangements of the standards "I Want to Be Happy," "Indiana," "I've Got You Under My Skin," and "Pennies from Heaven.")

Only in 1949, as a collective that had been known for three years as "the Eight" transformed itself into "the Dave Brubeck Octet," would Brubeck emerge as the group's de facto leader. The name "the Eight" had consciously riffed off Les Six and was a label, Smith thought, that spoke more precisely of the group's core identity as jazz musicians and improvisers who were also inspired by modern composition. "When we were try-ing to make a go of the octet, around 1949, 1950 in San Fran-cisco," remembered Smith,

> we'd play gigs in Chinese restaurants, but no one was inter-ested in hiring a group called "the Eight." We would show up one week as the Bill Smith Octet and get fired; we'd go back a while later as the David Van Kriedt Octet and get fired again. Eventually it became obvious that we needed to call ourselves the Dave Brubeck Octet if we were to going to get any reg-ular work. Dave had started to have a little success outside the octet, and using his name made sense to us all. But by the mid-1950s he had become such a major part of jazz that, when people were starting to think about the octet again, the nuances of what originally the Eight had been were lost—this despite Dave's careful explanations in interviews about our background and history.

The artist and illustrator Arnold Roth,[24] who would create a series of memorably droll covers for Dave Brubeck albums, set the tone for his collaborations with the pianist with the cover

---

24. Born in 1929, Roth created cover art for Brubeck, Cal Tjader, and Pete Seeger, and illustrations and cartoons for the *New Yorker*, *Playboy*, *Punch*, and *National Lampoon*.

art he drew for the Fantasy compilation of octet sides, which could be read as wry commentary upon the group's sustainability as a commercial entity. We see a haggard-looking Salvation Army band, with instruments including tuba, cornet, and tambourine, knocking on the door of two rakish jazz hipsters, cigarettes drooping idly out of their mouths. One is holding an alto saxophone, the other a guitar, and through the window a double bass has been leaned against the wall. Octet music, this image tells us, cuts right across anyone's expectations of "formal" music and jazz. Roth's jaunty, proto–Hanna Barbera lettering announced that this album was by the "Dave Brubeck Octet" while, positioned immediately underneath, the tag "featuring Paul Desmond, Cal Tjader, David Van Kriedt, Dick Collins" was a subtle attempt at steering this music toward the same informed jazz audience inclined, hopefully, to buy "new" Brubeck: *Jazz: Red Hot and Cool* and *Dave Brubeck and Jay & Kai at Newport* by the Brubeck Quartet, and the solo piano *Brubeck Plays Brubeck*, had all been recently released.

Bill Smith's name was excluded from the roll call because he had spent the years 1951 to '53 in Paris and in 1956 was preparing to take up an academic position in Rome, and, unlike Dick Collins or Paul Desmond, his was not a name familiar to jazz fans. Airbrushing such an important contributor to the octet as composer, arranger, and clarinet soloist from the front cover of the Fantasy LP feels harsh, although Smith did fare better than some. Another local alto saxophonist, Bob Cummings,[25] filled in whenever a paying gig kept Paul Desmond from octet duties. Desmond, in fact, appears on only one octet track from 1946 ("I Hear a Rhapsody"), while Cummings played the entire 1947 session that produced "Schizophrenic Scherzo"—a major contribution that went uncredited in 1956.

---

25. The only African American musician to play with the octet, Cummings later worked with bandleader Sun Ra, playing bass clarinet on the early 1960s albums *Cosmic Tones for Mental Therapy* and *When Angels Speak of Love.*

Down in the engine room, more confusion. Brubeck's sleeve notes implied that Jack Weeks played all eighteen tracks, when we know, because he's listed on *Old Sounds from San Francisco*, that Ron Crotty played bass on the 1950 session. (It seems likely that Weeks would have led his own "Prisoner's Song," and he must have played on the 1946 pieces, recorded before Brubeck met Crotty. But he did not play the 1950 session.)

Cal Tjader's personal fingerprints were all over the drumming, but the drummers Richard Saltzman and John Markham both played live engagements with the octet during this era. Markham would later work with Nat King Cole, Ella Fitzgerald, Benny Goodman, and Frank Sinatra, and in the quartet pianist Vince Guaraldi formed in 1955, with Jerry Dodigon on alto saxophone and one Eugene Wright on bass. Saltzman became a fixture on the local San Francisco scene with his own groups, and occasionally backed visiting stars like Charles Mingus, and sold furniture as a sideline to help pay his bills. Could we be listening to another drummer altogether on some octet tracks? Markham, it seems, played only one live concert with the octet, but Saltzman had first refusal on live gigs whenever Tjader was otherwise engaged—and on recordings, too? There are, it seems, too many imponderables and faded memories to supply any definitive answers. Brubeck's inclination, in his sleeve note, to skate over doubts about who played on which octet track, and when, was perhaps due to limitations of space, or the feeling that the majority of people buying the record didn't care, or perhaps he himself could not fully remember.

In a 1953 letter to Brubeck,[26] Van Kriedt wrote of a "nucleus" within the membership of the octet—the same word that, in a 1980 essay written to accompany a Book of the Month Club compendium of his earliest recordings,[27] Brubeck used to

---

26. David Van Kriedt to Dave Brubeck, September 23, 1953. Personal Correspondence, Brubeck Collection.

27. Dave Brubeck, "Early Fantasies," booklet included with Book of the Month Club boxed set of LPs, catalog number 20-5566 (1980).

describe an octet core of Smith, Van Kriedt, Dick Collins, and Weeks, which also helps explain his hesitancy in identifying the rhythm section. It suited the narrative in 1956, and would no doubt have pleased the Fantasy sales team, to imply that Paul Desmond had been part of the octet inner circle. But Desmond and Tjader came from outside the close coterie of students that had surrounded Darius Milhaud at Mills. They had been studying at San Francisco State College—part of a circle of budding jazz musicians that included the pianist Richard Wyands, who would later play with Kenny Burrell and Gene Ammons—and their voices were added *to* the core octet. In his 1980 essay, Brubeck wrote of Jack Weeks needing to swap between bass and trombone if Bob Collins was unavailable,[28] and also said, "We had several drummers, finally ending up with Cal Tjader, whose versatility later proved so valuable in the Trio."

This reinforces the case that the octet existed as much as an idea about music, carried around inside Brubeck's imagination, as a dependable reality. The Eight played their first concert as a benefit at Mills College for the World Student Service Fund (a scheme designed to fund scholarships) in March 1947, and then a whole two years passed before they played in public again—this time before a paying audience at the College of the Pacific in Stockton, California, from which Brubeck had graduated in 1942. Two months later, on March 6, 1949, the group—under the billing "New Sounds in Modern Music with the Jazz Workshop Ensemble"—played an ambitious program at the Marines' Memorial Theatre in San Francisco. The concert was designed to show off the full range of the octet's capabilities: jazz standards in the first half and, after an intermission, a set of fully composed music that included Smith's E. E. Cummings pieces, a Paul Verlaine setting by Jack Weeks, and Brubeck's *Miniature Dance Suite*. The Smith and Weeks pieces

---

28. A pre-echo of the bass/trombone multi-instrumental role that Brubeck's son Chris would fulfill in the 1980s version of the Dave Brubeck Quartet.

were sung by a guest vocalist, Joyce Bryant, who would later find fame as a jazz and opera singer and as a sex symbol regularly referred to in the press as "the black Marilyn Monroe."

A repeat performance a month later in Berkeley included the first live performance of Van Kriedt's "Fugue on Bop Themes," but two other compositions performed that day went unrecorded—Jack Weeks's "Four Quiet Preludes" and a Smith piece tailored around Dick Collins, "Concertino for Trumpet." It was at the Marines' Memorial Theatre that they appeared under the moniker "the Dave Brubeck Octet" for the first time, allaying the fears of promoter Ray Gorum that a group with such an anonymous name as "the Eight" was likely to succeed only in blowing tumbleweed through the box office.

# Chapter Three

# IDEAS OF ORDER

"In ghostlier demarcations, keener sounds."

WALLACE STEVENS, "The Idea of Order at Key West," 1934

"Iola! What was the name of that guy who promoted the octet, who wanted us to use my name?" The bus's rapid approach toward the London suburbs is gathering speed, with only an hour to go before the Brubecks are dropped back at their flat in Maida Vale, West London, home from home for the duration of the quartet's tour. Dave is trying to remember Ray Gorum's name, but he looks around to find his wife asleep. He shrugs. "I'll ask her when she wakes up; Iola's much better with names than me.

But the other guy who became important around this time, changed everything in fact, was Jimmy Lyons. I think Paul [Desmond] met him first and somehow we persuaded him to act as a kind of master of ceremonies [for the Marines'

59

Memorial concert], which was a good idea because at the time Jimmy had his own radio show, very popular, and he helped bring people in. Jimmy himself was very taken with what he heard, probably preferring the jazz to the classical, but he understood, I think, what we were about as a group, and he began talking to people he knew at NBC. He talked about us as both a jazz and a classical group, and the people at NBC were so taken with that idea that we landed ourselves an audition. Jimmy narrated "How High the Moon," and we also recorded my "Playland-at-the-Beach." They liked it but couldn't see how they could afford to pay eight musicians to play a radio show. They thought about it for a while, then asked if I could do something with a trio, which they could pay for. So I used Ron Crotty and Cal [Tjader] from the octet and we played on Jimmy's show a few times, weekly at one stage. But always my hope was, the trio goes down well, NBC might use the octet.

Although Lyons's intervention with NBC did not work out as planned, his proselytizing on behalf of the octet did produce some unexpected windfalls, including a plum gig opening for an acknowledged jazz master. In his 1980 essay for the Book of the Month Club, Brubeck shared fond memories of opening a concert for the Woody Herman Orchestra at the San Francisco Opera House in 1950 and being warmly applauded by Herman's musicians as they walked off stage; "Coincidentally, just in the past year," he wrote, "the Dave Brubeck Quartet has played three concerts followed by Woody's youthful band; and each time my mind has raced back to that concert 30 years ago when everything seemed to ride on our acceptance." (Lyons would also, five or six years later, save Brubeck's life. The Brubecks were visiting undeveloped land near the Lyons home, on a mountaintop above Big Sur, near Monterey, when Brubeck sat down, very narrowly avoiding a rattlesnake. Lyons ordered him to freeze. Chris Brubeck finishes the story: "Jimmy said in a very serious tone, 'Dave, I am about to tell you something, and it is extremely important that you do not move at all. Try to stay calm, but there is a rattlesnake right behind you. Don't move, but when I tell you to jump off that ledge, make one quick move and jump. Do you understand?' Then we waited a little and Jimmy shouted, 'JUMP!' My dad went flying off that ledge down the hill slope like he had been shot out of a cannon. The snake did strike at my dad's back, but he was already six feet down the hill, flying through the air."[1])

But that eagerly hoped-for call requesting the octet never came, and received wisdom has supposed that the octet's 1950 recording session was also their final hurrah—that shortly afterward the group folded without fanfare as economic realities finally overcame youthful idealism. But Brubeck's papers reveal that his commitment to making the octet viable stretched far into 1953—after the Dave Brubeck Quartet had recorded *Jazz at Oberlin* and only a year before he signed with Columbia Records.

During the summer of 1953, Larry Bennett at the Associated Booking Corporation wrote a detailed response to Brubeck's inquiries about a potential octet tour.[2] Associated Booking Corporation—ABC—was Chicago-born Joe Glaser's artist management agency, with which Brubeck had signed at the end of 1950. Glaser would represent Brubeck throughout the years of the classic Dave Brubeck Quartet, their association ending only with Glaser's death in 1969. The correspondence between Brubeck and Glaser—and Glaser's assistant managers, Larry Bennett and Bert Block—gives compelling, in-depth insights into Brubeck's world. Glaser, you suspect, had zero interest in

1. Conversation with Chris Brubeck, January 15, 2018; followed up by email, May 30, 2018.
2. Larry Bennett to Dave Brubeck, August 11, 1953, Business Correspondence, Brubeck Collection.

polytonality and polyrhythm. The clean-cut Brubeck and his business-minded manager—whose alleged links with the mob reached as far as Jack Ruby, who, in 1963, was charged with the murder of John F. Kennedy's assassin, Lee Harvey Oswald[3]—made an odd couple. Their written exchanges were generally warm and affable, with intermittent grumbles of mutual irritation. Unforeseen humor rippled to the surface, too, as when, in response to Brubeck's admiring his Cadillac, Glaser dropped a line into a letter that is pure Tony Soprano: "If you ever want me to get you immediate delivery on a Cadillac, it will be a pleasure to do so or to do anything I can for you at any time."

Although the balance of power switched noticeably when Brubeck's unswayable popularity eventually gave him license to call the shots, Glaser was the dominant partner during the 1950s and early 1960s. He viewed the Dave Brubeck Quartet as an investment he needed to protect, and curbing its leader's more quixotic enthusiasms was a key concern. In his letter, Larry Bennett—presumably acting on Glaser's instructions—stomped on the madness of thinking that the octet had any commercial promise. After opening with some good news about quartet bookings, Bennett raised the subject of the octet gently. "I am happy indeed to hear about the great success the Octet is having at the Sunday afternoon sessions," he said, before humoring Brubeck. "I feel, Dave, you will be able to perform at colleges and concert halls with the Octet after you have firmly established yourself as a top name in the small band field. I think you need one more tour through the East with

---

3. Connections between Glaser and Ruby date back to Glaser's early days in Chicago, although when Ruby visited the ABC offices in 1964 to ask for "favors," Glaser dismissed him and later described him as a "mental case," "a phony," and a "namedropper." US Congress, House of Representatives, Select Committee on Assassinations, *Findings of the Select Committee on Assassinations in the Assassination of President John F. Kennedy in Dallas, Tex., November 22, 1963*, 95th Congress, 2nd session, January 2, 1979, https://archive.org/stream/HouseSelectCommittee OnAssassinations/Volume%209_djvu.txt.

your quartet to achieve the stature in your particular field so you might return next time on a tour with the Octet." Bennett concludes with a reminder that "the remmerative [*sic*] aspect must be of prime consideration because of the costs involved in transporting and paying salaries to seven top-flight musicians besides yourself." His letter concludes with the customary "kindest regards to Oli and yourself."[4]

It comes as no surprise to learn that ABC was agnostic about the money-guzzling octet, but that the group was still playing in 1953 comes as an unexpected bolt from the archives. As preparations were underway to tour with Charlie Parker and Brubeck was leading his quartet toward *Jazz at the College of the Pacific,* the octet was an ongoing project, with regular Sunday afternoon sessions hosted by the Black Hawk Club in San Francisco. A program booklet has survived from December 19, 1953—only five days after *Jazz at the College of the Pacific*—that announces, "The Dave Brubeck Octet in a benefit performance for the Emerson School Music Program. Berkeley Little Theatre. Saturday, December 19th—2.30pm." The lineup, we're told, "includes Dave van Kriedt, William Smith, Jack Weeks and Dick Collins, in addition to the personnel of the Quartet. Occasionally Bob Collins, brother of Dick, comes in to play trombone." This booklet was likely standard issue across all octet concerts, with built-in generalities to account for the last-minute substitutions of players. There is no mention of Cal Tjader, who, by 1953, was enjoying successes of his own; and if this latter-day octet was essentially the Dave Brubeck Quartet (Ron Crotty, bass, and Joe Dodge, drums) with added horns, then Jack Weeks would often have found himself surplus to requirements.

The booklet also posed a crucial question. What sort of jazz would an audience member attending an octet concert expect

---

4. Letters from ABC were always scrupulously polite, even when conveying bad news or trying to persuade Brubeck to do something he didn't necessarily want to do. "Oli" was a pet name for Iola, used by family and close friends throughout her life.

to hear? Their style, the notes reported, had been "variously described as 'postbop,' 'cool jazz' and 'cerebral swing,'" before Paul Desmond was called upon to provide some clarity: "At its best [the octet contains] the vigor and force of simple jazz, the harmonic complexities of Bartók and Milhaud, the form (and much of the dignity) of Bach, and at times, the lyrical romanticism of Rachmaninoff." Desmond's neat analysis chimed with claims elsewhere in the booklet that the octet was "probably the most serious minded group of jazz musicians on record. But jazz is a classification they protest, since their purpose is 'to create music, not categorize it.'" Four years later, in *DownBeat* magazine, Brubeck set the terms of a debate about the octet's place in the wider context of jazz history that never fully went away.[5]

Quizzed by the writer Ralph J. Gleason[6] about the Miles Davis Nonet—which recorded for the first time in January 1949 and whose collected output, released under the title *The Birth of the Cool* in 1957, was heralded as a radical post-bop reboot for jazz—Brubeck enthusiastically acknowledges it as "a great group. I liked it very much," before adding the disclaimer: "I know that the octet predates that group, as far as a unit, but they recorded before us."

The implication, in reviews and articles, that the octet had been Brubeck's response to the influence of Davis's nonet displeased him, and quite reasonably so. In 1946, the year the Eight had begun their experiments, Miles was still a Charlie Parker sideman, and there's no shame in that at all—but the language and musical innovations of the *Birth of the Cool* sessions were a future concern. The historical lineage is, admittedly, complex. The octet made their first commercial recording in 1950, and therefore technically the Davis Nonet

5. Ralph J. Gleason, "Brubeck—'I Did Some Things First," *DownBeat*, September 5, 1957.

6. Writer and founding editor of *Rolling Stone* magazine (1917–1975) whose attention gravitated from jazz toward the West Coast rock of Jefferson Airplane and the Grateful Dead. He wrote the sleeve notes for Miles Davis's *Bitches Brew*.

*did* record first. But Brubeck's octet had that impressive library of student and audition recordings dating back to 1946, which, although never designed for public consumption, was eventually released in 1956. But even as late as 2000, this chronology was muddled. In *The Essential Jazz Records: Modernism to Postmodernism*,[7] the British writer Eric Thacker damned the octet with faint praise. The group was indeed deserving of wider recognition, he wrote, but only because of "their strange—perhaps uncanny—seismograph of tremors from the earliest Miles Davis Capitol nonet recordings"—a line that came loaded with misleading innuendo that the octet had borrowed liberally from the nonet.

Like the Brubeck Octet, the Davis Nonet started as a loose collective of personalities and eventually coalesced around a figurehead. In 1947, the apartment on West Fifty-Fifth Street, in midtown Manhattan, home of the pianist and arranger Gil Evans, was the place where New York's more adventurous jazz musicians went after gigs to debate the future of music. Evans took his open-house policy to a charitable extreme by leaving his front door permanently unlocked, and he would routinely return home to find the likes of Miles Davis, Gerry Mulligan, John Carisi,[8] Lee Konitz, John Lewis,[9] and George Russell[10] shooting the breeze about music.

7. Max Harrison, Eric Thacker, and Stuart Nicholson, *The Essential Jazz Records: Modernism to Postmodernism* (London: Mansell Publishing Limited, 2000), 623.

8. Trumpeter (1922–1992) most famous for two compositions recorded by Miles Davis: "Israel," with his nonet, and "Springsville," on *Miles Ahead* (which also included Brubeck's "The Duke"). He performed with Cecil Taylor on *Into the Hot*.

9. Pianist (1920–2001), former Dizzy Gillespie sideman and arranger, and leader of the Modern Jazz Quartet.

10. Pianist, composer, and theorist (1923–2009) whose book *Lydian Chromatic Concept of Tonal Organization* was a catalyst for Ornette Coleman's personal theories about harmony. He also made a string of fine albums including *Stratusphunk*, *Ezz-thetics*, and *Electronic Sonata for Souls Loved by Nature*.

Evans was paying his way, just, as the arranger and music director for bandleader Claude Thornhill, whose orchestra was famed for its silky, pastoral tone colors. Although bebop was integral to the group—Thornhill's orchestra recorded agile reimaginings of Charlie Parker's "Yardbird Suite" and "Anthropology"—his own lingering composition "Snowfall" typified the new sensibility that his orchestra was nurturing. Adding French horns and tuba gave the Thornhill ensemble a spongier base than the traditional big band. The French horns placed a sonic buffer between brass and saxophones, replacing big-band muscle with more ductile timbres. And it was this aspect of the Thornhill Orchestra that Evans wanted to develop inside a small-group context—a plan that immediately captured Miles's imagination.

The Brubeck Octet had binged on Milhaud, Bartók, and Stravinsky, while the *Birth of the Cool* band more obviously revisited the finespun instrumental shimmer of Debussy and Ravel. Evans's writings for French horn—played variously by Junior Collins, Sandy Siegelstein, and Gunther Schuller—and tuba—played by Bill Barber—were the most obvious manifestations of his borrowings from classical orchestration, but he also understood a deeper truth. For Debussy timbre and harmony were *not* separate concerns. Extended harmonies could best be appreciated by listening to an ensemble that took time to resonate. French horn and tuba bolstered the front line of trumpet, trombone, and two saxophones, giving the *Birth of the Cool* band extra weight and resonant depth. Gerry Mulligan's composition "Rocker"—a reconstituted "Sleigh Ride" that wove Leroy Anderson's melody around itself—and Davis's own "Boplicity" were typical of the rather delicious way the front line sashayed across the rhythm section, like a dainty elephant dancing on the head of a flower. But John Lewis's arrangement of Bud Powell's "Budo,"[11] decidedly hot, acted as a reminder

---

11. Originally recorded by Powell's trio in 1950 under the title "Hallucinations."

that the *Birth of the Cool* band was never about repudiating bebop—group members were interested in repositioning the harmonic and rhythmic richness of bebop inside a music where formal arrangement and composition were given equal billing to improvisation.

"Post-bop," too, was a curious descriptor for the Brubeck Octet. Van Kriedt aside, nobody in the octet had ever been committed to bebop; and no group, surely, can be "post" a genre that it had never played. The Davis Nonet versus Brubeck Octet debate was ultimately a phony war: a battle of words long after the event over an argument that was never fought between the musicians themselves. Both ensembles imported elements from European composition and the time-signature obstacle course of Gerry Mulligan's *Jeru*—4/4 interspersed with runs of 2/4, 3/4, and 6/4—was octet meat and drink. Yet both groups had arrived at their discoveries independently. The *Birth of the Cool* band was entirely a product of New York bebop shaking hands with French new music, mediated through Claude Thornhill. A neatness to their articulation, and a drilled precision, derived from the expertise of musicians with extensive experience working in bebop small groups and big bands. Brubeck's octet was, equally, a creature of the West Coast. In a pattern that would replay throughout his career, Brubeck felt it necessary to defend himself. Confusions over dates was understandable, if annoying, but Brubeck could never let the suggestion that he had taken directly from Miles, with the intention of creating a lighter spin-off, stand.

By the time of his September 1957 article for *DownBeat*, Ralph Gleason had already bumped heads with the Brubecks over the octet. In a letter to the magazine's editor, Iola Brubeck complained, very much in sorrow *and* in anger, that Gleason had willfully played fast and loose with the facts, especially dates, in an earlier piece about the octet published on

August 8 the previous year.[12] Another bone of contention was Gleason's finger-wagging assertion that "critics who did not like [Brubeck] had only themselves to blame for not speaking out before he had arisen into prominence," a blame game from which Gleason absolved himself by claiming that he had refused to endorse Brubeck. But Iola pointed to the liner notes Gleason had written for the Dave Brubeck Trio's first record in 1949—and "everyone knows that writing album notes is tantamount to an endorsement," she said, before aiming a kick directly at the critical solar plexus: "But then that was for a fee and perhaps integrity has a price to Mr. Gleason." She signed off by observing that, in his review of the octet reissue, Gleason had claimed Bob Collins's solo on "Body and Soul" was the outstanding performance—but that "particular tune did not appear on the record, but was mentioned by mistake on the jacket." In 1961, when Brubeck appeared on Gleason's *Jazz Casual* television series, neither man appeared especially comfortable in each other's company—and now we can guess why.[13]

To those on the inside, the octet had long since outgrown its origins as a student workshop ensemble to become a noble cause, and one well worth fighting for. Van Kriedt's letter to Brubeck, in which he identified an octet "nucleus," was written only six weeks after Larry Bennett's letter had attempted to cool Brubeck's octet ambitions. In the context of the Bennett letter, Van Kriedt's words could be interpreted as a request for a stay of execution—the Dave Brubeck Quartet's remarkable success was likely to mean the end of the Dave Brubeck Octet, especially with dollar-hungry agents now in the loop.

"While you are in LA," he wrote, "you are probably organizing views, and objectives, and are planning considerably so that

---

12. Iola Brubeck to *DownBeat*, August 18, 1956, Business Correspondence, Brubeck Collection.

13. The April 6, 1955, issue of *DownBeat* showed how deeply conflicted Gleason was over Brubeck's music: he confessed to not liking the trio but also said, "I still have to respect the fact that he did it in his own way."

your enthusiasm for [the future of the octet] is going to have a lot to do with the enthusiasm of the total group. . . . The more I have thought of this the more impressed I am and would like to do everything to make [the octet] a success."[14] In other words, the quartet was likely to be eating so much of Brubeck's time that the octet's very survival depended now on the combined energy and input of everybody else involved.

Van Kriedt felt dangers lurking, he said, in the current jazz scene, to which the octet could provide a necessary antidote. "For the past 10 years 'jazz' has been going through a period of degeneration so that the young musicians of today lack directions and guidance," he wrote.

> Not only has it degenerated but it has also elapsed into a sort of passivity particularly caused by the overwhelming forces of our peculiar economic structure and because of the world shaking forces of conflict which effects people down to their very guts. The economic system in particular has caused people to develop a reliance on materialism which has achieved psycotic [*sic*] proportions. These are some of the major problems which hit at the core of jazz and which make it a vital force within the structure of this society. Each member of the octet (the nucleus) is aware and is deeply entwined in these problems and have their talents geared toward the serious attitude of trying to bring some resolution to this problem. The phenomenon of this group is indeed a miracle and even though its effects have been felt in a rather limited scope its potential staggers the imagination.

But the trail runs cold in Brubeck's papers following the octet's December 19, 1953, concert, which likely marked their final appearance. Van Kriedt pursued his belief in the

---

14. David Van Kriedt to Dave Brubeck, September 23, 1953, Personal Correspondence, Brubeck Collection.

progressive potential of jazz by joining Stan Kenton's orchestra in 1955, and he played on Kenton's classic *Contemporary Concepts* album. In 1985 he emigrated to Australia, taking the octet scores with him, and, much to Brubeck's regret, they were damaged when his garage flooded. Following Van Kriedt's death in 1994, Brubeck became embroiled in an argument with his estate over the octet library: "Even if it's got ink all running, we could put it together," he said in 2007. "But they won't cooperate, the sons and relatives that could have done me a great favor and sent [the scores] back after Kriedt died. So we lost so many classical compositions and jazz compositions. If we hadn't recorded, we'd have nothing."[15] This unfortunate episode aside, Van Kriedt's death brought an inevitable moment of reckoning for the surviving octet members. "It is so sad to lose David Van Kriedt," Dick Collins wrote to Brubeck.[16] "Anyone who had anything to do with the Octet remains in the deepest part of my being. The late '40s into the '50s were one of the most exciting and beautiful times of my life. Kriedt and I (and sometimes Weeks) had fun in Paris. . . . I think we all heard death-bells when Dave [Van Kriedt] started sending photos, letters and tapes. I only regret the failure to see more of his music recorded or any of it published."

As a metaphor for the octet's improbable fortunes, the indignity of flood damage in a suburban Australian garage feels sadly apt: the octet had always been a commercial washout, and opportunities for the octet's material to live, breathe, and develop during live performance were so rare that the group was never able to discover what might have been.

15. Dave Brubeck, interview with Ted Gioia, Smithsonian Jazz Oral History Program, August 6–7, 2007, transcript, http://amhistory.si.edu/jazz/Brubeck-Dave/Dave_Brubeck_Transcript.pdf.

16. Dick Collins to Dave Brubeck, October 25, 1994, Personal Correspondence, Brubeck Collection.

Synchronous thinking would, soon enough, lead to many octet techniques and sounds becoming fixtures within the lingua franca of modern jazz. The Modern Jazz Quartet was anchored around pianist John Lewis's fascination with Bachian counterpoint, likewise Gerry Mulligan's so-called pianoless quartet with Chet Baker. The emergence of a so-called third stream during the late 1950s—the term coined by Gunther Schuller to describe a synthesis of jazz and compositional techniques like polytonality and twelve-tone music—was documented on the Columbia Records releases *Music for Brass* (1957) and *Modern Jazz Concert* (1958), albums that showcased long-form compositions involving improvisation. John Lewis, J. J. Johnson, George Russell, Charles Mingus, and Jimmy Giuffre found themselves sharing the albums with the post-Schoenbergian purist twelve-tone composer Milton Babbitt and the more Stravinskian-minded Harold Shapero. The Greek conductor Dimitri Mitropoulos, then music director of the New York Philharmonic, shared the conducting duties with Schuller. But this trend arrived too late for the octet, whose experimental music had needed a sympathetic environment to grow, and that, in the San Francisco of the early 1950s, had proved impossible to find.

However, seeds were sown in the minds of Dave and Iola Brubeck that new audiences needed to be found—and that younger, more receptive minds, open to the idea of serious listening, could be found, perhaps, on university campuses. Inspired by the octet's concerts at Mills College and College of the Pacific, and an appearance at the University of California, Berkeley, Iola decided to write to every university and college within drivable distance of San Francisco, offering the services of the quartet. She included a list of the quartet's modest requirements and waited to see if anybody would bite. But in the meantime Brubeck's own father, Pete, had inadvertently given the octet warning of the hard times ahead when, emerging from their College of the Pacific concert in 1949, he barked to a newspaper reporter, "That's the damnedest bunch of noise I ever heard."[17]

These days, 3255 Lakeshore Avenue in Oakland, California, tries hard not to draw any attention to itself. Blinds, lowered behind the window in the front door, block out the light, while a curtained hexagonal window set inside a spherical facade that encircles the front of the building guards against any opportunistic peeking. Lakeshore Avenue skirts Lake Merritt and today comes with all the expected trappings of gentrification; number 3255 sits adjacent to an artisan bakery.[18] But seventy years ago this part of town was considered undesirable and 3255 Lakeshore housed the Burma Lounge jazz club, where, beginning in December 1949, at "almost every midnight," as the posters put it, the Dave Brubeck Trio played "sensational jazz concerts."

A regular gig at last, and another reason to be grateful to Jimmy Lyons. "Things had been tough, really tough," Brubeck recalls as the bus weaves through central London, with Maida Vale in the near distance.

> There was no chance of work with the octet, but, especially with kids, you got to work. Then one day Jimmy called and told me about the Burma Lounge in Oakland, and that he could get me a job there with the trio. The money wasn't great—they paid what they called "scale"—but it was steady work. We were originally booked for a couple of weeks, then they kept us on for six months. And because we were playing every night,[19] the trio began to cohere as a group. You play the same set of tunes

---

17. The newspaper article in which Pete's quote appeared has apparently been lost, but Brubeck relished telling this story in interviews about the octet.

18. This was the scene on October 3, 2017, during the author's visit to Oakland.

19. Later, a more manageable three nights a week.

night after night, that's when they change and develop; you can't play them the same way each time.

The Burma Lounge was a small, dark room. Clint Eastwood used to come down when he was underage and he said they never troubled him because he was tall and because it was so dark nobody could really see him. Some months later, Jimmy got us a job at the Black Hawk in San Francisco, and this felt like a step up. Jimmy's radio show was popular with the navy, and some nights at the Burma Lounge I'd look into the audience and it was like *On the Town*—sailors everywhere. But the crowd in San Francisco was, I guess, more in tune with modern jazz than in Oakland. Dixieland was very popular there, Turk Murphy[20] and all those guys, but then guys like George Shearing had begun to open things up, and perhaps, without Shearing, those audiences would not have been so receptive to a small group led by a pianist playing modern jazz.

After the Burma Lounge, the Black Hawk felt at first like a vast concert hall, but actually, it wasn't that big. It had been a local deli or neighborhood store, something like that, then they turned it into a club by making a small stage and putting chairs around. It had been a comedy club, but my trio played the first night the Black Hawk opened as a jazz club. The money was slightly better than at the Burma Lounge. We'd play a few months at a time, every night, then take some months off, and during that time I'd try to figure out some new music and how to develop the group.

As a jazz venue, the Burma Lounge is lost to history—no recordings made there have been officially released. But the Black Hawk, which closed in 1963, remains an indelible and vital part of modern jazz mystique, a name that, like the Village Vanguard in New York City, has attached itself to an imperial

---

20. Trombonist (1915–1987) who was the West Coast's leading Dixieland jazz musician.

batch of classic live jazz on record: *Thelonious Monk Quartet Plus Two at the Blackhawk*, Shelly Manne's *At the Black Hawk* (volumes 1 to 4), and the Miles Davis Quintet's *In Person Friday Night at the Blackhawk* (and a Saturday night sequel).[21] The Brubeck Quartet album released in 1953 under the title *Jazz at the Black Hawk* (subsequently retitled *Two Knights at the Black Hawk*) only contained one track ("Jeepers Creepers") actually recorded at the venue, but from Sunday afternoons with the octet to extended residencies with his trio and eventual appearances by the Dave Brubeck Quartet, the Black Hawk would be crucial to Brubeck's career.

By May 1947 matters had become so desperate that the Brubecks—Iola heavily pregnant with Darius—had put out feelers about a possible move to Alaska. Writing on May 13 to Lloyd Herberlee,[22] the secretary of the local musicians' union in Anchorage, Brubeck (who politely enclosed a self-addressed stamped envelope) inquired about "the prevailing wage scale for members of a small combo—piano, sax and bass, for example? What is the usual salary for a pianist, playing singles? Is there a demand for musicians in your area?" Brubeck ended his letter by asking about work opportunities in other areas of Alaska and how "musician's wages compare with the present cost of living in Alaska"—more information than necessary for a casual working visit.

But biding his time in San Francisco, hoping for better times ahead, would ultimately pay off. Among the get-rich-slowly schemes Brubeck initiated in the meantime, before Jimmy Lyons's phone call, was the sandwich delivery business he ran with David Van Kriedt. Brubeck's interest in having Van Kriedt on board was purely pragmatic: the saxophonist's brother owned a truck, meaning there was no need to pound

---

21. "Black Hawk" and "Blackhawk" were used interchangeably on album covers, but the two-word spelling is correct.

22. Dave Brubeck to Lloyd Herberlee, May 13, 1947, Business Correspondence, Brubeck Collection.

that hot San Francisco pavement. "Unfortunately, though, Kriedt's brother was a terrible driver," Brubeck says. "He'd accidentally hit the accelerator, or mess up the gear change, and all the sandwiches and orange juice would spill out on the floor [and] we'd have to dust them off before we arrived at the next office building." File under Steve Reich and Philip Glass's furniture removal firm, which was how they made a living before minimalism became all the rage.

Abandoning San Francisco would also have meant leaving behind his colleagues from the octet: times were hard, but at least Brubeck was surrounded by pairs of sympathetic ears that understood his predicament. Bill Smith and his then wife shared living space with Dick Collins and his wife (the Smiths upstairs and the Collins on the bottom floor) in a building described by Brubeck in his notes as being "over a fish store and behind a Chinese laundry."[23] For a while the Brubecks lived in an apartment downstairs from Denise McCluggage, a reporter for the *San Francisco Chronicle* who would later find fame as the first successful woman race car driver, and Brubeck would regularly borrow her piano for practice sessions.[24]

And he had plenty to practice. For the only sustained period in his life, Brubeck was taking piano lessons to finesse his keyboard technique. His teacher was Fred Saatman, a local concert pianist with a repertoire rooted in Debussy, Ravel, and Isaac Albéniz. In the 1920s Saatman had lived in England, where he played "hot" music in Bert Ralton's Savoy Havana Band. Brubeck studied with him from the end of 1947 to the beginning of 1949 and lessons were, it seems, often focused around Chopin. He considered this period of study to have been very beneficial, but, in 2000, Brubeck responded to a complaint from an LA-based correspondent that Saatman had been willfully airbrushed out of his biography. "Fred's name was always

---

23. Dave Brubeck, handwritten journal, undated entry, Brubeck Collection.
24. Obituary of Denise McCluggage, *New York Times*, May 9, 2015.

mentioned [when I was first performing]," he wrote. "[But] as the bio grew and the audience reading it was no longer just the San Francisco Bay area, somehow it was dropped, not by any bad intention on my part, but probably because whoever it was at Columbia Records or Associated Booking writing my publicity blurbs simply didn't know who Freddie was and omitted it. As the years went by, it didn't seem to matter to anyone except perhaps Freddie or me."[25] Brubeck explained that when his bassist Norman Bates joined the quartet, "he also studied piano with Fred. So the respect was great throughout the jazz community."

Brubeck also explained that his decision to discontinue his piano lessons had coincided with Milhaud's return to California, after his year in Paris: "[I] decided that I would concentrate on my piano playing rather than composition in Milhaud's absence. When Milhaud returned to Mills the following academic year, I returned to lessons with him. The simple fact is that I could not afford both teachers." Brubeck concedes that Saatman must have been hurt by his decision—why else would he have mentioned it to his correspondent? "Obviously, it bothered him. . . . I'm sorry for that."

In January 1949, Milhaud invited the Brubecks for dinner to celebrate his return, and during the evening Brubeck asked him about private study. Milhaud purportedly offered to tutor him free of charge ("Just do not tell anyone"),[26] which does not square with Brubeck's account of events in 2000, although we can't know whether Brubeck took Milhaud up on his offer of pro bono lessons. Confined to a wheelchair due to incapacitating arthritis, Milhaud was also complaining of discomfort in his arms and, although only fifty-seven, told Brubeck that he felt

---

25. Dave Brubeck to Gerry Collatz, June 22, 2000, Personal Correspondence, Brubeck Collection.

26. Dave Brubeck, handwritten journal, undated entry, Brubeck Collection.

ready to die. This was the only time he saw his mentor down-hearted, Brubeck reported[27]—but Milhaud would, in fact, live until the age of eighty-two to enjoy every moment of his star pupil's dizzying success. Brubeck peppered his notes about this period with other tantalizing snapshots.[28] We learn that, with Bill Smith and David Van Kriedt, he played an audition for the swing-era vibraphone veteran Red Norvo, who once recorded with Dizzy Gillespie and Charlie Parker and had recently moved to the West Coast; and also that a friend with connections to Mills, identified as "Grutzie," performed a piano piece of Brubeck's for the modernist composer, conductor, and polemist Pierre Boulez (who had recently completed his landmark Piano Sonata no. 2) during a visit to Paris. Neither situation led anywhere, but finding Brubeck caught somewhere between swing and modern composition feels spot on—a portent of things to come.

When the Dave Brubeck Trio entered the Sound Recorders Studio in San Francisco later that year, one day in September, they seized the moment . . . or tried to. As the recording engineer struggled to set the speed of a previously untried brand of tape, most of their three-hour session was wasted, and the trio ended up recording four tracks during the remaining thirty minutes. Octet arrangements limited the scope for soloing, but now Brubeck properly stretched out, his polytonal thinking given extra edge thanks to Fred Saatman's buffing up of his piano technique. In the evening the trio played either the Burma Lounge or the Black Hawk, and in the daytime they recorded over five sessions, producing a set of twenty-four standards that were refashioned and harmonically rerouted through Brubeck's increasing mastery of polytonal harmony.

---

27. Dave Brubeck, handwritten journal, undated entry, Brubeck Collection (uncataloged).

28. Ibid.

One night at the Burma Lounge, Cal Tjader transformed the trio into a quartet when, much to Brubeck's surprise, he turned up with a vibraphone (later in his career Tjader was celebrated more as a vibraphonist than as a drummer). Brubeck quickly realized the musical potential of this new instrumental setup, figuring that if a piano-vibraphone front line could prove a hit for George Shearing's quintet (in which Marjorie Hyams played vibraphone), then some of that stardust might rub off on his group. The trio's second studio session, in March 1950, introduced a trademark piece of choreography: as the final flourish of a vibraphone solo rang in his ears, Tjader would jump to his drum kit and start playing time behind Brubeck—without ever missing a beat. In an early sign of Tjader's burgeoning interest in Latin percussion, bongos and congas also became a constituent part of the Dave Brubeck Trio sound.

Shearing's raffish quintet had leaned heavily on the phraseology and the repertoire of bebop—"bop relaxing in the lounge with an aperitif," as the jazz writer Richard Cook memorably put it[29]—but Brubeck had no interest in stock bop phrases, and sometimes no one sounded more surprised at where his harmonic detours were leading him than Brubeck. The ghost of Art Tatum's 1940s trio can be heard benevolently haunting those long, winding arranged lines around which some pieces are pinned. Brubeck and Tjader (on vibraphone) executed "Sweet Georgia Brown," "Undecided," and "Too Marvelous for Words" in flawless unison, in a manner indebted to the quicksilver fingerwork of Tatum and his guitarist, Tiny Grimes—a fluidity of line that anticipated Brubeck with Desmond.

"Tea for Two," "Body and Soul," "Too Marvelous for Words," "Avalon," and "You Stepped out of a Dream" could have been Tatum's set list, too, although Brubeck obstinately nudged

---

29. Richard Cook, *Richard Cook's Jazz Encyclopedia* (London: Penguin Books, 2005), 569.

these pieces into the future.[30] "Laura" was recalled from the octet book, and those same six thunderbolt clusters were incorporated into an expanded vision of his 1946 solo, complete with quarreling tonalities churning up unease. In the notes Brubeck wrote for a concert in San Jose that saw the trio opening for the octet, he revealed the complexities, emotional and musical, of his relationship with the tune: "I first heard 'Laura' overseas [in the army]," he wrote. "I liked the melody very much, but as we could not get copies of sheet music or records and the score never seemed to use the same chord progressions twice, I remembered the melody and the chords you hear . . . are an approximation of the original."[31]

The three other pieces cut that same day, "Blue Moon," "Tea for Two," and "Indiana," have nothing of the menace of "Laura" and bathe instead in pastoral warmth and an occasional wink of whimsy, although the relentlessly probing harmony counts against any too-easy sentiment. "Blue Moon" launches with Brubeck's polytonal thrusts juddering against the rhythm section. A dramatic interjection from Tjader's drums propels Brubeck into an eddy of swirling block chords as Ron Crotty's bass holds the harmony firm underneath. The theme, when it reappears, makes landfall in a wholly unexpected key, leaving our sense of tonal perspective gleefully disoriented. "Indiana" begins with the aw-shucks daydream of a leisurely introductory piano soliloquy before Brubeck changes gear, accelerating toward a roaring improvisation in which urgently hammered repeated notes are hit against rapid-fire flurries. Brubeck's arrangement of "Tea for Two" skillfully balances the lesser-known verse against the famous chorus, and his improvisation weaves together strains from both.

---

30. The trio also recorded test pressings of "Idaho" and "Button Up Your Overcoat," which were never issued commerically. The latter track is the first recorded example of Brubeck accompanying a vocalist—most likely Barbara Ritchie.

31. Concert Programs, 1950–1951, Brubeck Collection.

Brubeck was also furthering his ideas about time. Tjader's accompanying "That Old Black Magic" and "Perfidia" on bongos and congas rotates strong and weak beats around the bar as if he was stirring together a whole pot of mambos and sambas, and Brubeck luxuriates in the rhythmic carpet being rolled out underneath him. These arrangements have a conceptual looseness that suggests they had at some point been worked out on the fly, while "Singin' in the Rain," "'S Wonderful," "Sweet Georgia Brown," "Undecided," and "I'll Remember April" had clearly been figured out meticulously on manuscript paper. Newly written heads, extrapolated from the original melody lines, have the air of well-ordered chamber music. Brubeck creates the impression of different perspectives on a song that are occurring simultaneously as sped-up versions of lines are overlaid against slowed-down melodic loops.[32]

"I'll Remember April" knits together two superimposed readings of the melody: Brubeck outlines a version at the actual tempo, while Tjader's vibes double the note values. "Singin' in the Rain" begins innocently enough at a bright tempo, the melody line splashed with an occasional polytonal chord. But then Brubeck and Crotty double the tempo, running the theme in counterpoint between them, with displaced accents wrenching the music out of 4/4 and into shell-shocked bars of 6/8. "Too Marvelous for Words" splutters into life inside a metric no-man's-land; Brubeck and Tjader (on vibes) slither around beats, leaving Crotty's bass to catch the "one" of the next bar like a conductor catching a ballet dancer midleap. The familiar melodic hooks of "Sweet Georgia Brown" are similarly chewed over, then pulled around the beat like strands of chewing gum.

Time was moving further out, and Brubeck's polytonal alchemy had positioned him as a pianist with a unique ap-

---

32. Speeding a line up by shortening the notes values is diminution and slowing a line down is augmentation—and Brubeck had learned both by studying how Bach had deployed them in his fugues.

proach and sound; meanwhile, an alto saxophonist named Paul
Desmond was preparing himself to reenter the story. Brubeck's
trio records hint of this quartet future. The harmonic patterns
behind his version of Rodgers and Hart's "Spring Is Here"
sound like a preparatory sketch for one of his most famous
compositions, "The Duke," while Brubeck's trading lines with
Tjader on the fugal finale to "How High the Moon," based on
the octet arrangement, is a direct antecedent of the quartet.
Brubeck takes the title of "I Didn't Know What Time It Was"
literally as his introduction bends and distends time, the beat
a bullet dodged. After the systematic, compositional approach
of "I'll Remember April" and "Singin' in the Rain," Brubeck is
playing with the fiber of sound itself.

And people were listening. In a letter dated November 15,
1950, Brubeck responded to an offer from Cliff Aronson, a West
Coast representative of the New York–based Associated Booking
Corporation, an offer that, after all the hardships of the previous
two years, ought to have been irresistible. "I have just received
the contract and your letter asking me to sign . . . for a period
of three years," he wrote. "I am flattered by your apparent faith
in me, but I do not wish to make jazz my career unless I see the
possibilities of becoming a top name in the country. . . . If the
national future of the trio does not look promising, I intend to
return to San Francisco, teach in some college and be a 'local
boy almost made good.'"[33]

Brubeck added that he understood the desirability of being
represented by a booker who also handled Shearing, Norvo,
Parker, Hampton, Armstrong, et al., but he hoped that the corporation wouldn't be committed to "pushing those established
groups first. I feel at present I am equipped with a library and
the musicians to become a top name in American jazz with my
octet and trio, if handled correctly. . . . I absolutely will not sign

33. Dave Brubeck to Cliff Aronson, November 15, 1950, Business Correspondence, Brubeck Collection.

a three year contract with ABC, but I will sign for one year with the intention of renewing the contract after each year that has been satisfactory for both parties. I hope you can understand my position on this matter. Yours sincerely, Dave Brubeck."

Given that Brubeck had few bargaining chips—a trio, a local success only, and an octet without any consistent track record of work—his reply to America's leading talent agency demonstrated full-on confidence and self-certainty. He wanted success, but only on his own terms. Foraging an existence as a middle-ranking local player, making the round of the same old, same old gigs, held few attractions for him. It was time to make this thing work properly—or live some other life altogether.

*Chapter Four*

# MANHATTAN TRANSFER

"The terrible thing about having New York go stale on you is that there's nowhere else. It's the top of the world."

JOHN DOS PASSOS, *Manhattan Transfer*, 1925

Another day trip, all roads leading to Manchester. Randy Jones is telling Brubeck that there is a definite trace of John Coltrane's *A Love Supreme* in his composition "Crescent City Stomp,"[1] which the quartet has been breaking in during this current tour. Iola is keeping her head down inside a two-day-old copy of the *New York Times*; Russell Gloyd is shuffling paperwork; Militello snoozes. All the scenes you'd expect from a midmorning commute.

---

1. Recorded in December 1964, *A Love Supreme* is considered one of John Coltrane's masterworks. And Randy Jones was right: "Crescent City Stomp" shares something of its restless harmonic wanderings.

Then the conversation turns to Paul Desmond. The evolution from trio to quartet involved more than simply adding Desmond's alto saxophone to the existing Dave Brubeck Trio. This was a period of significant transition for which very limited recorded evidence exists, none in public circulation. So we need to talk about Desmond, about how the pair first met—when Brubeck's attention was focused on his trio and he doubted that a "Dave Brubeck Quartet" could ever flourish—and about how their initially testy relationship blossomed into one of the closest personal and musical friendships in jazz.

Desmond and Brubeck were utterly different personality types. Desmond was a man about town who, in 1963, took up residence in a newly built midtown Manhattan apartment at 77 West Fifty-Fifth Street, from which, as devoted New Yorkers do, he basked in the city's night-owl jazz clubs, bars, and eateries. He smoked and drank (sometimes to troubling excess) and experimented with cocaine and LSD. When his three-year marriage to an aspiring actress, Duane Lamon, ended in divorce in 1949, after they decided their relationship wasn't working and that they should split before things turned nasty,[2] Desmond concluded that he wasn't the marrying kind. He then involved himself in a string of relationships with women to whom he could never ultimately commit;[3] an affair with Sue Sahl, wife of his friend the comedian Mort Sahl, another regular on the bill at the Interlude in Los Angeles, along with Lenny Bruce, ended in inevitable tears. Desmond, you feel, would have been happy to walk away from his life on the road with the quartet at any point and spend his time instead kicking back with a glass of whiskey

---

2. Lamon remarried and moved to Montreal, where she became a radio disc jockey. Desmond contacted her whenever he played in the city, but they eventually lost touch.

3. At the quartet's concert in Brighton on April 23, 2003, an elegant lady came backstage to see Dave and Iola—she was introduced as "Paul's English girlfriend."

at Elaine's or Bradley's,[4] his favorite NYC hostelries. But he was also a naturally gifted writer who, until the Brubeck Quartet had established itself, was genuinely unsure about whether to pursue a career in music or writing. After the group folded in 1967, his eagerly anticipated memoir, tentatively entitled *How Many of You Are There in the Quartet?*, was never completed.[5] Desmond was more suited to the instant satisfaction of jazz improvisation than to putting in the hours required to finish a demanding book project: all those drafts, that endless finessing of text, all that hard work.

Desmond wasn't originally Desmond. Born Paul Breitenfeld in San Francisco in 1924, he never convincingly explained his nom de plume: his reasoning that "Breitenfeld" was too long to fit on a 78 rpm record was all about deflecting, not answering, the question. Desmond's father, Emil, had also worked as a musician, while his mother, Shirley, struggled with a crippling psychological problem that left her with a terror of physical touch, a phobia that extended to close physical contact with her son and only child.[6] While Shirley coped, just about, Emil made his living as an arranger and as a cinema organist who accompanied silent film and found minor fame with his song "The Last Long Mile," written for a 1917 stage show, *Toot! Toot!*; the song was later recorded by Charles Hart and the Shannon Four. The art of finding appropriate music to accompany silent film scenes involved mentally flicking through an inventory of prelearned songs and instrumental pieces—then editing, collaging, blending, and cutting them in sync with the action onscreen. This plundering of existing material wasn't improvisation exactly, but the knack of weaving networks of musical associations together was hardwired, clearly, into the

---

4. Desmond bequeathed his piano to Bradley's, the much-loved Greenwich Village jazz club that opened in 1969 and closed in 1996.

5. Titled after an actual air stewardess's question, only one section of Desmond's memoir ever appeared, in the British magazine *Punch* in January 1973.

6. Emil died in 1964; Shirley took her own life in 1966.

Breitenfeld genes. And Paul, as a child, spent many hours perusing his father's mighty collection of sheet music, imprinting standard tunes into his memory.

Brubeck preferred the relative peace of living in Connecticut, in the small town of Wilton, to New York. He didn't smoke at all or drink heavily, disapproved vigorously of drug taking, and certainly was the marrying type—his marriage to Iola would last seventy years. After the quartet folded at the end of 1967, he demonstrated a capacity to lock himself away in a room, alone with his thoughts and pads of paper, for hours, days, and weeks as he created *The Light in the Wilderness*, the first in a series of extended-form works for voices and orchestra, which also incorporated jazz improvisation. Brubeck was driven, Desmond less so, but more has been made of how their differing personalities manifested themselves musically than is wise or fair—to either man.

A column in *DownBeat* published February 11, 1953, under the pseudonymous byline "jack," reflected what had already become critics' shorthand for describing the Brubeck Quartet. "[Desmond] seems to be quite superior to the leader as a jazzman, yet the leader is taking on almost mystic qualities. . . . That [Brubeck] is oftimes loud and pounding and seemingly at a loss for melodic ideas is probably just one reporter's opinion."[7] But it wasn't. By the time critic and *DownBeat* editor Ira Gitler reviewed *Time Out* in 1960—filed alphabetically in between releases by Patti Bown and Duke Ellington (his classic *Side by Side*)—he considered Desmond's solo on "Blue Rondo à la Turk" about "as jazzy as it gets," while "substituting bombast for swing is a Brubeckian credo," he claimed.[8] Writing about "Strange Meadow Lark," Gitler described Desmond's solo as "wistful" and "sensitive" and found it within himself to

7. jack, "Coronation Ceremonies Nearing for Brubeck," *DownBeat*, February 11, 1953.

8. Ira Gitler, "In Review," *DownBeat*, April 28, 1960.

praise Brubeck, albeit inversely: "Brubeck doesn't pound here, and he develops some melodic ideas, something he rarely does at faster tempos." As a critical response to the complex chemistry of the quartet, turning Desmond into an attack dog with which to bite Brubeck had become standard practice. But an unfortunate, and presumably unintended, by-product of such critiques could be to reduce Desmond's role to adding mere melodic seasoning to the main Brubeck-Wright-Morello meat—while also fatally misunderstanding Brubeck's role as anchor and guiding light of his own group.

"Paul and I met [for the first time] far earlier than many people think," Brubeck says,[9] "and often I'm asked whether we bonded immediately, and the answer to that is no. I was already in the army. So 1944, I guess. I hadn't been sent overseas yet, and my one chance to avoid being sent to Europe was to audition for a place in the army band.

David Van Kriedt was already in the band and would often talk about this alto player he knew, Paul Breitenfeld. When I showed up for the audition, which was in a military base over [by] the Golden Gate Bridge, Dave and Paul had put together some guys for me to play with, a bassist and a drummer, and they had their horns ready. Somebody suggested we get into a blues, and I started getting into a polytonal thing—probably G in my left hand, B-flat in my right—and Paul kind of froze. He didn't understand what I was putting behind him, hadn't heard anything like it, and I remember him shaking his head slowly from side to side.

Later, he said in an interview somewhere that he thought I was absolutely crazy—mad! Fair enough. But the story, I think, grew through the telling. Next I'm stark raving mad—and I've got wild hair. Then I've got wild hair *and* I'm wearing a bright-purple army jacket. After we played Paul insisted

---

9. Interview with the author, May 1, 2003.

he said to me, 'Man, wigsville—those crazy changes really grooved me,' and I'm supposed to have answered 'White man speaks with forked tongue.'[10] Paul would tell that story over and over until people believed that was how we first met, but I'm not certain I remember it like that. I liked his playing, but I remember him being quiet. But playing polytonality in an audition wasn't very wise—I didn't get the job, and a little while later I was sent overseas.

After I was discharged from the army and at Mills, and we needed an alto player for the octet, Paul was the obvious choice. Kriedt had kept in touch with him, and that's how we were reintroduced. But even in the octet, neither Paul nor I sensed what was in the future. Bill Smith and Van Kriedt were part of Milhaud's class and they were writing arrangements and compositions for the octet, and, thinking about it now, I probably paid them more attention than Paul. But Paul recognized something in my playing that he liked, and then he started turning up to every job I played, especially with the trio, asking if he could sit in. That would have been around 1949, 1950, but [some years] earlier Paul had really made life very difficult for me, and the family, and I told Iola that I never wanted to see him again—"If he turns up at the house," I said, "do not let him in."

While I was studying at Mills and for a while afterward, I was playing in a group called the Three Ds. Darrell Cutler played [tenor] saxophone and operated a [hi-hat] cymbal with his foot, we had a vocalist called Francis Lynn and a guy called Don Ratto, bass, who was quickly replaced by Norman Bates when the Musicians' Union stopped Don from working because he

---

10. The source of this reported conversation seems to be an article by Marian McPartland, "Perils of Paul: A Portrait of Desperate Desmond," in the September 15, 1960, issue of *DownBeat*. McPartland has Desmond describing Brubeck's changes as "nutty" rather than "crazy"; Desmond also claims the first tune they played was "Rosetta," not the blues.

wasn't a member.[11] We started off in a club in Stockton and then got a regular gig at a club in San Francisco called the Geary Cellar, and that's when Paul started showing up, asking if he could sit in. It was good to have him play, but then, suddenly, Paul had a job of his own at a place called the Band Box in Stanford and hired Norman and Francis. He wanted me, too, and I ended up playing for Paul for half the money I had been making with the Three Ds. And then Paul got another job at a place called the Russian River near Reno and decided to take a different piano player. I tried to make something good out of the situation by coming up with a new group [to play at the Band Box]—based around me and Bill [Smith]—but Paul refused to let his job go. So there I was—no job, with two young children to feed, and a lot of anger directed toward Paul. To this day, I'm sure he took that job so that he could be near Reno, where he could gamble—he was obsessed with gambling back then.

This was the lowest point of all. We all ended up living in a corrugated iron tent, just about big enough, next to Clear Lake [more than a hundred miles north of San Francisco], where I'd managed to get work at a place called the Silver Log Tavern playing with [trumpeter] Rudy Salvini. Man, that tent was *hot*. It had no ventilation, and the only way to keep the children cool was to spend all day at the lake. They could float in the water, and then some nights we'd sleep outside to keep cool. That's when Jimmy Lyons called offering me the job at the Burma Lounge.

Paul was working in New York with [guitarist] Alvino Rey when he heard one of the [Dave Brubeck] trio records on a

---

11. No recorded evidence of the Three Ds has come to light, but their repertoire was based around Broadway tunes and standards. There is no trace of Darrell Cutler or Don Ratto following a career in music after the Three Ds. Francis Lynn, who died in 2008, went on to perform with Charlie Barnet and Gene Krupa; Norman Bates would later become a regular bassist in the Dave Brubeck Quartet.

local radio station. By that point we were living in San Francisco [on Eighteenth Street, in the Eureka Valley neighborhood] and one afternoon there was a knock on the door; Iola answered and there was Paul. Now you have to remember what Paul had put us through. Clear Lake, the hot iron tent, had all happened because he had left us in the lurch. Now that things were going well with the trio, the last person I wanted to see was Paul Desmond. I was hanging up diapers on a clothesline in the back, and, had I answered the door, Paul would not have been invited in. But he charmed Iola, who had always thought we belonged together musically—so perhaps he didn't need to do too much charming.

Then we talked and I knew right away that Paul was working to turn the trio into a quartet. He had learned all the trio arrangements, he said, and had worked out horn parts—he even offered to babysit and wash the car, not that he ever did. And gradually, I guess, he wore down my resistance and I remembered the good work he did with the octet and thought that perhaps he was right—a quartet might be a good idea. But I couldn't turn up suddenly at clubs with a quartet. The trio records we were making were doing well and people wanted to hear that group live; they didn't want to hear the trio with Paul sitting in. Also, club owners had hired three musicians and had no interest in paying somebody else. But Paul persisted. When we were playing at the Burma Lounge or in San Francisco, Paul would turn up, sit in, and he knew there was no chance of being paid.

The bus pulls into a service station. Jones and Militello exit for a hasty cigarette, and Brubeck, never appreciative of cigarette smoke, turns the other way to fill his lungs with air. Then the bus continues on its way and Brubeck picks up where he left off.

Ron Crotty was called up for military service and had to quit the trio, and I hired Jack Weeks in time for a job in Honolulu, a few weeks playing in a club [the Zebra Lounge]. Paul decided to come along, even though he had to pay his own way and he'd be playing for free. The first couple of weeks were terrific—then disaster. I took the kids swimming on Waikiki Beach, and I remember cheerfully saying to them, "Look at Daddy!" as I dove into a wave. But there was a sandbar right in front of me. I turned to avoid hitting it with my head, and all my weight went onto my neck, very nearly breaking it.

I knew, immediately, that I was in serious trouble. The ambulance arrived and I heard the drivers talking about how they were bringing in a DOA. The main hospital refused to take me—I didn't have money or insurance—so instead they took me to the army hospital [Tripler Veterans Administration Hospital] where they would take people from the services. I was put on a gurney and told to keep absolutely still or else I'd be paralyzed for the rest of my life—assuming I survived at all. After that I spent nearly a month in the hospital, in traction. Which was bad news for the trio. It would be four months or more before I could play again. Cal and Jack had to find other work and began recording with Vince Guaraldi,[12] and I felt very betrayed, I have to say. So the trio came to an end, and once again, I had no job, no money, and nowhere to live— before we left for Honolulu I'd put a deposit down on a house, but the deal fell through and all our possessions were in storage. I wrote to Paul from the hospital when still in traction and told him we should form a quartet. I told him exactly the bassist and drummer I wanted him to hire, and that I'd let him know when I could play again.

But before that could happen we needed, somehow, to get back to California. The doctors insisted I couldn't fly—sitting for all that time would have put too much pressure on my back. We'd have to go by boat, but we didn't have any money.

---

12. *The Cal Tjader Trio* (Fantasy Records 3-9), with Jack Weeks (bass) and the piano chair shared between John Marabuto and Vince Guaraldi.

The money I'd earned before the accident had all gone, but I thought there might, if we were lucky, be a few dollars left in our account. When I got to the bank I was amazed to find we had five hundred dollars in the account; even when I explained to the clerk that I hadn't deposited any money, he shrugged and said, "It's definitely here, you might as well take it." That's how we bought tickets for the ship back to San Francisco, but I'm not sure to this day how that money came to be in the account. I asked Joe Glaser, my dad, everybody I could think of—but nobody knew anything about it.[13]

A year earlier, nobody had wanted to hear Paul play with the trio, but almost as soon as the quartet began playing, people started saying that this was a great new sound and approach. Soon we were winning awards and playing on the East Coast. Financially it was tough for a while still, but I was certain of this new direction and that we needed to give it everything we had.

𝄞

At the beginning of 1954, with the Charlie Parker package tour and the release of *Jazz at the College of the Pacific* behind it, the Dave Brubeck Quartet was edging toward the threshold of big-time success. Within a few months Brubeck would be signed to Columbia Records and *Brubeck Time*, the quartet's first studio album for this most major of major labels, would represent a summation of everything hitherto achieved: eight tracks, every note made to count. Progress from the Brubeck Quartet's first session in August 1951, which produced "A Foggy Day," "Somebody Loves Me," "Crazy Chris," and "Lyons Busy,"

---

13. This strange episode was never definitively explained, although in a 2007 interview with Ted Gioia, Brubeck speculated that Doris Duke might have deposited the money (interview with Ted Gioia, Smithsonian Jazz Oral History Program, August 6–7, 2007, transcript, http://amhistory.si.edu/jazz/Brubeck -Dave/Dave_Brubeck_Transcript.pdf). Duke (1912–1993) was a wealthy heiress and philanthropist who adored jazz and often visited jazz clubs in San Francisco and Los Angeles. She later donated sizable sums to AIDS research.

through *Jazz at Oberlin* and *Jazz at the College of the Pacific*, had indeed been prodigious. By the time the quartet recorded *Time Out* in 1959, the moods, textures, and designs of their music had changed radically once again, and yet it was all recognizably Brubeck. But how so? What were the boundaries under which the quartet operated—and how did those boundaries license new and unforeseen freedoms? What transformed three musicians led by Dave Brubeck into the Dave Brubeck Quartet?

"Almost as soon as the quartet began playing, people started saying that this was a great new sound," Brubeck said on the bus to Manchester in 2003, but there had been a number of false starts. One plan had been to retain the spirit of the trio by supplementing a piano–alto saxophone–bass core with a Latin percussionist—despite the hurt Brubeck felt over Tjader's and Weeks's behavior following his swimming accident, he still carried a torch for the sound and feel of playing like Cal Tjader's. But when that idea faded away, in came drummer Herb Barman, who had been working with Paul Desmond in Alvino Rey's band. He was "loud," Brubeck said, and "he swung like a bastard,"[14] a view corroborated by Barman's recordings with the quartet. You can't help but wonder what might have been had Barman not left a year later to be replaced by Lloyd Davis.

The much-sought-after Ralph Peña, who had been working with Stan Getz, Art Pepper, and Charlie Barnet, was Brubeck's first choice for bass, but he was unavailable. When two other bassists, Roger Nichols and Gene Englund, quit in quick succession,[15] Brubeck was drawn toward Fred Dutton, who usefully doubled on bassoon. Dutton's bassoon, he thought, could bring an enticing new instrumental color into the octet, and

---

14. Dave Brubeck to Paul Desmond, May 1951, cited in Doug Ramsey, *Take Five: The Public and Private Lives of Paul Desmond* (Seattle: Parkside Publications, 2005), 131.

15. Nichols left jazz after his short tenure with Brubeck; Gene Englund had a distinguished career that included stints with Anita O'Day, Stan Kenton, Jimmy Giuffre, Art Pepper, and Maynard Ferguson.

his bass playing was the right side of impressive. Also under consideration, Wyatt "Bull" Ruther had studied alongside Paul Desmond at the San Francisco Conservatory of Music, and the two men had worked together in a local swing band led by the drummer Billy Shuart. Ruther later worked with Erroll Garner, George Shearing, Buddy Rich, and Count Basie, and was the first black musician to play with the Brubeck quartet. Unable to choose between Ruther and Dutton, Brubeck used both men throughout 1951 and 1952, depending on their availability, and on that August day in 1951, when the Brubeck Quartet recorded for the first time, Barman was on drums and Dutton played bass and bassoon.

Not all aspects of the music flowed smoothly. Dutton's spluttering tone retched with the grace of a smoker's cough as he struggled gallantly to keep his bassoon in tune, especially in its mid range. But the degree to which Brubeck imposed his personality and musical sympathies over all aspects of the music—while handing Desmond all the space and freedom he needed to express himself—is immediately apparent. This was a leadership trait that Brubeck shared with an elite of jazz greats, Ellington, Miles Davis, Charles Mingus, and Ornette Coleman included, and was as true in 1951 as it would be fifteen years later, when the classic quartet delivered their final handful of albums to Columbia Records: *Time In, Anything Goes! The Dave Brubeck Quartet Plays Cole Porter*, and *The Last Time We Saw Paris.*

Handing musicians pieces that were negotiable through simple musicianly instincts—that led players into a comfort zone of stock harmonic and rhythmic patterns—held no interest for Brubeck. He expected his players to work at it, hard, and his greatest compositions, as catchy as they were—"Blue Rondo à la Turk," "Three to Get Ready (And Four to Go)," "Unsquare Dance"—set musical riddles and puzzles. "Blue Rondo" required Desmond learn how to switch gears suddenly between the complexities of Brubeck's written line in 9/8 and two improvised bars of the blues in 4/4—then back again.

"Travelin' Blues" talked the blues eloquently, but Brubeck took a discursive walk around the traditional twelve-bar blues structure, stretching the form into sixteen bars (twenty bars at the end, including the coda), which reshaped the cyclic symmetry of the chords that would ordinarily be expected to underpin a blues. Familiar forms, relandscaped with their markers repositioned, heightened the responses of his musicians and counted against improvisation by rote. Brubeck's strategy—like those of other great jazz composers, ranging from Jelly Roll Morton and Charles Mingus to Anthony Braxton—was to use composition as a means of lending improvisation a context.

And having worked hard to internalize the notes, Brubeck's musicians gained a certain ownership over the material, and then, when pieces had been performed to the point that familiarity was in danger of denting their impact, Brubeck raised the stakes: witness the evolution of "Take Five" from a modest, medium-paced miniature in 1959 to the grandstanding, pumped-up-tempo versions of the mid-1960s (which, by the early 1970s, had evolved once again into epic performances, the chimerical trance set by bass and drums reminiscent of the ecstatic and sensual energy of John Coltrane's extended latter-period meditations on "My Favorite Things.")

The four pieces Brubeck recorded in August 1951 reveal aspects of his quartet's artistic makeup waiting to blossom. "Crazy Chris"—dedicated to his third son—is one of those riddles wrapped up inside a jazz mystery. Brubeck had abandoned his own compositions in favor of standards during the fourteen months the trio recorded, knowing that he couldn't feed his family on originals, and "Crazy Chris" was the first of his own pieces to be committed to disc since the octet had recorded "Curtain Music" and "Playland-at-the-Beach" in the late 1940s. And, like those earlier pieces, this was an artfully constructed montage. Dutton, we soon realize, is looping around the sprightly opening riff from Chu Berry's "Christopher Columbus." After Desmond enters with an impish theme of his own,

Brubeck slips the opening bars of Spencer Williams's "Royal Garden Blues" underneath him. Such a whip-smart, clever composition fools you into questioning, at least for the three minutes it takes to play, why would anyone *not* want to work "Christopher Columbus" in counterpoint to "Royal Garden Blues"—and therein the riddle of "Crazy Chris." In the B section, counterpoint gives way to block harmony as Brubeck—in unison with Desmond—rotates the phrase borrowed from "Royal Garden Blues" around like a geometric shape flirting with a set square.

This starting point is prophetic. The classicism by association of Dutton's spirited, if clunky, bassoon riding above Barman's immaculately played swing time (brushes swiveling against snare drum) symbolizes a shared background in jazz and classical music, while Brubeck's solo on "Crazy Chris" demonstrates the breadth of his own musical concerns. His loquacious opening phrase curls around a veiled allusion to "The Peanut Vendor," then a more explicit reference to "I Want to Be Happy" proffers a digression that Brubeck chooses, on second thought, not to follow. Instead he picks up the "Christopher Columbus" riff and lassos it into an eight-to-the-bar hoedown, leaving holes in the texture through which Dutton inserts funky bass asides. Then, suddenly, Brubeck's sparse, balletic chords are dancing around the spry walk of Dutton's bass in a note-perfect allusion to Count Basie and Walter Page—a fitting endpoint for a composition sewn together from references to other music.

"Lyons Busy" was written as the theme song to Jimmy Lyons's radio show on NBC, the same program that had featured the trio, and the quartet would use a truncated version of the piece as their theme when they broadcast from the Storyville Club in February 1952. Brevity didn't stop Brubeck packing his come-hither fanfare with points of interest: a gnarly polytonal flourish prefaces a more courtly second theme that is pockmarked with displaced accents. "A Foggy Day" and "Somebody Loves Me" attempt to graft ideas incubated during the earliest days of the octet onto the quartet, with Dutton's bassoon acting as an effective fifth member. "Foggy Day" is the better of the two. Brubeck divides Gershwin's sixteen-bar structure into two groups of eight, with Dutton (joined by Desmond in the repeat) carrying the theme in a rather operatic manner, a mood that abruptly switches to a skipping swing feel for the second eight bars. Desmond is catapulted into his solo via a piano trill delivered with pile-driver force, which he immediately transforms into a visceral Stravinskian squawk colored by a nasal quality *so* bassoon-like that you wonder whether this might, in fact, be Dutton's solo. Later Desmond adopts a "correct" classical tone that would have made Adolphe Sax's day as he brings this particular foggy day in London town to a close by intoning the bells of Big Ben.

"Somebody Loves Me" suffers an unfortunately inelegant and messy opening as alto saxophone and bassoon attempt to navigate counterpoint extrapolated from the first phrase of Gershwin's theme. Desmond's unflappable playing throws cruel light on the fragility of Dutton's technique, but the record redeems itself when, after the solos, that same fragment of counterpoint flowers suddenly to reveal the theme in full for the first time. Then Brubeck steers it toward a fugal ride-out, played in three-part counterpoint, with Dutton sounding much more comfortable pushing a bass line out through the bowels of his instrument.

In the early 1950s, if a jazz fan who admired Parker, Gillespie, and Monk walked into a record store in either New York City or Los Angeles and came away with these four newly released sides by the Dave Brubeck Quartet, what would he or she have thought about how this music lined up against other modern jazz? Brubeck's "modernism"—the Schoenberg and Milhaud backstory in particular—had, as in the program book published to accompany his 1953 tour with Charlie Parker, often been manipulated as a marketing tool. "The Modern" and "Modernism" were sexy concepts at the time, and ripe for sensationalism. When Stravinsky toured the US in 1937, the mythology surrounding this "exotic" purveyor of modern sounds proceeded him. The *Cleveland Press*, trailing a pair of Stravinsky concerts in Ohio, ran with the headline "IGOR STRAVINSKY— SMALL BODY BUT A GIANT BRAIN," which, accompanied by a satirical cartoon, "perfectly encapsulated the image of a stunted alien with freakish intellectual powers," according to Stravinsky biographer Stephen Walsh.[16]

When, two decades later, Columbia Masterworks released an LP of Edgard Varèse's *Arcana*, *Déserts*, and *Offrandes*,[17] the composer's wiry gray hair was photographed against a backdrop of neon lighting on the cover, the intention being to depict him as a scientist, a mad one presumably; meanwhile the refrain "A Sound Spectacular" invited people to listen with amazement to this sonic science fiction. *Modern* was a word heavy with connotation, and nowhere more so than in jazz, where, if you weren't a modernist, people might mistake you for a Dixieland revivalist. The relative merits of traditional and modern jazz were debated passionately all through the 1950s. Modernists ridiculed Dixieland musicians for dumbing down jazz into a quaint, twee museum piece. Trad players, meanwhile, castigated modernists for sacrificing the purity of 1920s classic jazz, and in interviews and elsewhere Brubeck relentlessly pressed the case for modern jazz.

"You ask about Dixieland today," he told *DownBeat* in 1953.[18] "I don't see any challenge in it for a young kid. Makes me sick to see a young kid playing Dixie . . . if that's all he can play. From an audience standpoint it's even worse; there's so little challenge

16. Stephen Walsh, *Stravinsky—The Second Exile: France and America, 1934–1971* (London: Penguin, 2010), 58.

17. *A Sound Spectacular: Music of Edgard Varèse, Volume 2* (Columbia Masterworks MS 6362, 1962).

18. "The Jazz Scene Today," *DownBeat*, June 3, 1953.

in it. Then you're limited to tonic, subdominant, dominant chords in practically all the tunes." But Brubeck was presenting an argument more nuanced than "traditional jazz bad, modern jazz good." He raised an objection to use of the word *progressive* as shorthand for modern jazz, as his admiration for Jelly Roll Morton, whose work, like Stan Kenton's, had been progressive and forward-thinking for its time, was spelled out. His complaints were never aimed at pioneers like Louis Armstrong and Morton who had advanced the language as they had found it but toward bands, like Turk Murphy's, that in the 1950s were trying to faithfully re-create the music of King Oliver, Armstrong, or Morton—a pointless rewind, Brubeck thought, back through history. The most traditional thing about tradition was that tradition never stood still.

Brubeck also brought distressing news for those who considered that Kenton, or bold-ideas man Lennie Tristano,[19] whose recordings had involved daring experiments with counterpoint and free-form improvisation, were doing anything new—in the wider scheme of music, they weren't, he said. "I don't think [Kenton] or any of us are doing anything today that hasn't been done before by Stravinsky or Bartók," Brubeck maintained. Tristano's achievement in reviving counterpoint, a lost art during the swing era, and making it "atonal, the chord progression[s] more intriguing and challenging," was praiseworthy. But "Hindemith and Schoenberg are much farther out on the atonal limb than he, or any of us."

This was fighting talk, no question about that, and people were entitled to ask how far Brubeck's own music had traveled out on a limb, atonal or otherwise. Littered throughout

---

19. Chicago-born pianist and composer (1919–1978). Tristano established himself in New York City as an independent jazz thinker whose chromatically complex compositions, often built around standard tunes, also used daring rhythmic relationships. He also assembled pieces in the studio using overdubbing, the first musician in jazz to do so. His protégés included saxophonists Lee Konitz and Warne Marsh.

Brubeck's papers are tantalizing glimpses of connections with the vanguard of modernist composition. Stefan Wolpe—a former student of the serial composer Anton Webern, and teacher of composer Morton Feldman and John Cage's pianist of choice David Tudor—wrote to Brubeck in 1954 after reading the famous cover feature in *Time* magazine[20] devoted to his work. "I am, of course, well acquainted with what you do," Wolpe wrote,[21] "and feel very keen about it"; Wolpe wished to send Brubeck a new record, on the Esoteric label, of his works including a *Quartet for Trumpet, Tenor Saxophone, Percussion and Piano* and Sonata for Violin and Piano—he concluded "I am very eager to get your reaction to this music." In a letter from Max Weiss of Fantasy Records (undated, but probably sent in 1954), there's an intriguing suggestion that Brubeck had expected to take part in a recording at Mills College of music by Harry Partch, a composer who designed his own instruments based around his intricate division of the octave into forty-three different tones. The role Brubeck was meant to assume is not made clear, but in the event his exclusivity to Fantasy prevented his appearance; "this production which is being recorded by the backer cancels out any tiein [sic] with you."[22]

In a 2007 interview, Brubeck recalls attending a Harry Partch concert "where he [Partch] was on a huge . . . it was like a structure with instruments that you had to climb way up," he said.[23] In the same interview, Brubeck also remembered his brother Howard inserting household implements inside a grand piano at Mills College when John Cage performed there—transforming it into a "prepared piano" upon which Cage could play

20. Carter Harman, "The Man on Cloud No. 7," *Time*, November 8, 1954.

21. Stefan Wolpe to Dave Brubeck, November 27, 1954. Personal Correspondence, Brubeck Collection.

22. Max Weiss to Dave Brubeck, undated. Business Correspondence, Brubeck Collection.

23. https://tedpanken.wordpress.com/2011/08/11/an-interview-with-dave-brubeck-july-23-2007/.

perhaps his *Sonatas and Interludes,* or another composition like *Totem Ancestor* or *In the Name of the Holocaust.* In November 1962, Brubeck and Cage were among the musicians chosen by *FM Listener's Guide* magazine to comment on the music of Claude Debussy.[24] Their comments appeared on the same page, next to those of the songwriter Harold Arlen. Brubeck commented on how Debussy's harmonic, melodic, and rhythmic devices had "influenced jazz tremendously" and how "The first usage of African rhythmic sounds in classical music that ever met my ears . . . came from Debussy's String Quartet," while Cage observed "Debussy was the first to state that henceforth any tones or combinations of tones could be used for musical purposes in any sequence. Substitute any sounds for tones and you have an expression of what is nowadays thought and acted upon." The other musicians asked to contribute were Cole Porter, Darius Milhaud, and Edgard Varèse.

Anybody arriving at Brubeck's earliest quartet records expecting—or fearing—that his thoughts about Schoenberg, Bartók, and Stravinsky would translate into literal repurposings of the compositional techniques behind Schoenberg's *Pierrot lunaire* or Bartók's *Music for Strings, Percussion, and Celesta* as jazz were destined to be left disappointed—or relieved. But Brubeck's comments in his 1953 *DownBeat* interview acknowledged a new reality. Life had changed. During the war, Schoenberg, Bartók, and Stravinsky, and his own teacher Darius Milhaud, had all been given sanctuary in the United States. Bartók and Schoenberg had since died, but their legacy endured. This was now the atmosphere inside which American jazz was evolving; Brubeck, as a GI, had witnessed Europe at its lowest ebb, and this new music from Europe represented thinking that was both fresh and constructive.

For a musician of Brubeck's status in the early 1950s, successful but still on the rise, putting jazz out on any sort of atonal limb

---

24. "Claude Debussy," *FM Listener's Guide* magazine, November 1962.

would, in truth, have finished him, and to that extent he was presenting a straw-man argument. Duke Ellington had taken to presenting extended-form pieces, some of which pushed the tonal envelope, during annual appearances at Carnegie Hall in New York—*Black, Brown, and Beige* in 1943, *Perfume Suite* in 1944, *Liberian Suite* in 1947, and *The Tattooed Bride* in 1948. Brubeck's *Jazz at Oberlin* and *Jazz at the College of the Pacific*—and his second record for Columbia, *Jazz Goes to College*—were recorded on campus, in university concert halls, where people could be expected to listen. But his working life was otherwise centered overwhelmingly around jazz clubs. His debut album for Columbia had been *Dave Brubeck at Storyville: 1954*, recorded at George Wein's club in Boston, and his next live album was *Jazz: Red Hot and Cool*, assembled from various appearances at the Basin Street East club in New York City during 1954 and '55. Music by Hindemith and Schoenberg was designed specifically for the concert hall, but in jazz clubs, art found itself locked into an uneasy alliance with the expectation that it would entertain.

Brubeck was, of course, not the only jazz musician who needed to reconcile this apparently irreconcilable problem, although his experiences trying to promote the octet as a commercially viable unit had no doubt smoothed this sharp learning curve. A week before the Brubeck Quartet's first studio session, Thelonious Monk and his musicians walked into the WOR Studios on Fortieth Street in midtown Manhattan to record a set of six pieces—five original compositions ("Four in One," "Criss Cross," "Eronel," "Straight No Chaser," and "Ask Me Now") and one standard ("Willow Weep for Me")—that would be released by Blue Note Records in 1952 under the title *Genius of Modern Music, Volume Two*.[25] Note that flag-waving use of the term *modern* again, and imagine these adventures in modern music by Brubeck and Monk sitting alongside each other in record-store racks.

25. Blue Note LP 5009.

Monk, who was three years older than Brubeck, had worked with Parker and Gillespie and had recorded with Coleman Hawkins,[26] a master of an earlier age, but was still considered a resolutely underground figure: a first volume of *Genius of Modern Music*,[27] a compilation of recordings made in 1947, had sold very poorly, and securing live gigs remained a constant struggle for Monk. The fearsome technical difficulty—some might have said "impenetrability"—of his music, typified by the high-speed spaghetti-junction construction of "Four in One," was befitting of a musician who had involved himself in bebop. But Monk was no bop purist or stylist. He would encourage his musicians to improvise on the *melodies* of his compositions, whereas bop musicians usually constructed their improvisations around the chords that flowed beneath a song. Improvising on a Monk composition required musicians to tease out the essence of pieces invariably defined by their jagged corners, structural booby traps, and twists in the tale when the melodic flow was suddenly turned inside out (or was it outside in?). Nothing compromised Monk's music more than unthinkingly applying conventional bebop orthodoxy to his music while failing to absorb the melodic specifics of his compositions.

Herb Barman might have been "a bastard," but Monk's drummer Art Blakey[28] swung like a true motherfucker who was unafraid to sex up his playing with eruptions of capriciously unpredictable noise: the opening of "Eronel" was powered forward by the sheer damn attitude of Blakey pummeling his sticks against the rim of his snare drum. Where the Monk group charmed, cajoled, and lashed out, the Brubeck records

---

26. On Coleman Hawkins Quartet, *Bean and the Boys* (Prestige Records 7824, 1944).

27. Blue Note LP 5002.

28. Blakey (1919–1990) was Monk's drummer of choice during the early part of his career; he founded the Jazz Messengers in 1956, which mentored generations of jazz musicians (Lee Morgan, Wayne Shorter, Keith Jarrett, Joanne Brackeen, Wynton Marsalis) in the ways of hard bop.

were obsessively tidy and functioned like jewel-box chamber pieces (the more bellicose "Lyons Busy," a *pièce d'occasion*, being a rule-proving exception).

When Duke Ellington introduced Brubeck at the 1955 Newport Jazz Festival, he spoke of his quartet belonging to "the Darius Milhaud school, with a very strong modern French influence."[29] French-school neoclassical composition—typified by Milhaud's *Scaramouche* or Stravinsky's Concerto in E-flat (*Dumbarton Oaks*)—could feel emotionally detached, as musical forms borrowed from the past were rechanneled through a mid-twentieth-century sensibility. Stravinsky, in particular, had problems with what he perceived as the misnomer that music amounted to emotion played out in sound. In his 1936 *Autobiography*, he wrote, "I consider that music is, by its very nature, essentially powerless to express anything at all, whether a feeling, an attitude of mind, a psychological mood, a phenomenon of nature, etc. Expression has never been an inherent property of music."[30] *Dumbarton Oaks* offered a correspondingly objectified view of musical architecture: laying out the beauty of form and proportion for all to hear.

Like Charlie Parker during his interview on WHDH radio in 1954, Ellington identified instincts that set the Brubeck group apart stylistically from the lingua franca of modern jazz: another lineage, taking a different approach from ensembles led by the likes of Thelonious Monk or Bud Powell. But Ellington, like Parker, was also astute and generous enough to appreciate the quartet for what it already was, rather than laying down the law about any jazz they "ought" to have been playing instead.

The side of his music that Brubeck presented in August 1951 exhibited a cool detachment, a lightness of touch matched by a relaxed, languid rhythmic sashay. These same records might

29. Ellington's speech can be heard on Dave Brubeck Quartet, *Birdland 1951–52/Newport 1955* (Solar Records 4569967).

30. Igor Stravinsky, *An Autobiography* (New York: Simon & Schuster, 1936), 66.

have led some listeners to believe that the blues, which coursed through Monk's musical DNA and helped mold each improvised utterance, had barely touched upon Brubeck's consciousness or entered his musical vocabulary. That riff Brubeck had snatched from Chu Berry's "Christopher Columbus" could have quite easily been worked up into a conventional blues, but his harmonic thinking spun the piece in a multitude of other directions. Brubeck's solo—taking its cue from the B section of his theme, where polytonality shifted the earth from under "Royal Garden Blues"—organized itself as a mismatch of disjoints that shone in each other's reflection rather than forming a neat narrative arc. Phrases were parked on the ends of chromatic cliff-hangers; nothing quite resolved where expected.

Having heard the evidence, that customer in the 1950s record shop had a choice. Those four Brubeck records were not bebop, nor were they audibly grounded in the blues, considered to be the spiritual backbone of jazz. But was there enough within them to satisfy head and heart while persuading the jazz fan that they were indeed listening to jazz? This question, and variations upon it, would be raised persistently throughout Brubeck's career—to the point that Brubeck bashing became a critical blood sport. By March 1956, in an opinion piece published in the *Philadelphia Jazz Digest*, Billy Root was arguing that Brubeck was not cool—to someone like him, who "first learnt about jazz in the funky little clubs around Philadelphia . . . not on a college campus from a pseudo hip chum," he was "cold."[31]

A tenor saxophonist himself, and a soon-to-be associate of Charlie Parker's trumpeter Red Rodney, Root aimed to put clear water—blue water—between his idea of jazz and what he

31. Billy Root, "Cool? Dave Brubeck Is Cold!," *Philadelphia Jazz Digest*, March 1956.

called Brubeck's "pseudo jazz." Root took exception to Brubeck's "scuffl[ing] through some 'Bachish'-sounding things
[and consequently] the hippies think he's inserting the classics." Counterpoint and fugue "don't mean a thing to jazz," he
continued, and anyway, "Dave has horrible time. He sounds
like he's jumping up and down on the piano with his feet."
Root questioned why "Brubeck fans think they have to 'study'
his music. The very title of one of his albums, *Jazz Goes to College*, is ridiculous. You shouldn't have to sit around and analyze
and scrutinize every note as if you were listening to the Philadelphia Orchestra playing Bartók's *Concerto for Orchestra*." His
claim that "most Brubeck fans don't know what Bird was" was
unfortunate given that Charlie Parker had himself expressed
enthusiasm for Brubeck's music. No one, he said, need analyze
Parker's music—"You could *feel* what he was playing" [italics
mine]. Meanwhile, Brubeck's reliance on classical techniques
ran only skin deep—"He's neither a good classical nor a good
jazz pianist. . . . Don't settle for halfway people. I'm afraid I
must consider Dave Brubeck one of these."

Root relished his chance to let off steam in print, although
whether his argument was fortified or weakened by asides such
as "His group plays like little girls tripping over the meadows" is
an open question. The implication that Brubeck was a classical
music dilettante was unfair: studying with Milhaud had wholly
transformed his musical language. Questionable also was the
notion that people only "felt" Parker's music. Until the rise of
John Coltrane, no jazz musician's solos were poured over, transcribed, learned, and absorbed into jazz language more than
Charlie Parker's. The hoary old stereotype that black jazz was
"felt," while music that could be analyzed and scrutinized was
the domain of the white musician, did little to recommend
Root's writings.

Charles Mingus, for one, would have disagreed with him. A
few months earlier, in November 1955, when Mingus penned
his "Open Letter to Miles Davis" in *DownBeat* magazine, he

defended the physicality and the feel of Brubeck's playing. Arguments about whether Brubeck swings or not are "factually unimportant," Mingus wrote, "not because Dave made *Time* magazine—and a dollar—but mainly because Dave honestly thinks he's swinging. He feels a certain pulse and plays a certain pulse which gives him pleasure and a sense of exaltation because he's sincerely doing something the way he, Dave Brubeck, feels like doing it. And as you said in your story, Miles, 'if a guy makes you pat your foot, and if you feel it down your back, etc.,' then Dave is the swingingest by your definition, Miles, because at [the] Newport [Jazz Festival] and elsewhere Dave had the whole house patting its feet and even clapping its hands."[32] A few paragraphs later, Mingus pulled rank on Davis in a way only he could have gotten away with: "Remember me, Miles? I'm Charles. Yeah, Mingus! You read third trumpet on my California record dates 11 years ago on the recommendation of Lucky Thompson. So easy, young man."

Brubeck's 1956 solo album, *Brubeck Plays Brubeck*, gave notice of his increasingly deft compositional touch. This was the album that established "In Your Own Sweet Way" and "The Duke" as standards, as well as "Two-Part Contention" and "One Moment Worth Years" as regular pieces in the quartet's repertoire. "Two-Part Contention" was an explicit nod toward J. S. Bach. "In Your Own Sweet Way," "The Duke," and "One Moment Worth Years" were all primed with the harmonic colors of what Ellington called "the French school": Debussy, Ravel, Milhaud. But throughout, and not only in "Two-Part Contention," Brubeck offset polytonal block chords and sumptuous chordal flourishes against two-part keyboard textures borrowed from Bach. So unified, in fact, were the album's gestures and harmonic foundations that *Brubeck Plays Brubeck* could be transcribed and played note for note as a concert item: like a through-conceived

32. Charles Mingus, "An Open Letter to Miles Davis," *DownBeat*, November 30, 1955.

piano suite in the tradition of Milhaud's *Scaramouche* or Stravinsky's *Serenade in A*. This was Brubeck at his most classical.

With the experience of *Brubeck Plays Brubeck*, and in particular "Two-Part Contention," behind him, this strain of classicism swam to the surface again during the quartet's 1958 album *Jazz Impressions of Eurasia* in a piece Brubeck called "Brandenburg Gate," which, three years later, he transformed into a multisectional concerto grosso on his album *Brandenburg Gate: Revisited*: the quartet in a call-and-response conversation with a chamber orchestra conducted by Howard Brubeck, Dave's elder brother. Suitably emboldened, at the end of 1963, Brubeck recorded his own first custom-built composition designed for his quartet with orchestra. "Elementals" was a punctilious seventeen-minute composition, positioned as the set-piece finale of his album *Time Changes*, and Brubeck filled a large canvas with some of his very favorite things. Teasing rhythmic ambiguities; the busy counterpoint of the octet and the still center of chorale-like harmony based around Bach; improvisation—both real-time and the "heat" of improvisation written into the fully scored orchestral music—all found their place inside a structure that wantonly played one block of activity off against another.

Classicism was operating deep inside Brubeck's most popular music, too. Although he would suggest later that he regretted the wordiness of "Blue Rondo à la Turk"—"I should have called it 'Blue Rondo' and left it at that"[33]—his title spelled out a convergence of cultural reference points: a rhythm heard in Istanbul meets classical form. "Rondo" (defined as a musical form held together by one recurring principal theme interrupted by contrasting episodes) was used frequently during the eighteenth and nineteenth centuries, and Brubeck's title invoked the famous "Rondo alla Turca" movement from Mozart's Piano Sonata No. 11 in A Major, K. 331. Meanwhile

---

33. Email to the author, February 9, 2004.

his unaccompanied introduction to "Strange Meadow Lark" borrowed the wavering out-of-tempo malleability typical of a classical cadenza (the moment in a concerto when the soloist combines and paraphrases themes, usually in an out-of-tempo stream of consciousness), his fingertip sensitivity pitching up somewhere between Debussy and Chopin; and "Three to Get Ready" opened like a witty Haydn minuet.

Within a few weeks of the US release of *Time Out* on December 14, 1959, the Brubeck Quartet recorded a pair of albums that yanked the creative tension in Brubeck's music between classical music and jazz into sharp focus. On February 16, 1960, the quartet was at the CBS 30th Street Studio in New York City recording an album with the legendary blues singer Jimmy Rushing, who had built his following as Count Basie's vocalist during the '30s and '40s; and twenty-four hours later, on February 17, they were in that same studio recording an extended four-movement composition with the New York Philharmonic conducted by Leonard Bernstein.

*Bernstein Plays Brubeck Plays Bernstein* was released on July 4, 1960, and *Brubeck and Rushing* on December 12, 1960. The extended piece was by Howard Brubeck, who, like his younger brother, had studied with Darius Milhaud. His *Dialogues for Jazz Combo and Orchestra* pasted together a smorgasbord of Romantic orchestration, twelve-tone technique, neoclassical harmony, and a showstopping Chopin-like ballad—choppy stylistic waters through which the Brubeck Quartet sailed calmly. The B side— the "Brubeck Plays Bernstein" part of the equation—consisted of quartet reimaginings of four songs from *West Side Story* (and one piece from an earlier Bernstein musical, *Wonderful Town*), which, in contrast to equivalent projects by Oscar Peterson or André Previn,[34] avoided "jazzing up" Bernstein's already jazz-infused score.

---

34. Oscar Peterson Trio, *West Side Story* (Verve V-8454, 1962); André Previn and His Pals, *West Side Story* (Contemporary S7572, 1959).

There was no "Jet Song," "Cool," or "Dance at the Gym," *West Side Story* at its jazziest, in Brubeck. Instead he stripped "I Feel Pretty," "Maria," "Somewhere," and "Tonight" down to their constituent parts, divorcing the notes themselves from Bernstein's overt stylistic borrowings. "Somewhere" found itself recast as a canon while the quartet didn't so much play "Maria," *West Side Story*'s central love song, as find a way into inhabiting and developing its restless, lovesick yearning. Brubeck's solo massaged the ripples of Bernstein's harmony. He morphed a melodic hook in the bass line into a new shape that was molded around oncoming chords as he tenderly merged and expanded the harmonic material while never losing sight of the song's original structure. That this same quartet, Brubeck's chords stabbing like a big band, had only a day earlier been roaring through classic blues with Jimmy Rushing— "Blues in the Dark," "Evenin'," "River, Stay 'Way from My Door," "Am I Blue"—registers as an unlikely parallel universe. "I've been listening to you for years and I know we can make a great album," Rushing reportedly told Brubeck.[35] And if Jimmy Rushing heard something inside Brubeck's music that not only did he admire but with which he actively wanted to work, this is reason enough to rewind through the early history of the quartet to hear their work through the ears of a great singer steeped in the blues.

At their second session, in November 1951, the quartet wailed. Fred Dutton had left, taking his bassoon with him, and Wyatt "Bull" Ruther quickly demonstrated that he was able to operate on a whole other level. His chunky, boomy tone was rooted in the strident funk of Jimmy Blanton, who had done so much to revolutionize the bass player's art during his all-too-brief tenure with Duke Ellington's orchestra between 1939 and '41. Brubeck's solo on "Me and My Shadow" bounced between

---

35. Cited in the sleeve notes to Dave Brubeck Quartet and Jimmy Rushing, *Brubeck and Rushing* (Columbia Records CL1553, 1960).

gymnastic stride piano and quivering tremolos that scrunched the harmony back into itself, a nimble pianistic display no doubt facilitated by Ruther motoring away underneath him like a circuit of spring-loaded pistons. Elsewhere, Ruther's swaggering, albeit short, solo herded "At a Perfume Counter"—a treacly ballad recorded by Jimmy Dorsey's orchestra in 1938,[36] which Brubeck's arrangement transformed into something tarter— toward its climactic peak. And the session also reconnected the quartet with the Latin spirit that Cal Tjader had once embedded into his trio. Their take on "Frenesi," which had provided Artie Shaw with a hit record in 1940,[37] used sudden turnarounds of Latin and swing rhythms to crank up the tension, Barman swapping between congas and his drum kit with deft ease. We hear Brubeck sitting deep inside a Latin groove—and then he's cutting loose, stretching his rhythms along the spine of Barman's swing patterns. But this performance really belongs to Desmond, whose biting, ecstatic tone is reminiscent of Charlie Parker—until he squeezes notes out from far beyond the accepted upper range of the alto saxophone, turning the dial from hot to boiling.

We can't know, of course, whether Rushing had heard these records or dreamed up the idea of collaborating with the quartet after some other Brubeck records came his way. But this second session highlighted another nascent trait in the quartet's armory: something unexpected was often lurking behind the politest of veneers. "At a Perfume Counter" might have neutered the candied sweetness of Jimmy Dorsey's record, but Brubeck's rerouting of its melodic line, spreading buttery passagework between piano and alto saxophone, resonated more with the objectified aloofness of neoclassicism than anything Monk would have understood as jazz. Yet, lurking underneath the surface, Ruther's soulful bass added a shade of something

---

36. Decca 1724.
37. RCA Victor 26542.

blue that also tinted Brubeck's and Desmond's solos. "Me and My Shadow" filtered a theme made famous by Al Jolson through Stravinskian rhythmic displacements, in the manner of Brubeck's trio arrangements of "'S Wonderful" and "Sweet Georgia Brown." But then Brubeck's solo answered the rhythmic questions posed by his arrangement with those gymnastic finger-busting stride piano moves.

It's more likely, as a Columbia Records artist himself, Rushing acquired his taste for Brubeck from the quartet's earliest records on the label, and *Jazz Goes to College, Brubeck Time, Jazz Impressions of the USA, Jazz Impressions of Eurasia,* and *Dave Digs Disney* were filled with those signature veneer-slipping moments. One can imagine Rushing's delight in "Keepin' Out of Mischief Now," a Fats Waller tune that was slapped right into the middle of the otherwise-studious *Brubeck Time,* with Brubeck's solo sending runs of stride piano over a structural and harmonic obstacle course; or the grooving "History of a Boy Scout" from *Jazz Impressions of the USA*; or the slow-burn gathering of feel and rhythmic momentum through *Jazz Impressions of Eurasia*'s "Nomad." The list goes on, and Rushing would also have heard authentic blues. Producer George Avakian's sleeve note for *Jazz Goes to College* describes "Balcony Rock" as "the first plain old blues to be played by the Quartet," and variations on its melodic and harmonic framework turn up again as "Back Bay Blues" on *Dave Brubeck at Storyville: 1954* and then, most famously, as "Audrey" on *Brubeck Time.* Each performance ends with Desmond urbanely slipping the minor harmony into the major, with each version finding its own route toward that blissed-out coda. Brubeck's bucolic solo on "Balcony Rock" could not have been further removed from the granite force of his solo on the pacier "Back Bay Blues," recorded four days later, on March 30, 1954. "Audrey," recorded in October 1954, was exquisitely delicate and introverted, and all three records unearthed radically different perspectives on Brubeck's idea of the blues.

With its lazy, hazy impressionism and placid disposition, "Audrey" could be thought of as exemplifying "cool jazz," the label liberally applied to lots of 1950s modern jazz—music by Gerry Mulligan, Chet Baker, Shorty Rogers, Lee Konitz, Stan Getz, Jimmy Giuffre, Chico Hamilton—that did not sound obviously like bebop. Even musicians with a background in bop, who still played the music in some contexts, might find themselves categorized as "cool"; then confusion reigned as "cool jazz" often became synonymous in the popular press with "West Coast jazz," another overused and ill-defined envelope term. In reality, the West Coast "cool" versus East Coast "hot" paradigm broke down soon enough when people actually listened to the music. But whenever the specter of "cool jazz" was raised, Brubeck felt uncomfortable, fearing that the term misrepresented the range of his work. Put him on the spot, and he would invariably cite his quartet's 1951 record of "Look for the Silver Lining," captured at the Surf Club in Hollywood, as upsetting every assumption about his group and its allegedly "cool" sound.

Desmond, his tone as hard as steel, heckles and hollers as he turns somersaults around the chord changes of "Look for the Silver Lining," racing over a frenetic, reckless even, tempo. Brubeck's labyrinthine solo maintains one flowing line as others swarm around it like bees, before he takes a dramatic plunge down the keyboard, grabbing a lolloping chain of melody that gleefully evades the regular metric plod of the bar line. As his solo reaches burnout, Brubeck shouts "Play!" at Desmond, who enters by quoting, tongue firmly in cheek, "We're in the Money." Improvised counterpoint, even at this formative stage in their history, was common quartet practice. But here the musicians sound as surprised as anybody else by the heat they are igniting: piano and alto saxophone burning with the energy (if not the notes) of a Dixieland band in full cry. This record was *hot* and highlighted the freedom that operated at the core of this Brubeck Quartet—and which would permeate through later incarnations of the group.

*Freedom* was about to become a loaded word in jazz, and a sometimes-elusive concept, but Brubeck was discovering that freedom *from* could open a door into being free *to*. Charlie Parker had already taught musicians how to fly free of stock harmonic sequences. The next generation of jazz innovators, including Miles Davis, John Coltrane, Cecil Taylor, and Ornette Coleman, would give chapter and verse on various ways in which improvisers, who felt habit and routine to be antithetical to their art, could free themselves from regular patterns of harmony and pulse. And in those earliest records, Brubeck gave us an inkling of his own idea of what it was to be free. Connecting what he had learned from Milhaud, and from a wider enthusiasm for modern composition, to the sounds and techniques of those 1920s and '30s pianists rooted in swing and stride piano he admired, including Fats Waller, Duke Ellington, Art Tatum, and Teddy Wilson, had taken Brubeck directly to his art, bypassing the prevailing influence of bebop.

During his quartet's first working trip to New York City, in 1951, to perform at Birdland—where the clue about the music normally played there was very much in the name—Brubeck felt free to bring along a group that had no audible allegiance to bop. Patrons grappling for a point of reference might have heard hints of the chamber-music sensibility of Benny Goodman's mid-1930s quartet, with Teddy Wilson (piano), Lionel Hampton (vibes), and Gene Krupa (drums), in the blend between Desmond's velvet tone and the leader's piano, while the ghost of Art Tatum haunted Brubeck's reharmonizations and those elegant, swishing lines that were interwoven through the quartet arrangements of "That Old Black Magic," "This Can't Be Love," and "I'll Remember April."

But if Brubeck's quartet didn't fit the bebop profile, nobody was likely to mistake it for a swing group either. Brubeck's reharmonizations did more than add splashes of decorative color: his disruptive alterations of chords permeated everything, boring down into the structure of solos. That velveteen ensemble shimmy, which, in the absence of bebop, might have led some listeners to recall the Goodman Quartet as a point of reference, rarely lasted long. "That Old Black Magic" and "How High the Moon," captured during a broadcast from Birdland on December 15, 1951, start out innocently enough before chords alien to the basic harmony jut out provocatively. Whole phrases are dragged away from the reassurance of tonal gravity.

To some, the Brubeck Quartet's residency at Birdland in '51—bringing their idea of what jazz could (as opposed to "should") be to the East Coast—registered as a hawkish incursion into hallowed bop terrain. Line, in bebop, was everything. After listening and learning from Parker and Gillespie's approach to improvisation, bop pianists like Bud Powell, Dodo Marmarosa, and Duke Jordan took lines for extended walks. Brubeck, though, didn't seem especially interested in line. The backbone of his solos were block chords, which, depending on your point of view, had nothing to do with jazz—or brought something entirely fresh to the table. Paradoxically, had Thelonious Monk been more active on the New York jazz scene (1951 was Monk's *annus horribilis*, during which his cabaret card, effectively his license to play jazz clubs, was revoked following fabricated drugs charges), a precedent might have been set for a progressive pianist inclined to operate independently from the dominance of bebop. Because Monk, too, constructed solos around blocks of block chords with his roots in stride piano breaking through the surface.

For all Parker and Gillespie had clawed open hitherto-unheard complexities of relationships between chords, the art of bop improvisation remained moored around what George Russell would later term "the deadline of a particular chord."[38] Even when the sounds themselves might have wanted to wander elsewhere, knowing that a particular chord was on the horizon

---

38. George Russell, *The Lydian Chromatic Concept of Tonal Organization for Improvisation* (New York: Concept Publishing, 1959), 27.

tugged an improvisation toward a predestined direction; in bebop, the strict pattern of underlying chords around which a songs were structured could not bend easily to accommodate the whim of the moment. Although few people seemed to have noticed, early 1950s Brubeck demonstrated awareness of this limitation. When the spirit moved them, his quartet could improvise around an idea of the tune—a feeling, a mood, a melodic or harmonic hook of particular outstanding natural beauty—rather than on the specifics of the tune itself. "Over the Rainbow," recorded at the Storyville in Boston in 1952, conjured a new theme out of the air—which Brubeck would later call "Summer Song"—as he experimented with combining the A and B sections of the original song, and ended with Brubeck and Desmond homing in on the final eight bars of the tune, rather than concluding with a full chorus. Desmond's voice cut into the final bar of Brubeck's solo: "Eight out, all the changes," he says, which implies that he wanted Brubeck to play each chord change under his improvisation for maximum harmonic impact, rather than strip the harmonic sequence down to its essentials.

Extending an elegant phrase over the chord changes by defaulting to those prelearned phrases jazz musicians refer to as "licks" was anathema to quartet members. If the moment demanded, they were more inclined to displace chords within the bar and stretch bar lines, the emerging logic counting for more than cleaving to the changes. A case in point was Brubeck's treatment of "That Old Black Magic" from Birdland in 1951, during which he wrapped a carapace of harmonic digressions and diversions around its familiar melodic shapes and then, in his solo, attempted to reconcile his vision with the tune itself. Recorded three years later in Berkeley, on March 3, 1954, the quartet's deconstruction of Hoagy Carmichael's "Stardust"[39]

---

39. Originally released on *The Dave Brubeck Quartet* (Fantasy Records 3-230, 1956).

pursued matters further. This tune had long been a staple of their repertoire. The rhapsodic lyricism of the version they had recorded almost a year to the day before Berkeley is a high point of *Jazz at Oberlin*, but in Berkeley the group indulged in pure free associative logic. Following Brubeck's introduction, Desmond acknowledged only the broadest outlines of Carmichael's melody. His kneading of the line into a knurly paraphrase landed him on a sloping chromatic incline, which, a few bars later, Brubeck bounced back at him, leaving the whole piece suspended momentarily in midair. Desmond's disembodied utterances floated free from the harmonic groundings underneath, his whispers of melody leaning against ethereal trills. Brubeck, in his own minimalistic solo, also kept a discreet distance from Carmichael's theme as his harmonies sailed toward the tonal borderlands. Even an unexpected, slammed cluster proved no great upset. The quartet was playing so freely that any gesture or theoretically prohibited note could be made to work.

Three musicians led by Dave Brubeck metamorphosed into the Dave Brubeck Quartet based on an understanding that, while boundaries existed and to a certain extent set the frame, spontaneous flexibility was also crucial to the mix. Rules were free floating, never predetermined or prescriptive. New quartet members needed to feel their way, their experience of playing Brubeck's music adding to the internal discussion of boundaries rather than accepting the structures as they already existed. With freedom came responsibility, and the Berkeley "Stardust" demonstrated an intensity of listening, each musician sensitive to the needs of fellow quartet members. Reviews of the period tended to highlight the classicism and formal compositional procedures—all those fugues, canons, and counterpoint—while overlooking these freer impulses. But an implicit understanding that formal structures were balanced against free thinking embedded a performance tradition inside the quartet that would carry it far into the next decade. Even at its most popular, when "Take

Five" opened doors closed to most other jazz musicians, the Brubeck Quartet was quite capable of slipping its structural berths, entering a zone where musicians with records in the charts normally feared to tread.

𝄞

The year 1954, in which everything changed for Brubeck, began with a problem that threatened to get *Jazz at Oberlin* pulled from record stores. "This is one letter I hate like the devil to write to you," Joe Glaser wrote Brubeck on January 8, "as [I'm] sure you are aware of the fact that if it is ever possible to give you any cooperation at all and to do anything for you, it will always be my pleasure to do so, but I was definitely of the opinion that you had answered Petrillo's office pertaining to the recording date at Oberlin College."[40]

During the early 1950s the American Federation of Musicians, led by Caesar Petrillo, was still thinking through the seismic consequences of recording for the music industry. Petrillo deplored what he damned as "canned music" and, rather than recognizing the recorded artifact as potentially the musician's greatest calling card, his instinct was to police recorded music. From 1942 to 1944, and again in 1948, the federation's draconian legislation extended to a blanket ban on recording in an attempt to protect the livelihoods of musicians employed by radio and theater. By 1953, when major labels like Columbia, Decca, and RCA Victor were finding themselves swept along in the postwar consumerist boom, regulations had been eased: there was more to be lost than to be gained. But Brubeck had fallen afoul of the remnants of Petrillo's earlier, more paranoid thinking. Recording contracts were still stringently controlled—and the AFM took an especially dim view of musicians' releasing material that they themselves had recorded;

---

40. Joe Glaser to Dave Brubeck, January 8, 1954, Business Correspondence, Brubeck Collection.

an unfair, unregulated practice too far, they thought, with the potential to leave their sidemen unpaid.

Glaser had assumed that the problem had been settled by Larry Bennett while Glaser was on a business trip to Tokyo, and he was surprised to have received a follow-up letter from Petrillo himself, dated January 6, threatening to charge Brubeck for willful violation of the regulations. "Now, Dave," Glaser continued,

> since I have been given to understand the record [*Jazz at Oberlin*] is out and being sold on the open market, which you realize you are not supposed to do, and since you are aware of the fact, since you contacted me after the record was released and being sold, I would appreciate your writing me in detail, upon receipt of this letter, as to how you want me to proceed to handle this matter, as I am definitely of the opinion that if the matter is presented in the proper way that some sort of deal can be worked out with the Federation, whereby everyone concerned will be happy.

In a postscript, Glaser warned: "I do not want you to answer PETRILLO personally. Answer me so I can take care of the matter personally."

Petrillo and Glaser spoke the same language when it came to business. Following the payment of a fine, the matter was considered resolved, and *Jazz at Oberlin* remained in record stores. A few months later, in a letter mockingly addressed to "the Honorable Dave Brubeck," Glaser described how Brubeck had been "granted permission by Mr. James C. Petrillo's representative, Clare Meter, to use the tapes. Think it was three or four tapes, and hope I am not mistaken in stating 3 or four (and not 14) which you admitted having made."[41] This crisis

---

41. Joe Glaser to Dave Brubeck, April 6, 1954, Business Correspondence, Brubeck Collection.

had been averted, but the lesson was clear—Fantasy Records, the independent label that operated out of San Francisco and which had released Brubeck's octet, trio, and early quartet records, was too small, and its business practices too quaint, to push Brubeck's career to the next level.

For the first time in Brubeck's career, the East Coast began to exercise its pull. The subtext of Glaser's correspondence, as he wrote from his ritzy suite of offices at 745 Fifth Avenue in Manhattan, was clear. In the January 8 letter, he expressed surprise that Brubeck had already passed up offers of recording contracts from Norman Granz and Eddie Mesner: Mesner's Aladdin Records, which had Lester Young and Illinois Jacquet on its books, was a far bigger outfit than Fantasy, while Granz's Clef and Norgran labels (soon to be incorporated into a new label, Verve) would become a preeminent rival to Columbia, Brubeck's eventual label. Glaser was diplomatic: "I personally think that you should definitely and positively have some sort of understanding with Fantasy. First, pertaining to release of your records throughout the United States, second, pertaining to monies due you on royalties etc., and third and most important of all, as to how long you are going to remain with Fantasy." Glaser ends his letter with an offer to meet to "help you decide as to what you are going to do about your recording situation in the future."

Brubeck's continuing loyalty to Fantasy had been due partly to his own financial stake in the company. Fantasy was founded by two brothers, Max and Sol Weiss,[42] as a subsidiary of the plastic molding business they ran in San Francisco. Brubeck had met the brothers during one of his residencies at the Black Hawk, although jazz was, at best, only of passing interest to the Weisses. When, in 1948, they decided to plug an obvious gap in the market by pressing vinyl, having realized no other company in San Francisco was providing a similar service, this was

---

42. Sol Weiss (1916–2002), Max Weiss (1925–2007).

a natural extension of their plastics company rather than any-thing to do with loving music. And, in 1949, when they launched Fantasy, again it was strictly business: releasing records was a way of offsetting profits from their core plastic business against taxes, so that they could claim a tax loss.

Despite their indifference to jazz, the brothers recognized the potential of the Dave Brubeck Trio. The trio's first four sides—"Blue Moon," "Tea for Two," "Indiana," and "Laura"—had originally been released on Coronet,[43] the tiny indepen-dent label that the Dixieland trombonist Jack Sheedy[44] had set up primarily as an outlet for his own trad band. Although the normally sympathetic Jimmy Lyons had introduced Brubeck to Sheedy, Brubeck's music was never likely to sit comfortably inside a catalog devoted to Dixieland jazz. But there were finan-cial problems too. When Brubeck complained that his sidemen had not received their fees, the business-minded Weiss broth-ers were astute enough to connect the dots. Sheedy's claim that Brubeck's records had yet to make enough money to pay any-one was an expedient fib: in fact Dave Brubeck Trio records—as plugged regularly on Jimmy Lyons's radio show—were subsidizing Sheedy's releases of his own band, which had never sold in great quantities. Coronet was failing, and the Weisses strongly advised Brubeck to buy back his master recordings before the whole ship—and possibly his masters—sank with-out a trace. This was cogent advice: just before Coronet hit the buffers, Brubeck paid somewhere in the region of $300 to $400 for his masters.[45]

---

43. Coronet 103, 104.

44. Sheedy (1923–2001) was a minor player, although he did persuade Paul Desmond to participate in a 1950 recording session with his band. Desmond doubled on clarinet and alto saxophone on "How Long Baby How Long," "The Man I Love," and "Down in Honky Tonk Town"; Norman Bates and Bob Bates, both later Brubeck Quartet members, played bass. He moved to New York in the 1980s, where he continued to play jazz and wrote plays and poetry.

45. In different interviews, Brubeck remembered $300, $350, and $400.

In an interview for *Billboard* in 1967, Max Weiss recalled: "That's how we met Brubeck. He was on the Dixieland label we were pressing, only he wasn't playing Dixieland. Jimmy Lyons had introduced him to the owner of the label. Apparently Dave was told his records weren't selling, but we knew better, so we started a label just for him."[46] The brothers launched their label—which initially they called Circle Records—by reissuing the first four Brubeck Trio records and then inviting the group to record more. But their mercenary attitude toward music justified Glaser's hunch, four years later, that a talent like Brubeck's was deserving of something more professional and empathetic.

Music on Fantasy tended to thrive despite, not because of, the label. The brothers thrived on gallows humor. A running joke in their Natoma Street office—that they ought to have called their label "Reluctant Records"—might have tickled their funny bones, but they genuinely feared the prospect of Fantasy becoming too successful in case the extra cash flow upset the delicate balance of their tax affairs. Brubeck was disconcerted to hear them refer sarcastically to his music as "garbage" during a studio session;[47] to the brothers it was merely a disposable commodity. Everything about Fantasy—from sometimes jokey, pseudo-hipster sleeve notes and garish cover art to its very name, styled after a kooky sci-fi magazine—implied a lack of serious thinking at the top.

And yet Brubeck recognized that the label represented an opportunity that he would have been foolish to pass up. Alongside producing records of his own, he brought other fledging jazz musicians to the label. The Gerry Mulligan Quartet (featuring Chet Baker) recorded live at the Black Hawk in September

46. "Local Labels Build Acts, But . . . ," *Billboard*, May 6, 1967.

47. Dave Brubeck, interview with Ted Gioia, Smithsonian Jazz Oral History Program, August 6–7, 2007, transcript, http://amhistory.si.edu/jazz/Brubeck-Dave/Dave_Brubeck_Transcript.pdf.

1952,[48] and in 1954, Red Norvo made records with his trio and with strings for Fantasy,[49] all by Brubeck's recommendation (and Cal Tjader recorded for the label under his own name for the first time in the aftermath of Brubeck's swimming accident.)[50] But Brubeck was unquestionably the label's star and premier artist. "Blue Moon" was handed *Metronome* magazine's "record of the month" rosette in December 1949, and the quartet's "Singin' in the Rain" followed suit in May 1950. The response from *DownBeat* was more cautious. The trio's first four sides were given three out of a four possible "notes." But the (unnamed) reviewer at least noted, via a backhanded compliment, that Brubeck was doing something out of the ordinary with rhythm and time: "[He is] more easily separated from the beat than the average jazz pianist, yet with still a very good combo sense of what can and cannot happen to a musician devoted to the slogging 4/4."[51]

Brubeck's idealism about music was always destined to put him on a collision course with the Weiss brothers, who conspicuously failed to hide their concern at how well the quartet's *Jazz at the Black Hawk* was doing—sales at this level were dangerously close to upending their tax arrangements. The Weisses had been canny enough to see through Jack Sheedy's double-dealing, but now they had a nasty surprise of their own for Brubeck. Contracts between Brubeck and the brothers had been built around an understanding that they would share the costs of record production: Brubeck would pay the musicians (without taking payment himself) and then all other costs, including studio time and distribution, would be met by the brothers. Brubeck had assumed, naively, that this arrangement amounted to a full-scale partnership, but he was shocked to discover, at some point during 1953, that the brothers had retained full ownership of

---

48. Fantasy Records 522.
49. Fantasy Records 3-19; Fantasy Records 3-218.
50. Fantasy Records 3-9.
51. Reviews, *DownBeat*, January 27, 1950.

the name Fantasy Records and the only stake he had was 50 percent of his own records.

Everything connected with the Weiss brothers feels, in retrospect, odd and unfathomable, but their baiting of Brubeck financially, when the rationale behind their venture had initially been to absorb tax liability, is the strangest behavior of all. Were the brothers preparing to run the label on a more professional footing, which necessitated clarifying Brubeck's position? If so, they handled the situation with a characteristic lack of grace. But their next move—hiring Saul Zaentz in 1955—suggests they knew they needed to sharpen up their act. Zaentz had worked for Norman Granz, under whose guidance he had managed tours for Duke Ellington, Ella Fitzgerald, and Stan Getz while he learned the machinery of the record business from the inside. Zaentz was charged with boosting sales and distribution while casting his net wide for new artists and smaller labels that might be absorbed into Fantasy. And he made such a success of the label that he bought out the Weiss brothers in 1967. Zaentz added classy jazz labels like Riverside and Prestige to the Fantasy family, and then increased the label's visibility by signing the rootsy hard-rock group Creedence Clearwater Revival.

But Zaentz's arrival came too late for Brubeck, whose fingers had been bitten by Jack Sheedy and now by the Weiss brothers too. Tough lessons had been learned, and as he found himself at the center of talks between Joe Glaser and George Avakian, head of popular albums at Columbia, he kept the coolest of heads. The self-assurance and confidence that had surfaced when he was negotiating his contract with ABC at the end of 1950 emerged once again. Brubeck wanted to be part of the Columbia roster—what jazz musician didn't? But even as Glaser begged him to sign, Brubeck dragged his heels. Nothing would be signed until his every last requirement had been satisfied.

George Avakian's name turns up with increasingly regularity in Brubeck's correspondence from April 1954 onward, but the story, often put about, that Avakian discovered the Dave Brubeck Quartet in the summer of '54, when he chanced upon the group at the Black Hawk during a vacation in San Francisco, oversimplifies a complicated slice of history.[52]

By 1954, Avakian had been working for eight years at Columbia, where he had devoted a sizable proportion of his time and energy to carving out a convincing niche for jazz within a company lacquered by the huge profits they made from classical music, popular singers, and Broadway shows. When, in 1948, Columbia shifted production from the ten-inch LP to the long-playing 33⅓ rpm, twelve-inch vinyl disc, two years after Avakian joined, they bought time—literally. Those extra two inches made all the difference, and releasing a full original cast recording of Rodgers and Hammerstein's *South Pacific*[53] became feasible—as did records of complete classical works performed by a roster of artists that included Bruno Walter, Eugene Ormandy, and Vladimir Horovitz, and extended-play albums of pop songs sung by heartthrobs like Frank Sinatra, Doris Day, Tony Bennett, and Rosemary Clooney. But the company's interest in jazz was restricted to their Hot Jazz Classics series: salable and relatively cheap-to-produce reissues of 1920s and '30s material by Louis Armstrong, Bix Beiderbecke, Teddy Wilson, Earl Hines, and Bessie Smith—78s transferred onto ten-inch LPs.

Day to day, Avakian was based in New York City, but, unlike many major label honchos with an interest in jazz—who tended

---

52. Avakian (1919–2017) was a record producer who was hired by Columbia while still a student at Yale. At Columbia he produced Brubeck, Davis, Erroll Garner, Ravi Shankar, Eddie Condon, Tony Bennett, Lotte Lenya, Mahalia Jackson, and Louis Armstrong. He later worked at RCA Victor, where he signed Paul Desmond, Gary Burton, and Sonny Rollins. He also independently produced *The 25-Year Retrospective Concert of the Music of John Cage*, now a prized collectors' item in its original form.

53. Columbia A-850.

to consider New York the only place to be—Avakian made regular summer trips to California. His wife, Anahid Ajemian, was a distinguished concert violinist with a particular leaning toward challenging contemporary repertoire. With her sister Maro on piano, a typical Ajemian Duo concert might consist of music by John Cage, Lou Harrison, Charles Ives, Henry Cowell, or Elliott Carter—and during the summer months Anahid prepared and rehearsed her programs for the coming year with Maro, who lived in Berkeley. Avakian would fly out to be with his wife and had met the Brubecks socially at Maro's house. But when he heard the quartet live, he recognized both the artistic integrity of Brubeck's music and the group's commercial potential.[54]

Brubeck was signed by the end of 1954; Miles Davis would follow a year later, and over the next five years the Columbia jazz list increased exponentially to include Louis Armstrong, Duke Ellington, Charles Mingus, Billie Holiday, Jimmy Rushing, and Gerry Mulligan. This was an impressive roll call, but equally important to Brubeck's story, and to the general evolution of jazz on record, was Avakian's hunch that the twelve-inch LP required more sensitive handling than its ten-inch counterpart. As he explained in 2010: "[The] 12-inch LP [was] no longer simply a collection of singles. It was a journey, with a start and a finish. People put it on and sat down expecting a performance, a range of moods, a sequence."[55]

Avakian's campaign to give jazz visibility at Columbia had been fought using his natural charm—but also by showing tangible results, as the music gradually gained the trust of his superiors. In 1950, a double-LP set of Benny Goodman's historically momentous 1938 concert at Carnegie Hall was released, and for

---

54. In a line cut from the *Time* magazine cover story in 1954, Brubeck said, "If George was smart enough to marry Anahid Ajemian and have Maro as a sister-in-law . . . I decided, that's the guy I want to produce me." Carter Harman, "The Man on Cloud No. 7," *Time*, November 8, 1954.

55. George Avakian, interview with Marc Myers (part 4), JazzWax, March 18, 2010, www.jazzwax.com/2010/03/18/.

the first time jazz fans were given access to a concert they would certainly have read about but never heard.[56] Then, to demonstrate the potential of recording new material, on December 18, 1950, Avakian brought Duke Ellington's orchestra into the studio. *Masterpieces by Ellington* placed "The Tattooed Bride," his extended composition from 1948, in the context of reimaginings of "Mood Indigo," "Solitude," and "Sophisticated Lady": classic Ellingtonia expanded and developed to fit the LP format, no longer bumping up against the three-minute ceiling of the 78.[57] The Goodman and Ellington albums sold well, which gave Avakian leverage as he began to think about signing Brubeck, then Miles Davis. And his decision to bring Johnny Mathis to the label, at around the same time as Miles, no doubt helped reassure his bosses that the Columbia checkbook was safe in his hands.

*Brubeck Time*, which was recorded over four sessions at Columbia's 30th Street Studio in New York City between October and November 1954, showed how much the quartet benefited from being rigorously produced: Avakian's sensitivity to the craft of shaping an album and balancing instruments acoustically in the studio were a world away from the Weiss brothers' slapdash production values. And yet, as Glaser and Avakian hammered out a contract to satisfy all parties, Brubeck's obstinate determination to retain a working relationship with Fantasy clearly exasperated both men. In a letter sent when most of *Brubeck Time* was already in the can, Avakian advised Brubeck: "Remember that <u>YOU</u> are in the driver's seat. You can do great without Fantasy; Fantasy can't do much without you."[58] But two concerns were eating away at Brubeck. Columbia wanted new material, and he had surmised, rightly, that the company had no interest in repackaging his old octet or trio records. Buying

---

56. Columbia SET SL-160.
57. Columbia Masterworks ML 4418.
58. George Avakian to Dave Brubeck, October 29, 1954, Business Correspondence, Brubeck Collection.

back the masters might have been an option, but Avakian warned Brubeck to be cautious: "If you ever decide you want to buy back your old Fantasy masters, you will have to first depress their value or you will get held up on the matter of price."

If his older material was to remain in circulation, keeping Fantasy onside was essential, but Brubeck's insistence on retaining the freedom to release new albums on Fantasy irked Avakian, who regarded the prospect as commercially unhelpful. To fulfil his obligations to Fantasy, Brubeck had agreed to record a further three albums for the label (the last of which, *Near Myth*, a quartet session with Bill Smith in place of Paul Desmond, wasn't recorded until 1961),[59] which Avakian accepted as fair enough (and he would face a similar problem a year later when clawing Miles away from Prestige). But Brubeck's insistence that any tapes rejected by Columbia might be submitted to Fantasy for release—and then to a third company in the event that Fantasy rejected them or went bust—horrified Avakian, who worried about Brubeck diluting the impact of his major-label status and about multiple albums, containing multiple versions of the same tunes, leading to muddle and misunderstandings in record stores.

Brubeck also had his knuckles rapped by Alfred B. Lorber, from the Columbia legal department. "We are somewhat chagrined at this point that our proposed contract has not been promptly signed and the deal put to bed," Lorber wrote to Joe Glaser on May 3, the climactic thrust of an angrily worded letter.[60] On the vexed question of whether Brubeck might take recordings to a third company, Lorber was empathic: "He would then be in the same position as all of our other exclusive artists, no matter how important they are to our roster. That is, he would have to . . . ask specific permission." Lorber explained

59. Fantasy 3319.

60. Alfred B. Lorber to Joe Glaser, May 3, 1954, Business Correspondence, Brubeck Collection.

that any third company would need to prove their stature and fair business practices before Columbia would entertain the idea. By allowing Brubeck an ongoing relationship with Fantasy, "Dave has already received . . . a tremendous concession, and one we do not give to any of our other artists." And he was seeking a further concession: in the circumstance of an album being deleted from the Columbia catalog, Brubeck negoti- ated the right to gain control of recordings after a period of time, as Lorber explained, "for his own use and profit." Lorber explained that, assuming Columbia had recouped production costs, Brubeck would be charged only for the production of a master tape.

Lorber's tone evidently caught Glaser unawares, who, concerned that Columbia was about to walk away, immediately forwarded the letter to Brubeck—who promptly refused to back down. On May 13 he told Avakian:

> It seems that we have gotten nowhere with my request for a rider on the contract, and if I were in an argumentative mood I could be very caustic about some of the things included in a recent letter from Mr. Lorber, forwarded to me by Mr. Glaser. As he does not want to reword the contracts or add a rider, in your return letter will you kindly state that if FANTASY rejects any of my records, or goes out of business, the minor label chosen by COLUMBIA must be of comparable importance in jazz and have 29 or more distributors, which approximates FANTASY and other minor records labels.[61]

As a final thought, Brubeck added: "Does Columbia have a subsidiary label?" (Glaser's nerves might have been fortified by a Western Union telegram from Jack Lewis, head of jazz at RCA

61. Dave Brubeck to George Avakian, May 13, 1954, Business Correspondence, Brubeck Collection.

Victor, dated April 14, asking if Brubeck had definitely signed to Columbia—there were, apparently, always other options.)[62]

In reality, Fantasy and Columbia were in this together. During the handover period Avakian exchanged businesslike, but always cordial, letters with the Weiss brothers, and perhaps Brubeck need not have been so worried about Fantasy—in his 1967 interview with *Billboard*, Max Weiss proclaimed that he was untroubled when rapacious major labels lured away artists in which Fantasy had invested: "The artist's catalog suddenly comes alive when he gets the major buildup and promotion that such majors as Columbia are able to provide."[63]

Brubeck's first releases for Columbia, *Dave Brubeck at Storyville: 1954*[64] and *Jazz Goes to College*, were assembled from tapes that would otherwise have been released by Fantasy. The quartet's concert at Oberlin College on March 2, 1953—which, once the Weiss brothers had managed to acquire the tapes, became *Jazz at Oberlin*—had been recorded by student engineers using magnetic tape. Brubeck quickly recognized that this was a win-win situation. On condition that he retained the rights and was given the tapes immediately after the performance, the still-cash-strapped Brubeck walked away with a free recording of his performance, and colleges got to broadcast live relays of his on-campus concerts. This arrangement then became standard policy: any college booking the quartet could relay the concert, so long as the tapes were handed over and no copies were made. *Jazz Goes to College* was put together from recordings made at the University of Michigan, the University of Cincinnati, and a return visit to Oberlin College during 1954; Iola's pitches to university campuses offering the quartet had paid off. Initially Avakian's horse-trading with the Weisses was about securing those tapes and ascertaining whether the appropriate

62. Jack Lewis to Dave Brubeck (c/o Joe Glaser), telegram, April 14, 1954, Business Correspondence, Brubeck Collection.
63. "Local Labels Build Acts, But . . . ," *Billboard*, May 6, 1967.
64. Not to be confused with the 1952 *Jazz at Storyville* (Fantasy 3240).

permissions had been granted to circumvent a further clash with Petrillo—then the terms of any continuing relationship with Fantasy needed to be defined.

On March 3, Max Weiss sent a breakdown of how royalties were paid against record sales (to carn $18,000 Brubeck needed to sell sixty thousand LPs), which Brubeck immediately forwarded to Avakian with a message scrawled in pencil on its reverse side: "George, Should I get my own record licence from A[merican] F[ederation] of M[usicians]??"[65] Avakian's strategies for dealing with Fantasy soon became clear. Sol Weiss wrote on July 26 to tell Brubeck that Fantasy and Columbia were trading tracks—"'[At a] Perfume Counter' and 'Crazy Chris' [are] all squared away against 'Le Souk' and 'Gone with the Wind,'" he reported.[66]

A dazzling example of the Brubeck Quartet improvising spontaneously off the mood of the moment over any preconceived form, "Le Souk" would, alongside "Balcony Rock," prove a highlight of *Jazz Goes to College*. The piece opens with an apparent suspension of Western harmony and tuning as Desmond proudly ascends to the top of his instrument, tracing a scalic pattern that, as Avakian writes in his sleeve note, suggests "ancient Eastern practice," while his correspondingly gamey tuning disfigures the usually clean-cut steps of note moving to note (and in retrospect sounds unmistakably like Ornette Coleman). Not for the first time, Desmond's devastatingly smart solo presents Brubeck with a challenge. Pianos, with their fixed tuning, are impotent when it comes to twisting notes out of Western tuning alignment, so Brubeck instead proceeds by fashioning graphic contrasts of chordal density. The piece has been seesawing between G minor and A minor, not because Desmond and Brubeck had necessarily decided that it would

---

65. Max Weiss to Dave Brubeck, March 3, 1954, Business Correspondence, Brubeck Collection.

66. Sol Weiss to Dave Brubeck, July 26, 1954, Business Correspondence, Brubeck Collection.

but because that is where the emerging sounds led them. In his solo, Brubeck throws G minor and A minor between his hands like a juggler, an ever-changing kaleidoscope of rhythmic and harmonic color. Avakian recognized the singularity of "Le Souk." Including the piece on Brubeck's Columbia debut was a must.

Because he had yet to sign his contract, the convoluted process of licensing "Le Souk" involved the technicality of Brubeck writing to offer Columbia "At a Perfume Counter" and "Crazy Chris," which they would formally refuse. Columbia could then take ownership of "Le Souk" because *not* using the longer "Crazy Chris" balanced out the duration of music that Columbia could license from Fantasy—set against the LPs of new or reissued Brubeck that Columbia had agreed Fantasy could continue to release . . . once Brubeck had signed on the dotted line.

This was no way to run a record label, and Avakian's pleas for Brubeck to sign the Columbia contract hit a crescendo over the early summer. With *Jazz Goes to College* due for release, he scribbled a note on the bottom of a letter in order to highlight the urgency: "Album comes out June 10 unless we fail to get contracts by [May] 25th. I have assumed we'll get them any day!"[67] But as May 25 arrived without the contracts, Avakian wrote again to raise a further problem. "Has Desmond really signed with Fantasy? This doesn't seem possible in view of what you told me a couple of weeks ago. What goes?"[68] Avakian wanted to protect and polish the Brubeck brand, not find it compromised by his celebrity sideman effectively setting himself up in competition. Perhaps Desmond could be signed to Columbia to record one album a year outside the quartet—or be persuaded to record for Fantasy under a pseudonym? "Have

---

67. George Avakian to Dave Brubeck, May 19, 1954, Business Correspondence, Brubeck Collection.

68. George Avakian to Dave Brubeck, May 25, 1954, Business Correspondence, Brubeck Collection.

you ever discussed aspects of this whole situation with Paul?" Avakian asked.[69]

As the summer rolled on without a completed contract, but with Desmond signing to Fantasy anyway (his eponymous debut as a leader used bassist Bob Bates and drummer Joe Dodge from the Brubeck Quartet and reunited him with the octet's Dick Collins and David Van Kriedt—and, for good measure, threw in the Bill Bates Singers),[70] Avakian kept the faith. As it turned out, the release of *Jazz Goes to College* passed with discussions about the contract still going back and forth, but Avakian pushed ahead nevertheless with plans for the next albums— *Dave Brubeck at Storyville: 1954* and an LP that, depending on how Brubeck viewed matters, might be called *Hi-Fi Brubeck* or *Dave Brubeck at Basin Street.*

Avakian's finely tuned ears—exemplifying the elite production values that would help Brubeck as he worked toward making tautly structured albums like *Jazz Impressions of Eurasia* and *Time Out*—knew what they wanted to hear from the beginning. On the *Storyville* album, Avakian told Brubeck that he had cut a solo bass chorus on "On the Alamo" because "the quality of sound on the bass was so poor and thumpy that it was criminal to leave it in. This splice is virtually undetectable."[71] Meanwhile the two men had obviously been discussing the problematic ending of "Back Bay Blues,"[72] where announcer John McLellan's radio chatter cut across the final bars,[73] making removing the dialogue with a neat edit impossible. On reflection,

69. George Avakian to Dave Brubeck, 1954 (undated), Business Correspondence, Brubeck Collection.

70. Fantasy 3-21.

71. George Avakian to Dave Brubeck, July 30, 1954, Business Correspondence, Brubeck Collection.

72. Avakian types "Boston Blues" before correcting it to "Back Bay Blues" in pen, suggesting, perhaps, that Brubeck was considering a range of titles.

73. McLellan (b. 1926), a jazz journalist and radio and television presenter, hosted a radio show live from Storyville every Tuesday evening on WGBH during the mid-1950s.

Avakian suggested that the ending would "be covered by rising applause" and that they ought to make a virtue of McLellan's sign-off—"For the last twenty-five minutes you've been listening to the Dave Brubeck Quartet"—by utilizing his words to carry the album toward a natural ending.

Was it Avakian's intention to use live applause already captured on tape? Or to edit applause in? From the context, it is impossible to know. A few weeks before the final session for *Brubeck Time*, Avakian presented Brubeck with two options: the quartet's newly recorded studio material could be worked up into *Hi-Fi Brubeck*, or adding crowd hubbub could make *Dave Brubeck at Basin Street*, a fabricated blend of studio and live tracks with overdubbed applause and ambience, all held together by the hope that nobody would notice the join.[74] Passing off studio tracks as music recorded in a jazz club feels inconceivable today, but this practice was an industry-wide norm during the 1950s. In 1956, Avakian would even toy with the improbable plan of asking Duke Ellington's tenor saxophonist Paul Gonsalves to re-create in the studio, note by transcribed note, the talking point of the 1956 Newport Jazz Festival—the transcendent twenty-seven-chorus solo he had taken on Ellington's "Diminuendo and Crescendo in Blue." When playing, Gonsalves, lost in the ecstasy of the moment, had pointed the bell of his saxophone toward the wrong microphone. Avakian worried that the sonics of the track weren't robust enough to sit alongside the rest of that Newport program—which had been restaged in the studio.[75]

Either way, live or studio, he needed Brubeck's decision by November 10, which, he added, with a weary tone, precluded

---

74. George Avakian to Dave Brubeck, October 29, 1954, Business Correspondence, Brubeck Collection.

75. The album appeared, with Gonsalves's original performance, in 1957 as *Ellington at Newport* (Columbia CL934). A 1999 reissue (Columbia C2K64932) used a newly discovered radio broadcast by Voice of America, which had captured Gonsalves's performance clearly.

"waiting for any deal with Fantasy for material they are holding." Avakian's personal preference was the studio album option, and the proposed set list he included for *Hi-Fi Brubeck*—which would eventually hit record stores as the more poetically titled *Brubeck Time*—was very nearly the album we know, but with "Fare Thee Well, Annabelle" where you expect to see "Pennies from Heaven." Brubeck concurred; they should put out a studio album, but the ordering of tracks, he advised Avakian, threw up an unusual problem. Three tunes in the key of C—"Keepin' Out of Mischief Now," "Brother, Can You Spare a Dime?," and "Why Do I Love You?"—would need to be programmed judiciously to avoid too much of the same tonality (although "Why Do I Love You?," Brubeck said, "starts and ends in C even though it modulates all over the hell.")[76] He also worried that "Jeepers Creepers" and "Keepin' Out of Mischief Now," which affectionately played off the jitterbugging energy of 1920s jazz, with Brubeck indulging his love for stride piano, needed to be separated: "They are very similar in feeling [with] a two-beat like gimmick ending," he said. But they were too good to lose—Avakian placed "Jeepers Creepers" as the second track on side A, and "Keepin' Out of Mischief Now" claimed the equivalent position on the B side.

The correspondence between Brubeck and Avakian reveals how fluid ideas about albums remained during the planning stage as all options were kept open. Unfortunately, Avakian reported, a live version from Basin Street of "I Get a Kick Out of You"—"A pretty fine job," he said—had been wasted: the engineers were changing tapes and missed the opening bars. Also in the running for *Brubeck Time* were versions of "I'm Afraid the Masquerade Is Over" and "Margie" recently recorded in Hollywood, which were dismissed eventually on the grounds that "neither . . . are worldbeaters." (Brubeck would pick up the

---

76. Dave Brubeck to George Avakian, November 23, 1954, Business Correspondence, Brubeck Collection.

threads again on "Margie" forty-four years later when a 1998 version appeared on the quartet album *Double Live: From the USA & UK*.)[77] Another *Brubeck Time* piece, "Stompin' for Mili," which had been improvised in the studio, revived the eight-bar introduction Brubeck had used when he recorded "Give a Little Whistle" in 1952 for Fantasy. Should his introduction be edited out? "The last eight bars are then all we would have to worry about and they'd have to acknowledge that it's the same thing, but different because it ["Stompin' for Mili"] was played in the minor."

With "Stompin' for Mili" linking back to an earlier recording, *Brubeck Time* also seeded his next album, where "Fare Thee Well, Annabelle" would finally appear, as plans to release material recorded live at Basin Street blossomed into *Jazz: Red Hot and Cool*, a far catchier title than *Dave Brubeck at Basin Street*. A live "Keepin' Out of Mischief Now" could have appeared on the Basin Street album, but Avakian preferred the studio version, with the caveat that to make take 1 usable, an ending would need to be patched in from elsewhere. Conversely, the idea of a studio version of "Fare Thee Well, Annabelle" was rejected. There were too many fumbled notes (bars three to eight of take 2 would need to be dropped into take 3), while a single note in bar 31, which Desmond played too softly, would need to be patched—a mash-up too far. Upon its release, *Brubeck Time*'s studio credentials were proudly flaunted on the front cover. This was the first time that fans could hear "High Fidelity Studio Recordings by the Dave Brubeck Quartet." And that left "Sometimes I'm Happy," "Indiana," and "Love Walked In," which might have been mixed in with the studio recordings, as the backbone of *Jazz: Red Hot and Cool*.

A few weeks after the final *Brubeck Time* session, on December 6—coincidently Brubeck's thirty-fourth birthday—a final

---

77. Telarc 2CD-83400.

exchange of letters between lawyers signed off on an "agreement between Columbia Records Inc. and David Brubeck."[78] But, through the protracted and complicated process, it seems that not every kink could be ironed out in writing. "I will be keeping my fingers crossed in the hope that at no time ever will any situations present themselves where there will be any misunderstandings between you and George Avakian on the verbal agreements that you have with George personally," Glaser told Brubeck on June 2.[79]

Two weeks later, on June 16, Glaser forwarded Brubeck a copy of the contract and hoped that "you have already received your check from Columbia in the amount of $6000."[80] This advance against royalties was no arbitrary sum. Brubeck's parents, Pete and Bessie, still had a mortgage to pay on the family ranch in Ione, a small town in California where Dave had spent the latter part of his childhood. Brubeck's advance was sufficient to clear their debt. "You see what a family guy Dave was?" Avakian reflected in 1993. "He wanted to do that as a gift to his parents, because he was so grateful for what they had done through the years, sending him through college and letting him be a musician and all."[81] From Columbia's perspective, $6,000 was a hefty sum to invest in a musician who might have swum proudly as a big fish on a small independent label but was now expected to stay afloat alongside some of the biggest names in American music.

---

78. James Tomlinson to Dale E. Schlager, December 6, 1954, Business Correspondence, Brubeck Collection.

79. Joe Glaser to Dave Brubeck, June 2, 1954, Business Correspondence, Brubeck Collection.

80. Joe Glaser to Dave Brubeck, June 16, 1954, Business Correspondence, Brubeck Collection.

81. George Avakin, interview with Ann Sneed, Smithsonian Jazz Oral History Program, September 28, 1993, transcript, https://americanhistory.si.edu/sites/default/files/file-uploader/Avakian_Goegre_Interview_Transcription%20%282%29.pdf.

But Avakian's faith paid off. When *Jazz Goes to College* was released on June 7, demand was great, and the record flew off record-store shelves. By the end of the same month, Brubeck had already paid back his advance—and there was cash to spare.

*Chapter Five*

# UNDERWORLD

"How memory conspires with objects of human
craft, pressing time flat, inciting a tender
reminiscence."

DON DELILLO, *Underworld*, 1997

Milky-white light is lapping lazily around Brubeck's beanpole
frame as Paul Desmond loiters in the shadows like Orson Welles
in *The Third Man*, a silhouette poised to deliver a memorable
line. This first sighting of the Dave Brubeck Quartet on film
was shot on October 12 and 13, 1954, at Columbia's 30th Street
Studio in New York City during the *Brubeck Time* sessions, movie
cameras making good on Columbia's plan to promote their
latest signing.

Also in attendance—alongside George Avakian and the
quartet (with Joe Dodge on drums and newest member Bob
Bates on bass)—was Carter Harman, a reporter from *Time* magazine who was writing a profile of Brubeck due to be published

on November 8 under the headline "The Man on Cloud No. 7." For the same magazine Harman would also profile Rosemary Clooney, George Balanchine, Maria Callas, and Duke Ellington, great names all; but his Brubeck article would leave the biggest impression, both as a subsequent historical point of reference and more immediately in helping to form opinions about an artist who was still something of an unknown quantity, especially on America's East Coast. And as Harman watched Brubeck, the filmmaker and photographer Gjon Mili watched Harman watching Brubeck, as his camera improvised contrasts of light and shade in step with the music.

In his capacity as a staff photographer for *Life* magazine, Mili had famously captured Pablo Picasso in 1949, and he already had experience with jazz. His 1944 short, *Jammin' the Blues*, was centered around a core of musicians associated with Count Basie's orchestra—Lester Young, trumpeter Harry "Sweets" Edison, and drummer Jo Jones—playing the blues and then sauntering through the standard "On the Sunny Side of the Street," and already he was thinking about how the tonal color of film and the channeling of light might be deployed as a visual metaphor for the movement and vibration of sound. But his ten-minute Brubeck film—given the title *Stompin' for Mili*— would prove his masterwork, and Mili's transformation of light and shadow—Rembrandt shaking hands with John Cassavetes—remains mesmerizing all these decades later.

Harman's article saturated *Time* readers in atmosphere, and his words could stand as a frame-by-frame description of the opening minutes of Mili's film. "Brubeck bends his lanky torso over the keys, concentrating like a child on a jigsaw puzzle, but his eyes are closed," Harman wrote.[1] "The other members of the quartet . . . go to work. Desmond's tones are plaintive and pure, the rhythm of drum and bass is as rich and firm as a deep-pile carpet." The film announces itself with an urgent

---

1. Carter Harman, "The Man on Cloud No. 7," *Time*, November 8, 1954.

call to attention, a cymbal smash of the type more commonly used to declare the opening of a detective movie, the edgy noir of Raymond Chandler. But the bass line that walks away from that reverberant cymbal clash grounds what we're about to hear in the blues. The credits roll. "Stompin' for Mili. A film by Gjon Mili" wobbles into view, followed by a familiar surname: Aram Avakian, brother of George, is credited for his "technical assistance."

And now we see the quartet, and they are playing "Audrey." Brubeck has been positioned carefully at the center of the screen, with Desmond silhouetted at the far right of the picture, the bell of his saxophone just about visible through the fog of light. Mili's camera momentarily pans toward the elegant curvature of Brubeck's fingers, but then, suddenly, we're looking at Desmond's profile reflected against the lid of the piano, the velveteen timbre of his saxophone rhyming with the plush light that flickers against the shining wood of the piano lid; Bob Bates's fingers caress his bass, and Dodge's brushes circle the skin of his snare drum. As Brubeck solos, his hands and the piano keyboard are reflected inside his own spectacle lenses, as if the music were being looped back into his brain. Brubeck wears an enigmatic Mona Lisa smile, which deepens ever so slightly as Desmond slides the harmony from the major into the minor.

The next piece picks up directly on the tail of "Audrey." The tempo is brighter, the lighting correspondingly so, and Brubeck shouts "Hey!" as his left foot launches the quartet into a number they would later call "Stompin' for Mili," from which the film would borrow its name. We view the quartet from a new angle. Dodge's busy checked shirt, its patchwork of squares, jars incongruously against the expanses of space placed around each musician. To accentuate the heartbeat of the music, Mili captures the drummer's foot kicking rhythm into his bass drum as the up-down up-down of his sticks is reflected against the floor—you see the pulse, you hear the pulse. As Dodge suddenly swaps from a conventional ride cymbal to his Chinese cymbal, an electrifying jolt intensifies the groove: "The rhythm seems to take hold of everybody in the room," Harman tells his readers. "Drummer Dodge feels it and starts to bang on his Chinese cymbal (an instrument studded with loose rivets that buzz like a dozen sizzling steaks)."

His sizzling Chinese cymbal would become Dodge's signature sound,[2] and his igniting of the groove coincides with the start of Brubeck's solo. Mili rotates the camera speedily between Bates's fingers and Desmond's approving nods and captures Brubeck's right leg gyrating in time with the music: the quartet moving as one as the rhythm takes hold. Brubeck's fingers are scampering and marching across the keyboard. Unlike Thelonious Monk, whose fingers tended toward ramrod straightness, notes like nails he was knocking in with ten hammers, Brubeck curves his fingers as classical technique decrees. But he pushes the sustain pedal only sparingly, which keeps the surface of his playing dry and bumpy. Smoothing over harmonic tensions, using the pedal to blend chords too obsessively, would rob the playing of its urgency.

As Brubeck ratchets up the block chords that will eventually end his solo, Mili films under the piano stool, and we see Brubeck's feet rocking in rhythm as they send waves of energy coursing through his ecstatically gyrating body. No classical teacher, Fred Saatman or otherwise, would have approved. The emotional peak of Brubeck's solo is answered by a sequence of shapely drum fills. In the last, Dodge winds the tension down by transferring all the rhythmic momentum into his sticks, which he moves away from his kit and gently clicks together, and Mili follows his every move in detail. As the music enters what Harman calls a stretch of "polyphonic banter," Brubeck and Desmond alight, for whatever reason, on allusions to the

2. Whether a conscious nod to Dodge or not, Randy Jones brought the sound of the Chinese cymbal back to the Brubeck Quartet when he joined in 1978.

"Song of the Volga Boatmen." Mili lunges the camera toward Brubeck, meeting his hands on exactly the first beat of the bar as, their polyphonic fugue over, the quartet bring the piece to a close. When it's over, Brubeck stands up from the piano stool and strolls into the middle distance, and the camera floats up toward a ceiling light and fades. The end.

Two weeks after the session, Avakian told Brubeck, "The film is going to take time to edit, of course, but Al[3] and Mili think that in about 3 weeks they will have a fairly smooth job. Let's hope it has the impact we all think it will. It's a wonderful film artistically, anyway."[4] Nobody involved, including Brubeck himself, could have foreseen the eventual significance and wider connotation of that word *time*. *Brubeck Time* was a title that implied, "Time now to take notice." The more directly musical meaning of *time* in *Time Out* and *Time Further Out*, to do with uncommon time signatures, was for the future. But the synchronicity of events—*Time* magazine sensing that the time was right to make a splash about Brubeck as an album called *Brubeck Time* was being readied for release—feels like he was destined all along to be associated with concepts of time. Columbia fixed it so that everything linked together. Boris Artzybasheff's memorable illustration from *Time* magazine was incorporated into the montage-like cover for *Brubeck Time*, juxtaposed against stills of Desmond, Bates, and Dodge taken from Mili's film. And lest people had forgotten, Avakian also included small thumbnail reproductions of the covers of *Jazz Goes to College* and *Dave Brubeck at Storyville: 1954*, the latter labeled "Best Seller No. 2." Impact was everything.

On the album, "Audrey" and "Stompin' for Mili" appeared note for note from the soundtrack of Mili's film. Only Bates's

---

3. Aram Avakian (1926–1997) was familiarly known as "Al." He worked with director Bert Stern on the film *Jazz on a Summer's Day* and became known as a film editor.

4. George Avakian to Dave Brubeck, October 19, 1954, Business Correspondence.

bass preamble to "Audrey" was cut, and the first thing listeners to *Brubeck Time* heard, therefore, was the group already in motion, the sonorous touch of Brubeck's chords balanced to giddy perfection against a swaddling of translucently recorded bass and drums. Compared to the hard-driven, acicular hit of other classic jazz albums recorded during 1954—Art Blakey's *A Night at Birdland* on Blue Note, *Thelonious Monk and Sonny Rollins* on Prestige, or *The Max Roach Quartet featuring Hank Mobley* on Debut—the sound world of *Brubeck Time* established a tranquility that set the tone for later quartet albums like *Dave Digs Disney* and *Time Out*. Mili's empathy with Brubeck's music managed to illuminate its hazy pastoral colors, even though he was using black-and-white film—tricks of the light that would not have served the bare-knuckle smack of Art Blakey or Sonny Rollins as faithfully.

All of which opens a Pandora's box. The fine-grain pastel coloring of "Audrey" displayed a harmonic sensibility untypical within modern jazz, and represented the sound those who claimed that Brubeck played diluted modern jazz with the harder edges smoothed down, for pure commercial expediency, had in mind. But the argument can't go both ways, and Ira Gitler's barbed comment about Brubeck's "substituting bombast for swing" or Billy Root's complaints about his "jumping up and down on the piano with his feet" could not be applied to the warm, misty timbres of "Audrey," and therefore suggested a degree of selective listening.

Truth was, the unusual range of Brubeck's playing resisted easy categorization. For every melting moment like "Audrey" (or "Someday My Prince Will Come," from *Dave Digs Disney*, or *Time Out*'s "Strange Meadow Lark") there was the sharp-angled polytonal dissonance, raucous stride piano, and jabbing notes of "Keepin' Out of Mischief Now," or the prickly coating Brubeck placed around his solo on *Time Out*'s "Pick Up Sticks." The quartet's next studio album, recorded in November 1956, *Jazz Impressions of the USA*, was more obviously extroverted, hot even, due in part to Joe Morello's arrival. But with the increased visibility that accompanied his Columbia contract, questions about the apparent mismatch between Brubeck's pianistic instincts and commercial success rained down relentlessly around him. Desmond's cultivation of an authentically beautiful sound—so exquisite it moved far beyond being decorative or generically pretty—slotted with ease into this ideal of warm, misty timbres, but his leader's piano far less obviously so. How could someone who played piano like *that* reach so effortlessly into the mainstream?

One person who needed convincing was Gjon Mili, and the picture-perfect glow of his film belied the nerve-jangling tensions that brewed during those two days in the studio. To prepare himself for the filming, Mili had spent an evening listening to the quartet perform at Basin Street, but he came away unimpressed, confirmed in the opinion gained from their records that whatever the Brubeck Quartet played, it wasn't jazz. And Mili felt unable to keep that opinion to himself in the studio. In a sleeve note written as a faux letter of reminiscence to Avakian, Brubeck recalled how, as they started to play, Mili's blatant hostility left the group feeling "shaky" and "nervous"—and the more shakily the quartet played, the more angry Mili's demeanor became, which stoked the group's nervous state of mind.

This downward spiral was only heading one way—until Brubeck's patience finally snapped. The opening bars of "Stompin' for Mili" were played, he wrote, as an entirely spontaneous "musical expression of rage and frustration" after Mili snarled, "My first impression was right. You're no good." By the end of this piece, which would eventually bear his name, the story goes that Mili had been completely won over. Brubeck's sleeve note tells us that he jumped from his chair shouting, "You're hot! By God you're hot! Don't stop now!" And now apparently smitten, and responding to Avakian's suggestion that the quartet ought to play something as a counterbalance to the wrath of

"Stompin' for Mili"—a minor blues, perhaps—Mili set the mood by invoking Audrey Hepburn, whom he said he would like to see "walking through the woods." Registering the glazed look in Desmond's eyes, who had a serious crush on Hepburn, Brubeck counted the quartet in: "And we played it. Hence, the title. Its significance, I trust, will not be lost to the male population."

Mili's road-to-Damascus conversion has become part of the quartet mythology, although events cannot have played out entirely as Brubeck outlined. The dates don't fit. "Audrey" was recorded on the quartet's first day in the studio, bookended by "Jeepers Creepers" and "A Fine Romance," but "Stompin' for Mili" wasn't recorded until the next day, directly before "Brother, Can You Spare a Dime?" Nor can the impression left by Brubeck's notes that "Audrey" was plucked out of the air be quite the whole story. Bates's bass introduction suggested a certain degree of preplanning, and while the temperament and ambience of "Audrey" were unique, the piece was a variation on "Balcony Rock" and "Back Bay Blues." "Stompin' for Mili" and "Audrey" showed two sides of the Dave Brubeck Quartet, playing music that was both red hot and cool. "Audrey" was a refashioning of their freely evolving ideas about the blues. But "Stompin' for Mili" was a spontaneous finding of form.[5]

Nowhere else on record is there another example of a Brubeck "contrafact." Many bebop pieces—like Monk's "52nd Street Theme," Charlie Parker's "Koko," and Tadd Dameron's "Hot House"—were contrafacts: fresh melodies constructed above the chord sequence of an already-existing song, tunes that evolved on the bandstand as the original melodic shapes of "I Got Rhythm," "Cherokee," and "What Is This Thing Called Love?," worked over during long after-hours jazz sessions, became melodic putty in the bopper's hands and imaginations.

---

5. The quartet performed another version of "Stompin' for Mili" at Basin Street in February 1956, but it never became a regular part of their set list.

Contrafacting was an instrumentalist's shortcut for generating new material suited instantly to the purposes of improvisation, edging out of the equation compositional ideals that were dear to Brubeck. But with the pressure on and tempers fraying, Brubeck dug into his jazzman's instincts, and "Stompin' for Mili" sparked into life over the chord changes of "Lady Be Good"—complete with that self-borrowed introduction from "Give a Little Whistle" and a ride-out figure that inconspicuously blended a riff from the Benny Goodman Sextet's 1940 record "Wholly Cats" into the flow.

The joins were seamless—you'd expect nothing less from such a well-oiled unit as the quartet—but behind the public smiles of satisfaction were creative strains. At some point during Bob Bates's yearlong stay in the quartet, Brubeck wrote a document that he labeled "The DB Quartet—Principals [*sic*] and Aims," which, judging from its tone, had been prompted by frustration, either generally or by what Brubeck considered a particularly ineffective or lazy performance. Part mission statement, part reaffirmation of some basic musical principles, Brubeck's words give the clearest insight yet on the inner workings of his quartet—how he expected, and needed to hear, polytonality and polyrhythms nurturing his music, and his irritation when musicians fell short. His salvo of instructions was written over five sheets of paper. Some thoughts disappeared into a thicket of cross-out while one sentence, added as an afterthought, curls around the rest of the text. With topics ranging from the emotional content of an improvisation to appropriate deportment while on stage, the document makes clear that, musically, Brubeck felt the weak link in his quartet's expressive chain was the bass.

"This summary is written to help clarify to the members of this group the purpose and individual responsibilities of each man," he began. "Group feeling must be the basis without destroying the individuality of each contributor to the whole.

The soloist must predominate. If it is a drum solo the drummer should dictate if the bass is playing or piano."[6]

Brubeck's comments about Bob Bates could be misinterpreted as an attempt to rein in his bass player's creativity, but the point is made soon enough that a bassist in a group working so intently on polytonality carries very particular individual responsibilities.

> The bass must be basic and simple playing on the changes that
> are agreed on and written and established as the right ones. All
> bass note mistakes on records so far have been when the bass
> man deviates from the agreed on change. This practice makes
> you neither a hero or a fool whereas if you play the change you
> can only be one thing—right. You must understand the basis
> of polytonality which gives the soloist the right to superimpose
> on the original change and tonality any other change or tonal-
> ity. Polytonality is weakened if the bass man modulates or goes
> with the soloist. Bob should play the most simple changes until
> I feel he is ready to expand from a well grounded understand-
> ing of how we move harmonically in each tune.

The pressing need for a bass player who could reliably hold the harmonic fort *and* be superlatively creative would not be fully resolved until the arrival of Eugene Wright in 1958.

Next, Brubeck discussed how the boundaries imposed on the bassist were aimed toward the greater good of freeing up the front line. "The emotional content of the group can come from rage or pleading which is primarily the reason for success of the last 4 years," Brubeck continued. "The true music we wish to create must come from freedom of the soloist to express his emotion of the moment within the reason of musical intelligence and understanding with complete utmost cooperation

---

6. Dave Brubeck, "The DB Quartet—Principals and Aims," n.d., Biographical Writings, 1940–1969, Brubeck Collection.

of the group." (Brubeck added later, "Simplicity of background gives complexity of solo. . . . Feel when [the] group is in a groove and can allow you freedom.")

Brubeck offered an aide-mémoire of the ground rules when the group was improvising counterpoint, indulging in what Harman called "polyphonic banter." "Never forget your importance in improvised counterpoint[,] the basis of which is Bach," he wrote. "I suggest that the group become familiar with the [Bach] Inventions and a review of the Bach chorales should give a ground work in bass lines (one rule being that the fifth should never be played where the root belongs)."[7] Important as all these rules were, Brubeck also appealed to their sense of adventure—looking beyond what they already knew how to play was essential to the true spirit of jazz: "Each tune every night should be approached as a new musical experience and any emotion of soloist should be felt by the group and the group should reach and adjust intelligently."

Other directives included the minor minutiae of stagecraft. Desmond should leave the stand during trio numbers, and Brubeck served Bates with a written warning about his maddening habit of audibly beating his foot in a steady 4 when the music was speeding ahead in 2. He also offered some listening recommendations, including "folk material of all countries" and the percussion music of the Far East. But whatever crimes and misdemeanors his quartet had committed on the bandstand that persuaded Brubeck he needed to prepare a pep talk, ever the diplomat, he concluded on an upbeat note: "I am in the process of setting up a group in which it will be easier for me to improvise and have no mental strain on the job. I am not happy with this group [but] nor have I ever been happy with any group I've had so far. [But] this group has more potential because there are more individual [voices]."

---

7. Brubeck is referring to a basic rule of Bachian harmony: the fifth of a chord is weaker than the root, and therefore should not be used as the bass note.

Brubeck then signed off with the hope that he hadn't created any bad feeling.

♫

Brubeck's decency and his moderate habits were sometimes used as a stick with which to beat him by those who felt the life force of jazz was synonymous with the macho, gladiatorial atmosphere of New York jazz clubs—those moderate in their personal habits, some thought, were unlikely to thrive in an arena where musicians expressed extremes of joy, sorrow, or anger.

In 1993, when Brubeck recorded in a jazz club for the first time in three decades, he spoke of how "it was like a return to my beginnings, back to that wonderful atmosphere that you find only in a well-run jazz club." But playing for six nights, two sets each evening, at the Blue Note in Greenwich Village in 1993 was a very different proposition than playing Birdland or Basin Street in the early 1950s. By 1993, Brubeck had serious status. A whole decade before the city introduced its smoking ban, Brubeck initiated one of his own: performing at the Blue Note was conditional upon a blanket ban on cigarette smoke. But forty years earlier, like every other musician with a club date, Brubeck had had to tolerate the unsocial hours, the smoke, the clinking of glasses, people who considered music as mere background to their own conversations—and also the uneasy reality that even if a club wasn't under the thumb of the mob directly, jazz clubs tended to attract the darkest elements of the crime underworld. Musicians controlled by their own drug addictions, and the impressionable hangers-on who aspired to their lifestyle, were willing cash cows, there to be milked for years.

The implication that Carter Harman implanted inside his readers' minds as he enticed them inside his *Time* profile was this: anyone who wanted to know how Brubeck stood apart from the jazz community need look no further than his attitude toward jazz clubs. Brubeck was "a wigging cat with a far-out wail," Harman began, a rather lame attempt at hipster talk that switched gear midsentence into a line guaranteed to please the Columbia PR department: "Conventional critics [view Brubeck] as probably the most exciting new jazz artist at work today."[8] But whatever the pros and cons of that claim, Brubeck had "strong ideas about how his audiences should behave while he plays. There should be no loud joking or talking; no table-hopping; no eating. Drinking, if absolutely necessary, should be done in moderation. 'Some people,' [Brubeck] says with horror, 'plunk a full bottle of Bourbon down on a table right in front of the bandstand—you know the sort that will order a whole bottle.' Brubeck does not feel that way because he is egotistical but because he takes his work with a deep, almost mystical seriousness." Disrupt his concentration, Harman continued, and you'd better watch out: "Normally as peaceable as a lullaby, Brubeck has been known to come off the bandstand in the middle of a number and threaten to silence a noisy customer with his muscular hands, which, until a few years ago, were expert at roping cattle.[9] But it has been quite a while since he has been forced to such extremes with audiences. Nowadays, people listen." And they listen, Harman emphasized, "in garish cellars and august concert halls." Over the last year, he reported, the quartet had played clubs in Los Angeles (Zardi's), Boston (Storyville), and Manhattan (Basin Street)—and "a fortnight ago they listened and cheered him in Carnegie Hall." The Brubeck Quartet was riding a wave of popular adulation, and the small West Coast clique that once appreciated his music was now a "coast-to-coast crowd." But Harman felt it his journalistic duty to place on the record that Brubeck's vision of jazz would not appeal to all comers. "Not everybody likes Brubeck's intense, quiet music; a lot of

8. Carter Harman, "The Man on Cloud No. 7," *Time*, November 8, 1954.
9. An apocryphal story—no evidence exists to support this.

Bourbon drinkers still prefer the wilder, louder jazz that thrives on full bottles." Which was a coded way of saying that Brubeck's music was more temperate and diagnostic than anything else, from the swing-band swagger of Benny Goodman and Count Basie to the bright bounce of bop likely to be experienced in a jazz club.

The correspondence between Brubeck and Associated Booking Corporation makes clear that club dates were central to Glaser's strategy for pushing his new client: one of his jazz groups playing a residency in a jazz club, in New York especially, was a group that was turning over regular income. But the Brubeck Quartet's first New York club appearance had nothing to do with Glaser. In December 1951, the group played the Hickory House, on Fifty-Second Street, under the recommendation of Duke Ellington.

Ellington had taken a shine to the Brubeck Quartet that summer when he visited the Black Hawk in San Francisco, which had become the go-to after-show hang for visiting musicians. Brubeck's first encounter with Ellington had been as a tongue-tied twentysomething at a concert in Stockton, California, ten years earlier. From his seat in the auditorium, he noticed that his friend Junior Raglin[10] was playing bass—but Brubeck froze when Raglin took him backstage to meet Ellington. There was so much to say that there was nothing he could say. Now, though, Ellington was offering his advice—"Come to New York." And when news reached Glaser of Brubeck's impending visit, he fixed it for the quartet to play Birdland after their Hickory House engagement.

Birdland was named after Charlie Parker, the Hickory House after the specialty of the kitchen—lavish steaks, which, plated up, would be brought to patrons' tables as they listened to the

10. Alvin "Junior" Raglin (1917–1955) replaced Jimmy Blanton in Ellington's orchestra, worked with the band from 1941 to 1945, and returned for short periods later.

music. The Hickory House, which opened in 1933, sat on the same block, between Sixth and Seventh Avenues, as Kelly's Stables, where William O. Smith had played in Vicki Zimmer's band six years earlier. Clubs like the 3 Deuces, the Onyx, the Famous Door, and the Hickory House were the beating heart of what had become known as Swing Street, or simply "the Street"—where, on any given night, jazz fans might hear Billie Holiday, Art Tatum, Coleman Hawkins, Charlie Parker, or Thelonious Monk. Birdland had opened its doors in 1949 and was situated a block away, just north of Fifty-Second on Broadway. Having never strayed much further than the San Francisco Bay Area and Los Angeles as a professional musician, Brubeck was about to receive the toughest initiation possible into the ways of New York jazz clubs.

The classic brownstone buildings that once housed those Fifty-Second Street jazz clubs have long since been razed to the ground in favor of a more anonymous corporate architecture, but bassist Bill Crow's 1992 memoir *From Birdland to Broadway: Scenes from a Jazz Life* effervesces with period atmosphere, the atmospheric sounds, sights, and smells that Brubeck would have encountered brought back to life. Although Crow and Brubeck never played together, their working lives had numerous points of connection. Crow played bass in the J. J. Johnson and Kai Winding Quintet, which shared the split LP *Dave Brubeck and Jay & Kai at Newport*; he had played at the Hickory House with pianist Marian McPartland[11] and drummer Joe Morello, soon to join the Brubeck Quartet; and he was Gerry Mulligan's bassist of choice for much of the 1960s, until a few years before Mulligan began working regularly with Brubeck. And he considered Birdland his alma mater.

---

11. British-born pianist Marian McPartland (1918–2013) arrived in the US shortly after the war. She was married to cornetist Jimmy McPartland and played in his Dixieland band, but she soon became fascinated by bebop and led a trio at the Hickory House. She later embarked on an affair with Joe Morello and developed a close friendship with Dave and Iola Brubeck.

Crow's arrival in New York was timely. Three weeks later, on December 15, 1949, Birdland opened its doors for the first time, and Crow recalled waiting eagerly all day until the anointed hour—8 p.m.—when he sprinted inside the club and descended into its innards via a long carpeted staircase, which became his nightly ritual. Once inside, Crow might have been greeted, as Brubeck would have been two years later, by Pee Wee Marquette, Birdland's master of ceremonies, a three-and-a-half-foot-tall dwarf, rumored to be a woman. His notoriously waspish tongue and extreme rudeness felt out of all proportion to his diminutive stature, an anomaly that led Lester Young to dismiss him as "half a motherfucker."

Finches, suspended in cages behind the bar, met the saddest of ends in the early days of the club, when the unfortunate creatures started choking on the stale air and smoke and the birds that survived were removed. The preeminent jazz photographer Herman Leonard, whose photographs of jazz musicians in action—including Charlie Parker and Lennie Tristano—were proudly displayed as a backdrop, reinforced Birdland's core identity more reliably. The club itself was divided into three sections. Customers who sat at the bar or the tables were required to pay a cover charge for food and drink, while those on a budget were herded toward a cordoned-off section, variously nicknamed "the bleachers" or "the bullpen," where seventy cents bought you the right to sit tight until four in the morning, soaking in the music, undisturbed. And all sight lines coalesced around a bandstand draped in plush red curtains, under which the Dave Brubeck Quartet played its first Birdland residency.

Crow preferred not to ponder the darker side of clubland in his memoir, but from menacing men in dark suits pedaling drugs in the bathrooms to institutionalized criminality, it loomed inescapably. The premises that Birdland occupied—1678 Broadway—had once been the Clique Club, whose proprietor, Joseph "Joe the Wop" Catalano, would later be described in FBI papers as "a top New York hoodlum"[12]: a loan shark and drug dealer, with grand larceny and receiving stolen goods also chalked up on his rap sheet. At the start of 1949, Catalano sold the basement of 1678 Broadway to a group of eight young men, including brothers Morris and Irving Levy, who intended to transform the site into a jazz club—a purchase that was funded, at least in part, with Mafia cash.

Morris Levy quickly realized that one certain way to control musicians, and extract the maximum amount of cash from their talents, was to own a stake in every part of the music business: clubs, recording, publishing, and record retail. Because his tentacles spread everywhere, Morris became known as "the Octopus," and when his brother Irving was stabbed behind the bar of Birdland in January 1959, as the Urbie Green Big Band performed onstage, rumors spread that a rival mob gang had assassinated the wrong man. Morris rapidly expanded his portfolio of clubs, and then he "helped" cash-strapped musicians by paying a token amount for the rights to their songs, which he demanded they play on his premises, which allowed him to pocket their royalties—a strategy that paid even greater dividends once he began the invidious practice of adding his own name to the composer credits.

In 1957, Levy founded Roulette Records and, in 1976, the Strawberries chain of record stores, and he sat behind the scenes, shunning the limelight, as he pulled strings and made musicians jump. Count Basie foolishly borrowed money from Levy and found himself working extra weeks at Birdland until the debt was paid off. Another Levy line of attack was to persuade, usually through strong-arm threats, a more reputable record company to renege on a deal with a promising

12. A. J. Weberman, "Ruby Telephones Joe 'the Wop' Cataldo, Colombo Family Mafia Underboss" http://www.academia.edu/28822628/RUBY_TELE PHONES_JOE_THE_WOP_CATALDO_COLOMBO_FAMILY_MAFIA_UNDER BOSS_JOE_COLOMBO_WOUNDED_IN_COLUMBUS_CIRCLE_ON_COL UMBUS_DAY, accessed February 2018.

musician, at which point he would "rescue" their career—with a virtually worthless contract that condemned them to a life of producing one generic record after another. Evil genius that he was, Levy used Roulette to wrap himself in a cloak of respectability: because any label that released music by Basie, Sarah Vaughan, Billy Eckstine, and the only recorded collaboration between Duke Ellington and Louis Armstrong *must* be legitimate.[13]

It took time, but the law eventually caught up with him. In September 1986, Levy was arrested at a hotel in Boston in connection with an unpleasant incident that involved financial extortion and assault. The day after his arrest he appeared on the local television news, looking every bit like a hoodlum sent from central casting, but he kept a lid on his temper under questioning. "Federal authorities yesterday described you as godfather of the American music business," the interviewer probed, "the connection between the mob and the music business."[14] Levy denied there was any link, but the FBI—which had been tapping his phone conversations—begged to differ, and in December 1988 they secured his conviction. Also convicted was Dominick Canterino, a member of the Genovese crime family, one of the so-called Five Families of mobsters that controlled organized crime in New York City—the same family that had financed Levy's share of the Clique Club purchase in 1949. Life had come full circle, and then it ended. Levy died from cancer on May 20, 1990, aged sixty-two, two months before he was due to begin serving his ten-year jail sentence.

On the evening of Saturday, December 15, 1951, as the quartet skipped gracefully into "At a Perfume Counter" at Birdland,

---

13. Roulette also released two albums (*England's Ambassador to Jazz* and *Jazz from Abroad*) by the British saxophonist Johnny Dankworth, whose son Alec would join the Brubeck Quartet as bassist in 1999.

14. CambridgeOneStop, "Morris Levy Interview 1986—Strawberries Records / Roulette Records," YouTube video, 6:40, December 28, 2011, www.youtube .com/watch?v=DCdMCWzmMXQ.

they betrayed nothing of their reaction to their unfamiliar surroundings. They had driven coast to coast to reach New York, a
journey fueled as much by nerves as by gas, but once his group
took to the bandstand, Brubeck's confidence in the validity of
his music overrode any jitters. The Hickory House had helped
the quartet acclimatize, and the music that has survived from
Birdland is pure Brubeck: no tailoring of the music for East
Coast tastes, no chance of playing it safe as standards wrapped
in polytonal harmony were relentlessly interrogated through
improvisation.

Twelve precious pieces, recorded during live broadcasts at
Birdland over two nights in December and during the quartet's
return visit at the end of January 1952, have survived.[15] The
pieces were recorded by a Bronx-based jazz obsessive named
Boris Rose, who devoted much of his adult life to recording jazz
in clubs and from the radio. Rose engaged his tape recorder
only when the music started. The ambience and atmospheric
buzz of New York jazz clubs, part of his everyday experience,
were, he thought, not worth documenting. So we don't get
to hear Pee Wee Marquette introduce Paul Desmond as "Bud
Esmond," not because he tripped over the name but because
Desmond—unlike Brubeck, Wyatt Ruther, and Herb Barman—had refused to tip Marquette the requisite fifty cents he
demanded to pronounce any musician's name correctly.

By the time of *Jazz at Oberlin* and *Jazz at the College of the
Pacific* a year later, the concerns of the old Brubeck Trio had
been fully integrated inside the quartet, but at Birdland, a
replay of the trio was featured as a band within a band. Com-
plying with the "DB Quartet—Principals and Aims" rulebook,
Desmond would have presumably left the bandstand as Brubeck, Ruther, and Barman played "That Old Black Magic"
and "Spring Is Here" in arrangements lifted straight from the

---

15. The tracks are usefully compiled on Dave Brubeck Quartet with Paul Desmond, *Birdland 1951–52/Newport 1955* (Solar Records, 4569967).

trio's book. Barman's command of Cal Tjader's drum parts was absolute. His barreling rhythmic impetus, with Ruther holding the harmony secure—while resisting the urge to modulate or otherwise "go with" the whim of the improvising soloist—gave Brubeck total support as his pinprick dissonances oozed like ink seeping through paper into the mainframe of "That Old Black Magic." In 1951, the audience would have likely associated the song with Glenn Miller and the Modernaires or with Judy Garland,[16] but Brubeck's polytonal chords, superimposed over the original changes, wove another spell altogether.

With Desmond back on the bandstand, the quartet offered up a cross section of their in-progress repertoire, including "How High the Moon," "Jeepers Creepers," "Crazy Chris," "Line for Lyons," and "Tea for Two." The starting point of "I'll Remember April" turned out to be the trio's 1950 record, with Tjader's vibraphone lines transferring comfortably to Desmond's alto saxophone. Brubeck's solo blew a through-draft of sustained melodic lines around references to "Gone with the Wind" (which feels like it wants to morph into "April in Paris") and, later, to the zesty chromaticism of "Undecided," his soft touch skimming across the meniscus of the harmony. Karate-chopped block chords deliberately dragging *against* the steady pulse of bass and drums, which Brubeck deployed as he soloed on "Crazy Chris," delivered more of what customers who had read about Brubeck in the jazz press might have expected to hear. But "I'll Remember April" demonstrated the futility of generalizing about Brubeck. Whatever anyone said, his music seemed not to care, and it did as it pleased.

By the time of the quartet's next documented appearance at a New York jazz club, Bob Bates and Joe Dodge had replaced Ruther and Barman, and the interior world of the group, and their litheness of harmonic and rhythmic interplay, had

16. Glenn Miller's version appeared in 1942, Judy Garland's in 1943. The classic Frank Sinatra version appeared in 1961 on his album *Come Swing with Me!*.

matured perceptibly. Although George Avakian likely edited studio material into the final mix,[17] the material released on *Jazz: Red Hot and Cool* was otherwise recorded between fall 1954 and summer 1955 at Basin Street, a club hosted inside the swank ballroom of the Shelton Towers Hotel on Lexington Avenue—a world away from the grime and crime of Birdland. Basin Street would become Brubeck's favored New York jazz club and was where, in 1962, he recorded with Carmen McRae.

*Jazz: Red Hot and Cool* introduced the world to "The Duke" but pointed toward the future in many other ways too. The sprightly (and fiendishly difficult to execute) canonic introduction to "Fare Thee Well, Annabelle" harked back to the language of the octet, but Brubeck's solo was restless in its determination to look beyond what he already knew could be achieved through improvisation. This solo, and his epic outing on a ten-minute reading of "Little Girl Blue," emphasized his delight in free-associative chains of thought. With polytonality moving Brubeck outside the changes, a sudden harmonic declutter was enough to bring him back inside.

In the midst of "Little Girl Blue," Brubeck drove his solo into a tangle of compressed Jackson Pollock–like zigzags that defied harmonic analysis. This was precisely the sort of gesture that so pained his detractors; just why would a pianist work hard to establish a head-bopping improvisational flow only to decisively trash the momentum by throwing his solo into a self-induced crisis of confidence? Even when Joe Dodge doubled down on his Chinese cymbal, Brubeck took that as license to fragment and warp the harmonic logic further, moving outlier chords against patterns related to the harmony and leaving the rhythm section behind as he plundered the chordal depths. Not worrying too much about the overarching architecture, Brubeck kept his solo in a state of continuous exposition by

---

17. A producer's note on the 2001 CD reissue of *Jazz: Red Hot and Cool* tells us that "the original master tapes were destroyed."

molding the chords of "Little Girl Blue" around the emerging direction of his solo—the tail gleefully wagging the dog.

Mess with harmony and the dominos fall around your fingers, waiting to be scooped up again; but that moment of harmonic crisis wasn't, in fact, any crisis at all. It was Brubeck interjecting the thrust of an argument into his improvisation. As a composer he knew all about advancing and broadening a musical argument by challenging an existing statement with contrasting material, ripples of structural disruption waiting to be pursued. The next chorus was fueled by cross-rhythms that ricocheted between his hands with the trembling force of a pinball machine. Cross-rhythms colliding against unexpected beats had the effect that the expected correlation between melody note and supporting bass note below was wrenched out of place—which gave Brubeck leverage to push further into the harmonic unknown. Brubeck being Brubeck, though, his experiments with unpicking rhythm and harmony were charming rather than confrontational.

"Lover," the opening track of *Jazz: Red Hot and Cool*, delivered another innovation with far-reaching consequences for how the quartet felt and divided up time. Brubeck played his unaccompanied introduction in a lopsided 4/4, which Dodge eventually straightened out with a steady 4/4 pulse that motored relentlessly onward as it doubled up on Brubeck's tempo. There were two rhythmic sensations with which to contend—4/4 layered against double-time 4/4—and then, suddenly, there was a third. Phrasing around Dodge's insistent pulse, Brubeck, Desmond, and Bates played Richard Rogers's theme in 3/4 time. The mathematical permutations of 3/4 interlocking with 4/4—adding up to ever-changing patterns of strong and weak beats colliding and rebounding against each other—floated the piece free from any single anchoring beat. "Lover" would provide a point of departure for many further adventures in time.

"People forget that, during the 1950s, this was the way jazz clubs were run in America."[18] Nearly fifty years later, on the road to Manchester, Brubeck is as surprised as anybody to be opening a book on this part of his life. A look of utmost seriousness from Iola betrays that this is not especially comfortable terrain for Dave. But he goes there anyway, treading cautiously.

Nervous laughter surrounds his memory of the time a mafioso type approached him outside a jazz club—he can't remember which one—holding a large brown envelope stuffed with dollar bills. "Ten thousand dollars for you, Mr. Brubeck, a gift," the heavy mumbled as he compelled Brubeck to accept by thrusting the envelope into his hands. The inference was clear enough: take this gift, enjoy it, and we'll call when you can do us a favor in return. But Brubeck, horrified at the idea, moved his hands out of the way and narrowly avoided sending $10,000 spewing over the sidewalk. A Marlon Brando look-alike in a heavy coat giving the come-on to a jazz musician who he assumed would be drug-ravaged and desperate for cash could be from a Mel Brooks spoof. While he's able to laugh at the obvious absurdity, there is a part of Brubeck that still finds the incident disturbing: a troubling reflection on the world in which his working life once existed and a reminder of how different his life might have been had success not winched him out of harm's way.

In lowlier days, scavenging for gigs during the earlier octet period, Brubeck had discovered that "in certain clubs you could only play a few Stephen Foster songs, and boy would you get sick of 'Jeannie with the Light Brown Hair.' There was no time for art or original compositions, but if guys didn't work in clubs then they didn't work."

In later years, there was no escaping the smoke, noise, and bleary-eyed late nights, but the Burma Lounge, Black Hawk, and Storyville clubs were generally decently run establishments;

---

18. Interview with the author, May 1, 2003.

and the mosh-pit ethics at Birdland, the lawless bubble in which some New York clubs existed, caught Brubeck by surprise. "Birdland was controlled by the underworld, and there are events and guys I won't talk about even now," he says, shaking his head regretfully. Brubeck doesn't mention Morris Levy by name, but the villain of the following situation is clear enough: "A small example of the way they tried to control musicians—when I worked there, I was told that I must play 'Lullaby of Birdland' at the beginning and end of every broadcast. It's a great tune and George Shearing and I were friends then, and still are. But I didn't like being told what to play and said I wasn't prepared to do that. It caused a great deal of trouble, but by then I'd got to a point where they couldn't get at me." And George Shearing's 2005 autobiography, titled after his most famous song, revealed one very good reason why Levy was keen to push "Lullaby of Birdland" at every opportunity: he owned the publishing rights, and, as Shearing put it, when the tune opened and closed every broadcast from the club, those royalties added up to "something worth having."[19]

"If guys had a contract on you, Joe Glaser was the only person who could negotiate on your behalf, and usually he'd solve the problem," Brubeck continues.

There were some very popular musicians who'd signed contracts that would only let them play in clubs run by a particular gang, and if the mob found a way to worm their way past your defenses, then you had big problems. I found out that if you were straight they'd normally leave you alone. But Charlie Parker's a sad example of what could happen. These guys exploited Charlie's addictions, and finally he wasn't even allowed to play at Birdland—the club named after him.

19. George Shearing with Alyn Shipton, *Lullaby of Birdland* (London: Continuum Press, 2005).

I used to tell people—never accept anything from these people to promote your career or else you'll pay for it dearly later on. On tour buses I'd see guys I admired so much as musicians reduced to such a pitiful state, running off the coach after a long journey to try to find an immediate fix of whatever it was they needed to get them through. When we toured with Charlie Parker, he'd pawn his horn for money to buy drugs, then run around trying to find Paul to borrow his—and Paul would worry about having nothing to play the concert on, because Charlie might sell his horn too.

There were two Charlies, I learned. On a good day he'd want to talk about Stravinsky, Debussy—and about what I'd learned from Milhaud. And he could recognize how drugs were making his life a mess, and he felt very guilty that other musicians were following his example, like he was responsible for their choices. One night, he got very emotional and told me all sorts of things about his life, about what had led him to drugs and how easy they had been to come by. On a bad day, though, you couldn't reach him. I used to think, boy, this guy, with whom I'd had the deepest conversations about music, he's a nervous wreck: shaking, sweating, eyes rolling in his head. Man, he used to suffer. One of the saddest things I ever saw in my life was Charlie losing control during a concert. He walked onstage and the crowd went wild. They couldn't believe that Charlie Parker was about to play. That audience was under his spell and he could have played wonderfully, like he had other nights. But instead, he started the band going and then decided to goof around, waggling his tongue at girls in the audience, then sticking his head out from the curtains at the side of the stage and making faces. He was like a child. And people started walking out. They weren't going to put up with that. His conduct worried them—and seeing people leave upset Charlie even more.

Brubeck mutters an afterthought about how behavior along similar lines had at times come uncomfortably close to home before realizing enough is enough. In 2003 Ron Crotty and Lloyd Davis were still alive, and their personal stories were not Brubeck's to share: their predicaments were on that list of things he wouldn't talk about "even now." But a letter lodged in the archives fills the gaps of an extraordinary saga.

In April 1977, Brubeck received a letter from municipal court judge John A. Marlo of Watsonville, California. Marlo had been presiding over a case in which Crotty was charged with drug possession and wrote to inform Brubeck of Crotty's desperate circumstances and to ask for his advice. (When Marlo died in 2015, aged eighty-one, many tributes were paid to his congenial and compassionate disposition.[20]) Brubeck began his reply with some background:

> Ron, of course, was always his own worst enemy in his young and adult life and all the lecturing I did about drugs and drinking was to no avail. He came from what I considered to be a loving home and had very attractive lady friends and what seemed to be a bright future. He was even a good athlete and was a pitcher on one of the Oakland teams when he was about 16. He went to work for me when he was 18 or 19, did his military service in Germany and on his discharge from the Army re-joined me in New York.[21]

Which was when his problems began:

> I thought his future as a musician looked extremely good, but then he was caught some way being involved with drugs. Some very understanding people from a narcotics division called me and informed me that two out of the four members of my

20. Obituary of Judge John Marlo, *Santa Cruz Sentinel*, May 27, 2015.
21. Dave Brubeck to John Marlo, April 25, 1977, Personal Correspondence, Brubeck Collection.

quartet were using drugs. They said they didn't want to make bad publicity for me in that they knew Paul Desmond and I were not involved. . . . They told me they would relocate these two men and try to organize their lives into a less stressful social environment, removed from night clubs and the temptations of the world they were living in . . . all this with the understanding they would not be charged if they would agree to reshape their lives.

In the strictest confidence I will tell you that one of the musicians, Lloyd Davis . . . was placed with the San Francisco Symphony where he functioned very well and I think is still with that organization in the percussion section.[22] Ron was told he should be a landscape architect and they found him a job on the Peninsula near Redwood City. I think Ron eventually drifted back to San Francisco and started playing bass again and this may have been the start of a decline, because when I would ask about him, people would shake their heads and say "Ronnie isn't doing too well."

Brubeck recalled Crotty phoning him out of the blue: "He seemed very down and confused and asked me what I thought he should do. I asked if he were still involved in landscaping and he said he was trying to make it in clubs and bars in the city. I advised him to get back to landscaping and take care of his health. This was the last I heard until your letter." Brubeck enclosed a check for $200 "for you to administer in such a way that it would be used to help him most, whether that be food, clothes, or to enroll him in some program such as TM [Transcendental Meditation] . . . whatever you feel could help him most to 'turn around.' Ron is intelligent and may respond to TM or some of the programs that reshape lives and attitudes. By nature he

---

22. Lloyd Davis joined as timpani for the San Francisco Symphony's 1955–1956 season and then continued as percussion from 1956 to his retirement in 1989. (Confirmed by Kate McKinney, the San Francisco Symphony Orchestra's public relations coordinator, in an email to the author, December 4, 2018.)

has a very loving attitude and in all the years I knew him, I never saw him knowingly harm anyone." Brubeck ends by asking the judge to "relocate [Crotty] where he can grow to the full goodness that I know is in him. He might even find this in jail, if he could work with a chaplain or someone trained to help." Partly through Brubeck's gentlemanly discretion, and partly because the well-mannered image projected by the classic Dave Brubeck Quartet would come to embody the group's entire history, personal foibles have been largely written out of the group's history. It has been assumed that decisions were taken for either directly musical or practical reasons—but, in truth, Brubeck's group was no more able to remove itself from the realities and temptations of the 1950s jazz scene than any other ensemble.

Until Joe Morello arrived in the latter half of 1956, then Eugene Wright in 1958, the quartet's rhythm section was a revolving door. Within the first year Fred Dutton, Wyatt Ruther, and Herb Barman all came and went. Lloyd Davis and Ron Crotty lasted a little longer, but Brubeck's niggling doubts about the Bob Bates/Joe Dodge lineup was a contributing factor to Bates's eventually being replaced by his more rhythmically and harmonically astute bass-playing brother Norman.

Ruther left the quartet officially on December 20, 1952, after a concert in Pittsburgh, although he agreed to "remain as an employee of David W. Brubeck until the arrival of my substitute, Ron Crotty, at a salary of $200 per working week." Crotty's and Davis's rapid departures—having been made an offer by the narcotics division that they were in no position to refuse—required swift action on Brubeck's part.

Norman and Bob, the two bass-playing Bates brothers,[23] originally from Idaho, had been a fixture on the Bay Area jazz

---

23. After the release of Hitchcock's *Psycho* in 1960, the name "Norman Bates" gained a certain notoriety. As Eugene Chadbourne has pointed out, the stuffed fish that Norman keeps in the Hitchcock film is a bass, and the film's titles were designed by Saul Bass (and in *Strangers on a Train* Hitchcock makes his cameo carrying a double bass onboard a train).

scene for many years. It was Norman who had stepped in to replace Don Ratto, the original bassist of the Three Ds, when Ratto fell afoul of the Musicians' Union; and he also served time as bassist and pianist in Jack Sheedy's Dixieland band. The close friendship that formed between Norman and Paul Desmond, based on their mutual appreciation of music and of spending their free time loafing around San Francisco cinemas, even weathered the storm of falling in love with the same woman. Peggy Nilsson, a chorus girl and would-be actress, appeared in their lives when they were in the pit band accompanying a review show at the Playland Ballroom at Playland-at-the-Beach in San Francisco. It was Norman's charm that in the end prevailed, and the Bateses' marriage would last for fifty-two years. In 1953, when Brubeck needed a new bass player, Norman was the obvious first choice, but he was two years into a four-year stint in the air force, and the job went to his brother Bob almost by default. (Another Bates bassist, Jim, enjoyed a varied career, playing with jazz, country, and dance bands and symphony orchestras—but he never worked with Brubeck.)

Naturally a reserved and cautious man, with a family to feed, Joe Dodge was initially reluctant to relinquish his steady job at a Los Angeles bank when the call came to replace Lloyd Davis at the end of 1953. Desmond considered Dodge his ideal drummer, prepared to accompany unobtrusively as Desmond floated his improvisations above timekeeping that was reliably tasteful and neat. David Van Kriedt had introduced the two men, and Desmond encountered Dodge again while he was working the San Francisco Bay Area big-band circuit after the war, and he had deputized for Cal Tjader when the octet opened for Woody Herman at the San Francisco Opera House in 1950. Dodge required assurances that the quartet had sufficient work to sustain it, and him, but soon realized there was nothing to worry about: at the start of 1954, a chain of one-night stands took the quartet all around America.

Bob Bates was dedicated to the cause but his musical vocabulary was limited, and he balked at the prospect of playing a solo. The increasing demands placed on his technique by Brubeck's polyrhythms and embedded nests of time signatures were stretching Dodge beyond his comfort zone, and he had never reconciled himself to spending long periods on the road, away from home. Losing one rhythm section might be unfortunate, but losing another, after only a year, starts to look careless; but the transition from Bob to Norman Bates—once Norman was released from the air force—was seamless and without rancor. And miserable as Brubeck found New York jazz clubs, Fifty-Second Street was about to deliver him a new drummer. Paul Desmond had heard a drummer working at the Hickory House in pianist Marian McPartland's trio and reckoned Brubeck ought to check him out. And they both really liked Joe Morello.

On April 21, 1954, Larry Bennett wrote to update Brubeck about forthcoming club dates and a possible package tour with Stan Kenton, but he began with an apology: "I had a specific reason for not taking your call at 5 o'clock [a few days earlier]. First of all, there were some people in my office at the time and I did not want them to overhear any conversation with you, secondly, Joe Glaser was out of the office and I expected him back within an hour and probably thought you had some questions in mind . . . and it would make more sense to talk to you when he was present."[24]

The suggestion that Brubeck might tour as a featured guest with his orchestra had come from Stan Kenton himself, but the proposed dates clashed with a return visit to Birdland and also a concert at Carnegie Hall. Glaser himself followed up on Bennett's letter and dropped the subtlest of hints that he was

---

24. Larry Bennett to Dave Brubeck, April 21, 1954, Business Correspondence, Brubeck Collection.

unhappy about Kenton approaching Brubeck directly instead of routing his request through ABC. He set Kenton's management a tight deadline to confirm the tour—or call the whole thing off—and then threw Brubeck what he considered a far juicier offer: "I personally have every intention of including you and your wonderful band in the first package show we expect to set up to book through our agency. In fact, I have already discussed in detail with DUKE ELLINGTON[25] personally the possibility and importance of including you in a package show with DUKE."[26] The next time Glaser wrote, on May 20, the prospect of a Kenton tour had been discarded and, instead, an Ellington tour had been scheduled to start in the middle of September or early October—a minimum of forty or sixty dates, in a package that now also included Gerry Mulligan and "one or two other attractions" to be confirmed.

In a letter written a month later, Glaser concluded that his package tour "should prove to be very lucrative," and for a tour lasting up to eight weeks, Brubeck would net $5,000 a week[27]—equivalent to $47,000 today—a sum that tells of how dramatically his fortunes had risen within such a short period. Glaser tells Brubeck what he can expect to earn for a "location engagement"—between $2,000 and $2,500 for a club, college, or concert date—but adds a gentle reminder that it is incumbent upon Dave to give ABC the "green light" as to his availability, which would have left Brubeck pondering how much free time he could allow himself. Further opportunities—like an appearance on *The Ed Sullivan Show*,[28] easily the most popular

25. It was a convention at ABC to capitalize the names of artists in correspondence.

26. Joe Glaser to Dave Brubeck, May 7, 1954, Business Correspondence, Brubeck Collection.

27. Joe Glaser to Dave Brubeck, June 16, 1954, Business Correspondence, Brubeck Collection.

28. Which was delayed for a year due to a clash of dates—the quartet eventually made their first appearance on *The Ed Sullivan Show* on October 16, 1955, playing "Smoke Gets in Your Eyes" and "Jeepers Creepers."

entertainment show in America at the time—were under discussion, and soon Glaser was in the enviable position of being
able to play Birdland off against Basin Street, a risky business
given Morris Levy's reputation as a bruiser, and in truth only
Glaser could have got away with it. He had negotiated a deal for
Brubeck to play Basin Street for two weeks at $2,250 per week
(during which some of *Jazz: Red Hot and Cool* was recorded)
against a week at the Blue Note for $2,000. Bert Block also
wrote to inform Brubeck "that Basin Street has turned into one
of the top rooms in the country. Benny Goodman just played
there and LOUIS ARMSTRONG is currently there."[29]

During Brubeck's initial contact with ABC, back in November 1950, he had expressed the concern that an agency repre-
senting stellar figures like Louis Armstrong, Lionel Hampton,
and George Shearing might not be fully committed to an
unknown pianist from California with little commercial pedigree and a taste for far-out harmonies; there was no money in
polytonality.[30] But Brubeck was now walking the same stages as
Benny Goodman and Louis Armstrong, and, as Larry Bennett
wrote in a letter dated December 10, 1954,

> It is a very pleasant feeling to see all the things materialize now
> that you and I have been planning these past few years, but as
> far as I am concerned this is only the beginning. I feel that it
> is possible now if we make the right moves as we have done
> these past few months, that you may firmly establish yourself as
> one of the very few music name personalities accepted whole-
> heartedly as part of Americana not just in the jazz field—but
> long hair, short hair, crew cut or no hair at all. In a similar way
> BENNY GOODMAN accomplished this feat in his numerous

29. Bert Block to Dave Brubeck, August 12, 1954, Business Correspondence,
Brubeck Collection.
30. Dave Brubeck to Cliff Aronson, November 15, 1950, Business Correspondence, Brubeck Collection.

appearances with top flight symphony orchestras throughout the country I think you can accomplish something much bigger than this and I know, Dave, that is what you really want.[31]

The first night of the package tour with Ellington—which now also included Stan Getz's quintet—was in the building where Civic Grand Opera performed in Philadelphia. The next day the tour reached New York, with an eight thirty concert at the Mosque Theatre in Newark, New Jersey, followed by a midnight show at Carnegie Hall, during which performances by Getz's and Brubeck's small groups were let down by the microphones, which had been placed in readiness for Ellington's larger group. Only ten years earlier Brubeck had been too shy to talk with Ellington in Stockton, but now he was sharing his dressing room and watching in awe as a dresser carefully unfolded Ellington's suit from a large carrying case and draped it around his large, elegant physique.

When the tour reached Denver a month later, there was a knock at seven o'clock in the morning on Brubeck's hotel room door. Ellington was standing in the corridor, waiting to hand him a copy of *Time* magazine. "You're on the cover. Congratulations, Dave," he said, and gave Brubeck his copy. Brubeck would often speak of his deep embarrassment. Carter Harman had also been working on a profile of Ellington, and Ellington's appearing on the cover before Brubeck would have represented the natural order of things—the greatest innovator first and then everybody else. But Brubeck's own hero had handed him the proof that yes, indeed, his time had come.

---

31. Larry Bennett to Dave Brubeck, December 10, 1954, Business Correspondence, Brubeck Collection.

*Chapter Six*

# ANOTHER COUNTRY

"I think you've got to be truthful about the life
you have. Otherwise, there's no possibility of
achieving the life you want."

JAMES BALDWIN, *Another Country*, 1962

On July 23, 1955, as the Dave Brubeck Quartet performed at
Basin Street, President Dwight Eisenhower was winding up
the last day of the Geneva Summit—five days of talks during
which the leaders of the so-called Big Four countries tried to
warm Cold War relations. In attendance were British Prime
Minister Anthony Eden, French Prime Minister Edgar Faure,
and two representatives from the Soviet Union: Premier
Nikolai Bulganin and First Secretary of the Communist Party
Nikita Khrushchev. Also present were the future British Prime
Minister Harold Macmillan, in his then capacity as foreign
secretary, and John Foster Dulles, Eisenhower's secretary of
state, whose scornful views on Communism led him to term

it "godless terrorism." Top of the agenda were trade and the disarmament of nuclear weapons and other weapons of mass destruction, while Eisenhower proposed his Open Skies policy—an independent international monitoring system designed to discourage countries with nuclear capability from stockpiling deadly weapons in secret.

Meanwhile, in Anaheim, California, Mickey Mouse, Minnie Mouse, Donald Duck, and Huey, Dewey, and Louie were the "big four" attractions at Disneyland, which had opened its doors to the public on July 18, the same day the Geneva Summit had kicked off. Disneyland was the American dream played out as real-time cartoon make-believe, a fantasy utopia of smiles, parades, and cotton candy, where nothing bad could ever happen—but then the brutal homicide of a teenage African American boy only four weeks later shook America to its core and became an enduring symbol of Deep South racism.

Emmett Till, a fourteen-year-old boy from Chicago, was on a family visit to Money, a rural community located deep in the Mississippi Delta. Although Emmett had attended a segregated elementary school in Chicago and knew all about strict codes of segregation, white supremacist prejudice was ingrained into the collective psyche in Mississippi beyond his everyday experience. Four days before his murder, Till had walked into the local candy store where he allegedly whistled suggestively at a white woman, Carolyn Bryant, who alleged that the boy had made lewd comments and touched her sexually. Forty-eight hours later he was kidnapped in the early hours of the morning by Bryant's husband, Roy, and his half brother John William Milam, known as "J. W." After terrorizing Till by driving him around in the dead of night, the two men, with their accomplices, savagely beat and tortured him, crushing his skull, gouging out his left eye, shattering his thigh bone, and ripping off a section of his ear before shooting a bullet directly into his brain. Then they stripped him and used barbed wire to tie a cotton-gin fan to his lifeless body, which they rolled into the Tallahatchie River.

Once his corpse was recovered, the Mississippi authorities were keen to bury his body as soon as possible to minimize the scandal, with no thought for due process. But Till's mother, Mamie Bradley, had other ideas. After viewing her son's disfigured body, she decided that he should be buried in an open casket: the world needed to bear witness to this unimaginably brutal act. *Jet*, an African American magazine based in Chicago, published a photograph of Emmett's mutilated corpse lying in his casket—an image that repulsed America. National shame was compounded when an all-white jury, which deliberated over the case for less than an hour, arrived at a verdict of "not guilty." Carolyn Bryant eventually withdrew her allegations against Emmett Till, and the case became a turning point in the struggle for civil rights. Nobody was ever brought to justice for the young boy's murder.[1]

As he moved toward the next phase of his career, Brubeck's work would be shaped by Cold War politics and the rise of civil rights consciousness. If the quartet's 1957 album *Dave Digs Disney* was viewed by some as capitulation to corporate America, a world outside America would exert direct influence on the material Brubeck recorded on *Jazz Impressions of Eurasia, Time Out, Countdown—Time in Outer Space*, and *Brandenburg Gate: Revisited*. Key compositions on *Jazz Impressions of Eurasia, Time Out*, and *Brandenburg Gate: Revisited* were conceived when the quartet was on a state-sponsored tour of Eastern Europe and the Middle East in 1958. *Countdown—Time in Outer Space*, recorded in 1962, was dedicated to the astronaut John Glenn, who, in February of that year, became the first American to orbit Earth on the *Friendship 7* mission—rivalry over space exploration was woven intimately into the narrative of Cold War posturing between the US and Soviet Russia.

1. Timothy B. Tyson, *The Blood of Emmett Till* (New York: Simon & Schuster, 2017).

*Southern Scene*, the album that followed *Time Out*, featured the quartet in a program of songs associated with the Deep South. If anyone had expected that Brubeck would use the opportunity to vent his explicit anger at events in Mississippi, they were disappointed. But *Southern Scene* did contain a subtle nod of solidarity: Brubeck's prayerful arrangement of the traditional African American spiritual "Nobody Knows the Trouble I've Seen" was followed by "Happy Times," an original by his African American bassist, Eugene Wright, which Brubeck's sleeve note described as an antidote to the history of trouble expressed in "Nobody Knows the Trouble I've Seen": "I think Gene's bass solo expresses the Wright attitude to life—amiable, relaxed and smiling," he concluded. Brubeck was saving up his thoughts about race for *The Real Ambassadors*, the opera he designed for Louis Armstrong, performed and recorded in 1962, which posed the following unsettling question: On what moral basis could the State Department parachute jazz musicians into Eastern Europe and the Middle East, with the intention of lecturing others about freedom, when racial inequality was enshrined in law back at home in a segregated America?

The instant Joe Morello joined the quartet in October 1956, Brubeck found himself brokering the peace in a cold war of his own. Desmond had brought Morello to Brubeck's attention, but his new drummer and his saxophonist eyed each other with disdain throughout the new quartet's first live performance, at the Blue Note in Chicago. The gig ended with a furious exchange of words backstage—if Desmond had his way, Chicago would have been Morello's first and last performance with the quartet.

With Marian McPartland's group at the Hickory House, Morello had used wire brushes (not sticks) almost exclusively, and Desmond had assumed that if ever he were to join the quartet, that would remain the case. As McPartland explained in her 2005 autobiography, her then bass player Bob Carter had a "soft but compelling sound" that obliged Morello to mute his dynamic levels—especially as Carter played acoustically into a microphone in the days before bass amplification became standard: "Everything [Bob Carter] did would be a stimulus to Joe to weave intricate figures, first with the brushes," she reflected.[2] Morello's interlocking rhythms with Carter suggested that he was conceiving of rhythm in a way that was guaranteed to find favor with Brubeck.

Joe Dodge had been loyal and inventive to the best of his abilities, but there was no going back now. Brubeck felt certain that the musical development of his group depended on reconciling the differences that had arisen unexpectedly between Morello and Desmond. When McPartland met Morello for the first time, she thought "he looked more like a young physicist than a drummer," she wrote, "but when he played everyone was astounded by his tremendous technique and sensitive touch." By general consent, Morello's rhythmic sensibility brought something new to jazz, and his technical skills were widely considered to match those of Buddy Rich, the benchmark drummer of the mid-1950s. "Once in a while," McPartland recalled, "on [four-bar breaks] he'd do something totally off the wall, which would make me lose my place in the tune. He really would work hard to accomplish this. Having made me miss a beat, he would then get a tantalizing little smile on his face."[3]

Like Brubeck's pianism, Morello's drumming pulled together multifarious musical interests. Describing himself as a "melodic drummer,"[4] Morello understood how the architecture of melody worked from the inside. Born in Springfield, Massachusetts, on July 17, 1928, he started taking violin lessons at the age of five

2. Marian McPartland, *All in Good Time* (Champaign, IL: University of Illinois Press, 2005), 26.

3. Ibid., 26–27.

4. Interview with the author, April 24, 2002. Published in "Sounds In and Out of the Loop," *Jazz Review*, June 2002.

and by age nine had become proficient enough at his instrument to give a complete performance of Mendelssohn's Violin Concerto in E minor, Op. 64, with the Boston Pops Orchestra. A few weeks later Morello met violin great Jascha Heifetz through his own violin teacher.

"Heifetz was a real gentleman and a true artist," Morello reminisced in 2002.[5]

> But hearing him play, hearing that great sound he had, was enough to convince me to put the violin aside: I could never have come anywhere near his genius. I'd already started percussion lessons, with a guy who played drums in vaudeville, and I assumed I'd have a career as a classical timpanist or percussionist, standing at the back of an orchestra. My first experience of jazz came through a local piano player in Springfield. I also grew up with Phil Woods,[6] and we played together a few nights a week with Sal Salvador.[7] I was continuing to have percussion lessons in Boston and eventually I had to make a decision whether to go to New York or not. It was frightening. People told me that drummers in the city would eat me alive. But I decided to try it for a year.

Jo Jones, Big Sid Catlett, J. C. Heard, and Gene Krupa were Morello's favorite drummers, but the affection he expressed for Dave Tough reflected the peculiar strengths of Morello's own playing. Tough was the man who'd had the unenviable task of replacing the charismatic Krupa in Benny Goodman's orchestra in 1938, which meant taking it on the chin whenever the Goodman band showed up without its superstar drummer and people were unable to hide their disappointment. Tough's

5. Ibid.

6. Alto saxophonist (1931–2015) most closely associated with Charlie Parker, whose widow, Chan, he married in 1957.

7. Bop-minded guitarist (1925–1999) who worked with Stan Kenton and Sonny Stitt.

playing was trim and economical; he swung bands hard without ever wasting a gesture—an attribute that Morello respected enormously.

Life in New York was impossibly hard at first. Morello arrived in 1952 but didn't work for a whole year until Sal Salvador, newly arrived from Springfield himself, began introducing him to musicians. And once musicians heard Morello's touch and feel for time, his playing became self-recommending. He began sitting in with Marian McPartland, and McPartland recommended him to the guitarist Johnny Smith, who signed Morello up for his first regular job. Later, Morello worked three weeks at Birdland with Stan Kenton, deputizing for his regular drummer, Stan Levey, and it was during this three-week stint that McPartland booked Morello as her regular drummer. "After I'd been with Marian's trio at the Hickory House for three years," Morello recalled, "I decided I wanted to move on."

At that time Benny Goodman was organizing a band and wanted me to join. *The Benny Goodman Story* was about to come out and I guess it could have been a good job. But I didn't like the way Benny's band sounded, and he got very upset when I told him I wasn't going to join. I'd really wanted to go with the [Tommy] Dorsey band, and one night Louie Bellson came into the Hickory House and said Dorsey was looking for a new drummer. When I auditioned he'd already been through, and rejected, thirty bebop drummers, and so I got the job. But Dorsey was doing one-nighters up and down the country and I could earn more staying in New York, so I decided not to go.

Ever faultless in his timekeeping, Brubeck happened to make his approach just as the deal with Dorsey went sour. Morello had become irritated by the Dorsey management's lack of clarity about payment, and by the time Dorsey came back with what Morello considered a reasonable offer, it was too late—he had decided to go with Brubeck, who sent Morello a telegram confirming "the hiring of your services for the period starting approximately October 12th ending definitely November 26th 1956 at fifty dollars per day payment [which] will be made also on any day off if any occur which is equal to the agreed on $350 per week."[8]

"I'd met with Brubeck at his hotel, the Park Sheraton,[9] near Birdland, and we talked about how me joining the quartet might work out," Morello recalled. "I was interested, certainly, in Dave's offer, but I explained that I'd seen the quartet play a few times at Birdland and that Joe Dodge had never taken so much as a four-bar break. The spotlight had all been on Brubeck and Desmond, with the bassist and drummer in the dark in the background. I told him that wouldn't work for me, wouldn't hold my interest. I wanted to develop my ideas about rhythm, and I wanted to solo. Dave listened and said he'd feature me on each album and in concerts, and so we agreed."

Their initial agreement committed Morello to a trial period, but when Brubeck wrote to Morello on December 17, 1956, to formally offer him a permanent job, the Dave Brubeck Quartet was in a state of crisis—quite possibly on the brink of disintegrating in its current form. In 2002, with hindsight, Morello was able to identify the source of the problems his hiring stirred up. "Paul had his very identifiable flute-like sound on the alto saxophone," he said, "and I had my recognizable sound—and he felt threatened by that. I became very close to Paul later, but he didn't talk to me at all for the first six months, and Dave got caught in the middle. It took Paul a year, I'd say, before he learned to share the space."

My first day with the quartet, in Chicago, actually started positively. We played a TV show without anybody falling out, but

8. Dave Brubeck to Joe Morello, telegram, September 17, 1956, Business Correspondence, Brubeck Collection.

9. The site, a year later, of the murder of mobster Albert Anastasia, shot while having his hair cut in the hotel barbershop.

that evening at the Blue Note, Dave, remembering that he had promised to feature me and also wanting to show off his new drummer, gave me a drum solo. Paul wasn't used to sharing the spotlight with anybody apart from Dave, and he got very jealous. I received a standing ovation for my solo, and the next thing I know, Paul is storming off the stage. I could sense from Dave panic and horror, like he just knew how difficult the next few months were going to be.

In 2003, Brubeck picks up the same story from his perspective: "Paul thought he was getting a drummer who liked to play with brushes and who would never think of getting in his way or, as he liked to put it, 'drop bombs.' But Joe wanted to be featured, and he and I had talked about polyrhythms, and that the quartet could now get into a lot of areas that would have been impossible with Joe Dodge, who wanted to stay swinging in 4/4."

That day in Chicago, Joe flew in from New York and his plane was delayed, so there was no time to rehearse, but I had sent him the record of my piece "I'm in a Dancing Mood," which is difficult because there are a lot of time changes and switches in the tempo, and he played it perfectly. The first night, at the Blue Note, after Joe's drum solo, Paul walked offstage and started shouting, "Either Morello goes or I go," and I said, "Paul, he's not going anywhere." I explained to him that, with Joe, we could get back into the different time signatures, the things we'd started to explore in the octet and that I'd worked on with Cal Tjader.

But he wouldn't listen and told me that he was leaving— and taking Norman Bates with him. I didn't know if Paul was talking out of anger or whether he really meant it. The next afternoon, Columbia had booked a session at a studio in Chicago, and Paul and Norman turned up but refused to play; they stood awkwardly in the control booth next to the sound guys, so Joe and I played ourselves for about two hours. When

I went to the job that night, I had no way of knowing whether Joe and Norman were going to show up, and if they stayed away, was that the end of the group? But they came into the club just as we were about to go on and walked to the bandstand, and that was that—Paul never mentioned it again.

Which didn't mean he was happy. It took months before he would even speak to Joe, and it was exhausting having these two star players in the group who didn't get along. Had Paul not come back to the club that night, what would I have done? I might have started something new with Joe, Bill Smith, and a new bass player. But I knew that Joe was a phenomenon who could take this group new places. The way he kept different rhythms going and controlled the kit—I'd never seen anything like it. And even though Paul was upset and hurt, I think, deep down, that he knew all that too.

Brubeck's letter of December 17 gave no hint of this turmoil. He told Morello that he had picked through the budget and was willing "to take whatever gamble is involved in paying you at the rate of $1,350 per month,[10] beginning December 31, 1956."[11] But Brubeck urged Morello to think matters through carefully before he signed on the dotted line:

> I am having a contract typed, and will have it ready when you arrive. [But] before you sign the contract, I think you should know that this business is not as fat as a lot of people think, and unless you will really be happy with this guarantee over the next couple of years, you probably should not sign with me, because I don't see any hope of being able to better this salary very soon without giving up the slack time which means more to me than any amount of money. Whatever you decide,

10. Equivalent to approximately $13,000 today.

11. Dave Brubeck to Joe Morello, December 17, 1956, Business Correspondence, Brubeck Collection.

I think you are a great musician, and your contribution to the Quartet is deeply appreciated.

Sending Morello seasonal greetings, Brubeck also threw in a Christmas bonus: "This year I am giving each of the guys a new suit for Christmas, a suit that can be worn as a uniform. So when you arrive in San Francisco introduce yourself to Royal Park Custom Tailors so that your measurements can be taken."

That quarrelsome October 1956 evening at the Chicago Blue Note, when everything nearly fell apart, was not preserved on tape. But Brubeck's persistence in mending fences between his drummer and alto saxophonist feels vindicated when listening to a March 1957 broadcast from the same venue. The difference Morello made to the group was immediate, dramatic, and electrifying.

"In a Dancing Mood" was an obscure Tommy Dorsey record[12] that Brubeck had arranged to showcase the full range of his quartet's rhythmic capabilities, a piece to play on TV shows and during broadcasts to tell the uninitiated, in under three minutes, what to expect from the Dave Brubeck Quartet. One melody note was flattened to open up the too-sweet-for-its-own-good melody line harmonically, but otherwise Brubeck's arrangement darted between sudden switches of meter and tempo.

Joe Dodge's playing had neatly alighted on the dovetails of meter and tempo, but Morello ambushed listeners with rhythm, his roaring, torrential energy flowing around the different sections, making the piece sound less episodic. Recorded during that same gig, "The Song Is You" featured Desmond, who, despite the offstage infighting, was clearly enjoying himself. Desmond had been allowed as much space as he needed,

---

12. Victor BS-03084, 1937.

sometimes more, by Brubeck's previous drummers, but Morello's more assertive style heightened the tone of internal discussion—between Desmond and his own solo, and within the group as a whole.

Those who hadn't witnessed the quartet in concert would need to wait until 1957 to hear Morello with Brubeck, when Columbia released *Jazz Impressions of the USA*, his debut record with the group. Compared to *Brubeck Time* from two years earlier, something tangible had changed, even if it took a while to figure out exactly what.

Most obviously, *Jazz Impressions of the USA* was the first Brubeck Quartet album to be built entirely around original Brubeck compositions. The florid, formally arranged counterpoint typified by *Brubeck Time*'s "Why Do I Love You?" and "Brother, Can You Spare a Dime?" (and "Fare Thee Well, Annabelle" from *Jazz: Red Hot and Cool*) was superseded in this latest album by the crystalline clarity of compositions in which each note and harmonic gear-change move had been deliberately plotted. A quartet into which Joe Morello was injecting so much new activity didn't require such busy arrangements, and the opening track of *Jazz Impressions of the USA* spun the quartet in a dynamic new direction. The musical evolution of the group was about to become inseparable from Brubeck's development as a composer.

Nothing could have been more fundamentally F minor than the first bar of that opening track, "Ode to a Cowboy," in which Brubeck's melodic line raised up the notes of an F minor chord, a starting point of harmonic security from which he moved his melody step by step, keeping strictly within the tonal boundaries. But in bar 8 a sudden jolt—at exactly the midpoint of his sixteen-bar structure—as this most minor of melodies was parked on a major chord; and when the melody repeated, it rebounded from this correspondingly distant vantage point, far outside F minor. And this harmonic shift *was* the piece. Without it, "Ode to a Cowboy" would have been a pleasant enough riding-bareback-through-the-prairies theme; with it came depth and variety. The learning that Milhaud had instilled into him ten years earlier, as they worked together on "Playland-at-the-Beach," was still taking Brubeck in new directions.

As he wrote regular new compositions for the quartet, turning them around at speed, there was immense satisfaction to be had from letting one well-chosen harmonic step, or a cycle of harmonic shifts, do all the compositional heavy lifting. That major chord side step became as emblematic of "Ode to a Cowboy" as the catchy earworm opening phrase of "Blue Rondo à la Turk," which migrated between the home key of F major and a move three steps higher. Strategic shifts in harmony—and where they might lead improvisers—were becoming the very fabric of Brubeck's music.

Track three, "History of a Boy Scout," engineered a beautifully complex composition around one such harmonic shift. In his sleeve note, Brubeck relayed how the title was dreamed up "by our own wit-master Paul Desmond with an elaborate salaam in the direction of Stravinsky and *Histoire du Soldat*," and Stravinsky himself would have surely appreciated Brubeck's compositional savvy. "History of a Boy Scout" began with an almost identical melodic flourish to "Ode to a Cowboy": a rising triadic figure that dropped one step as it reached the first beat of the next bar but then brought the most illegal melodic interval of all into play.[13] Under normal circumstances the note C-flat would need to recuse itself from any piece in B-flat minor. On a piano, C-flat is the same note as B natural, which, once sounded, has the effect of undermining

---

13. The next two tracks—"Plain Song" and "Curtain Time"—were also cut from that same melodic cloth, enough to make you wonder whether Brubeck was thinking about unifying his album melodically over its forty-minute duration. It would be satisfying from a musicological perspective to claim that that were so; however, the pieces were not all written at the same time, and nowhere else did Brubeck attempt such a thing. But each composition does fit convincingly into the whole, that bond of melodic unity helping whether Brubeck was conscious of it or not.

the innate "B-flatness" of B-flat minor; it is the furthest possible port of call. Brubeck's melodic line yearned to return to B-flat minor but, having already slipped the harmonic moorings so comprehensively by resting his melody on C-flat, he introduced further instability by routing his journey home via a circuitous, tonality-busting tritone.

A tritone; a natural where the ear expected to hear a flat—obvious points of resolution were dodged as Brubeck kept his line retracing its own steps, turning around its own axis like an Escher staircase. He also gave careful thought to how best to place his melodically itinerant melody onto the instruments of the quartet. Morello opening with a steady 4/4 marching accompaniment lent some stability as Desmond introduced a précis of the theme over the drums as an introduction. But without feeder chords from the piano, and as he outlined a theme still to be revealed in full, the full harmonic context was left intriguingly open. It fell to Brubeck himself to fit all the pieces together by delivering his reptant theme; then, as Desmond prepared to solo, Morello jumped the quartet into a double-time swing feel—which released all of the harmonic and rhythmic tension that had accrued.

The next piece, "Plain Song," grew from killing time on the road as the quartet traveled, Brubeck's sleeve notes said, between South Dakota and Iowa City on a bus. Brubeck noted that "the monotonous revolution of wheels upon a journey which has no end" seeded what we hear in the rhythm section: "the insistent thump of the bass and the mechanical rhythm of the drums." Portraying monotony in music is high risk, the problems cogently summed up by the great Argentinean composer Mauricio Kagel, who once declared that "if someone tells me they want to produce boring music as a philosophical point of view then I accept it—but the boringness must be exciting,"[14]

14. Philip Clark, "Mauricio Kagel, Theatre of War," *The Wire*, June 2003.

and Brubeck pushed through monotony to induce a hypnotic, trancelike state.

As soon as he began to solo, Desmond would have felt the ground shifting under his feet as Bates started to accent, forcefully, the second and fourth beats of every bar, and then upped the intensity by accenting every offbeat. A boogie beat shuffled into being, supported by Morello, which elicited a lusty "yeah" from Brubeck. Did those increasingly adamant offbeats evolve as the group rehearsed? Or had Brubeck conceived this role for his bass player as an integral part of the composition from the get-go? A clue lurks within the rhythmic cracks of the very first beat of bar 1: Morello sneaked a brushed snare drum strike onto the actual first beat of the bar, pushing Desmond to the offbeat—which opened up the expectation of a swerve across the beat. Desmond shaped Brubeck's line by displacing melodic or rhythmic regularity with slurs and accents, and dropping in little grace notes.

Morello's first-beat interjection acted like a light suddenly switched on that illuminated a long and winding road, an illusion of joining a performance already in motion. The elation Brubeck expressed, pleasure mixed with surprise, as Bates and Morello nailed down that boogie beat was the sound of a composer exhilarated by where his material was leading his musicians creatively. He was handing over music that brimmed with potential, which, pored over and figured out in the studio, led to magic moments like Bates's bass line and Desmond's treatment of his theme. "Plain Song" also pointed to the future in another important way. Working in the studio, George Avakian captured Desmond's every breath and fluctuation of vibrato, purposely contrasting the diaphanous beauty of his sound with Brubeck's drier percussive attack: a key ingredient of "Take Five."

*Jazz Impressions of the USA* wasn't all based on deep minor modalities. For contrast, Brubeck included a jovial reworking of

"Tea for Two" called "Yonder for Two"[15] and the razzmatazz of a musical sketch of Broadway entitled "Curtain Time." The latter tune was lightweight compared to the musical and emotional complexities of "Plain Song," although Desmond's sneaky reference to Bob Hope's hit song "Thanks for the Memory" certainly raised a smile.

But those contemplative minor tunes—"Ode to a Cowboy," "History of a Boy Scout," "Plain Song"—lodged themselves in the memory most forcefully. The tenebrous shadings of "Plain Song" looked two ways at once: there were echoes of the wistful yearning of "Audrey" at the same time as it prepared the ground for the compulsive rhythmic loops of "Pick Up Sticks" from *Time Out* and the haunted, Edward Hooper melancholy of *Time Further Out*'s "Bluette" and "Blue Shadows in the Street." Brubeck's most praised composition to date, "In Your Own Sweet Way," had pinned its distinctive turns of phrase on the conventions of popular song form. Thelonious Monk's early song "'Round Midnight" also hung off popular song form, before his latter-period compositions like "Trinkle, Tinkle," "Ugly Beauty," and "Crepuscule with Nellie" rethought the idea of form as something that emerged out of the shape and direction of the material; form was not a preset mold into which material could be poured. Likewise, in "Ode to a Cowboy," "History of a Boy Scout," and "Plain Song" new forms sprang out of the vividness of Brubeck's harmonic imagination and his ability to transform a melodic cell—altering one crucial note enough to irrevocably transform the character of a phrase.

Brubeck's sleeve notes for *Jazz Impressions of the USA* signed off by reminding everyone, Desmond included perhaps, that

15. This piece was originally called "Tea Down Yonder for Two," which was changed to "Yonder for Two" when the album was re-pressed; when Brubeck played it live at the Newport Jazz Festival that year he called his tune "Tea Down Yonder." Suspicions that Brubeck had stumbled into a rights issue seem to be confirmed by the published sheet music album of *Jazz Impressions of the USA*, which omits the tune altogether.

Morello was here to stay, and the album's last quartet track made good on his promise to feature Morello on record.[16] "Sounds of the Loop," Brubeck wrote, "introduces the remarkable melodic drumming of Joe Morello. His forceful, individual style of drumming has noticeably influenced the over-all 'sound' of the quartet since he joined us in the fall of '56"— all of which was true, but this first version of "Sounds of the Loop" felt disappointingly tepid. Neither Brubeck nor Desmond gave the melodic line much of a rhythmic kick, problems amplified when Morello's solo began by tripping over a clumsy edit and losing rhythmic continuity.

Once the piece had weathered subsequent live performances it became more convincing, but the most important aspect of "Sounds of the Loop" was that Morello was now firmly established as a solo voice within the quartet. "We played 'Sounds of the Loop' for about two years," he said in 2002.[17] "During the solo I'd drop into either 3/4 or 5/4, or perhaps alternate between them—and 'Take Five' really had its roots there." Many factors would contribute to the chart-busting popularity of "Take Five," but its signature sound—a loose-limbed melodic line in which every note had a place and function, and that sfumato minor tonality—rested on discoveries made during the recording of *Jazz Impressions of the USA*.

*Dave Digs Disney*, recorded over the summer of 1957, would be the last quartet album to feature Norman Bates, who, like Joe Dodge before him, was tiring of the relentless recording and touring schedule. Bates's association with Brubeck stretched all the way back to the Three Ds, and Brubeck trusted his responsive and resourceful musicianship implicitly.

---

16. The album ended with a brief Brubeck solo piece, "Home at Last."

17. Interview with the author, April 24, 2002. Published in "Sounds In and Out of the Loop," *Jazz Review*, June 2002.

Earlier in 1957 concurrent histories had overlapped when the current Brubeck Quartet recorded a reunion album with David Van Kriedt. Bates never worked with the octet (and it was his brother Bob who had played on Desmond's debut as leader on Fantasy with Dick Collins, Van Kriedt, and Joe Dodge), but he sounded very happy to be part of this trip down a memory lane that he hadn't personally walked. Van Kriedt, who contributed all the compositions, revived "Prelude" from the old octet book (the same piece that had given Desmond his first recorded solo in July 1950), and Bates secured the harmony with his low bowed notes, which rumbled like a church organ. He also led the funky riff that opened "Divertimento" and then forked into two-counterpoint, double bass against Desmond's alto saxophone. Van Kriedt pepped up his writing for double bass with athletic octave hurdles over which Bates skipped with ease, a lightness of touch that rebounded into his solo.

The session was released by Fantasy under the title *Reunion*, and the prospect of having new Brubeck to release no doubt made Max and Sol Weiss salivate, especially as the record would be indirectly supported by Columbia, which was promoting the likes of *Brubeck Time* and *Jazz Impressions of the USA*. But the album, while enjoyable enough, was no match for the airy freshness of *Dave Digs Disney*. Where Brubeck had applied Milhaud's teaching to a range of new contexts, out of which he had divined a musical vocabulary of his own, Van Kriedt was still operating within the basic octet format, making microadjustments to ideas he had ingested a decade earlier. (And *Reunion* would no doubt have benefited from the presence of Bill Smith and/or Dick Collins.)

Van Kriedt's charts looked backward at precisely the time West Coast pioneers like Gerry Mulligan, Shelley Manne, Chet Baker, and Jimmy Giuffre were broadening the expressive base of their music. The Gerry Mulligan Quartet's consummate *What Is There to Say?*, recorded between December 1958 and January 1959, placed the question "whither West Coast jazz?" under a microscope.[18] With Art Farmer (trumpet), Bill Crow (bass), and Dave Bailey (drums), ensemble textures that dredged classic 1920s jazz for inspiration bumped into Mulligan's moreish "As Catch Can," which felt like the best Thelonious Monk composition that Monk himself never wrote. "Blueport" and "Utter Chaos" were strident, badass funk; "Festive Minor" and "My Funny Valentine" were lyrical and exquisite. The album was a demonstration that the argument had moved on, leaving Van Kriedt's charts to sound a little musty.

The significance of *Dave Digs Disney*, compared to *Reunion*,[19] was that Brubeck was playing a game entirely of his own making, which removed him from the generalities of debates about the development of West Coast jazz. His thoughtful reinterpretations of "Alice in Wonderland," "Give a Little Whistle," "Heigh-Ho!," "When You Wish Upon a Star," "Someday My Prince Will Come," and "One Song" had appeal because the themes themselves were so familiar, reworkings that had learned from *Jazz Impressions of the USA*. Improvisations were complex and intricate, while presentations of themes peeled the original songs to their essence.

*Dave Digs Disney*'s latter-day reputation (and the reputation of the album that followed it in October 1958, *Jazz Impressions of Eurasia*) has been skewed by *Time Out*'s popularity, which blocked out the light on anything that surrounded it. Before "Blue Rondo à la Turk" and "Take Five," the controversies the Disney album provoked had nothing to do with time signatures and classically influenced forms becoming that little bit *too* classical for some tastes. Before Miles Davis and Bill Evans followed Brubeck's lead with their own versions of "Someday My Prince

---

18. I'd argue that, alongside *Time Out*, Miles Davis's *Kind of Blue*, John Coltrane's *Giant Steps*, Charles Mingus's *Mingus Ah Um*, and Ornette Coleman's *The Shape of Jazz to Come*, Mulligan's *What Is There To Say?* is the other great 1959 jazz album.

19. *Dave Digs Disney* on December 30, 1957; *Reunion* was released in February 1958.

Will Come" and the John Coltrane Quartet recorded "Chim Chim Cher-ee," and transformed "My Favorite Things" into a jazz anthem, the question *Dave Digs Disney* raised was: Why would any serious-minded jazz musician choose to work with twee songs written for children's movies?

George Avakian's sleeve note recounted the story of Brubeck—by then a father of five—calling him from a phone booth in Disneyland during a family outing. Had things panned out in accordance with their initial telephone conversation, Columbia would have released an album called *Jazz Goes to Disneyland*, with a front cover featuring all five Brubeck children posing next to a Disneyland exhibit alongside their father's quartet. But rights issues (Disney already owned their own Disneyland record label) and someone's suggestion for an attractively alliterative album title handed us the record we know: *Dave Digs Disney*, with, on its front cover, a beaming Dave surrounded by pencil sketches of Mickey Mouse, Pluto, and Donald Duck.

Disney tunes had been part of the Brubeck repertoire since at least 1952, when the quartet (then with Wyatt Ruther and Lloyd Davis) recorded "Alice in Wonderland" and two separate versions of "Give a Little Whistle" (one during the same session that produced the classic "Over the Rainbow" and one on the live tapes from which Fantasy would cull *Jazz at the College of the Pacific*). But back then there had been no grand "Project Disney" in the offing. "Alice in Wonderland" might have been designed with Desmond's love of sensually lyrical melodies in mind (file under "Stardust" or "These Foolish Things"), while a skittish melody like "Give a Little Whistle" appealed to the same side of Brubeck that gravitated toward "Lulu's Back in Town" or "Frenesi" as material for improvisation. These were songs the Brubecks played to keep their children entertained while driving between gigs.

Each song he chose for *Dave Digs Disney* was artfully personalized. "Someday My Prince Will Come" further developed the overlay of 4/4 against 3/4 introduced on *Jazz: Red Hot and Cool*'s "Lover" to become the album's most talked-about track. But anybody keen to count the beats might have been thrown off the scent by claims in Avakian's sleeve note that "Dave introduces 4/4 and 2/2 against the rhythm section 3/4." The juxtaposition of one pulse against another was, in fact, far more complex. Bates was tasked with maintaining a steady 3/4 groove over which Morello superimposed a speedier 4/4 beat; and, as had happened in "Lover," the rhythm section levitated around the overlapping intersection of strong and weak beats.

For no better reason than that the waltz feel of the original song was so ingrained, most listeners would have felt the rhythm primarily in 3—but that layer of 4/4 was more than a cosmetic trimming. Morello's exacting brushwork, which rarely peaked above medium-soft, helped oil the fluid rhythmic motion while pumping nervous, anticipatory energy into what would otherwise have been an uncomplicated waltz: not inappropriate given the lyric.

Brubeck's unaccompanied piano introduction was expansive and tapped directly into the sentiment of the original with cascading, tinsel-draped arpeggios. With Desmond's seductive reading of Frank Churchill's theme and the rhythm section on their furtive rhythmic maneuvers, Brubeck's tidy and precise emphasizing of the waltz's "two, three" punctuated the texture with the matter-of-factness of secretarial typing. When Brubeck landed solidly on "two," which he sustained for a whole bar, light beamed through the texture and the groove was given a little bounce; and, as his patterns became more irregular, he moved rhythm and space around the quartet. In his solo, solid 3/4 waltzed against striding 4/4 time, while other bars could be argued (and counted) rhythmically either way—a lesson in hairsplitting rhythmic ambiguity.

The quartet's "Heigh-Ho!" found a soulful side to a song not normally celebrated for its emotional depth, while a soft-spoken, downy lyricism radiated through "Alice in Wonderland." But that touch-type rhythmic figuration at the beginning of "Some-day My Prince Will Come" planted the most important seed of all. Similar patterns would become a feature of Brubeck's accompaniments whenever he needed to maintain rhythmic order. And two years later, during the summer of 1959, when the quartet was attempting the seemingly impossible feat of stitching together a new piece in 5/4 time, the best thing Brubeck could do, he realized, was provide unobtrusive rhythmic support with another tidy, neat vamp.

On January 3, 1955—two months after publishing their Brubeck cover feature—*Time* magazine named John Foster Dulles, President Eisenhower's hawkish secretary of state, Man of the Year 1954. This accolade was largely in recognition of Dulles's role in masterminding the Southeast Asia Treaty Organization: the founding principles of NATO applied to Southeast Asia, where it was hoped an alliance of democracies with interests in the region would put a restraint on the ambitions of Communist countries, especially China. SEATO would be Dulles's final grand political gesture. By the time of the Suez crisis in November 1956, ominous signs of the colon cancer that would kill him in May 1959 were making themselves felt. And as Eisenhower mulled over Suez—what to do about Egyptian president Gamal Abdel Nasser's decision to close the Suez Canal and Israel's military intervention—Dulles was convalescing after stomach surgery. Once recovered, though, he lashed out at Nasser and pushed him toward forging closer ties with Moscow. Dulles's shouty form of diplomacy and brinkmanship led the comedian Mort Sahl—Brubeck and Desmond's old friend from the Los Angeles club circuit—to deadpan in the *New Yorker*, "Whenever John Foster Dulles visits a country, the State Department sends the Dave Brubeck Quartet in a few weeks later to repair the damage."

Over on the other side of the political spectrum, Adam Clayton Powell Jr., the charismatic congressman for Harlem, was pushing for another form of international diplomacy that replaced angry rhetoric with culture—jazz in particular. Powell represented everything that the establishment Dulles wasn't. A black Democrat with a background in hard-left politics—his sympathies with Soviet Russia had lasted until Stalin signed his nonaggression pact with Hitler in August 1939—Powell reveled in preaching truth to power. In April 1955 he attended the Bandung Conference in Indonesia as an observer—a conference convened by countries excluded from SEATO, including Indonesia, Ceylon, Burma, and India, to protest the dominance of Washington and Moscow; "There are others, too, in the world," said Prime Minister John Kotelawala of Ceylon, "and the main concern among these others is peace."[20] Powell's intention to attend threw Dulles and Eisenhower into a panic. Dulles's office tried to persuade him to withdraw, arguing that sending a US delegate would lend the conference legitimacy. But Powell left for Indonesia anyway, telling reporters at the airport, "It will mark the first time in history that the world's non-White people have held such a gathering, and it could be the most important of the century."[21]

Foremost among the many reasons why conference delegates believed the US should think twice before playing the world's policeman was the country's own lamentable record on race. The Declaration of Independence had aspired to establish a land where "all men are created equal . . . endowed by their Creator with certain unalienable Rights . . . among these . . . Life, Liberty and the pursuit of Happiness." But Eisenhower was presiding over a country warped by segregation,

---

20. John Kotelawala, opening address, Bandung, Indonesia, April 18, 1955, www.cvce.eu/content/publication/2015/10/20/1d96efd4-aaae-49b6-b3f9-bc298741462c/publishable_en.pdf.
21. Norman Otis Richmond, "The Legacy of the Bandung Conference," Black Commentator, n.d., www.africaspeaks.com/reasoning/index.php?topic=2989.0;wap.

where inequality was written into law and the lynching of black people was commonplace.

Powell told it like it was: racism was America's shame, and Eisenhower's decision not to send a delegate was myopic and misguided. "America must clean up her own race problem as swiftly as possible in order to reassure the people of Asia," Powell asserted—but equally, lectures on freedom had little value, he declared, coming from repressive Communist regimes. Powell spoke optimistically about the grounding virtues of American democracy and returned home as man of the moment, feted by Democrats and Republicans alike; Eisenhower invited him for talks at the White House.

Using this newfound status as leverage, Powell acted quickly. The best way to promote an image of America working hard to right the divisions of racism, he reasoned, was to send jazz groups on tours overseas. The State Department's current strategy was all wrong, he argued. Dropping institutions like the New York Philharmonic and Cincinnati Symphony Orchestra behind the Iron Curtain was white America importing European culture back to Europe. But jazz was America taking pride in its own black culture, and bands in which black and white musicians worked together would be viewed as a metaphor for democracy and racial equality.

The State Department leaped on the idea enthusiastically. At the time Powell was married to the pianist and jazz singer Hazel Scott, who had recorded with Max Roach and Charles Mingus and whose television program, *The Hazel Scott Show*— the first US network television series to be hosted by a person of African descent—had been a ratings winner until her appearance before the House Un-American Activities Committee in 1950 led to sponsors' pulling the plug and the cancellation of her show. Scott had introduced her friend Dizzy Gillespie to Powell—and now Powell persuaded Gillespie to undertake the first state-sponsored tour by a jazz musician.

Beginning in March 1956, Gillespie and his eighteen-piece big band embarked on a ten-week trip through Iran, Pakistan, Lebanon, Turkey, the Dominican Republic, Yugoslavia, and Greece. The band's arrival in Athens coincided with a student demonstration against Eisenhower's support for Greece's right-wing government, but Gillespie received a hero's welcome nevertheless—Powell's hunch that if you couldn't be diplomatic you could at least bebop seemed well founded.

But the next State Department tour floundered before a single note could be played. In September 1957, nine black students defied segregation laws by trying to enroll in their local high school in Little Rock, Arkansas. The governor of Arkansas, Orval Faubus, remained resolute in his determination to keep the school "for whites only"—but a court order ruled against him. In response, Faubus ordered the Arkansas National Guard to form a ring of "protection" around the school, and Eisenhower refused requests to send federal troops to ease the situation. Interviewed that same night by Larry Lubenow, a twenty-one-year-old student journalist working for the *Grand Forks Herald,* Louis Armstrong rounded on Faubus and Eisenhower. The governor, Armstrong said, was a "motherfucker" (which Lubenow euphemistically changed to "uneducated plough boy" in the final article), while the president had capitulated to racism and had "no guts." "The way they are treating my people in the South, the government can go to hell. It's getting so bad, a colored man hasn't got any country," Armstrong concluded.[22]

These words, from a man who presented such a genial, smiling face to the world, always were going to cause a storm. Charles Mingus wrote "Fables of Faubus," a Kurt Weill–like dirge with a mocking lyric as a gesture of solidarity, and Lena Horne and Eartha Kitt spoke out in support of Armstrong; but some radio stations, content to play Armstrong records

---

22. Larry Lubenow, Associated Press, September 17, 1957.

when he was conforming to their idea of how a black entertainer ought to behave, issued a ban on the grounds that they thought it inappropriate for him to enter the political arena. His state-sponsored tour was still under discussion, but Armstrong had made it clear to Lubenow that, under current circumstances, an ambassadorial trip to Russia was unthinkable: "[When] the people over there ask me what's wrong with my country, what am I supposed to say?"

When Armstrong relented in 1961 and undertook a state-sponsored tour with his All-Stars, he was unaware of a CIA plot to assassinate the left-wing president of the Congo, Patrice Lumumba, one of the countries on his schedule, which rather took the "good" out of "goodwill tour"; in 1963, during Duke Ellington's tour of the Middle East, the police commissioner of Birmingham, Alabama, Bull Connor, set fire hoses and attack dogs on black protesters, children included, an act that Ellington condemned unequivocally. State-sponsored tours, it was becoming apparent, could not be cushioned from the surrounding politics, and parachuting free-thinking jazz musicians into politically volatile countries came with risks both diplomatic and personal.

Armstrong's vocalist, Velma Middleton, died a few weeks after suffering a stroke in Sierra Leone, and All-Stars clarinetist Barney Bigard was of the opinion that Armstrong and Joe Glaser had failed in their duty of care; Middleton should have been airlifted to better hospital facilities in France, he maintained. Benny Goodman's tour of the Soviet Union in 1963 was marred by the King of Swing's nagging neuroses. Squabbles over money and his condescending attitude toward the superb array of musicians he had hired—hardly the hoped-for model of fair-minded American democracy—very nearly derailed the tour, and Goodman's miserly spirit was satirized by one of his sidemen reversing film of the clarinetist on walkabout in Red Square, making it look as though Goodman was taking money *off* beggars.

Compared to the trials and tribulations suffered by Armstrong and Ellington, and Goodman's self-inflicted traumas, the quartet's 1958 tour was logistically flawless, and with the final concerts approaching, Brubeck needed to rein in the State Department's desire to extend because he had engagements to fulfill back in the US. The quartet was on the road for a total of three months, February to May. Before the State Department leg of the tour, the quartet played concerts in England, Scotland, Germany, Holland, Belgium, and Denmark, before leaving Western Europe for Poland, and then onward to Turkey, Afghanistan, Ceylon, Pakistan, India, Iran, and Iraq. The 1958 tour is primarily remembered for three things: Brubeck hearing, on a street in Istanbul, the 9/8 rhythm that would lead to "Blue Rondo à la Turk"; Brubeck and Morello jamming with Indian classical musicians in Delhi and Madras; and Brubeck's Chopin-inspired composition "Dziekuje," which, the first time it was performed, wowed an audience in Poland. Remembered now only in photographs, press clippings, and memories, the music hasn't been made public. But Brubeck considered the tour a highlight of his career—a three-month period of great learning about music and cultural exchange.

Behind the scenes, John Foster Dulles himself had pulled the strings. In 1957, making his initial approaches to embassies in Eastern Europe, Dulles had emphasized some sound reasons why a visit from the Dave Brubeck Quartet might be desirable: the group's popularity at home was unprecedented; their leader was a fine pianist, conservatoire trained, equally at home in jazz and classical music; and he was pursuing and developing jazz as a "serious" art form. Although he chose his words carefully, Dulles also let it be known that the quartet was all white, which, he thought, conveniently swept issues of race under the carpet.

Then Norman Bates left, and before leaving for England at the start of February 1958, Brubeck needed to resolve the problem of his replacement. The prospect of touring for three months in some of the world's most inaccessible places had been the tipping point for Bates, who had decided to return to his family in San Francisco. Brubeck had heard Eugene Wright play with Cal Tjader, Red Norvo, and Buddy DeFranco and had been impressed;[23] meanwhile, Joe Morello's gut instinct that the quartet could not do any better than Wright would prove spot on.

Wright was the first bass player from outside the milieu of Mills College and the octet that Brubeck hired. With technique in abundance and unquenchable musical curiosity, Wright relished the imminent arrival of those complex time signature pieces while he never lost sight of his jazz roots. Born in Chicago in 1923, Wright had an approach to his instrument that was grounded in the Kansas City mold of Count Basie and of the bass player who had helped define the Basie orchestra's unique approach to feel and groove.

Walter Page—who died from pneumonia on December 20, 1957, two months before Wright joined Brubeck—spent the years 1935 to 1942 with Basie, during arguably the orchestra's greatest period. Although the Basie Orchestra would develop a reputation for the throbbing, rapturous swing of "One O'Clock Jump," "Kid from Red Bank," and "Jumpin' at the Woodside"— the brass section gnawing like a pack of Rottweilers at the wailing saxophones—the Basie sound was a carefully cultivated blend of personalities and musical methods. The emotional yin and yang of Basie was personified by the tenor saxophone partnership of Herschel Evans[24] and Lester Young—Evans's galvanic energy and guttural tone often pitched against Young's breezy, singing impressionism.

---

23. Dave Brubeck, handwritten journal, undated entry, Brubeck Collection (uncataloged).

24. Tenor saxophonist (1909–1939) and early star of the Count Basie Orchestra whose career was tragically cut short by heart disease.

The Basie rhythm section—Page alongside Basie himself on piano, with Freddie Green (guitar) and Jo Jones (drums)—swung ferociously, but their dynamic level rarely rose above medium-loud, and when Jo Jones broke cover with a drum fill, it punched above its weight. Eugene Wright took from Page an awareness that articulating the beat crisply and clearly did not mean hammering each strong beat; he imported Page's elegant, skipping tone directly inside the Dave Brubeck Quartet.

Wright had played with Basie himself between 1948 and '49, his tenure frustratingly coinciding with a recording ban, and also with two saxophonists grounded in pure blues: Gene Ammons and Arnett Cobb. The prospect of a bassist so intimately tied to the blues and to Basie's Kansas City style making any meaningful contribution to Brubeck's quartet might have felt unlikely. If the quartet's idea of the blues was the silky pastoral shades of "Audrey," what part could Wright play in that?

Recorded in January 1957, almost exactly a year before he joined Brubeck, the Cal Tjader Quartet's *Jazz at the Blackhawk*[25] bears witness to the versatility of Wright's musicianship. Rocking "Bill B."—Tjader's blues dedicated to Basie—to its core, his own "Two for Blues Suite" (an antecedent of his "African Times Suite," which the Brubeck Quartet would record during their twenty-fifth anniversary concert tour in 1976) offers further proof of his prowess as a bluesman. Tjader's arrangement of "I'll Remember April" finds Wright projecting a singing line through an intricate contrapuntal texture, and he brings a light chamber music sensibility to quartet pianist Vince Guaraldi's piece "Thinking of You, MJQ" (referencing the Modern Jazz Quartet). Far from Wright's Kansas City credentials precluding him from working with Brubeck, his ability to hold the foundations together solidly, swinging lightly or robustly as required, made him a natural for the quartet.

---

25. Fantasy Records 3241.

Which is not to say that Wright was the only bass player who had the right stylistic pedigree. Bill Crow, the highly-thought-of Red Mitchell, and Carson Smith, who had played in Charlie Parker's group during the 1953 package tour with Brubeck, might have been contenders for the job, and Wyatt "Bull" Ruther made a direct approach to his former boss. "What ever gave you the Idea that I did not want to work with you again?" he wrote. "I read In the trade mag. that once again you had changed Bass Players and I have yet to be asked. I think that Father Wright Is by far one [of] the best choices for the group, however If the occasional should arise again, and a Bass player Is needed with the group I'd be indeed grateful to you If you phone . . . and offer the job to me, If you have no objections."[26]

But Wright's sunny temperament lightened the mood by balancing out Morello's brooding, and the chemistry felt instantly right. Wright ironed out the problems with the role of bassist that Brubeck had identified in his "The DB Quartet—Principals and Aims" document by turning them to his advantage. "I liked his solid bass lines that grounded that group," Brubeck wrote.[27] "[It was] possible to play other tempos and do polyrhythmic things and he wouldn't budge from this grounded beat. Oftentimes Joe, on drums, would be playing a different counter-rhythm to what Gene was playing. Paul and I might be playing in a different rhythm from either of them. Gene would never budge [and] as it got further and further complicated . . . Joe would say [that] on a wild night the more complicated it got the bigger Gene's eyes got."

"Many bass players would have objected to having to play in such a restricted and demanding way," Brubeck continued—but Wright, a disciple of Walter Page and Jo Jones, quickly developed a working rapport and rhythmic empathy with

26. Wyatt "Bull" Ruther to Dave Brubeck, May 19, 1958, Personal Correspondence, Brubeck Collection. (Capitalization of letters all Ruther's.)

27. Dave Brubeck, handwritten journal, undated entry, Brubeck Collection (uncataloged).

Morello, and the two men began referring to themselves as
the "Section." Brubeck reported Wright's cry of victory whenever he felt a groove lying naturally under his fingers—"I've got
'em, Joe"—and his mantra that staring at Morello's bass drum,
rather than following the movement of his hands, helped shore
the group up: "If my bass and your bass drum are together,
nothing gonna move it."

The evening before the quartet left for Europe on a mission
to spread the good word about American democracy, an incident at East Carolina College in Greenville, North Carolina,
on February 5, 1958, left Brubeck questioning why his group
was welcome to perform in authoritarian states in Eastern
Europe but not on a college campus in the United States. College officials thought they had hired an all-white quartet (with
Norman Bates), and their naked prejudice when a mixed-
race group showed up was heightened by post–Little Rock
paranoia, and the symbolism was crushing, especially during
Wright's first week with the quartet.[28] The dean of the college
informed Brubeck, backstage moments before the concert was
due to begin, that there must be no repeat of Little Rock on
his watch—Wright could not perform. Without his bass player
there could be no concert, Brubeck countered, and as he continued to argue, students began to stamp their feet and chant
Wright's name. Realizing that canceling the concert might
equally provoke trouble, the university authorities relented—
but this new quartet had received a first taste of the difficulties
they would face whenever they toured the Deep South.

A little over a week later, Brubeck was sitting in the lounge
of a Manchester hotel before a concert at the city's Free Trade
Hall, drinking tea and eating cake as he talked to a reporter
from the *Manchester Guardian*, who noted his "very friendly

---

28. This performance has sometimes been cited as Wright's first concert with
the quartet, although a tape exists of a concert recorded at the Massachusetts
Institute of Technology on February 2, during which Brubeck introduces Wright
as the group's new bassist and says, "It's his first concert."

and relaxed" composure. Of the incident in North Carolina a few days earlier there was no mention. Instead Brubeck gave a digest of how his jazz differed from other approaches—"My whole idea in jazz is superimposing rhythm on rhythm, and harmony on harmony," he said—before the reporter asked him about the palm court orchestra, a feature of upmarket British hotels at the time, which was "sawing relentlessly" in the background. Would Brubeck prefer to hear a jazz group? "No, I don't think so. Not while you're eating. It might give you indigestion," he quipped.[29]

Selections from their March 4[30] concert at the Tivoli Concert Hall in Copenhagen were recorded for release under the title *The Dave Brubeck Quartet in Europe*, and Frank Loesser's tune "Wonderful Copenhagen," from the film musical *Hans Christian Andersen*, was given the full *Dave Digs Disney* treatment: its melody superimposed over the 4/4 against 3/4 rhythmic grid borrowed from "Someday My Prince Will Come." In Hannover on February 28 the quartet played "Someday My Prince Will Come" itself, and on both occasions Wright's nimble-fingered trot breathed air through the rhythmic maze, helping the pieces swing naturally.[31] Other bootleg performances from this European leg of the tour—from Manchester on February 14[32] and Berlin on February 25[33]—are crowned by a near-twenty-minute version of "Take the 'A' Train" recorded in Berlin, where Desmond's epic solo was followed by Brubeck refitting Billy Strayhorn's original tune with an array of audacious harmonic leaps of faith.

While the giddy enjoyment of those earlier evenings radiate through even these lo-fi recordings, a whole other level

29. "The Art of Dave Brubeck," *Guardian*, February 17, 1958, www.theguardian .com/music/2017/feb/17/dave-brubeck-jazz-interview-1958.
30. Not March 5, as the album sleeve claims.
31. Moosicus Records 1302-2, 2013.
32. Solar Records 4569900, 2011.
33. RLR Records 88636, 2008.

of creative intensity was achieved in Copenhagen. Why, that night, did Brubeck decide to call the standard "Tangerine"? The Hannover, Manchester, and Berlin concerts captured multiple readings of "St. Louis Blues," "Take the 'A' Train," "For All We Know," and "Gone with the Wind," but a tune from outside the regular set list forced open new lines of inquiry— Brubeck knew that Desmond loved to improvise on its changes. Knowing that George Avakian wanted new tunes that the quartet hadn't recorded before no doubt focused Brubeck's mind; and "Tangerine" followed "Wonderful Copenhagen" and "Like Someone in Love" as fresh entries in the Brubeck discography.

From the very first note of "Tangerine," the mood was searching and inquisitive. Brubeck chose a tempo that made his musicians, Desmond in particular, think bigger than just the notes. Were they playing a ballad with a foot nudging the accelerator or an up-tempo tune running in slow motion—or both simultaneously? Morello (on brushes) and Wright phrased with the lightness of bubbles bursting, and Desmond played like he wanted everyone to know how much Johnny Mercer's theme amused him. In Berlin he had shaped his solo on "Take the 'A' Train" as a marbled network of interlinked episodes: new panels, fresh perspectives. But now, in Copenhagen, he took a single train of thought for a ten-chorus ride, injecting tension into the structure by bouncing and splicing his line between different octaves. Preparing the way for the mother of all octave leaps, Desmond left the idea dangling over a cliff—a gesture turned on its head later as the solo climaxed around a three-note falsetto yelp. Falsetto squeaks didn't merely jump the octave; they pushed sound outside the accepted frame of his instrument.

Brubeck's smiles were almost audible, his understated but omnipresent accompaniment drunk with enjoyment. As a counter to his saxophonist's note-y busyness, Brubeck's solo was spare and spread out. The hint of a line in straight, swinging 4/4 was, like Desmond's mother of all octave leaps, tossed over a cliff's edge as Brubeck departed rhythmically from the rhythm section and the thrill of dislocated continuity took hold. Single notes were swatted at. Smashed-up hunks of melody were chewed over and squished into crumpled, ragged tremolos. Brubeck dragged phrases ever tauter over bar lines until they snapped, stretching time with a subtlety beyond even his landmark "Little Girl Blue" solo from *Jazz: Red Hot and Cool* three years earlier.

In a solo designed, in part, as a riposte to Desmond, Brubeck's sign-off—a neat, in-time tremolo that obeyed the underlying tonality—matched the conceptual thinking behind Desmond's squeak, a desire to reclaim logic by turning the anti-logic upside down. Another contribution to the performance was made by the rapt attention of the audience, who sensed that if they missed a single note, they'd live to regret it.

Even for a musician of Brubeck's stature working under the auspices of the US government, travel through Eastern Europe was not immune from the deadweight of bureaucracy. An oversight at the State Department left the quartet without the necessary transit visas for crossing the border into Poland. Then someone on the ground came up with an audacious plan: if Brubeck was prepared to be smuggled into the Communist sector of Berlin, he could collect all the required paperwork in person. As he crouched behind the back seat of a car, stories of Westerners who had been "disappeared" in East Germany replayed through his mind as signs forbidding entry raced past the vehicle. The car stopped next to a soulless, vast municipal building, and Brubeck was herded into a waiting room where, nerves almost getting the better of him, he waited for two hours. Then a scruffily dressed official came into the room looking for a "Mister Kulu." "But I'm Mr. Brubeck" came the panicked response. The official pointed at his copy of a Polish newspaper, with its photograph of Brubeck and the headline

Dave Brubeck (far left, standing), aged 17, August 1937, at Ione CA Union High School. The caption on the original photo tells us that Brubeck had been elected "Treasurer Student Body." *Photo never before published.*

The Dave Brubeck Trio, c. 1949, with Cal Tjader on drums.

*(Facing page)* The Dave Brubeck Quartet—with Paul Desmond, Ron Crotty, Joe Dodge—on campus, location unknown, c. 1954.

*(Facing page)* The Dave Brubeck Quartet—with Paul Desmond, Norman Bates, Joe Dodge—1956.

*(Above)* A flyer issued by Fantasy Records in 1953, advertising *Jazz at Storyville* and *Jazz at Oberlin*. Artwork by Arnold Roth.

*(Left)* Official tour program book: the Duke Ellington Orchestra and the Dave Brubeck Quartet, with Stan Getz and Gerry Mulligan, 1954.

## Associated Booking Corp.

| 8619 SUNSET BOULEVARD | 745 FIFTH AVENUE | 203 NORTH WABASH AVE. |
| HOLLYWOOD 46, CALIF. | NEW YORK 22, N. Y. | CHICAGO, ILL. |
| *Phone* Crestview 1-8131 | *Phone* PLaza 9-4600 | *Phone* Central 6-9451 |

FROM CHICAGO OFFICE

December 23, 1954

Mr. David Booker
2203 Park Avenue
Kansas City, Missouri

Dear Mr. Booker:

The FOUR TUNES are available for you January 14, 15 and 16. Would
you be interested in playing them in Omaha, Topeka, Kansas City or
Wichita?

The fabulous DAVE BRUBECK QUARTET is available for you Saturday,
February 26 and also Sunday, March 27.

LOUIS ARMSTRONG AND HIS FAMOUS ALL-STARS are available for you
Sunday, March 13 for either a concert of dance or combination of
both.

Hope that I may hear from you and with all best wishes for the Holiday
Season, I remain

Sincerely yours,

Paul Bannister
ASSOCIATED BOOKING CORP.

PB:jmr

A letter from Joe Glaser's Associated Booking Corp., dated December 23,
1954, offering dates for the Dave Brubeck Quartet and Louis Armstrong
and His All-Stars, and autographed by both artists.

The Dave Brubeck Quartet in the studio, taken during the *Gone with the Wind* sessions, April 1959, Los Angeles. *Photos never before published.*

The Dave Brubeck Quartet in the studio, taken during the
*Gone with the Wind* sessions, April 1959, Los Angeles.
*Photos never before published.*

A characteristic
shot of Dave
admiring a phrase
coming from Paul's
horn. The Dave
Brubeck Quartet,
Wisconsin Club,
Milwaukee,
August 1961.

Dave Brubeck,
Willis Conover,
Leonard Feather.
May 1960 in
Baltimore.

Dave Brubeck receives a traditional Maori greeting after arriving in New Zealand, 1963.

Dave Brubeck poses at home, mid-1960s.

Dave Brubeck and Count Basie, 1970s.

Dave Brubeck, Joe Morello, Dizzy Gillespie, c. 1959.

Dave Brubeck and Louis Armstrong eating lunch during *The Real Ambassadors* sessions, 1961, Columbia 30th Street Studios, New York City.

A new quartet—Dave Brubeck and Gerry Mulligan, c. 1968.

We're all together again for the first time—Dave Brubeck,
Gerry Mulligan, Paul Desmond, 1971, Boston.

The New Brubeck
Quartet, 1970s.
*Photos never
before published.*

The New Brubeck Quartet with Iola Brubeck, 1976, Houston.
*Photo never before published.*

Three generations of Brubeck reedsmen—Perry Robinson,
Paul Desmond, and, in the background, Jerry Bergonzi, c. 1973.

The mid-1980s quartet—a bearded Brubeck with Bill Smith,
Chris Brubeck, and Randy Jones.

The final quartet—
with Bobby Militello, Michael Moore, and Randy Jones, 2005.

"Mr. Cool Jazz." For once in his life, Brubeck didn't quibble about being categorized as a "cool school" jazz musician, grabbed the papers, and beat a hasty exit.

Poland, in the dead of winter 1958, truly put the "cold" in "Cold War," especially for Americans acclimated to the California sunshine. Iola, with sons Darius and Michael, then aged ten and eight,[34] joined Dave and the quartet for this part of the tour, and photographs show the family swaddled in their thick winter coats. The Brubecks spent twelve days in Poland, playing concerts in Szczecin, Gdańsk, Warsaw, Wrocław, Kraków, Łódź, and Poznań, and also immersing themselves in local culture and politics. Darius's scrupulously written and colorful travel journal, alarmingly astute for a ten-year-old—"Some people seem to forget that not all Poles are Communists, but have it imposed upon them"[35]—teleports us far inside the atmospheric sights and sounds of late 1950s Communist Poland.

Young Darius's descriptions, like the mists in a Sherlock Holmes story, are permeated with cold. Arriving at their hotel in Gdańsk, the icy stone floor felt like "cold cucumbers" under their feet; the hotel in Kraków had no central heating, and maids kept a large stove, positioned in the center of their suite, stoked with coal. As the Brubecks traveled, Darius and Michael took bets on how long it would be before their dilapidated bus broke down (two days). On the trains that transported them between big cities, the sounds of soldiers shouting, their rifles clanking against the ground, was something completely alien. Perhaps officials kept running into the Brubecks' railcar and staring, Darius speculated, because they hadn't seen Americans before. The travel cases into which Morello had packed

---

34. Michael celebrated his ninth birthday in Poland; Darius gifted him a chess set.

35. Audio recordings of Iola reading Darius's journal are available from the University of the Pacific. Darius Brubeck's Travel Journal, Jazz Diplomacy Tour 1958, Brubeck Collection, Holt-Atherton Special Collections, University of the Pacific, https://scholarlycommons.pacific.edu/jdttj/.

his drum kit were frisked on the train to Szczecin in case they contained a bomb. And all around them, buildings crippled during the war acted as silent reminders of recent history.

The morning after their arrival in Poland, over breakfast in their hotel, Iola and Michael had a chance meeting with Roman Waschko, who, as president of the Polish Jazz Federation, would be responsible for emceeing the quartet at some of their concerts. But Waschko's enthusiasm for Brubeck's music, which he had first heard during Willis Conover's *Voice of America Jazz Hour* broadcasts, far outstripped his official duties, and he considered himself very fortunate indeed to be chaperoning the quartet during their stay.[36] Waschko—and their official guide, Adam—quickly became like part of the family, Darius wrote, and the conversation about music flowed. During one of two concerts in Szczecin, Waschko encouraged Darius and Michael, who had been watching the performance from the wings, to join the quartet onstage as they were about to play "Take the 'A' Train." Michael animatedly pounded out a rhythm on the drums as Morello gently guided him. Darius sat on the piano stool next to his startled father, who told his son, "Play the melody, stupid!" This first live meeting in concert of two generations of Brubecks "didn't sound too bad," Darius concluded.

In Gdańsk, the Brubecks spent a convivial evening at the home of a local musician. Food and drink were served, and the evening ended with their host playing music by Frédéric Chopin on his piano. Brubeck was captivated by the sophistication and grandeur of Chopin's harmonic thinking and by how that ambition saturated the keyboard with brilliant musical invention. Darius noted in his journal that the rebuilding of monuments to musicians, poets, and artists had often been

---

36. Willis Conover, Music USA #1664-B, Interview with Roman Waschko (audio recording), Music Library Conover Collection, University of North Texas Music Library, https://digital.library.unt.edu/ark:/67531/metadc824278/m1/#track/7.

prioritized over housing in a country still recovering from the devastation of war—culture mattered in Poland. After visiting the Chopin Museum in the composer's birthplace of Żelazowa Wola, near Łódź, where Chopin's pianos and death mask were on display, Brubeck poured his thoughts about Poland onto manuscript paper. Sitting on the train to Poznań, he composed a musical thank-you for all the warm hospitality his family had received—a composition that highlighted numerous points of connection with Chopin's approach to composing for the piano and jazz.

Brubeck called it "Dziekuje," the Polish word for "thank you," and the piece would appear for the first time on the album *Jazz Impressions of Eurasia*, recorded soon after the quartet returned to the US. Such was its emotional potency that Brubeck would return to it often. In 1973 a solo version rounded off the first album on Atlantic Records by Two Generations of Brubeck; in 1984 a blissful, beatific solo reenvisaging was included on the quartet album *For Iola*; and in 2011, approaching his ninety-first birthday, Brubeck performed it again during a guest appearance with Triple Play, the jazz-blues-folk group led by his son Chris.[37] Reducing the piece down to its harmonic essentials— with bitonal detours injecting the structure with tension and ending in a mist of swirling arpeggios—Brubeck's fingers overrode the frailties of advanced old age evident elsewhere on the album. This would be his final recorded performance, and "Dziekuje" communicated like a sacred work.

When, in 1960, Brubeck published sheet music from *Jazz Impressions of Eurasia* under the title *Themes from Eurasia*, in an introductory note he listed the "typical Chopin devices" he had utilized: "arpeggiated chords in the left hand, and large strong leaps of melody, followed by a descending step-like motion in the left hand." Those compositional devices alone would not be enough to guarantee anyone music that

---

37. Blue Forest Records 11003, 2011.

summoned up the true spirit of Chopin, but, as in "History of a Boy Scout" and "Plain Song," Brubeck had organized every aspect of "Dziekuje" meticulously. Its opening melodic cell spelled out an octave leap that shadowed the spoken inflection of the word *dziekuje*. An answering motif distorted this octave with a melodic sigh that suggested yearning and not a little pain, before this first phrase ended with a chromatic tailpiece that implanted a hopeful major interval into the minor harmony. The middle section sat on the keyboard like a hymnal chorale: full-bodied chords in the right hand interlocking with pungent patterns in the bass.

Although an internal conversation between jazz and classical composition was never far from Brubeck's thoughts, the issue was reignited by an incident that occurred a couple of weeks before the quartet left for Europe. Willis Conover's Voice of America radio station, broadcasting to audiences overseas, approached Brubeck, via Associated Booking, to propose making a promotional film to be screened in the countries the quartet was to visit. John Foster Dulles had made Brubeck's background in classical music such a vital part of his initial pitch to foreign embassies in 1957 that the VOA thought it fitting that he should play "one classical number." Brubeck smarted at the thought. "[I] hope you have not given [a] false impression to [the] State Department. I cannot play classical piano," he replied in a swiftly written telegram addressed to Frances Church, another member of Joe Glaser's team.[38] In the event, the film was scrapped; the quartet's touring schedule made the logistics impossible. But this misunderstanding, by refocusing Brubeck's mind on his relationship with classical repertoire, perhaps helped pave the way for "Dziekuje."

Dulles, certainly no great thinker about music himself, had let a fundamental truth about Brubeck's art pass him by. His

38. Dave Brubeck to Frances Church, telegram, January 27, 1958, Business Correspondence, Brubeck Collection.

identity as a jazz musician was not a persona he could step outside of to perform a classical piece, even on a tour predicated on the benefits of exchanging cultural ideas. Jazz and classical music informed each other in his work, and during the quartet's final concerts in Poland, Brubeck demonstrated exactly how heady the exchange between these two traditions could be. Without time for rehearsal, Brubeck handed Desmond and Wright a lead sheet (a sketch of the melodic line and chord sequence) of his new piece, and that night in Poznań the quartet performed "Dziekuje" as an encore. Following Brubeck's visit to the Chopin Museum, Poland's national composer had penetrated far into Brubeck's soul, and the cat's cradle of arpeggios with which he accompanied his theme conjured up the restless, searching quality of Chopin's own harmonic language, typified by the famous Polonaise in A-flat Major or his Mazurkas, Op. 33. Desmond's solo cruised leisurely around the chromatic landmarks of Brubeck's theme—standing back to take a look and then zeroing in on especially alluring details—and then Brubeck's solo spaced the arpeggiated figures he had outlined at the beginning around the keyboard, building hybrid tonalities and ending with high-speed flurries to the top of the piano.

When it was over, the quartet was met with roaring silence. "I thought I had insulted the audience by linking the memory of Chopin to jazz," Brubeck wrote in the sleeve notes for *Jazz Impressions of Eurasia.* But then applause rained down from all corners of the hall. More than had he performed an actual piece of Chopin, Brubeck had refracted something of Polish culture through his own experience, and handed this audience a gift in sound—which moved them profoundly. The next day, as Brubeck's party left Warsaw, Roman Waschko gave Darius and Michael Easter eggs and sprinted after the train as it departed the platform, shouting, "Dziekuje!" Tears filled everybody's eyes.

In a letter addressed to "Iola, Dave, Dari and Mike," dated October 14, 1959, Waschko needed Brubeck to know about the transformational significance of the quartet's visit on Polish jazz. "You certainly know that your visit to Poland was the most important event in the history w[ith] our jazz movement here," he explained.[39] And "movement" was no accidental word choice. Until the "Polish October" of 1956, during which the Soviet Union under Nikita Khrushchev, reluctantly at first, had backed a new and less draconian government led by Władysław Gomułka, jazz had been considered to be the very definition of Western decadence: reactionary and imperialist. Poland's first major jazz festival took place in August 1956, in Sopot, which hinted at the thaw that was about to follow. But new records were all but impossible to acquire officially and jazz LPs smuggled into the country were precious indeed; and only the most determined Polish jazz fans could hear the music live.

Founded in 1951 by jazz-loving students from the National Film School in Łódź, Hot Club Melomani dished up a Dixieland style broadly comparable with British trad bands of the mid-1950s led by Humphrey Lyttelton, Ken Colyer, and Chris Barber. Their concerts, at first few and far between, would proceed only if the police charged with licensing live music failed to recognize their music as jazz—or were prepared to have their silence bought with hard cash or a glass of vodka. By the time Brubeck arrived in Poland, Melomani had disbanded: now that jazz bands were officially allowed and were engaging with more contemporary styles, film students attempting to play the music of Sidney Bechet and Jelly Roll Morton did not feel like such an enticing prospect. Younger Polish musicians, most notably the pianist Krzysztof Komeda, were thinking through the consequences of bebop and the West Coast jazz of musicians like Brubeck and Gerry Mulligan. Despite the more relaxed attitude of the new government, playing jazz still remained tinged

---

39. Roman Waschko to Iola Brubeck et al., October 14, 1959, Personal Correspondence, Brubeck Collection.

with cultural rebellion—and Polish jazz musicians considered themselves part of a "movement," both musical and political.

In his letter to Brubeck, Roman Waschko also talked about the "great thrill" of Willis Conover's visit to Poland in June 1959, during which Voice of America had recorded five hours' worth of Polish jazz for broadcast. Conover also interviewed Waschko for the same program, and the two men discussed the roots of Polish jazz and its future. Echoing the sentiments of his letter to Brubeck, Waschko called the quartet's visit "the greatest event in our jazz life [because] it was the first meeting with jazz musicians of such great [quality]."[40] He recalled an earlier visit from a band led by the former Glenn Miller drummer Ray McKinley—"Some would argue this is not jazz at all," he laughed mischievously. But Brubeck's visit, he argued, exemplified the necessity of contact with good musicians. "Listening to all our jazz bands, [there is the] influence of Brubeck," he explained.

Krzysztof Komeda had played in one of the final incarnations of Melomani before founding a sextet of his own that played music with an airy, folksy flavor that borrowed generously from the Modern Jazz Quartet and influences from West Coast jazz; in 1962 he reached a wider audience by scoring his first film for Roman Polanski, *Knife in the Water*, which led the two men to collaborate on *Cul-de-Sac*, *The Fearless Vampire Killers*, and *Rosemary's Baby*. As the Brubecks traveled through Poland by train, they noticed some of the same faces appearing at every port of call. Komeda and his wife Sofia attended all twelve concerts; other soon-to-be-prominent local jazz musicians who heard the quartet included the singer Wanda Warska, trumpeter Tomasz Stańko, and multi-instrumentalist and composer Andrzej Kurylewicz. Such was the devotion of the drummer Andrzej Dąbrowski to

40. Willis Conover, Music USA #1664-B, Interview with Roman Waschko (audio recording), Music Library Conover Collection, University of North Texas Music Library, https://digital.library.unt.edu/ark:/67531/metadc824278/.

Joe Morello that he earned himself the nickname "Mollerick," and Waschko even confessed, talking to Conover, that sometimes "the influence is too great—almost all modern musicians here [are in the] Brubeck convention."

Komeda kept in touch with the Brubecks, and the warmth of their letters is touching. "Our thoughts return many times to Krakow in the snow," Iola replied to Komeda in October 1959.[41]

> It is a beautiful city, with an atmosphere and personality of its own. I remember so well, you and Sofia, when you would surprise us by turning up in a different city. I wished that I could sketch, because the day that we had the long train ride, and Sofia slept with her head on your shoulder all the way to— where was it?—Poznan?—I thought this was a picture to capture forever. . . . It was on this same train trip that "Djiekuye" [*sic*] was jotted down. I remember Dave showing me the theme and whistling it to me. It is still one of my favorite pieces.

In 1970, when Brubeck returned to Poland to play that year's Jazz Jamboree with Gerry Mulligan, the Polish jazz community was still in mourning and reeling from the shock of Komeda's sudden death at age thirty-seven, the result of an injury sustained at a drunken party in Los Angeles the year before. Brubeck's new group rekindled the spirit of '58 by sharing the bill with Andrzej Kurylewicz's Contemporary Music Foundation, with Wanda Warska on vocals,[42] and the bond between Brubeck and his Polish friends would continue to burn bright. When the Darius Brubeck Quartet toured Poland in November 2018 to mark the sixtieth anniversary of the 1958 tour, during their

---

41. Iola Brubeck to Krzysztof Komeda, October 7, 1959, Personal Correspondence, Brubeck Collection.

42. Two pieces by the Brubeck group—"Jumpin' Bean" and "St. Louis Blues"—and three tracks by Andrzej Kurylewicz's Contemporary Music Foundation and Wanda Warska were released on the Polish label Polskie Nagrania Muza (SXL 0696) in 1970.

concert in Szczecin Darius was introduced to an elderly lady who remembered this now-seventy-one-year-old pianist scrabbling up onstage, aged ten, to play "Take the 'A' Train" with his father's quartet.

The Brubecks flew into Turkey via East Berlin. There were concerts in Izmir, Ankara, and Istanbul to play, and, as in Poland, the city's jazz musicians were keen to make contact and then hang out with their American visitors. In Ankara, the quartet was announced to the audience in a local jazz club, and an inevitable, and lengthy, jam session ensued. Desmond had left his horn at the hotel, but Brubeck, Wright, and Morello played, and Brubeck invited his new friends—a Turkish bassist, French horn player, French drummer, and Italian guitarist—to join the quartet the next night for their concert, which picked up from the previous night with a jam session finale, the tune of choice "All the Things You Are."

Istanbul's urban bustle, Darius wrote in his journal, reminded him of San Francisco "in the old days": San Francisco, perched on the Pacific Ocean, was a Western city geographically placed to absorb influences from the East. Istanbul defined itself by being divided between Europe and Asia: its historical center was on the European side, which was separated from the Asian part of the city by the Bosporus Strait. As they disembarked the airplane at Istanbul Airport, the crackle of a hi-hat cymbal alerted them to a welcoming committee of city jazz musicians playing Brubeck's arrangement of "Tea for Two." Their guide was a local musician called June Eight—styled after the day he was born—who took them to a mosque and to the Grand Bazaar, which the Brubecks returned to the next day to buy presents for family back at home. At Istanbul Radio, Darius recalled being impressed with the setup of the radio orchestra, which included a steel clarinet, something that looked like a zither, and an instrument that was bowed between the knees and closely resembled the human voice. The rhythm section included kettledrums, an instrument that looked like a tabla, and some tambourines, and the Brubecks heard a solo-ist improvising over a rhythmic carpet provided by the rest of the orchestra. Darius noted that the effect was like a concerto, but also "close to jazz." He also mentioned that the orchestra played in other more difficult rhythms—"like 9/8."

Although Darius didn't elaborate, this was not the equally proportioned 3+3+3 familiar from Western music of the baroque and classical eras; this 9/8 was divided 2+2+2+3. The oft-told story of Brubeck hearing this rhythm on an Istanbul street, taking a moment to rationalize what he had heard in terms of Western notation, and then asking the local radio orchestra to explain its origins, skirts over the cultural com-plexities. For Brubeck, who appreciated Milhaud, Debussy, Stravinsky, and Bartók, the *concept* of dividing up rhythms asym-metrically was not new; but the *actuality* of hearing a group of musicians who had internalized an asymmetrical rhythm to the point that it sounded innate and spontaneous was a new experience. June Eight explained that this rhythm, which Bru-beck perceived in 9/8, was as intrinsic to Turkish folk music as the blues was to America—and he asked the radio orchestra to demonstrate the point. Although Brubeck didn't respond immediately with a new composition, as he had with "Dziekuje" in Poland, he stored this information away—and a year later it handed him the basis of his greatest composition, "Blue Rondo à la Turk."

Iola, Darius, and Michael returned to the US after the quar-tet's final concert in Istanbul, on March 28, with a suitcase full of presents bought from the Grand Bazaar for the other chil-dren, Chris, Dan, and Cathy; another six long weeks would pass before Dave safely returned home. Next on the quartet's sched-ule was India—with concerts in Rajkot, Bombay, Delhi, Hyder-abad, and Madras—and with the mercury rising, Brubeck made good use of the lightweight suit he had bought from a tailor's shop in Istanbul.

And once again, the quartet discovered a community of musicians wowed by the prospect of hearing Brubeck live and eager to find points of affinity between their music and a modern jazz group. A review published in the *Hindustan Times* of the quartet's April 8 concert at the University Gardens in Delhi gave an inkling of the unprecedented nature of what local audiences had heard. "New ground was broken in the field of Western music concerts in Delhi on Tuesday," an uncredited reporter wrote, "when the Delhi University Music Society . . . presented for nearly two hours a delightful jazz concert by the celebrated US group, the Dave Brubeck Quartet. The concert, first of its kind in Delhi, was held . . . in the Delhi University gardens on an improvised platform in the open and was attended by thousands."

The writer from the *Times of India* used Indian classical music as a model to explain what he had heard the Brubeck Quartet play:

> We Indians are familiar with the usage that allows each artist to display his skill vis-à-vis the particular music being performed. Placing Brubeck as the principal artist, the pattern ran true to Indian type. Each artist showed his paces within the limitations of rhythm or music, and the instrumentalists each improvised on the fixed theme or fragment. The pianist was, of course, outstanding. The alto saxophonist has all the sax appeal (pardon me!) that he needs. The contrabassist is astonishing[ly] good and the drummer is nearly as good as some of our best Indian mridangists and tabalchis. That, believe me, is praise worth giving.[43]

---

43. These reviews were included in a digest of press reports and clippings forwarded to the Brubecks (with the heading "Re: Dave Brubeck Jazz Quartet in India") by the American embassy in New Delhi on June 6, 1958. Promotional Material, Brubeck Collection.

Having played their final concert in India the previous evening, on April 12, the quartet accepted an invitation from the local radio station in Madras to discuss music and improvise with Indian classical musicians, including one of the country's greatest virtuoso mridangam players, Palani Subramania Pillai.

Subramania Pillai opened proceedings with a long and elaborate solo that utilized the mridangam—a cylindrical double-sided drum—to juggle polyrhythmic patterns between his hands, which he coordinated against the bending and sliding of notes as he pressed down on the skins of his drum. As Brubeck and Morello, their ears suitably dazzled, prepared to play with Subramania Pillai, there was an unmistakable air of excited anticipation. The two percussionists set a ferocious tempo, Morello answering Subramania Pillai's percussive jabs and scrapes by firing rhythms back, his sticks ricocheting against the wooden rims of his drums. Having already learned the significance of 2+2+2+3 for the Turkish psyche, Brubeck wanted to test how compatible the blues and Indian music could be, and the improvisation soon turned into a blues. The opening of his solo was drowned out on the recording by Morello and Subramania Pillai's sweet thunder, but Brubeck's piano suddenly zoomed into focus and his light-touch, spidery lines steamrolled toward orotund block chords.

A photograph taken that evening shows Subramania Pillai sitting cross-legged on the floor with his mridangam balanced on his lap and Morello perched behind his kit; Paul Desmond sits in the background with his hands leaning on his saxophone case. The camera catches Morello and Subramania Pillai staring at each other intently, quizzically even, their deep musical communion obvious. Their improvisation began by trading phrases, and then they fashioned a unified maelstrom of sound, a labyrinth of spontaneous cross-rhythms that continually changed direction and shape. In Bombay, a week earlier, the quartet had improvised with the sitar master Abdul

Halim Jaffer Khan at the luxurious home of businessman Pra-
lhad Mehta, and both experiences made a profound impact
on the quartet, Brubeck and Morello in particular. Morello's
enthusiasm for hand drumming—displayed proudly during his
famous solo on "Castilian Drums" at Carnegie Hall in 1963[44]—
can be traced back to his meeting with Subramania Pillai.

Brubeck's own initial thoughts about Indian music found a
musical form on *Jazz Impressions of Eurasia* under the title "Calcutta Blues," a composition that learned from the motionless
harmonies typical of Indian music by abandoning chords in
favor of improvising around scales over static, drone-like bass
patterns. In the longer term, these experiences in India were
to have a profound impact on his spiritual growth. In Poland,
Turkey, and now India, Brubeck had discovered that there was
as much that unified musical cultures as divided them. The
scales and melodies of Turkish or Indian music had a gram-
mar of their own, but that didn't prevent a mutual understanding among jazz musicians—and rhythm was the common
denominator.

His hunch, when he heard *The Belgian Congo Records of the
Denis-Roosevelt Expedition* LP in the early 1950s, that rhythm
operated under different rules in cultures outside Western
notated music—that rhythm didn't need to be neatly contained inside symmetrical bars and, like fire, could find its own
form through improvisation—had been vindicated by his trip
to India. Three years later, interviewed by Walter Cronkite on
his CBS television program *The Twentieth Century*, he declared,
"What I did learn on [the 1958] tour [is] that rhythm is an
international language, not harmony and melody but rhythm.
Maybe the thing that binds humanity together is the heartbeat.
It's the first thing you hear—even before you're born, you
hear your mother's heartbeat—a steady pulse. You know, it's

44. Columbia, C2S 826, 1963.

the last thing you hear before you die."[45] Whenever Brubeck was faced with the agonizing reality of segregation and was told by concert promoters back in the US that Eugene Wright was not welcome to play, his belief that sound and rhythm bound humanity together helped fortify him. And the journey toward those multifaith, multicultural, large-scale oratorios he wrote during the late 1960s—*The Light in the Wilderness* and *The Gates of Justice*—started here.

After India and five weeks on the road, fatigue and illness began to take their toll. Desmond succumbed to a bug in Calcutta and missed the quartet's next concert two days later in Dacca, Bangladesh. He struggled through three concerts in Karachi, West Pakistan, and spent the next two nights in the hospital as Brubeck, Wright, and Morello played as a trio in Kabul, Afghanistan, and then traveled onward to Iran and Iraq, where they played the final concert of the tour at the Khàyyam Theatre in Baghdad. The enforced time off allowed Desmond to convalesce and also resolved the pressing problem that his Jewish heritage, which he had declared on his visa, restricted his passage through Islamic countries.

In Baghdad, Brubeck himself was sickening with the first signs of dysentery, which would be diagnosed once he returned to the US, and Iraq did not feel like an especially safe place to be. The stirrings of the 14 July Revolution—which established the Republic of Iraq by overthrowing the monarchy—were being felt, and barely forty-eight hours after Brubeck, Wright, and Morello checked out of their hotel, the building was attacked, killing many innocent civilians and tourists. But still the State Department insisted that Brubeck extend the tour, and later it emerged that John Foster Dulles had been unilaterally canceling the quartet's US engagements by writing

---

45. Dave Brubeck, interview with Walter Cronkite, *The Twentieth Century*, CBS, December 31, 1961.

ahead to universities and other venues. Southern Methodist University in Dallas eventually called Dulles's bluff. They had a contract with Dave Brubeck, and they fully expected that his quartet would show up as planned on May 17, or else. So an exhausted and emaciated Brubeck flew home. He had an engagement to keep.[46]

---

46. Brubeck was asked to undertake another State Department tour, this time to Brazil, in 1961, two years after the revolution that brought Fidel Castro to power. His existing performing schedule clashed with the proposed dates, and guitarist Charlie Byrd went instead.

# Chapter Seven

# TIMEQUAKE

"A plausible mission of artists is to make people appreciate being alive at least a little bit."

KURT VONNEGUT, *Timequake*, 1997

Having touched down at Idlewild Airport, Brubeck sought sanctuary and a week of much-needed rest and recuperation in a New York hotel room. Iola flew in from Oakland and wrote to Roman Waschko that Dave was spending healing time in bed to recover his strength and vitality. Apart from meals and the occasional stroll, he got up "only to take care of necessary business."[1]

And there was much "necessary business" to think about. From May 17, when Brubeck reunited with Desmond, Wright, and Morello to perform at Southern Methodist University in

---

1. Iola Brubeck to Roman Waschko, June 5, 1958, Personal Correspondence, Brubeck Collection.

Dallas, the quartet would be back on the (American) road, and there was also music to be written for their new album. *Jazz Impressions of Eurasia* would follow on from the broad concept of *Jazz Impressions of the USA* while setting a template for two further "impressions" albums, *Jazz Impressions of Japan* and *Jazz Impressions of New York*, both recorded in 1964. Dealing now with cultures not his own and wary of being categorized as a musical tourist pilfering sounds from traditions that he didn't fully comprehend, Brubeck made his aims and objectives clear in his sleeve note: "These sketches of Eurasia have been developed from random musical phrases I jotted down in my notebook as we chugged across the deserts of Asia, or walked in the winding alleys of an ancient bazaar. I did not approach the writing of this album with the exactness of a musicologist. Instead, as the title implies, I tried to create an *impression* of a particular locale by using some of the elements of their folk music within the jazz idiom." Around "Dziekuje," which opened side two, Brubeck plotted a musical journey based on his experiences in Kabul, Berlin, the Bosporous Strait in Istanbul, London, and Calcutta.

With the new album forming in his head, Brubeck was also being obliged to think through the significance, musical and cultural, of his tour for an article that would be published in the *New York Times Magazine* under the title "The Beat Heard 'Round the World." The piece was ghostwritten by Gilbert Millstein, a forty-three-year-old journalist who worked the Sunday edition of the newspaper and whose admiring review of Jack Kerouac's novel *On the Road*, published on September 7, 1957, had helped seal the author's reputation. His extended interview with Dave and Iola in their hotel done, Millstein edited himself out of the conversation and then wrote up the article, which the Brubecks eventually approved for publication. But the *Times*, recognizing the value of a byline "by Dave Brubeck," rejected their request that it be published as "by Dave Brubeck as told to Gilbert Millstein."

With the subhead "Jazz, says a well-known music man, is an American export with an international appeal, making friends wherever it goes," this new article was published eight years after Brubeck's speculative two-part "Jazz's Evolvement as Art Form" piece for *DownBeat*. His theories about jazz, folk music, and improvisation had been tested in the field, and now he spoke with the weight of experience. His opening statement mirrored exactly Adam Clayton Powell Jr.'s belief that jazz, as a working model for American democracy, could better represent America abroad than classical music:

> Jazz, our single native art form, is welcomed—not simply accepted—without reservation throughout the world and is felt to be the most authentic example of American culture. It would be fatuous of me to pretend to correlate its importance with the billions of dollars we have spent in restoring nations ravaged by war and in raising the living standards of underdeveloped countries, or the day-to-day spadework of statesmen and diplomats. But there is no mistaking its effect: it arouses a kinship among peoples; it affords them flashes of recognition of common origins, because of its basic relationship to folk idioms; and the forthrightness and directness of its appeal are grasped alike by the naïve and the sophisticated.[2]

Soon-to-be-familiar interview tropes, including the first mainstream print mention of a quote that would follow him around for decades to come, were introduced: "Somewhere in a set of program notes I wrote this sentence. 'I think of an audience as a co-creator, the fifth instrument in our quartet. How an audience chooses to play its part is determined anew each time musicians and listeners gather together.'" That a jazz group depended upon its audience was observably true: "Tangerine,"

---

2. Dave Brubeck, "The Beat Heard 'Round the World," *New York Times Magazine*, June 15, 1958.

from *The Dave Brubeck Quartet in Europe*, was an example of what could happen when an audience listened and concentrated as intently as the musicians. Against the background of the 1958 tour and the ideas Brubeck was expressing to Gilbert Millstein about the universality of jazz, this "fifth instrument" ideal began to assume global dimensions, like a hint of the global village four or five years before Marshall McLuhan.[3]

Jazz symbolized unity, Brubeck said, "and uninhibited, if sometimes wordless, communication. . . . Sources [of jazz] are world-wide—African, European, Asian, American—and therefore may be understood almost instantly, whether by a provincial group of Indians 500 miles inland from Bombay or a cosmopolitan audience in West Berlin." It followed, therefore, that the politics of segregation was an obvious abomination: "There are three white men in our quartet and Gene Wright is a Negro. . . . Jazz is color blind. When a German or a Pole or an Iraqi or an Indian sees American white men and colored[4] in perfect creative accord, when he finds out that they travel together, eat together, live together and think pretty much alike, socially and musically, a lot of the bad taste of Little Rock is apt to be washed from his mouth."

A trauma the scale of Little Rock being exorcised by jazz alone seems a little far-fetched, but this was Brubeck at his most idealistic. Racism was inward looking and gorged on its own malice, paranoia, and hatred; but a creative pursuit like jazz looked outward and was entirely dependent upon collaborative dialogue—and people who looked outward into the world were not responsible for lynchings or denying children their right to go to school.

Jazz embodied a model of how America could do better:

---

3. McLuhan began discussing his idea of the global village in his 1962 book *The Gutenberg Galaxy: The Making of Typographic Man.*

4. The words *Negro* and *colored*, considered unacceptable today, were still in standard use during the late 1950s.

I am convinced—though it may be no more than the prejudice of the jazz musician—that the effect of jazz on people is more profound than our serious music[5] or art or literature, for the reason that it is being created at the very moment it is played before an audience. The one element common to all religions, we are told, is the act of creation. For man to be creative is to be godlike. Now, the form and notes of a symphony are fixed; pictures have already been painted; books already written . . . but jazz is another matter. Musically, by its very nature, it is the most creative, the freest and most democratic form of expression I know.

And it was no coincidence, Brubeck added, that "wherever there was dictatorship in Europe, jazz was outlawed. And whenever freedom returned to these countries, the playing of jazz inevitably accompanied it." Reaffirming in interviews the centrality of improvisation would become increasingly important to Brubeck, especially as criticism rained down from some quarters that his music was becoming sclerotic, typified by Whitney Balliett's complaint in the *New Yorker* in 1966 that the quartet had been "as safe as IBM for over a decade [because Brubeck] hasn't seen fit to experiment by adding new instruments and new blood."[6]

The source of the ideas about rhythm that Brubeck would discuss with Walter Cronkite on *The Twentieth Century* in 1961 also comes into focus here: "I remember something the philosopher Gerald Heard told me.[7] The first thing a man is aware of, he said, is the steady rhythm of his mother's heartbeat and the last thing he hears before he dies is his own. Rhythm is the

---

5. Brubeck is referring to modern classical music.

6. Whitney Balliett, "Jazz Concerts: Monterey Journal," *New Yorker*, October 1, 1966.

7. The Gerald Heard website—www.geraldheard.com—includes the following quote from Brubeck: "Gerald Heard had a brilliant mind . . . I can truly say he broadened my vision of religion and spirituality."

common bond of all humanity: it is also the most pronounced and readily misunderstood ingredient of jazz."

Before Brubeck could start work on *Jazz Impressions of Eurasia*—recorded over two sessions in July and one in August—and fulfill his other summer engagements, including an appearance at that year's Newport Jazz Festival, there was a personnel problem to resolve. Eugene Wright had been contracted to play with the singer Carmen McRae that summer, and Brubeck hired Joe Benjamin as a temporary replacement. New Jersey–born Benjamin's playing history echoed Wright's. He had worked with Fletcher Henderson and Artie Shaw early in his career and had spent 1957 playing with Duke Ellington's orchestra and with Gerry Mulligan, in Mulligan's regular quartet and on the album he recorded with Paul Desmond in August 1957, which became known later as *Blues in Time*.[8] Benjamin slotted right into the quartet, and, during a rehearsal at the Brubeck home in Oakland, he also became an instant hit with the Brubeck children: it was Benjamin who correctly identified the song "Manhattan" in a phone-in radio competition, which won free pizza for Darius, Michael, Chris, Dan, and Catherine.[9]

*Jazz Impressions of Eurasia* was recorded at the 30th Street Studio in New York, and as Brubeck brought his new bass player to the session, there was another major change with which to contend. After twelve years at Columbia, George Avakian had decided to jump ship and spent a few months with the small independent label Pacific Jazz before creating a record company for Warner Brothers, for whom he signed the Everly Brothers and Bill Haley. A and R skills like those would be

---

8. Released originally as *Gerry Mulligan—Paul Desmond Quartet* in late 1957 on the Verve label, the album was later reissued as *Blues in Time*.

9. Darius Brubeck, conversation with the author, January 2019.

sorely missed at Columbia, and his departure made a greater impact on Brubeck's records, as he moved into the 1960s and the superstardom that came with *Time Out,* than has often been recognized.

For now, Cal Lampley, Avakian's protégé at Columbia, did an admirable job on *Jazz Impressions of Eurasia.* Lampley's sympathies, like Avakian's, ranged across jazz, pop, and classical music, and he approached working with Brubeck by applying the mold established by Avakian. Brubeck and Desmond had license to stretch and Morello was featured heavily, leaving Joe Benjamin to nail down the beats and tricky rhythms. Whereas the brilliance of "Ode to a Cowboy," "Plain Song," and "History of a Boy Scout" had been let down by the below-par "Sounds of the Loop" and "Curtain Time" on *Jazz Impressions of the USA, Eurasia* was the best and most consistent Brubeck Quartet album since *Dave Digs Disney.*

Mirroring those thoughts about improvisation from his *New York Times Magazine* interview, Brubeck's sleeve note made a startling admission. "The heart of any musical work, jazz or classical, is not the theme itself, but the treatment and development of that theme. And the heart and developmental section of these jazz pieces are the improvised choruses," he wrote—striking words from a composer, especially one who, only a year later, would be committing such carefully crafted compositions as "Blue Rondo à la Turk," "Strange Meadow Lark," and "Three to Get Ready (And Four to Go)" to record. Brubeck was articulating a truth about his approach to composition that the process of making *Jazz Impressions of the USA* had clarified. Composing for improvisers had different, more exacting demands than writing for classical performers. Chord progressions must flow naturally, Brubeck said, and liberate the soloist rather than boxing them in. And clarity was everything: "Many melodies, which could have been developed into compositions if our music were completely *written,* have been discarded," he wrote, "because in these jazz impressions of Eurasia the improvisations by the soloists are comparable to the developmental section of a composed work."

Bound together tightly by the ultraprecision of Brubeck's compositions and the complex responses they stirred in his musicians, the six tracks of *Jazz Impressions of Eurasia* played out over forty minutes. "Dziekuje" was its emotional hub but had evolved since the quartet played it for the first time in Poznań. This piece rooted in Chopin now embraced a more overtly "classical" sound world that excluded Desmond altogether but embraced Joe Benjamin's skills (which Eugene Wright didn't share) at bowed bass. Benjamin was handed a dual role: keeping time through the placid swing of the middle section, and then using his bow to accompany the out-of-tempo conclusion. Brubeck ended his solo with a polytonal flourish that opened the structure out rather than locking it down. Laying arpeggios on thick, Brubeck recapped his theme as Benjamin's "arco" bass seesawed through the texture, spiraling around the rich chromaticism with an intense, throbbing tone that projected like a whole section of cellos.

"Nomad" and "The Golden Horn" were both introduced by another instrumental sound from outside the usual jazz palette: Morello skipping across his tom-toms using felt-covered timpani sticks to produce a springier, more resonant tone than the slap of sticks against drumheads. Both pieces exhibited the clarity upon which improvisers thrived. Brubeck's oddball solo on "Nomad"—a piece inspired by the sight of nomadic Turks riding through Kabul on camels, playing string drums to scare off feral dogs—relayed information like the negative of a photograph. With Morello busily maintaining time and Benjamin sprinting around the changes, when not stroking the occasional chord, Brubeck was inserting long blocks of silence over the hectic motion of his rhythm section. Gradually he filled those silences with short bursts of chordal activity that spilled in wavelike blocks over bass and drums and then melted back into the texture—before flowing back with increasing force.

Brubeck's solo ran concurrently against the rhythm section but refused to be framed by it.

Like "Dziekuje," "The Golden Horn" and "Brandenburg Gate" derived their melodic pattern from local words for "thank you." Brubeck wrote in the notes for the accompanying sheet music album *Themes from Eurasia* that "'Choc Teshejjur Ederim' says 'thank you very much' in Turkey, and spoken rapidly becomes the rhythmic pattern of 'The Golden Horn.'" The title was not a reference to Paul Desmond's saxophone, he explained, but to the "narrow inlet of the Bosporus called the Golden Horn that divides Istanbul." Noting that Istanbul was the bridge between Europe and Asia, Brubeck devised a theme that used "a modal-like theme characteristic of Turkey, along with Western harmony." "Brandenburg Gate"—scored around the shape of "danke schoen"—subsequently became the basis of a rather fussy set of variations, with orchestra, on the album *Brandenburg Gate: Revisited*; but the piece never worked better than on this first quartet outing. Desmond set the tone by intricately reconciling Bach and the blues with the chromatic side steps that walked Brubeck's theme outside the boundaries of a Bach chorale; Brubeck's own solo, duly inspired, balanced on that same tightrope before heading toward a two-part dialogue between piano and alto saxophone. The next track, "Marble Arch," offered some good-humored relief by recalling the pompous bustle typical of the English light music composer Eric Coates in its opening bars, although, as the piece developed, Brubeck's eloquent melodic questions served up something more fertile than "Curtain Time," its equivalent on *Jazz Impressions of the USA*.

The placing of "Calcutta Blues" as the final track reflected the significance of Brubeck's experiences in India: everything else led there. His composition, unerringly simple on the page, dealt head-on with the most profound lesson Indian music had to teach. Where jazz, and nearly all Western music, used harmonic sequences to give sound a narrative shape—its beginning, middle, and end—Indian musicians used harmony to occasion a state of meditative grace by freezing time. The composer Terry Riley, whose composition *In C* helped kick-start the minimalist revolution in 1964, once argued that "Western music is fast because it's not in tune." Although Western music *is* in tune on its own terms, Riley was questioning the validity of how that music is tuned, and his suggestion that the subtle nuances of Eastern tuning systems embraced a more considerate and moderate way of living was not just an argument about sound. The aggressive speed of the West was draining the planet of its resources, polluting the environment, and creating wars. Western tuning—in particular, bland equal temperament[10]—signified this tendency toward homogenization, which served commerce well, Riley thought, but was bad for art.

Although the nitty-gritty of sociopolitical arguments like Riley's feel far outside the remit of the quartet, "Calcutta Blues" was a thoughtful and deeply felt response to the techniques, rituals, and slower pace of Indian music. Just as "The Golden Horn" superimposed a modal theme characteristic of Turkey over Western harmony, "Calcutta Blues" worked a cyclic theme—an "impression" of an Indian raga—over the conventional blues changes; that evening in Madras in 1958, when he and Morello had improvised with Subramania Pillai, was clearly in Brubeck's mind as he conceived "Calcutta Blues." In the studio, the piece found its shape as an improvisation lasting ten minutes, which Brubeck and Cal Lampley agreed should run at length, without edits.

Mother India had seeped into the most fundamental parameters of Brubeck's composition. The note C, which Brubeck

---

10. Equal tempered tuning divides the octave so that each adjacent note is expressed with an identical mathematical ratio, which allows musicians to move between keys without provoking overtone interference, which in equal temperament–think would knock the music "out of tune." Composers like Terry Riley and Lou Harrison have raged against equal temperament, claiming that it imposes a one-size-fits-all tuning system on music that could be tuned with more subtlety.

sustained with his left hand from the very first bar—and to which Joe Benjamin's pattern always returned—remained steady as the expected harmonic patterning of a blues was carried in the melody line. The piece turned out to be another sensitively drawn composition in a minor key, with a trademark Brubeck melodic hook that was reminiscent of "Ode to a Cowboy." When the theme reached the middle of its arc, Brubeck marked the moment by introducing a major melodic interval into his minor theme—like a blue note in reverse.[11] As the theme passed to Desmond, Brubeck introduced the scurrying, hurrying motion that would form the basis of his own solo—and the paradox that the melodic entanglements of his lines, becoming ever busier and protracted, were built on harmony that moved nowhere. Morello used his hands to slap, caress, and warp the heads of his drums in his solo; rhythm being the common bond of all humanity, this brought the album to a symbolically fitting resolution.

As the quartet was preparing *Jazz Impressions of Eurasia*—two rehearsal sessions, on July 28 and 30, leading to a final recording on August 23—they had recently presented a very different side of their work to audiences at that year's Newport Jazz Festival. July 3, the festival's opening night, as introduced by Willis Conover, was dedicated to Duke Ellington. The Brubeck Quartet performed alongside an all-star band of former Ellington sidemen led by trumpeter Rex Stewart, the Marian McPartland Trio, Mahalia Jackson, the Miles Davis Sextet (featuring John Coltrane, Julian "Cannonball" Adderley, and Bill Evans), and Ellington's own orchestra. And amiable chaos ruled. Brubeck and Ellington were last-minute additions to the bill, their presence required by the Voice of America, which wanted exclusive material for broadcast. Miles, apparently, didn't get the memo about the Ellington dedication and played material from his regular set list instead, including Monk's "Straight No Chaser"

---

11. Blue notes normally add a minor interval into a major scale.

and Gillespie's "Two Bass Hit." The evening was also plagued by technical hitches, including balance problems and badly positioned microphones. Brubeck's extra set led to Ellington's slot being delayed until one thirty in the morning, at which time his exhausted band played to an equally spent audience. Columbia released the Ellington, Brubeck, and Mahalia Jackson material over three separate LPs, which they hoped would be bought as a set: the artist Bob Parker had been commissioned to illustrate each LP with a playfully sketched, Raoul Dufy–like watercolor and all three LPs were given the title *Newport 1958*.[12]

Or, to be more precise, Columbia was indulging its penchant for facadism. Technical problems, combined with player fatigue, had rendered most of the live Ellington material unusable, and his album was a remake of the same program in the studio, with Conover's announcements and audience ambience left in place. Brubeck fared better. Unlike Miles, he had honored the occasion by preparing a program of songs by or associated with Ellington. "Things Ain't What They Used to Be," "Jump for Joy," "Perdido," and "C Jam Blues" (which segued into the theme of "Take the 'A' Train" to sign off) were taken directly from Newport, and, as they were rehearsing *Jazz Impressions of Eurasia* on July 28, the quartet rerecorded "Flamingo," "Dance No. 3" from *Liberian Suite*, and "The Duke," which were not salvageable from the live tapes. Since George Avakian had mixed live and studio recordings on *Jazz: Red Hot and Cool* three years earlier, praying that nobody would notice the join, Columbia had become more expert at covering their tracks: Brubeck's *Newport 1958* was passed off convincingly, from beginning to end, as "live."

As an antidote to rehearsing six challenging new compositions, *Newport 1958* basked in a party atmosphere and recalled something of the blithe spirit of old Fantasy dates like *Jazz at Oberlin* and *Jazz at the College of the Pacific*, when the tapes were

---

12. The Miles Davis performance wasn't issued until 2001.

kept rolling. "Things Ain't What They Used to Be" was the funkiest, dirtiest blues the quartet had recorded to date. Brubeck's high-energy solo riffed off the moxie of Harlem stride piano and landed blows with gargantuan polytonal chords that sounded bigger than his hands; Desmond's solo, unusually earthy, incorporated an uncanny impersonation of Ellington's star saxophonist Johnny Hodges. The finger-snapping groove of "Jump for Joy" did not prevent Brubeck from triggering his solo with a sneaky reference to the opening motif of Stravinsky's *Rite of Spring*, then he churned up the flow by jumping with joy between apparently unrelated keys. "Dance No. 3," recorded in the studio, rolled with the mood of *Eurasia* as Morello's drum patterns bounced between the wooden rims of his drums and hits on his drumskins that bent upon impact. On "C Jam Blues" Morello played a rabble-rousing, gutsy solo that thrilled the crowd—and prepared the way for the arrival onstage of Duke Ellington and his orchestra.

🎼

*Newport 1958* was produced by Teo Macero, who was readying himself to steer Brubeck through the next stage of his recording career at Columbia. It was Macero who would produce *Time Out*, *Time Further Out*, and *At Carnegie Hall*, and other major projects like *The Real Ambassadors* and the quartet's collaboration with Leonard Bernstein, released as *Bernstein Plays Brubeck Plays Bernstein*. And Macero stuck with Brubeck after 1967, after the classic quartet disbanded, working on the albums *Blues Roots* and *Compadres* by Brubeck's new group with Gerry Mulligan. But for every album like *Time Out* and *At Carnegie Hall*, where creativity felt limitless, records like *Countdown—Time in Outer Space*, *Bossa Nova USA*, and *Jackpot!* sounded uncared-for and rushed. Compared to the empathy between pianist and producer that had served *Brubeck Time*, *Jazz: Red Hot and Cool*, *Jazz Impressions of the USA*, and *Jazz Impressions of Eurasia* so well, Brubeck's relationship with Macero was more casual and workmanlike, and tensions occasionally spilled over. Avakian had signed Brubeck and understood his music from the inside; Macero's attention was too often elsewhere.

His initial point of contact with Columbia had been as a musician, not producer. In May 1956 Columbia issued some of Macero's own compositions on *What's New,* a shared LP with the composer and percussionist Bob Prince; and the two men, with John Lewis, Gil Evans, and Manny Albam, had also contributed arrangements to Johnny Mathis's eponymous debut album, subtitled "A New Sound in Popular Song,"[13] released that same summer. Macero had played tenor and alto saxophone on two albums with Charles Mingus, *Jazzical Moods* and *Jazz Composers Workshop,* during the early 1950s, and the work he released with Columbia in 1956 followed broadly in the wake of Gunther Schuller's third-stream experiments. *What's New* revealed a resourceful ear for orchestral timbre as Orlando DiGirolamo's accordion became the pivot point between jazz solos and waves of thickly compacted twelve-tone-based counterpoint merging into Varèse-derived block texture. It was the very definition of a period piece, demonstrating various composition techniques without ever satisfactorily answering the question "Yes, but why?"

Whereas Avakian never forgot when producing jazz records that he was a jazz fan, Macero's greatest strength could also prove a weakness. Macero was a composer who liked to involve himself in the creative process in a way that would ultimately redefine how record producers operated. Brian Eno, the composer and onetime keyboard player in Roxy Music, who was on hand to advise David Bowie in the studio and produced albums by U2, Devo, and the Talking Heads, talked in 1996 about his fascination with Macero's creative partnership with Miles Davis. Acting as a conventional record producer on earlier Davis records like *Porgy and Bess, Miles Smiles,* and *Filles de Kilimanjaro,*

---

13. Columbia CL 887.

by the time of *In a Silent Way* and *Bitches Brew*, recorded in 1969, and then moving up a gear in the 1970s as Miles recorded *He Loved Him Madly, On the Corner, Live Evil,* and *Tribute to Jack Johnson,* Macero was making decisions about not only how the music would sound on record but *what* music would appear.

It was Macero who shaped the raw tape reels of the *In a Silent Way* sessions into the compact, lean structure that was released in July 1969. Macero's decision to repeat some sections—dropping the same piece of edited tape back into the structure as a flashback—struck Eno as something profound: "[It] is very radical in jazz to use the same section a couple of times over. . . . And it's a very interesting idea, to take something that is all accidents and chance events, and then make it happen again. So suddenly you think 'Hold on—we've been here before.' It's like a strange déjà-vu thing."[14] In the late 1990s and early 2000s, when Sony began issuing "complete" box sets of the *In a Silent Way* and *Bitches Brew* sessions that restored the cuts,[15] Macero was outraged. The cut material—which he described as "bullshit"—had been cut for very specific creative reasons, he insisted. On the original 1970 double-vinyl release of *Miles Davis at Fillmore,* which comprised four heavily edited twenty-five-minute slabs of music, each tailored to fit comfortably onto one side of an LP, Macero reverse-engineered the live sounds by operating on them in the studio.

Macero's working relationship with Miles Davis endured for so long—from 1958 to 1983[16]—because he invested himself directly in the creative process in a way that could never happen with Brubeck or with Thelonious Monk, whom he had brought to Columbia in 1962. That same year, Macero contributed to Brubeck's *Bossa Nova USA* a tune, "Coração Sensível,"

14. Brian Eno, interview with Michael Engelbrecht, March 24, 1996, http://music.hyperreal.org/artists/brian_eno/interviews/me_intr4.html.

15. *The Complete in a Silent Way Sessions,* C3K 65362 (2001); *The Complete Bitches Brew Sessions,* C4K 65570 (1998).

16. Their creative relationship ended with *Star People* in 1983.

that was pure lounge music fluff, while the tune he foisted upon Monk, "Consecutive Seconds," on *Monk's Blues* in 1968, was banal Monk pastiche. Macero didn't try to pull the same trick on the notoriously volatile Mingus, whose classic *Mingus Ah Um* he produced in 1959, along with its follow-up, *Mingus Dynasty,* a year later. When Mingus returned to Columbia in 1972 to record an album of extended compositions, *Let My Children Hear Music,* his sleeve note even acknowledged Macero's "untiring efforts in producing the best album I ever made."

Brubeck's first studio project with Macero, *Gone with the Wind,* recorded on April 22 and 23, 1959, shows some traces of the difficulties that would beleaguer later albums like *Countdown—Time in Outer Space* and *Bossa Nova USA.* Eugene Wright had rejoined the Brubeck fold the previous fall, in time for the quartet's concert at the 1958 Monterey Jazz Festival, and *Gone with the Wind* was recorded at the American Legion hall in Hollywood as the group played a string of on-campus concerts around California. Compared to the more intimate-sounding 30th Street Studio in New York, the cavernous acoustics of the American Legion hall pumped air and space through the music, and the album's temperament is noticeably more easygoing than the serious-minded *Jazz Impressions of the USA* or *Jazz Impressions of Eurasia.*

This collection of tunes, designed to "evoke memories of the South," Macero said in his sleeve note, lent itself to uncomplicated swing and wistful reminiscence, but as an album, *Gone with the Wind* tried to look two ways at once. The opening three tracks—"Swanee River," "The Lonesome Road," and "Georgia on My Mind"—and the closing title track were closest to the heady concentration that had characterized *USA* and *Eurasia,* which left the remaining music feeling underproduced. After the first side ended with a two-minute sprint through "Camptown Races," the B side opened with a second take of the same piece. Macero's notes claimed that because each version "had its own special qualities, both were used," which was true, but, in reality, the piece needed time to gestate into something more substantial. Morello and Wright were given a short feature each—"Short'nin' Bread" and "Ol' Man River"—and very nicely played they were, but the stop-start structure of this second side felt disconnected and haphazardly strung together.

"Gone with the Wind" had appeared for the first time on a quartet album in 1954 on *Dave Brubeck at Storyville,* and the tune would remain a regular part of the group's repertoire. The innocence with which Desmond introduced the theme in this latest version was a front for his solo of considerable rhythmic and motific deviousness—including a surreal moment when, without warning, he hardened his tone and exaggerated his vibrato to manhandle in a quote from Sonny Rollins's famous calypso tune "St. Thomas." Brubeck's sly reference to "Anything Goes" when his solo came along was, perhaps, his coded retort to this moment of inspired madness.

"Swanee River" began with a call-and-response phrase that bounced between Brubeck and Wright four times, with each repeat becoming progressively softer and more muted, like a clock winding back to old-time America. The impressive "The Lonesome Road" also played subliminal tricks with time and structure. After outlining the bare bones of the theme, Brubeck took full advantage of the American Legion hall's mighty Bösendorfer grand piano by sustaining a throbbing low note, which he gently reengaged each time it faded away. The contrast between Desmond's hazy, gossamer-light tone and the gong-like attack of that note was Brubeck orchestrating at the piano, leaving Desmond to rotate around different centers of harmonic gravity at will.

Structurally, Brubeck's arrangement nested inside each other a sequence of interlocking episodes that darted between the original tempo and double time. Brubeck ended his first solo with a chordal crunch that propelled the quartet into the first double-time section. From there, the baton passed between Desmond and Brubeck until the quartet began to trade short phrases, solo breaks from Wright and Morello interspersed with Desmond picking up on, and extending, Brubeck's reference to *Rhapsody in Blue*. A single chord from the piano was enough to return the quartet to the original tempo, and the piece ended with Morello's drums counting the passing of time with a series of tick-tock clicks: this road, like the journey of "Plain Song," had been long and winding.

"Georgia on My Mind" was balanced carefully between the major and minor. As the second chorus of Desmond's solo was already leaning toward the minor, Brubeck gave him a little push via a descending chromatic shiver that Desmond answered with a visceral sob—and then his next phrase gravitated back toward the major. The second version of "Camptown Races" was elevated by a gloriously uninhibited Brubeck solo, a steaming bass line racing toward a gospel-infused shriek of block-chord joy. Morello's version of "Short'nin' Bread" carried the theme in its entirety across his tom-toms and cymbals, which developed out of *Newport 1958*, when he had dropped a hint of "Short'nin' Bread" into his solo on "C Jam Blues." Wright's brief outing on "Ol' Man River" was pleasant enough but slight, and the album's architectural curve could have been far sharper had an extended bass solo been incorporated into one extended take of "Camptown Races"—or instead into the breezily funky strut of a version of "Basin Street Blues," which, as things stood, felt marooned between these miniatures. Macero ought to have tightened the structural reins.

*Gone with the Wind* was a happy, carefree session that did not produce a major statement as *Jazz Impressions of the USA* or *Jazz Impressions of Eurasia* had, partly because it was never intended to. Word had reached Columbia HQ that Brubeck was planning an entire album based on odd time signatures—each track an original composition—with a piece of abstract modern art on the cover. Nerves wobbled, and *Gone with the Wind* was recorded as insurance that would allow Columbia to recoup their money when this next album, which Brubeck wanted to call *Time Out*, inevitably crashed and burned.

🎼

The more he was asked about it, the more fixed in his telling Brubeck became on the three summer recording sessions that produced the seven tracks—"Blue Rondo à la Turk," "Strange Meadow Lark," "Take Five," "Three to Get Ready (And Four to Go)," "Kathy's Waltz," "Everybody's Jumpin'," and "Pick Up Sticks"—released as *Time Out* on December 14, 1959. And the more certain his view, the less people were inclined to probe: after all, the one person guaranteed to know how *Time Out* was put together, especially after Paul Desmond's death in 1977, was Dave Brubeck. Unlike with Miles Davis's *Kind of Blue* and Charles Mingus's *Mingus Ah Um*, the other certified jazz classics recorded by Columbia in 1959, none of the *Time Out* rehearsal material, alternate takes, or studio chatter have ever been made public, and these hidden tapes, stored at the archive at University of the Pacific, reveal a more complicated truth about the evolution of *Time Out* than Brubeck ever admitted, or could remember.

Brubeck always prioritized talking about the present and the future over the past, and especially over nitpicking questions about a recording session that had taken place almost forty-five years earlier, even if it had brought into being his most famous music. In 2003, while on tour in the UK and on the move between major cities, there is a new quartet album recorded live in New York, *Park Avenue South*, to be discussed; a recently recorded double album of his extended sacred music, with the London Symphony Orchestra, is awaiting release; and he is thinking ahead to a new solo piano album. The world of *Time Out*—recorded during a roasting-hot New York summer— feels a long way from this dank English spring.

Heading back to London following his concert at the Cliffs Pavilion in the Essex town of Southend-on-Sea on May 7, 2003,

Brubeck is forthcoming when talking about *All the Things We Are*, the album he made with Lee Konitz and Anthony Braxton in 1974, but when the conversation turns unexpectedly to *Time Out* he stiffens, and his language becomes labored and formal. This twist in the conversation demands that Brubeck be the Dave Brubeck of *the* Dave Brubeck Quartet, and he knows that whatever he says, late at night after playing a concert, will likely achieve permanence in print.[17] As the custodian of his quartet's most widely loved legacy, he is being put on the spot. Giving false information would be a mistake, but too many details have faded from his memory, and so he listens to himself delivering a carefully rehearsed account of those three days in 1959 and their aftermath.

"I was very seriously advised, by people at Columbia, not to put *Time Out* out," he begins.[18]

Think of everything you've achieved over the last few years, they said: *Time Out* will not sell and, worse, it will damage your reputation and that of the quartet. The album was an experiment, and Columbia didn't know how to deal with it. I wanted to put an abstract painting on the cover, and that was new in jazz. But more of a problem was that it was all originals—and Columbia much preferred original tunes to be mixed with standards or, even better, all Broadway songs. Another problem was the time signatures—"No one will dance to something in 5/4 or 9/8," I was told. Columbia would have liked me to forget about *Time Out* and make another record, one they knew they could sell.

I persisted. I wrote letters. I knew this was a great record, and eventually the music found a public over the heads of Columbia. I gave the tapes to Goddard Lieberson, who was

17. An account of my experience shadowing the Dave Brubeck Quartet appeared under the title "Adventures in the Sound of Modernist Swing" in *Jazz Review*, July 2003.

18. Interview with the author, May 7, 2003.

Columbia's president. He was a musician himself, a composer, and I thought he might get it. I was right—he replied saying how tired he was of hearing "Body and Soul" and "I Got Rhythm" and that this sounded new and fresh. He was going to the West Coast and took "Blue Rondo" and "Take Five" with him to play for some company executives out there—but he came up against the same resistance as in New York.

But Goddard, as president, insisted it was put out, and that changed everything. Disc jockeys started playing "Take Five" and, very quickly, people were calling in to the radio stations to request it—so quickly that at first Columbia couldn't keep up with demand for records. Then they realized that they had something and I thought, "*Never* listen to the sales team!" The quartet was on tour in Europe when the single came out, and when we came back we soon realized we had a hit. We'd drive into a diner to eat when we were on the road, and it was playing on the jukebox; we'd arrive to play a concert on campus and hear it playing in the student buildings. I was so happy that something I'd put so much thought into—that was new and creative—the people liked it.

Brubeck's potted history poses as many questions as it answers, especially against the background of the music that Mingus and Davis were making for Columbia during this same period. *Mingus Ah Um* was recorded on May 5 and May 12, *Kind of Blue* on March 2 and April 22, *Time Out* over three sessions on June 25, July 1, and August 18, and all three albums consisted of original compositions, without recourse to Broadway standards (and the same had been true of the Gerry Mulligan Quartet's *What Is There to Say?*, in the can by January 1959). Brubeck had recorded many standards for Columbia since joining the label in 1954, but *Brubeck Plays Brubeck*, *Jazz Impressions of the USA*, and *Jazz Impressions of Eurasia* were, like *Time Out*, also collections of original compositions. So original compositions, per se, were not the problem.

Until 1959, the expectation that Columbia cover art would feature an image of the artist concerned was so ingrained that nobody had thought to question it. *Brubeck Time, Brubeck Plays Brubeck, Dave Digs Disney, Jazz Impressions of Eurasia,* and *Gone with the Wind* all featured Brubeck's smiling face, with or without the rest of the quartet; *Jazz Impressions of the USA* used a caricature of the quartet drawn by Arnold Roth, who had created all those characterful cover images for Brubeck's Fantasy albums. Putting the artist on the cover was marketing at its most basic: it put a face to the music, making a strong impression on those liable to part with their cash in a record store. One of the most memorable covers in jazz history, by photographer Jay Maisel, graced *Kind of Blue.* Miles in profile against a dark backdrop, trumpet in mouth, light leaking around his face.

In the case of *Jazz Impressions of Eurasia,* the connection between cover image and marketing had been more mercenary. The record's release, on October 15, 1958, ushered in Columbia's "Dave Brubeck Month"—November—during which the album was heavily promoted during a package tour: the Dave Brubeck Quartet on the same bill as the Sonny Rollins Trio (when Desmond likely heard "St. Thomas," which he quoted on the title track to *Gone with the Wind*) and Maynard Ferguson's orchestra. Also tossed into the promotional mix was Pan Am, which had provided four round-trip New York–Paris airplane tickets to be won by a lucky purchaser of Brubeck's new album. Brubeck had been required to show up for a photo shoot at San Francisco International Airport, where he stood dutifully in front of the tail of a Pan Am jet as two air hostesses plied him with Pan Am travel bags. Hardly a subtle image—and if this was how the Columbia marketing office was conceiving of cover art, what could they possibly do with Brubeck's choice of cover for *Time Out,* better suited perhaps to an album of music by Anton Webern or Edgard Varèse?

But, like the perceived problem with original compositions, Brubeck's decision to use an abstract painting turns out not to be the whole story either. *Mingus Ah Um* was also decorated with a trippy abstract painting, and both covers—obviously a pair—were by S. Neil Fujita, staff artist and head of graphic design at Columbia, who had also worked on the cover of Miles Davis's *'Round About Midnight* and the dramatic montage cover for *The Jazz Messengers*, Art Blakey's only Columbia album, recorded in 1956. Neither Mingus nor Davis had suffered at the hands of the Columbia sales team for the content of their records or their presentation. *Kind of Blue* was released on August 17, the day before Brubeck's final *Time Out* recording session, and immediately sold well; an anonymous reviewer in *DownBeat* gave the album the maximum five-star rating, and a review that began with the laudatory: "This is a remarkable album. Using very simple but effective devices, Miles has created an album of extreme beauty and sensitivity" ended with the poetic "This is the soul of Miles Davis, and it's a beautiful soul."[19] *Mingus Ah Um* also sold well when it was released on September 14—so Columbia knew they had nothing to fear from original compositions or abstract paintings.

Which left Brubeck's odd time signatures. Was the label seriously about to bury a new album of original music by one of their most bankable jazz stars because of 5/4 and 9/8 time? In isolation, had Brubeck decided to play "All the Things You Are" in 5, time signatures would not have raised concerns, but asymmetrical beats combined with original compositions and odd time signatures blew up into a perfect storm of confusion at Columbia about what *Time Out* actually was. *Kind of Blue* and *Mingus Ah Um* presented obviously as jazz albums. For all its melodic and harmonic innovations—modal jazz had never had it so good—Miles's record was at its core blues, soulful and joyful. Mingus originally intended to record a whole album of Jelly Roll Morton compositions, but instead *Mingus Ah Um* evolved into a state-of-the-nation address about the past and future of

---

19. Review of *Kind of Blue*, *DownBeat*, October 1, 1959.

jazz, from Morton to free jazz. Its opening track, "Better Git It in Your Soul," rooted proceedings in fundamental gospel truths; from there the album paid tribute to the recently deceased Lester Young ("Goodbye Pork Pie Hat") and offered an "Open Letter to Duke" before ending with two pieces that reconnected with the album's origins in Jelly Roll Morton—"Pussy Cat Dues" and "Jelly Roll."

In theory, Mingus's record ought to have tested Columbia's patience more than *Time Out*. Mingus had insisted on recording "Fables of Faubus," the ridiculing protest song he had aimed at racist Arkansas governor Orval Faubus after the Little Rock scandal in 1957, and Columbia had relented on the condition that it was recorded as an instrumental—his contemptuous lyrics were deemed too inflammatory for a mainstream jazz audience.[20] His group included three saxophonists—John Handy, Booker Ervin, and Shafi Hadi—who, like John Coltrane and Eric Dolphy, were flying with but also away from the legacy bequeathed by Charlie Parker. Mingus's composition "Bird Calls" caught them all midflight as high-speed bop changes overshot the runway toward harmonic freefall. The piece acknowledged the arrival of free jazz, sneaking sounds more associated with Ornette Coleman, still considered by many to be musically underdeveloped and a charlatan, onto Columbia. And yet it was the musical vocabulary of *Time Out* that, at Columbia HQ, was causing consternation and bewilderment.

Six decades later, *Time Out* has become so thoroughly absorbed into mass culture—piped into chain coffee shops and wafting around the soundtracks of countless television programs,

---

20. A version with lyrics was recorded on October 20, 1960, and appeared on the album *Charles Mingus Presents Charles Mingus*, released on the independent label Candid in 1961.

commercials, and movies—that *listening*, as opposed to merely hearing, can be a challenge. But listening properly, with concentration and a degree of objectivity, reveals something wonderful: what were problems in 1959 are the same factors that have allowed this album to endure and become genuinely loved.

Following those carefree *Gone with the Wind* sessions— eventually issued in August 1960, eight months after the release of *Time Out*—Brubeck went out on a creative limb, pouring everything he knew how to do into this new experimental album. Whereas *Mingus Ah Um* could be considered difficult and controversial in terms already being discussed in jazz, *Time Out* proved controversial in a way that often left people struggling for definitions. As Mingus was placing the free jazz revolution in the context of a history that stretched right back to 1920s New Orleans, and Miles was engaged in nothing less than reinvigorating the blues, the explicit classicism of "Blue Rondo à la Turk" and "Three to Get Ready" was being interpreted by some as a middlebrow indulgence—not even posing the right questions about "whither jazz," let alone providing any answers.

Ira Gitler's review in *DownBeat*—not published until the April 28, 1960, issue; *Time Out* had not made the editorial list of priority releases—used Brubeck's classicism as a weapon to bludgeon his new record. Dismissing the prevailing mood as "drawing room music" in his first paragraph, he went on to draw blood. "In classical music," he observed, "there is a kind of pretentious pap, sometimes called 'semi-classical,' which serves as the real thing for some people. As a parallel, Brubeck is a 'semi-jazz' player. . . . Take 'Blue Rondo à la Turk' in 9/8. After hearing that ersatz, corny Chopinesque he used for Polish representation in *Jazz Impressions of Eurasia*, I'm surprised he didn't play *In a Persian Market* here. 'Blue Rondo's theme is equally far from jazz. . . . In 'Three to Get Ready,' the thematic material is again alien to jazz, but the alternation of two bars of

3/4 with two bars of 4/4 does engender a different and effective kind of swing."[21]

As an unforgiving summary of the critical community's long-standing problems with Brubeck, Gitler's review, in a little under seven hundred words, delivered a stinging rebuke. Brubeck, forever the gentleman, gamely put rancor aside a few years later to pose for a goofy photograph at a festival in Detroit with Gitler and Cannonball Adderley, whose *Dish Here* had also suffered a lashing from Gitler's pen—Brubeck raises his fist in theatrical anger as Adderley laughingly wraps his hand around Gitler's neck. At the time, though, a demolition job of that magnitude in *DownBeat* was no laughing matter. When Gitler died in 2019, the jazz writer Gary Giddins remembered him as "the ideal critic of the bop era"[22]—but less ideal, arguably, for an album that had no connection with bebop. Gitler took *Time Out* apart by telling readers what the album was not, *not* what it was.

One inconsistency, although one that honestly reflected the problem of grasping for appropriate definitions, was Gitler's failure to convincingly reconcile his criticism of *Time Out*'s classicism and thematic material that he alleged was "alien to jazz" with Brubeck's ever-eager sense of how composed beginnings could serve the needs of the improviser. "Blue Rondo à la Turk" set up the expectation that *Time Out* would walk a tightrope between composition and improvisation as Brubeck's assiduously composed theme gave way to improvised blues choruses. As the composition of a West Coast musician who had never played a note of bebop in his life but had poured over the implications of polytonality with Darius Milhaud, "Blue Rondo"

---

21. Ira Gitler, review of *Time Out, DownBeat*, April 28, 1960.

22. Quoted in Howard Mandel, "In Memoriam: Ira Gitler (1928–2019)," *DownBeat*, March 6, 2019, http://downbeat.com/news/detail/critic-and-writer-ira-gitler-dies-at-90. The photograph of Brubeck with Gitler and Adderley, from the *DownBeat* archives, is included in feature.

feels flawless in its conception, and exactly the sort of music he ought to have been creating. But if your working definition of jazz was synonymous with East Coast bebop, then "Blue Rondo" would, by definition, miss the mark.

But Gitler was right about one thing. There could be no denying that *Time Out* behaved differently from how jazz normally acted and sounded, the recently completed *Gone with the Wind* included. *Time Out* was a *Harlequin's Carnival* of an album, playful but serious-minded, and very serious about being playful. Lines took acrobatic midair turns. Bright sunshine colors glowed against pockets of pastoral repose. A waltz, dedicated to Brubeck's daughter, began in 4, while another piece ostensibly in 3 (to get ready) reconfigured its own geometric shape as bars of 4/4 (to go) interrupted the count. The album's central drum feature rethought the basic nature of the drum solo; as solos by Max Roach and Art Blakey twisted through records like tornadoes, Morello's chiffon shuffle moved silence around a 5/4 vamp with as much impact as it did sound. It was an album that could melt into the background or send people to the dance floor but which also revealed, and continues to reveal, further harmonic, timbral, and melodic subtleties with each careful listen.

And as they pieced it together, the language and shape of *Time Out* had a habit of eluding members of the quartet, too, as gradually—painfully, sometimes—they discovered the music through a process of trial and error. "Three to Get Ready," "Kathy's Waltz," and "Everybody's Jumpin'" were the first pieces to be recorded, on June 25; "Strange Meadow Lark" and "Take Five" followed on July 1; and "Blue Rondo à la Turk" and "Pick Up Sticks" completed the sessions on August 18. The quartet played the standards "Someday My Prince Will Come" on June 25 and "I Get a Kick Out of You" on July 1 to warm up, and the June 25 session also included a version of "I'm in a Dancing Mood" to sign off. The technical difficulty of Brubeck's own compositions sometimes tripped the musicians up, and while they were quick to iron out the problems, reaching an understanding of the concept behind a piece proved trickier. It took time for the smoke to clear around "Blue Rondo à la Turk" and "Take Five," and for a well-defined picture of their musical architecture to materialize.

The recorded history of "Blue Rondo à la Turk" began unpromisingly, with Brubeck shouting "Balls!" as the quartet's first take fell apart shortly after Desmond entered. When they stopped in apparent puzzlement to ask what happened, Brubeck admitted that he had dropped a beat—"*I* missed it," he growled—and they went straight into a second take. Speaking from behind the glass, Macero called the piece "Turkish," which suggested that Brubeck was still pondering his title, and this new take was correspondingly work-in-progress. The passage that had led the first take to break down passed without incident, and the 2+2+2+3 rhythm (interrupted by 3+3+3 every fourth bar) bubbled along joyfully, with Brubeck and Desmond coaxing a balmy, pillowy tone from their instruments. Apart from Wright's briefly losing his way and stopping toward the end of Brubeck's theme, shortly before the arrival of the blues choruses, this was a flawless performance.

Although "à la Turk" was a throwaway reference to the title of the "Rondo alla Turca" movement from Mozart's Piano Sonata No. 11 in A Major, K. 331, the suggestion that Brubeck might have consciously shaped his melody around Mozart's theme is an urban myth; but the melodic shapes he deployed—plain scalic patterns and major thirds (the most singable, consonant melodic interval) were basic compositional Lego bricks that would have been familiar to any composer working in Vienna during the eighteenth century. The cubist, angular shapes and flattened fifths that jutted out like fish bones in bebop or Monk tunes took no role in "Blue Rondo à la Turk." Out of an almost embarrassingly simple melodic cell, Brubeck had fashioned a composition with a dazzling melodic and harmonic inner life, in which each note had a clearly audible function. In the first bar a two-note pattern (A dropping to F) repeated three times, followed by three notes that strolled up the scale, leaving the second bar to answer with an inverse: that same two-note pattern, with the three-note phrase at the end now descending (not ascending). Bar 3 was a literal repeat of the first bar, and the fourth bar picked up the scalic tailpiece that had ended the previous bars and ran three of them together, each marching further up the scale, which shifted the rhythmic pattern from 2+2+2+3 to 3+3+3.

Had it not been for what Brubeck placed in between his melody line and a bass line that obsessively reiterated the root of the chord on every strong beat, "Blue Rondo" might have collapsed into naked F major blandness. This inner line—a step-by-step slide along the chromatic scale that sounded in unison with his bass note—injected the thrill of unpredictability into the regular pattern of the theme. A sudden key change after nine bars of F major, which shifted the whole pattern up three steps to A, unleashed some glorious rays of bitonal sunshine. Brubeck had experimented with superimposing A major over F major in the first take, a possibility that he had rejected by the master take; but his abrupt switches between the two keys, mixed with the loose-cannon chromatic harmony underneath, created a strobing ripple that cascaded over the quartet as tonalities clashed and overtones ran wild. Clashing overtones— that audible buzz experienced when the waves of harmonics underpinning two different notes rub against one another— were an important ingredient of the field recordings that Brubeck had heard on *The Belgian Congo Records of the Denis-Roosevelt Expedition* LP, and there was a pleasing historical symmetry in the fact that asymmetrical rhythms that Brubeck had soaked up a decade previously were now replicating this rarefied acoustic phenomenon.

"Rondo" form, in classical parlance, denoted a composition in which a recurring principal theme was slotted around episodes designed for contrast, and Brubeck, working broadly within the rules of the eighteenth-century rondo, also rein-vented the form, as a jazz musician working in 1959 was duty-bound to do. The first contrasting episode announced itself by walking the opening two-note cell up—and in the next bar down—the scale. The second episode transformed mel-ody into harmony by bunching together the two-note cell to form a stabbing chord, which he raised further up the scale to build excitement. For his final episode, he constructed a mel-ody by verticalizing those same chords while upping the quo-tient of chromaticism. The 2+2+2+3 pattern now spelled out a churning bass pattern that propelled the music toward vast block chords, surging upward in the right hand and plummet-ing downward in the left.

The quartet's joy as they heard Brubeck's audacious com-positional plan lifting off the manuscript paper—his concept *actually* worked in sound!—is palpable. And the performance continued to go according to plan as the honeycomb intri-cacies of Brubeck's composed rondo were knitted inside his grander compositional plan: "Blue Rondo" turned out to be a rondo placed inside a rondo, as the quartet jump-cut three times between two bars of the blues and two bars of 9/8, before the space opened up for an extended contemplation of the blues. But finding a suitable way to improvise on the blues in the context of "Blue Rondo à la Turk" would only suggest itself once Desmond and Brubeck had lived with the material a little.

As seasoned jazz players, their instinct, and especially with so many melodic and harmonic byways to explore, was to improvise on the theme. But soon enough they discovered that improvising in the accustomed manner did not work in the context of a composition designed as a rondo that, by the time Brubeck had reconceived it, had turned into something resem-bling a mosaic—the latest manifestation of a compositional predilection that had started with his student piece "Playland-at-the-Beach." Mosaics define themselves by differences of shape, color, and texture between the various panels, but in this first complete take, both Desmond and Brubeck fell into the trap of trying to *unify* the structure by dealing directly with the melodic contours of the 9/8 theme in their improvisation.

Desmond's beefy, bluesy tone, darting between different keys as he attempted to wrap elements of Brubeck's theme around conventional blues changes, was a virtuosic feat of florid melodic invention; but it was also uncharacteristically forced and contrived. Brubeck's solo, his usual architectural sense of pace and place having deserted him, contained enough ideas for a whole album in itself as each chorus introduced new perspectives and material in an attempt to get things rolling. He tried flipping his theme between his hands, hoping counterpoint might shine a light; he consciously mashed his 9/8 theme into blues changes; he tested different tonal centers—but nothing caught fire. But then his hands chanced on a tumbling motif (beginning at 6:48) that, the next time we hear it, has become central to the familiar take of "Blue Rondo à la Turk."

Brubeck's and Desmond's solos on the master take were like light, airy line drawings that had been lifted from the crossouts and indecision of their messy first draft. Perhaps in discussion between takes they realized that the solution to making "Blue Rondo à la Turk" function as a polyvalent structure lay in maintaining the composition and the improvisation as separate entities. After the note-y industry of the composed element, their rejected solos were overcooked: too busy, too effortful, too much. The correctness of their revised thoughts was absolute. Desmond thinned his tone and pursued one single line of thought, each phrase unfolding logically from the consequences of the previous phrase over a pleasing-to-the-ear structural arc that ended with a sudden upward inflection, a question, which Brubeck immediately picked up.

Like Desmond, Brubeck had pared back: where once there was clutter, order and structural balance now ruled. Having established that superimposing his 9/8 theme over blues changes led nowhere but a cul-de-sac, Brubeck based his new solo around recasting that falling A-to-F motif, stretching it over the key-shifting footfall of the changing chords beneath. The unsung hero of this classic solo was Eugene Wright, whose springy walking bass line handed Brubeck unflinching support. Lines migrated toward block chords, a typical direction of travel. But Brubeck, not wanting to repeat the mistakes of earlier by overstacking his solo with information, made dramatic use of space, his block chords, lightly touched, at first drifting in and out of focus against Wright's all-immersive pulse. Brubeck raised the intensity—of course he did—but this was not to be one of those labyrinthine, multiheaded solos, like in "Little Girl Blue" or "Tangerine," that took off in different directions simultaneously. The graceful architectural curve of Brubeck's solo landed his soulful block chords against the arrival of the tumbling motif he had discovered during the first take, which he threaded through a reprise of the same phrase with which he had begun. His beginning was his end. Desmond interjected a two-bar phrase to direct the quartet back to the 9/8 theme, which throbbed with excitement—they had just created something unique and extraordinary, and they knew it.

Also recorded that day, "Pick Up Sticks" underwent a similar journey of transformation. The quartet already had a piece in 6/4 in their repertoire. "Watusi Drums" had been Brubeck's response to "Royal Watusi Drums," a favorite track from *The Belgian Congo Records of the Denis-Roosevelt Expedition* LP, and "Pick Up Sticks" found itself grafted over the top of its looping bass line. Why didn't the quartet simply record "Watusi Drums"? It had been featured heavily during the quartet's 1958 State Department tour and served as the final track of *The Dave Brubeck Quartet in Europe*, which ruled out a repeat appearance on *Time Out*. Yet the quartet, minus Desmond, recorded a complete take, which included a powerful solo from Morello.

There had been a sketchy, incomplete take in which Brubeck threw splintering clusters—think Ellington meets

Monk—against Wright's strident bass, which developed into jagged, smashed-up lines. This experiment broke down after only a minute, but you feel Brubeck searching for something beyond "Watusi Drums." His composed bass line was anchored around an entirely characteristic melodic twist: the sixth beat of the bar—a strong beat—was made to coincide with a weak melody note—a tritone—which gave the line a hiccup as it moved into the first beat of the next bar, tricking your sense of where the strong beat lay. "Pick Up Sticks" retained this tantalizing harmonic pun, but everything else was rethought.

Aside from its appearance on an earlier album, another likely reason why "Watusi Drums" was excluded from *Time Out* was because its chirpy melody—suitable fodder for a drum feature in the heat of a live concert—would have sounded ungainly, crude even, in the company of such sophisticated melodic constructs as "Three to Get Ready," "Strange Meadow Lark," and "Take Five." So Brubeck dialed back on the fiery energy and spiky piano figurations of "Watusi Drums," replacing the original melody with a repeating cycle of richly marinated polytonal chords that his right hand draped languidly over Wright's bass line, the regularity of the pattern gently disrupted every fourth bar by a ghostly echo, a shorter version of the cycle that entered a beat early. Such misty, painterly colors were a world away from the high-speed pyrotechnics of "Blue Rondo"—and yet there was also a unifying point of connection. Spaciously organized block chords hanging off Wright's bass had also dominated Brubeck's "Blue Rondo" solo, and *Time Out* would be an album in which colors lingered and faded, then melted into the surrounding space.

"Three to Get Ready," "Kathy's Waltz," and "Everybody's Jumpin'," recorded on June 25, all came together without the conceptual head-scratching of "Blue Rondo à la Turk" and "Pick Up Sticks" to become *Time Out*'s middle panel, the music that opened the second side of the LP. Like "Blue Rondo," "Three to Get Ready"— called "3/4, 4/4" by Macero from the control booth—placed one music inside another, both types defined by their different time signatures. The piece introduces itself as a waltz, and Gitler wasn't wrong: this thematic material was indeed alien to jazz. In his sleeve note, the British jazz musician and writer Steve Race described the theme as "a simple, Haydn-esque waltz theme in C major," although even this apparently "simple" twelve-bar melody was spiced with some wayward chromatic slippages in the left hand. As the melody repeated, the music began to alternate between 3/4 and 4/4: each 3/4 two-bar phrase was interrupted by two bars of 4/4 underpinned by Wright's Walter Page–light walking bass, a waltz morphing into jazz swing.

"Three to Get Ready" would achieve a special sort of popularity in France after the popular Toulouse-born singer-songwriter Claude Nougaro scored a hit in 1962 with a vocal version he called "Le jazz et la java," which tapped directly into a very French sensibility.[23] From Erik Satie's song "Je te veux" to Claude Debussy's *Valse romantique* and Maurice Ravel's *Valse nobles et sentimentales* and *Menuet sur le nom d'Haydn*, composed reimaginings of the waltz were hardwired into French culture, and Nougaro had reached inside Brubeck's original "Three to Get Ready" and extracted every possible trace of Milhaud and French neoclassicism, which he fused with a hip, New Wave, *À bout de souffle* sensuality. The ease with which Brubeck slipped in tritones and other clashes between melody and bass related to his experience of midcentury French neoclassicism. His quartet's first take bordered on hesitant, but they had at least grasped the essentials of the tune. Improvising over the shifting ground of 3/4 and 4/4 came naturally, and their second take proved the equal of the master take that would eventually appear on *Time Out*—nearly.

---

23. Accompanied by Michel Legrand and his musicians, the song was included on Nougaro's album *Le cinéma* (Philips B 76.559 R).

Brubeck made some microadjustments between takes. Morello's delicate cymbal chimes that struck at the end of each phrase would become integral to the arrangement, but they were barely audible during the first take, and Brubeck clearly told Morello to raise the volume. Also integral to the composition was each member of the quartet's improvising a break during the two bars of 4/4. As "Three to Get Ready" became part of the quartet's regular repertoire, those two-bar interjections became nimble and playful, and Morello's low-pitched tom-tom fill during the first take felt inappropriately ponderous. Those problems had been fixed by the second take, which was rejected nevertheless because Desmond's and Brubeck's solos hadn't quite hit their mark. But one more take, and "Three to Get Ready" was in the can.

"Kathy's Waltz" would appear again in an orchestrated version on Brubeck's 1961 album *Brandenburg Gate: Revisited,* and "Everybody's Jumpin'" would find itself repurposed, with added lyrics, as "Everybody's Comin'" on *The Real Ambassadors,* but neither piece would become a fixture of the quartet's regular set list. "Play that waltz no matter what I do!" Brubeck warned Wright and Morello as they gave "Kathy's Waltz" a spin. As a portrait of Brubeck's then-toddler daughter waltzing, enthusiasm overriding rhythmic self-assurance, "Kathy's Waltz" was a charming vignette, and the latest of Brubeck's pieces that overlaid 4/4 against 3/4 in the tradition of "Little Girl Blue" and "Someday My Prince Will Come." "Everybody's Jumpin'" settled into a confident groove from the beginning. Here the only alteration between takes was to fix contrasts of louds and softs. "I'm gonna play it a lot louder on this one," Brubeck warned Macero, referring to his climactic block chords, as the quartet embarked on what would become the master take. "A *lot* louder!"

"'TAKE FIVE' is a quick sketch in 5/4 intended mainly as entrance and exit for a pentagonistic drum solo by my favorite drummer, Joe Morrello [sic]," Paul Desmond wrote in an undated note typed on the headed stationery of the Hotel Wellington on Seventh Avenue in New York City.[24] His note was intended as an introduction to "Take Five"—but for whom exactly it was intended is unclear, and the missing date makes it impossible to know whether he was referring to "Take Five" on *Time Out* or to the subsequent single. Meanwhile, his punning invention of the word *pentagonistic* is your first clue that Desmond wasn't taking the task especially seriously:

> Joe's contribution here is unfortunately much shorter than at like concerts, but I guess you'll get the idea. If the problem of beating time to this disturbs you, and I don't see why it shouldn't, a good way is to tap your fingers, one at a time. (One is where the thumb is.) The melody, such as it is, was assembled rapidly in the studio, and consists of fragments which occurred to me here and there, mainly at a slot machine in Reno which produced an ominous but regular series of 5 clicks as the coins vanished. (The royalties from this will have to exceed $47 before I break even, but then that's show biz.)
> PAUL DESMOND

Desmond would have beamed broadly at the thought of anyone actually believing this cock-and-bull story about slot machines in Reno that chugged along in 5/4 time. But one aspect of his story rings true: "Take Five" always was intended to frame a drum solo, like "Sounds of the Loop" and "Watusi Drums" before it. With "Blue Rondo," "Three to Get Ready" and "Kathy's Waltz" already written, *Time Out* needed a piece in 5 to push it to the next metric level—and the task fell to Desmond.

---

24. Paul Desmond, undated note, Correspondence (*Time Out*), Teo Macero Collection, JPB 00-8, Music Division, New York Public Library.

Brubeck had heard Desmond responding animatedly to Morello's 5/4 rhythm as the two men warmed up together before concerts. But formalizing something on paper proved a different matter: "Paul resisted at first and said there was no way he could do that," Brubeck remembered in 2003.[25] "We had a rehearsal at my house and he played two different themes on my piano: if you don't like the first, you might like the second. And I realized that if we put those themes together—one following the other—we'd have a complete tune in 5/4 time." What became the B section of "Take Five," once Brubeck had deployed his composer's brain, showed a striking similarity in its elegant melodic curve to the Jimmy Van Heusen song "Sunday, Monday, or Always," which had been a hit for Bing Crosby in 1943 (and was subsequently covered by Nat King Cole and Pat Boone). Whether Desmond was conscious of the fact is an open question. This was precisely the sort of crooning pop song he would have likely found among his father's collection of sheet music; but whatever the truth, "Take Five" had a sound as fresh and zingy as newly cut root ginger, that might have been designed to show off Desmond's empathy with his instrument. The composer credits deservedly went to Desmond, but was his reticence in explaining "Take Five" because he, least of all, could account for the record's unparalleled sales and success? Was it Brubeck's vamp? His own melody? The tiptoe elegance of Morello's drum solo? Why did "Take Five" prove jazz catnip to so many listeners?

Attempting to unpick its backstory by listening through those never-released tapes only takes you so far: the tapes rolling as the quartet recorded their final thoughts on "Take Five"—the "session reels"—have gone missing,[26] which leaves all sorts of questions hanging. As Desmond concludes his solo

25. Interview with the author, May 7, 2003.
26. Confirmed by an email from Columbia, August 20, 2018. ("The session tapes themselves were not retained in the Columbia vaults. Only the master takes were retained.")

on the album version of "Take Five," a very obvious edit intervenes before Morello's drum solo. Had Brubeck taken a solo that was cut? Or is the "Take Five" we know two takes spliced together to take advantage of the strongest solos of the day? And why, when the quartet recorded another finished version of the piece on July 1, eventually released as the single a year after the album, did Macero not take the opportunity to fix a problem with Brubeck's vamp: a low E-flat initiates the first beat of each bar, but in bar 4, the note failed to sound.

Intriguing questions all, but a larger question overshadows everything else. Brubeck, to the day he died, insisted in interviews that the 5/4 "Take Five" beat— "Oom, chuk-a, chuck, boom, boom / Oom, chuk-a, chuck, boom, boom / Oom, chuk-a, chuck . . . "—was the same pattern that Morello had used to warm up before concerts. But as the quartet tried to fix together a piece that Macero was still calling "5/4," Morello was sounding another beat altogether. The "Take Five" theme had yet to settle into the shape we know, and Brubeck was still testing his vamp. But Morello's rhythm is furthest removed from the "Take Five" we know.

Had Morello stuck to this beat, best described as a lopsided Latin rhythm, it's highly doubtful whether "Take Five" would have become a hit; as the beat migrated from his ride cymbal to the clickety-clack wooden rims of his drums, its angular attack was a world away from the cushioning balm of his cymbal work on the released version. Morello also had great difficulty executing it. "How did I ever think of such a thing?" he groaned as yet another take fell apart. The beat clearly put him on edge and resisted his every attempt to slip into a relaxed groove—his unease trickled down through the whole group. As Brubeck counted off take after take—"1! 2! 3! 4! 5!"—the quartet wobbled rhythmically and Desmond kept tripping over the melodic furniture. Each attempt felt doomed to certain failure (and, yes, there was a "take five" of a piece then temporarily called "5/4"). Brubeck, as leader, saw it as his role to reassure and calm. "This is all rehearsal," he reasoned. "You're goddamn right it is!" Morello shot back. But after twelve attempts, some failing better than others, the law of diminishing returns led Brubeck to say, "Okay, let's try 'Waltz for Kathy.'"

On the tape, the group's relief at playing a rhythm that they fully understand is tangible, and their segue into "Kathy's Waltz" tells us that this intensive rehearsal of "Take Five" took place during the June 25 session. Hearing America's most popular jazz combo reduced to sounding like enthusiastic music students who have bitten off more than they can chew, as "Take Five" continues to outwit them, is alarming. Miserable because he was frustrated and frustrated because he was miserable, Morello suffered something of a breakdown behind his kit. "Oh man, I just forgot my beat," he sobbed after a further stumble, and Brubeck, again, comforted him: "It's very hard—we got all day."

During the studio chatter that followed another botched attempt, Brubeck declared, "At least we got a take!" but, in truth, not a note recorded that day could have been used; even when the quartet succeeded in completing a take, the music was tentative and coarse. The "Take Five" that they signed off on a week later, on July 1, had an intensely satisfying sense of internal proportion, as Desmond's melody ebbed and flowed around the minor scale and the B section gently twisted the harmony in a fresh direction. But indecision had ruled the week before as Desmond had attempted to give his melodic ideas a definitive shape. Phrases kept slipping into the major, and the elegant ascent and drop of the familiar melody sometimes appeared in reverse.

How to repair this car crash? Brubeck's musical instincts told him to fix Wright's bass part first and then resolve the shaky transition between the A section and the bridge. In discussion, Wright and Brubeck alighted on the bass pattern most likely to highlight the tune's primary-color harmonies, which, in turn, helped Brubeck feel the shift toward the bridge. "Go to

B in the bridge," he told Desmond, which he knew would give the harmony a lift: "Take Five" is in E-flat minor, and going to B lands the bridge on a tritone that feels less like a resolution and more like a fresh starting point. But even with the bass part and the bridge locked down, the quartet's struggles were far from over. Desmond's attempts to solo petered out into insignificance. Brubeck's efforts to construct a solo by shapeshifting the contours of his vamp felt oddly empty and overblown. Earlier, Brubeck had shouted out, "Crazy! This is such a ball, man. I really dig this!" An hour later, he'd have been forgiven for thinking otherwise.

The process mirrored to an uncanny degree the experience of working on "Blue Rondo à la Turk," as the quartet realized that the secret to unlocking "Take Five" lay in stripping notes back to their essentials. We can't know what discussions took place in the intervening week between June 25 and July 1 or what private thoughts the musicians had, but when the quartet reconvened, "Take Five" blossomed from an unkempt caterpillar into a beautiful butterfly. The game-changing difference was, of course, Morello's finding that now-familiar beat, which, when played at a more relaxed tempo, licensed everything else to slot into place. That first rhythm had overwhelmed "Take Five." Its boisterous energies had led Morello toward hectic, monolithic solos, cross-rhythms bouncing between his saber-rattling snare drum and tom-toms. But now his beat, molded around the rhythmic shape of Brubeck's vamp, oxygenated rather than suffocated the quartet, his bass drum gently but insistently punctuating the "one" of each bar as he danced the beat between taps on his snare drum and the reverberant depth of his ride cymbal.

Vamps are the throbbing heartbeat of popular music, and Brubeck's "Take Five" vamp exists among an elite of instantly recognizable vamps that make audiences go crazy: John Lee Hooker's "Boogie Chillen'," Muddy Waters's "Mannish Boy," Chuck Berry's "Johnny B. Goode," Lee Morgan's "The Sidewinder," The Kinks' "You Really Got Me," Led Zeppelin's "Whole Lotta Love." What determines that one vamp will be utterly addictive, enough to trigger a sensory rush, while others never quite catch on is the ultimate pop mystery. When Desmond tried to piggyback a hit off the back of "Take Five" by recording "Take Ten" in 1963[27] as the title track of a record of his own (produced by George Avakian), nobody cared much; and Lee Morgan faced similar disappointment when he cast "The Rumproller" in the image of "The Sidewinder."

To be fair, not even Brubeck recognized the potential of his vamp at first. It was mere rhythmic and harmonic glue designed to keep the quartet together, after the traumas of all those aborted attempts. Play the vamp neatly, quietly, and unobtrusively, and then absolutely nothing can go wrong, was the new strategy. But it was Brubeck's caution—his nervy determination to get it right—that led his left hand to brush past the first beat of the fourth bar of the vamp without making that low E-flat sound. By the next time it appeared on an official Dave Brubeck Quartet album—recorded live at Carnegie Hall in February 1963[28]—"Take Five" had infatuated hearts and minds, and the audience, already whipped into a frenzy by an ecstatic "Blue Rondo à la Turk," responded with a communal shout of joy. Improvising in 5/4 time by now had become second nature, and that once-inconspicuous vamp had been repurposed as a rallying call.

In the absence of those session reels, Brubeck's vamp helps open a window onto the sorts of discussions the quartet must have had on July 1. The "Take Five" single, released in 1961, was not, as is often assumed, an edit of the album version (on the B side was an edited "Blue Rondo à la Turk," minus the blues

27. RCA Victor LPM 2569.
28. There were, of course, various earlier bootlegs, and the quartet recorded a vocal version of "Take Five" on the album *Take Five Live* with Carmen McRae at Basin Street East on September 6, 1961. But the Carnegie Hall version was the first official instrumental version after *Time Out*.

solos, which was like a sandwich without any filling). On the single, Desmond turned in what sounds like a dress rehearsal, with many of those same sighing, falling motifs in place but without the connective tissue that made his album solo sound so effortless and chaste. Even at this eleventh hour, adjustments were still being made to the A section of the theme, which, on the album, was diverted around a slightly more complicated melodic route than on the single.[29] And it's that missing note in Brubeck's vamp on the album, as compared to the single, where it is proudly present and correct, that confirms that more than one take of "Take Five" was recorded on July 1.

With the single largely forgotten, or perhaps airbrushed out of history, the misnomer that "Take Five" was completed in one take on July 1 was reinforced when, in 2009, the fiftieth anniversary "legacy edition" of *Time Out,* coproduced by Russell Gloyd, omitted any alternate takes.[30] Assuming that any historically minded reissue would contain alternate takes was reasonable enough, given that the half-century anniversaries of *Mingus Ah Um* and *Kind of Blue* had been marked by deluxe CD editions with extra tracks backed up by sober commentary in newly commissioned booklet notes. During this era, when CDs were beginning to give way to downloads, Columbia's appetite for reissuing their back catalog of 1950s and 1960s jazz classics was insatiable, and it began to eat itself in 2010 with a Miles Davis box set, presented in the shape of a trumpet case, that boxed up all their previous Davis box sets.[31] Dollars could still be made, and had the session reels not been misplaced, Sony

29. Blink and you might miss it, but Desmond plays the melody on the single with bars 6 and 7 literal repeats of bars 2 and 3; on the album, bar 6 drops the sixteenth-note pattern of the last beat down a major third; bar 7 raises the same pattern up a major third, and the bar opens with a B-flat (E-flat on the single).

30. Columbia/Legacy 739852, released May 26, 2009. A second CD contained previously unreleased live performances of material from *Time Out* (and elsewhere)—but no alternate takes.

31. *The Genius of Miles Davis* (Columbia/Legacy 88697157662), released October 26, 2010.

would surely have given *Time Out*'s most celebrated track the same treatment as *Mingus Ah Um* and *Kind of Blue*.

Lacking the evidence to further the story of "Take Five" much beyond the June 25 rehearsal is frustrating. Did Brubeck take a solo that was cut from the master take of "Take Five"? Between Desmond's solo and Morello's, all the evidence points toward an edit or a cut. The giveaway is a sudden, artificial shift in the tone and pitch of Morello's cymbal that cuts across its natural acoustic resonance and could only be the result of an expedient splice. If those tapes ever turn up and the gaps can be filled, I'll be sure to get back to you, but in the meantime nothing can detract from the miracle of "Take Five." The impeccable intimacy of the recording captured every wavering breath of Desmond's saxophone, while the minimalism of Morello's solo and the choreography of Brubeck's vamp proved irresistible. The record's sound, its aura, and its harmonic intrigues overrode that momentary fumble in the vamp and the awkward editing—and any concerns Columbia might have had about odd time signatures—to hand the quartet the biggest hit that any instrumental jazz group had ever achieved.

Miles Davis's life wasn't changed by *Kind of Blue* to the extent that Brubeck's was changed by *Time Out*. The group that had recorded *Kind of Blue* soon reached a natural end point, after which Davis began the process of assembling a new quintet that eventually coalesced around Wayne Shorter, Herbie Hancock, Ron Carter, and Tony Williams—which still played material from *Kind of Blue* live as, in the studio, they created a string of new classic albums, including *ESP*, *Miles Smiles*, and *Nefertiti*.

Anyone expecting Brubeck to have similarly responded to *Time Out*'s unexpected success with another feast of math-based jazz would need to wait until *Time Further Out*, which was not recorded and released until 1961. *The Riddle*, for which Desmond temporarily made way for Bill Smith, who brought along eight of his compositions to the 30th Street Studio, was recorded a week before the final *Time Out* session, but it was quickly forgotten when it was released in 1960.[32] With Desmond returned, *Southern Scene* didn't pick up where *Time Out* had left off but followed on from *Gone with the Wind* with a program of tunes rooted in the Deep South. After *Time Out* was released on December 14, 1959, and the quartet had taken a well-earned Christmas break, they put down the first tracks for *Brubeck and Rushing* on January 29, 1960, and the very next day returned to the very same studio to record Howard Brubeck's *Dialogues for Jazz Combo and Orchestra* with Leonard Bernstein and the New York Philharmonic.

The all-seeing eye of George Avakian would have perhaps focused more intently on the ripples created by *Time Out* as "Blue Rondo à la Turk" and "Take Five" moved the musical language of the quartet forward while *Southern Scene*, entertaining as it was, repeated an old formula. The Rushing and Bernstein projects were, by accident or design, a valuable demonstration of the range of the quartet: Who else could have recorded blues on a Friday and a complex orchestral piece, involving a grand coming-together of big-band pizzazz, neoclassicism, and twelve-tone composition, on Saturday? But those albums, too, answered different questions to the important ones posed by *Time Out*. From *Jazz Impressions of Eurasia* to *Time Out*, each new recording project had been fresh and daring. In 1960, though, the quartet's recording activities lost a certain momentum, as though Brubeck was waiting for his audience—and Columbia—to catch up with the innovations of *Time Out*.

To claim that *Time Out* was released into a void at the end of 1959 would be to overstate matters—nothing on Columbia, by definition, was especially obscure or lost in the market. But *Time Out* was a slow burn until "Take Five" was released as a

---

32. Columbia CL-1454.

single on May 22, 1961, and, through the advocacy of radio DJs, took people back to the album. The paradox was not lost on Desmond that interest in *Time Out* had been sparked by an inferior take of "Take Five" that he never intended anyone to hear. In an interview published on the Artists House Music website in 2011, Macero remembered Desmond calling him shortly after the release of the single to complain that "you got the wrong take." Macero played dumb: "It can't be, I went over there and did the editing myself," he said, before turning the tables. "Have you been to the bank lately with the royalty statements?" Macero asked. "They're selling like hotcakes!" Desmond responded, Macero's cue to hang up with a cheerful "Bye, Paul!"—which implied that, although the single might not have been Paul's take of choice, any record selling in those quantities could never be the "wrong" take.[33] Macero's interview also hinted at festering tensions. He didn't always find working with Dave "the most pleasant," he said, because "he never wanted to take too much advice." He also felt that Brubeck never gave him due credit for "Take Five."

As Macero told the story, the upsurge in interest from DJs that Brubeck had noticed was no coincidence. It was his doing as part of a concerted campaign cooked up with an old associate during a business trip to Chicago. Before leaving New York, Macero had attended a disheartening meeting with Columbia's head of A and R, Mitch Miller, who was worrying that *Time Out* had only sold thirty-five thousand albums—a vast amount of records by today's standards, but small potatoes to Columbia in 1959. Arriving in Chicago, Macero chanced upon a local record promoter called Granny White. "You got a hit in there . . . 'Take Five,'" White spluttered, and, as a conversation ensued, the two men hatched a plot. Macero would prepare an edit of "Take

---

33. ArtistsHouseMusic, "Teo Macero on Working with Dave Brubeck and Miles Davis," YouTube video, 12:10, February 17, 2011, www.youtube.com/watch?v=2yK6kXSqB2k.

Five," and then White would send a telegram to the sales department at Columbia Records in New York requesting five thousand singles. Macero predicted that the sales department team would run into his office shouting, "Breakout in Chicago, we need to move right away!"—and he was right. "I had thirty-five or forty acetates ready that were shipped to Chicago," he remembered, "and they were passed all over town—and then that record sold a couple of million!" As he reported his conversation with Grady some fifty years after the event, Macero said he used the phrase, "I can't *get* a single out of that" [my italics]. Would "getting" a single out of the album version of "Take Five" have involved taking a knife to Desmond's structurally faultless solo and disrupting the cumulative impact of Morello's solo—could this be why Macero decided to edit the single from a different take?

On Sunday, July 5, 1959—only four days after completing the master take of "Take Five"—Brubeck appeared at the Newport Jazz Festival, sandwiched between sets by Stan Kenton's orchestra and the singer Pat Suzuki, and the Kingston Trio and Louis Armstrong and His All-Stars. That audience in Newport was the first to hear "Three to Get Ready," "Blue Rondo à la Turk," and "Take Five" live. "Three to Get Ready" quickly hit a strident groove, but although solos in "Blue Rondo" were powerful and driving, the quartet's presentation of Brubeck's theme barely avoided falling apart. More work was needed.

As Morello launched "Take Five," it's spooky to hear Brubeck project his vamp into silence. There were no cheers or applause—to this audience the vamp was attractive enough, but not worth acknowledging. Desmond began his solo by bouncing around melodic utterances familiar from the album, and then Morello claimed the part of "Take Five" that would forever be his own. After he opened by replaying the spacious meticulousness of his solo on the album, Morello's patterns soon became wilder, freer, and hotter. Brubeck shouted "Yeah!" and the audience whooped its approval as his solo reached its climax. Experiences like this confirmed Brubeck's view that *Time Out*, while considered experimental, also had the power to move audiences.

In terms of prestige and financial security, *Time Out* changed everything for Brubeck, and his concerts, from now until the end of his life, were given a definite shape: everything led toward "Blue Rondo à la Turk" and "Take Five." During the 1970s, the era when Brubeck was mixing it up with his sons in their group Two Generations of Brubeck and serving up an often-combustible concoction of jazz, free improvisation, abstract composition, and rock rhythms, the promise of "Take Five" would become a bond of trust with his audience. The royalty payments from "Take Five" might have gone to Paul Desmond—who bequeathed them to the Red Cross in his will—but *Time Out* handed Brubeck something just as valuable: complete creative control over his career.

As a family, the Brubecks' lives were about to change in other ways too. Writing to Krzysztof Komeda on October 7, 1959, Iola reported that the family had spent that summer on the East Coast—they would permanently relocate east the following year. She also told Komeda about their residency at the Lenox School of Jazz at the Music Inn, a summer school nestled in the Berkshire Hills in Massachusetts where some of America's youngest and brightest jazz musicians went to study with the jazz masters, a counterpart to the nearby classical summer school Tanglewood, where students could work with the likes of Aaron Copland and Serge Koussevitzky. "The teachers [at the Music Inn] are outstanding," Iola wrote. "John Lewis, and all the other members of the Modern Jazz Quartet, Jimmy Giuffre, Max Roach, Jim Hall, and teaching composition and arranging are Herb Pomery, Gunther Schuller, and George Russell. Marshall Stearns and Dr. Willis James teach jazz history, and Dr. James explores the folk origins of jazz."[34]

---

34. Iola Brubeck to Krzysztof Komeda, October 7, 1959, Personal Correspondence, Brubeck Collection.

During his stay at the Music Inn, Brubeck was relieved to hear a lecture by Willis James during which he demonstrated an African field holler. "He started to sing a very complicated but interesting song in a language completely foreign to me," Brubeck wrote in his unpublished journal. "When he finished he said 'This is an African folk song—can anyone tell me what time signature is was in?'" No one in that educated audience responded. So he said 'That African folk song is in 5/4 time and the DBQ [Dave Brubeck Quartet] is on the right track.' I felt vindicated. It was a happy day in my life."[35]

Iola told Komeda about *Gone with the Wind* and *The Riddle*, and that they had just completed work on a "musical play to star Louis Armstrong." But *Time Out* seemed especially significant. "Dave is quite excited about his new album, which is not yet available," she wrote. "It is called 'Time Out' and has in it many different experiments in rhythms. They improvise in 5/4, 9/8, 6/8, 3/4 alternating with 2/4—and they do it in such a natural way that the group still swings to a jazz beat. I find it very exciting." Little did she know.

Eleven summers later, on Saturday, August 29, 1970, at the Isle of Wight Festival—the UK's answer to the Woodstock Festival—the prog rock group Emerson, Lake & Palmer, who had just performed their reimagining of *Pictures at an Exhibition*, a composition originally for piano by the Russian composer Modest Mussorgsky but best known in an orchestral arrangement by Maurice Ravel, launched into a number they called "Rondo."

Earlier that same day, a disgruntled hippie called Yogi Joe had interrupted Joni Mitchell's set, delivering a rambling and incoherent speech before being dragged away by security. Miles Davis's group played a set drawn from his latest album, *Bitches*

---

35. Dave Brubeck, handwritten journal, undated entry, Brubeck Collection (uncataloged).

*Brew,* which had been released five months earlier, and following Emerson, Lake & Palmer came The Doors, The Who, and Sly and the Family Stone. The Davis group included two keyboard players, Chick Corea and Keith Jarrett, who had been influenced by Brubeck in their formative years, while anyone suspecting they heard traces of Brubeck in the full-throttle block chords that keyboardist Ray Manzarek brought to The Doors was not mistaken. While a student at DePaul University in Chicago in the mid-'50s, Manzarek had played piano in a student jazz band and organized a charity concert that featured two of his favorite jazz stars—Sonny Rollins and Dave Brubeck. The Bach-influenced counterpoint that introduced one of The Doors' greatest hits, "Light My Fire," could have been lifted directly from a Brubeck record. Another Doors hit, "Break On Through (To the Other Side)," had a bass line clearly indebted to Ray Charles's "What I Say" that also shadowed the harmonic contours of the "Take Five" riff. The harmonic twists and turns of Manzarek's solo makes the *Time Out* connection explicit; and you feel that, at any moment, drummer John Densmore would be happy to add in an extra beat, levering this funky 4/4 beat into 5/4 time.

As Corea, Jarrett, and Manzarek were absorbing the influence of Brubeck in the US, in Sussex, England, Keith Emerson was undergoing a similar learning. "My mother and father earned little and my meagre earnings from a newspaper and grocery round were put towards a stereo record player," he wrote in a message posted on his website in 2009 after seeing the Brubeck quartet perform in Southern California.[36] "That Christmas, my present from Mum and Dad was a single 45 vinyl record, 'Take Five.' On the B-side was 'Blue Rondo à la Turk.' I played the hell out of it." Then Emerson bought the sheet music and learnt the notes—which, all those years later, he played at the Isle of Wight.

36. https://www.keithemerson.com/MiscPages/2009/20090924-DaveBrubeck.html

Although "Rondo" is credited "Brubeck" on the album that resulted from ELP's performance,[37] the piece is far removed from anything that Brubeck, or Paul Desmond, or Wright, Morello, and Macero, could have envisaged. Beginning with forked slabs of electric sound, like a moment from Karlheinz Stockhausen's trail-blazing electronic *Kontakte* (1958–1960), Emerson then struck a huge gong before placing his hands on his Hammond organ, thrusting it backward and forward, to pump air through its innards. Then he launched himself into a furious keyboard solo out of which spilt a familiar theme: "Blue Rondo à la Turk," but with one major difference. Emerson squashed the 2+2+2+3 by playing the last "3" in the time of two, which recast Brubeck's original 9/8 pattern as a turbo-charged 4/4 rock beat. If the idea was to maintain a solid, grooving beat over which he, and then drummer Carl Palmer, could solo, Emerson succeeded. The performance was a roller-coaster ride. The cleanly executed keyboard lines with which Emerson began his solo soon congealed into a throbbing mass of electronic sound and, determined to squeeze out all the sonic juice possible, he jumped on top of his instrument and rode it like a rodeo horse. Palmer's drum solo crashed in at a moment of peak energy. Morello would certainly have admired his snare drum technique, but not his theatrical ripping off of his waistcoat and T-shirt as his solo reached burnout.

Before forming ELP, Emerson had tested the prog rock waters with a band called The Nice, in which covers of Bob Dylan songs bumped into arrangements of music by composers like Bach, Tchaikovsky, and Sibelius; and the first appearance of "Rondo" was on their debut album *The Thoughts of Emerlist Davjack*.[38] The Nice also had a chart hit with their version of Leonard Bernstein's "America" from *West Side Story*, a record

---

37. Emerson, Lake & Palmer, *Live at the Isle of Wight, 1970*, Manticore Records (M-CD-101).

38. The Nice, *The Thoughts of Emerlist Davjack* (Immediate IMSP 016).

which reportedly displeased Bernstein greatly because Emerson scrunched together the rhythmic subtleties of his song—6/8 alternating with 3/4—to produce a head-banging 4/4 rock beat. But Brubeck was more forgiving and, in 2003, after the same concert in Brighton that opened this book, signed Emerson's sheet music copy of "Blue Rondo"—"For Keith, with many thanks for your 4/4 version which I can't play."[39]

Prog rock was a term that materialized on both sides of the Atlantic in the latter half of the 1960s, triggered by albums such as The Beatles' *Sgt. Pepper's Lonely Hearts Club Band*, The Beach Boys' *Pet Sounds*, and The Kinks' *The Kinks Are the Village Green Preservation Society*, which aspired to create something more unified and compositionally complex than the string of musically unrelated songs typical of pop albums. Back in 1954, when he was on the brink of signing Brubeck to Columbia, George Avakian had conceived of the album in a similar way—which helped pave the way for Miles Davis's *Miles Ahead*, Charles Mingus's *Mingus Ah Um*, and, of course, Brubeck's *Time Out*. Emerson, Lake & Palmer, along with other British groups such as Genesis, King Crimson, Soft Machine, Henry Cow, Jethro Tull, Pink Floyd, and Yes had started to experiment with grand composition schemes, asymmetrical time signatures, and supplementing the standard rock band instrumentation with orchestral weight—anything to distance their work from the simple 12- or 32-bar pop song typified by something like The Beatles' "Lady Madonna."

Audiences, including some that had never been to a rock concert before, filled stadia as prog rock moved from a niche concern to a mainstream money-spinner for record labels and concert promoters—and the critics, generally, *hated* it. At *Rolling Stone* magazine, Loyd Grossman gave ELP's debut album a cautious thumbs-up, although his line "I suppose that your

---

39. https://www.keithemerson.com/MiscPages/2009/20090924-DaveBrubeck.html.

local newspaper might call it 'jazz-influenced classical-rock'"[40] was delivered with a discreet sneer. But there was nothing discreet about Lester Bangs's slamming of ELP's *Pictures at an Exhibition* release a year later—"If poor old Mussorgsky and Ravel can hear what Emerson, Lake and Palmer have done to their music," he wrote, "they are probably getting dry heaves in the Void."[41]

Bangs believed in the noble majesty of the simple—for which don't read "simplistic"—rock song. When Jon Anderson, lead singer of Yes, described prog rock as "really developing into a higher art form—building up the same way classical music did into huge works that last and stand the test of time,"[42] the instinct of critics of Bangs's persuasion was to prick what they considered to be colossal pomposity. Because the last thing honest-to-goodness rock music needed was grandiose self-aggrandizement and clever-dick "concepts." Another distinguished rock critic of the era, Robert Christgau, claimed "These guys are as stupid as their most pretentious fans" in a review of ELP's 1972 album *Trilogy*.[43]

As King Crimson put out *In the Court of the Crimson King* in 1969 and Mike Oldfield released *Tubular Bells* in 1973, critical factions became entrenched. The King Crimson album was jam-packed with bitonal shifts of harmony and lopsided time signatures; *Tubular Bells* was etched around a grid of shifting time signatures. Even ELP, despite their rhythmically square "Rondo" and "America," demonstrated their knack at playing other time signatures—if composed by Emerson. Their second album, *Tarkus*, opens with an extended composition in different movements, with sections in 5/4 time ("Eruption")

40. Review, Loyd Grossman, *Rolling Stone*, April 15, 1971.
41. Review, Lester Bangs, *Rolling Stone*, March 2, 1972.
42. Interview, Jon Anderson, *Sounds* magazine, 1971.
43. http://www.robertchristgau.com/get_artist.php?name=emerson+lake+and+palmer.

and 9/8 subdivided as Brubeck had shown them was possible ("Manticore").

Although prog rock was largely a British concern, Columbia Records intervened in 1973 with a compilation album they called *The Progressives,* obviously designed to reach out to prog rock fans who might like jazz/rock fusion (and vice versa).[44] British band Gentle Giant—more comfortable playing 5, 7, and 9 than 4/4—were represented with a track called "Knots," alongside other pieces by former Miles Davis guitarist John McLaughlin's Mahavishnu Orchestra, Weather Report, Charles Mingus, Ornette Coleman, and Keith Jarrett. British groups Soft Machine and Matching Mole were also featured.

And as the prog rock saga rolled forward—until the public fell out of love with it somewhere around 1976, when punk became the next big thing—much of the discourse and vocabulary used to give bands like ELP, King Crimson, and Pink Floyd a critical spanking feels spookily familiar to the Brubeck fan. Loyd Grossman supposing that "your local newspaper," which was almost certainly not as hip as *Rolling Stone,* might call ELP's music "jazz-influenced classical-rock" is Ira Gitler supposing, eleven years earlier, that *Time Out* was "drawing room music" and semi-classical pretentious pap "which serves as the real thing for some people." By hitching concepts from outside popular music, like Stravinskian ideas of rhythm and harmony, onto a form that communicated instantly—like the 12-bar blues, or verse/chorus popular song form—critics like Grossman, Bangs, and Christgau were arguing that something had been taken away from rock; the music had been robbed of its essence —which is precisely what Billy Root had argued in his 1956 piece for the *Philadelphia Jazz Digest*[45] about Brubeck in which he complained that counterpoint and fugue "don't

44. Columbia KG 31574.

45. Billy Root, "Cool? Dave Brubeck Is Cold!," *Philadelphia Jazz Digest,* March 1956.

mean a thing to jazz" and that "Brubeck fans think they have to 'study' his music. The very title of one of his albums, *Jazz Goes to College*, is ridiculous. You shouldn't have to sit around and analyze and scrutinize every note as if you were listening to the Philadelphia Orchestra playing Bartók's *Concerto for Orchestra.*" Brubeck in the 1950s, like ELP in the 1970s, stood accused of turning music that audiences ought to be able to *feel* in their gut into an over-intellectualized game.

The glitzy costumes of prog rock, Keith Emerson apparently dry humping his Hammond organ, the ornate stage sets together with the occasional burst of vainglorious pomp is where prog rock begins to part company with the Dave Brubeck Quartet: who were four studious men in smart suits playing chamber jazz. And yet traces of the impact Brubeck's innovations had on the compositional techniques deployed by leading figures of prog rock are not difficult to find; the *Concerto for Group and Orchestra* by Deep Purple's Jon Lord, performed at the Royal Albert Hall in September 1969, seems to pick up directly from where Howard Brubeck's *Dialogues for Jazz Combo and Orchestra* left off.

The links, musically and in terms of critical reception, between Brubeck and prog rock seem almost too good to be true—but let's not forget about The Doors' keyboardist Ray Manzarek, who followed ELP onstage that August night at the Isle of Wight Festival. You wonder if Emerson and Manzarek happened to meet backstage whether they might have discussed their mutual love of Brubeck's music—a conversation that Corea and Jarrett, from Miles Davis's group, might have overheard and joined in with. The miracle is that, as a random selection of rock musicians turned up at a countercultural music festival, so many of them not only had reason to respect Brubeck—but that respect was clearly audible within the fabric of the music they played.

The Doors was no prog rock group. They were a driving rock band, with the blues flowing through their veins. Their lead vocalist Jim Morrison would have had no time for the stage spectacle of prog rock shows, and yet, via Ray Manzarek, Brubeck's influence managed to filter inside their music in a subtle, understated way. In 2009, Ray Davies of The Kinks described how his drummer Mick Avory was obsessed with Joe Morello's playing,[46] which informed the sound Avory made in the band; meanwhile Davies himself spoke of how deeply he appreciated Brubeck and Desmond's playing; "I couldn't stop playing 'Take Five' when it came out. What a feel! What a band!" Tracing that love for Brubeck through into the music of The Kinks itself might be a leap too far, but not so for "Golden Brown," released by the British band The Stranglers in 1981.

This song pivots around E Minor and E Flat Minor (the key of "Take Five") and is based around a vamp—alternating between bars of 6/8 and 7/8—that pays obvious homage to Brubeck's most famous piano figuration; when, in bar nine of the introduction, the song reaches E flat minor, the echoes are eerie. A year later, listeners to Donald Fagen's—of Steely Dan—solo album *The Nightfly* heard Fagen sing "I hear you're mad about Brubeck / I like your eyes, I like him too / He's an artist, a pioneer / We've got to have some music on the new frontier." Fagen had written a song in which boy meets girl at a party and they bond over a shared love of Brubeck's music. And the connections keep coming. Sting's love for writing songs in unusual time signatures—"Love Is Stronger Than Justice" in 7/8, "I Hung My Head" in 9/8, "Seven Days" in 5/4—recurs throughout his work. In 2009, when Brubeck received the Kennedy Center Honors, Sting came to the reception afterward and sat by Brubeck's feet all evening[47]—he was basking in being in the presence of one of his heroes.

Brubeck's relationship to pop matters because it upturns the perceived wisdom that his work had negligible influence

---

46. Interview with the author, November 5, 2009.

47. I'm grateful to Cathy Brubeck, who was present at the same event, for this story.

or impact. True, there might not be a school of Brubeck in the way jazz pianists emulate Monk, Bill Evans, or Keith Jarrett; but look outside jazz and Brubeck's impact is heard in numerous vamps, melodic turns of phrase, and harmonic relationships. In 2019, the New York rap artist Nas (aka Nasir Jones) released "Jarreau of Rap" in which he sampled the jazz vocalist Al Jarreau's vocal version of "Blue Rondo à la Turk." And as Nas rapped in 9/8, the idea of musicians from outside jazz playing "Blue Rondo," which started at the Isle of Wight in 1970, found its extra beat.

*Chapter Eight*

# INVISIBLE MAN

"America is woven of many strands. I would
recognize them and let it so remain. Our fate is to
become one, and yet many."

RALPH ELLISON, *Invisible Man*, 1952

An elderly gentleman, made slow and gracile by the passing
of time, turns his wheelchair out of the galley kitchen of his
plush retirement pad in North Hollywood, spinning it toward
his living room—"If you want to know about Brubeck, I'm
gonna tell you!" he cries. It's October 2017 and Eugene Wright,
ninety-three, is the last surviving member of the classic Dave
Brubeck Quartet.

To get a feel for time and place, I've come to California to
talk to this most distinguished half of "the Section" and connect with the places central to Brubeck's childhood, his ado-
lescence, his career as a student, and the very earliest days of
his professional life as a musician. Los Angeles, Oakland (with

San Francisco in the distance), Concord, and the University of the Pacific in Stockton are on the schedule, and taking the short, early morning flight from LA to Oakland—a flight Brubeck himself no doubt took many times—is already an important lesson. In Oakland, the air feels different. From New York City, certainly, but also from Los Angeles. The pace, the restless itch, and the crammed-together architecture of Manhattan creates an energy that powers any music made there, whether by Charlie Parker, Edgard Varèse, Philip Glass, Debbie Harry, or Lou Reed.

From New York, the Atlantic tide leads toward Europe. In California, the Pacific looks toward Asia and the influence of the East. Places form imaginations, and in Oakland, circled by the San Francisco Bay and the greenery of the Oakland Hills, you're surrounded by, and aware of, vast expanses of space, and within a few minutes of my arrival, I understand Brubeck better. The unruffled spaciousness of *Brubeck Time, Jazz Impressions of the USA*, and *Time Out* feels as far removed from East Coast bebop as the works of John Cage, Lou Harrison, or Terry Riley—other great spirits who found their creative calling around Los Angeles and San Francisco during the 1940s and '50s—are from the East Coast modernism of Varèse or Elliott Carter. Could the main reason why New York–based critics like Whitney Balliett and Ira Gitler found Brubeck so problematic rest on this simple cultural misunderstanding?

Tall, elegant, and with a smile as inviting as a warm spa bath, Eugene Wright speaks quickly, his nervous hesitancy clearing as he formulates an idea—then words shoot out of his mouth with scattergun impulsiveness, leaving you struggling to keep up. Wright's mind, like that of many nonagenarians, wanders and drifts; 1963 fades back to 1955 without warning. He talks about taking the train from Pennsylvania to New York in the early 1950s with John Coltrane, then a young saxophonist afraid that a career as a musician might be beyond him; about his love for Walter Page's bass playing and the time he spent in the Basie orchestra; about the joy of working with Brubeck and the threatening underbelly of segregation. His bass is propped up against the wall, next to an upright piano. On the opposite wall is a framed golden disc celebrating sales of two million copies of *Time Out* surrounded by photographs of Brubeck, Desmond, and Morello. This feels unbearably moving. These colleagues and comrades with whom he shared so much are all gone now, leaving Wright as the last surviving witness and a guardian of so many memories.

"Joe Morello told Dave to get me for the bass."[1] Wright is thinking back to 1958, when Norman Bates quit the quartet.

"Dave, I don't take on jobs I don't know that I can do," so he said come over to the house. He'd just had a house built in Oakland, right up in the hills, and I borrowed Paul's car to get my bass up there. There was a big beautiful piano and Dave said, "What you want to play?" I know all the standards and he said, "Okay, 'Brother, Can You Spare a Dime?' He started playing his version of the tune[2] and we played the first chorus fine, but in the second chorus he made a mistake, which didn't happen too often. Now, I hadn't played with him before, but I knew how to listen and I had a good ear, and he carried on playing, and I waited until—bang—I caught up with him, made it right. Dave was delighted with how that afternoon went and offered me the job; I took it, and never looked back.

We played one concert before we left [for Europe], but we didn't rehearse. I'd heard the quartet and I knew a little bit about how Dave played, but once I began playing with him I learned that he knew all the old standards—he grew up knowing all that stuff—but then he got to that college where he

---

1. Interview with the author, October 2, 2017.
2. The version familiar from *Brubeck Time*.

realized he wasn't happy just playing jazz. His whole life, he wanted to play the things he could hear in his head. We didn't play keys a lot of the time—can you understand that? He'd start playing something and I'd hear it . . .

As we talk, Wright becomes animated. He likes talking; he likes talking Brubeck in particular. Sitting in his wheelchair, he starts to move to the groove of his reminiscences. He plucks melodic shapes out of nowhere, his long and still-agile fingers tracing the bass patterns of "Brother, Can You Spare a Dime?" in the air. After telling me that the quartet "didn't play keys a lot of the time," his mind wanders elsewhere, but I do understand: from their 1954 taking-apart of "Stardust" in Berkeley to Brubeck's solo on "Nomad" from *Jazz Impressions of Eurasia* four years later, the quartet's free-associative tendencies led them to swim around keys.

That one concert the quartet played before leaving for Europe was, of course, the now-notorious evening at East Carolina College when Brubeck stood his ground against the college authorities, who would not allow Wright to play. "If you want to talk history, we'll talk history, my friend!" Wright replies when I remind him of the incident.

We were waiting to go on for an hour, an hour and a half maybe, and man, when finally we went on, we smoked. That audience, they knew what had happened. They'd been kicking the floor and chanting because they wanted us to play, and, boy, I remember the roar when we hit the stand. After we finished the first song, they cheered for five minutes and we had to wait until they cooled off before we could carry on. Dave played like crazy that night, and Joe and I got it together right away. Dave laid out during one of Paul's solos, and Joe and I suddenly dropped behind him. In a situation like that you *don't* give everything right away; you start quietly, and Paul loved that. He had room to build a long solo, ten or fifteen choruses perhaps, and Joe and I moved it up a notch every few choruses. Paul took it to such a peak that Dave didn't take a solo.

What about other black musicians, former colleagues or acquaintances—did anyone question why Wright wanted to play with Brubeck? "One time we were playing a benefit concert in Carnegie Hall for the NAACP,[3] five or six different bands, and we opened the second half. Before we played one off the brothers said, 'Gene Wright! What are you doing with that group?' And I said, 'Well, I was offered a job.' Afterward he came up to me and said, 'Man, I owe you an apology, because you made Dave play harder than I've ever heard him play.'"

Wright reaffirms the importance of Walter Page and Basie to everything he brought to the quartet, a vital link to jazz tradition.

I'd played with everybody: Buddy DeFranco, Art Blakey, Monk on a dance job in New York, and everything I played with them I brought to Dave. My job was time; Joe's job was holding time and color, and I played just like Walter Page in that band. I'd loved Page before I even had a bass, when I heard the Basie band in Chicago. When I went to New York—and I was cleaning people's houses to pay the rent at the YMCA—I eventually got to play with Gene Ammons. Charlie Parker would come into the club where we were playing, and all the guys would tell Basie, "You got to go hear this bass player, he plays just like Walter Page."

After the classic quartet folded in 1967, Brubeck wrote Wright a reference that testified to how deeply he had come to rely on him as a musician but also, eventually, as the quartet's road manager, a role that Wright pursued vigorously. "This letter is to acknowledge the outstanding capability of Eugene Wright, who served the Dave Brubeck Quartet in the capacity of

3. National Association for the Advancement of Colored People.

road manager as well as bass player," Brubeck wrote. "Through nine years of concert performances and innumerable Columbia recordings, his musicianship speaks for itself. What is not so well known, perhaps, is the faithfulness with which he discharged all his extra-musical duties, such as handling souvenir programs, shipment of instruments, car rentals etc. His accounting has been conscientiously detailed and accurate. He has never missed a concert and he has never been late. As anyone with road experience can appreciate, this in itself is an outstanding achievement. I value Eugene as a musician, road manager and freind [*sic*]."

Brubeck's unpublished journal gives us a vivid account of the camaraderie between these four young musicians as they set off into the world. The derivation of Wright's moniker of choice—"Senator"—has long been shrouded in mystery, a mystery which Brubeck was happy to resolve. "Gene has been known for years as the 'Senator,'" he explained.

It has become more than a nickname and his letters and cards are signed that way. . . . I think it started on an airplane trip when J[oe] M[orello] said to a flight attendant that "the Senator" would be joining him. And because it made such an impression on the stewardess and surrounding passengers it was a phrase often used to get a special seat for his imposing 6'4" figure. Sometimes in an airplane Joe would speak in an accent that made people think that he was from India or Pakistan and Eugene would start with nonsense syllables and people would think he came from . . . Africa. He could keep this nonsensical dialect going for so long that it became so convincing that he had just come from some remote part of the Congo. Sometimes I would join in with a few words of native American I knew.[4]

---

4. Dave Brubeck, handwritten journal, undated entry, Brubeck Collection (uncataloged).

However much they enjoyed goofing around, though, the disquieting realities of segregation where never far behind and sometimes presented themselves in unexpected places. "I had told E[ugene] W[right] that some of the tours coming up would take us into parts of the country where segregation was still enforced. But a big surprise for the Q[uarte]t was when we worked at Lake Minnetonka, Minneapolis and E[ugene] was not allowed to stay any place close to the job or the lake. So Gene, Paul and Joe drove back and forth from M[innea]P[o]L[i]S every nite. Some place in the north I recall seeing a sign that said 'Don't let the sun set on any negro in this town.'"

"Don't let the sun set on any negro in this town"—more often "Negro, don't let the sun set on your head in this town"—was an old Confederate trope aimed at running black people out of town: *Go now, before the sun sets—don't wait until tomorrow.* After playing one concert at a military base near Enid in Oklahoma, the quartet was informed that they were not welcome to stay the night. "We were told . . . we would have to find something in town," Brubeck wrote.

So Joe, Gene and I drove into town [and] went to the most logical hotel where we thought we could stay the night. When the clerk saw us enter, he told me "no negroes allowed at this hotel." I used every argument I could think of, but nothing convinced the clerk that we could stay. So we walked out to the street and stood there discussing what to do next to avoid the only thing we could think of [which] was to sleep in the car.

Just then P[aul] D[esmond] pulled up in a white Cadillac. The driver got out and said, "What are you guys doing on the street?" I explained that they wouldn't take us at the hotel because of Eugene. He said, "Do you mind if I go in to talk to them?" . . . He came back out and said, "Go on in and register." I said, "What did you say different from what I said?" . . . "I told them that if you don't accept this group I'd foreclose on their little ol' hotel" . . . and he [also] said if we have any trouble getting out of here I have two jet planes that will be at your disposal. It turned out he was a president of an oil company from the Oklahoma area. He would often see J[oe] M[orello] for years after that.

Sometimes if a promoter found the problem of obtaining a hotel room for Wright insurmountable, he might end up in a luxurious country club, where the usual rules about segregation did not apply—accommodation considerably superior to the basic hotel where the rest of the quartet might stay. But this was a Pyrrhic victory.

Pressure to conform to racial codes came even from those who Brubeck might have expected would be sympathetic. On October 6, 1959, Bob Bundy, who worked alongside Larry Bennett at Associated Booking Corporation, wrote to Brubeck imploring him to replace Wright for a forthcoming tour of the South:

> A couple of weeks ago I wrote to you about playing 25 colleges and universities in the south and southwest during the month of February, sponsored by a newly formed organization. The chairman of this organization just called me and wanted to know if you had any colored boys in your group, which you do. My prupose [sic] in writing to you is to see if you could arrange to have an all white group to play these colleges and universities, because they will not accept you as a mixed group. Please let me hear from you immediately, as 25 dates for $1500 per concert are not to be sneezed at. This should be considered seriously, as college concerts are the backbone of your income.

To reinforce the message, Bundy added in his blocky handwriting, "You Need This" under his signature.[5]

---

5. Bob Bundy to Dave Brubeck, October 6, 1959, Business Correspondence, Brubeck Collection.

Brubeck refused, a principled stand that ended, inevitably, in a showdown with Joe Glaser, who balked at the idea of losing his commission. Out of the twenty-five dates, Brubeck decided that only two offered terms that he considered acceptable, which left a shortfall of nearly $35,000.[6] He rejected outright the proposal that Norman Bates take Wright's place for the other twenty-three concerts (and there were good musical reasons, too, for doubting whether Bates could have gotten his fingers around "Blue Rondo à la Turk," "Three to Get Ready," or "Take Five"). So the remaining concerts were canceled, leading Ralph Gleason, in the *San Francisco Chronicle*, to report, "Refusing to drop a Negro musician from his group on a month-long Southern tour is costing jazz musician Dave Brubeck an estimated $40,000 in bookings, The Chronicle learned last night. Brubeck disclosed here that Southern colleges and universities had canceled concert appearances by his quartet. . . . In New York City, the man who lined up the concert tour, Joseph Glaser, said 'they made no bones about it—they wouldn't play Brubeck because he has a colored bass player.'" Gleason also mentioned Louis Armstrong's canceling a concert in the South for the same reason. The article was headlined "Racial Issue 'Kills' Brubeck Jazz Tour of the South," and a headshot of Brubeck was captioned, "A matter of principle."[7]

The quartet, including Wright, could have played some of those twenty-five dates had Brubeck agreed to play to a segregated audience, but even this was a line he refused to cross. Brubeck's refusal to budge on the matter had also led him to cancel a promotional appearance on the highly popular *Bell Telephone Hour*, on NBC, when a producer insisted on filming the quartet with Wright out of the shot; the quartet was replaced by Duke Ellington. Brubeck's stance on racism might have hit

---

6. Equivalent to $350,000 today.

7. Ralph Gleason, "Racial Issue 'Kills' Brubeck Jazz Tour of the South," *San Francisco Chronicle*, January 12, 1960.

him hard in the wallet, but his physical safety wasn't threatened until one night in 1964 at the University of Alabama.

Two years earlier, in 1962, the university had overruled the student entertainment committee and canceled an appearance by Ray Charles that had been scheduled for the fall. Racism at the University of Alabama was systemic. The Ku Klux Klan had infiltrated both the student body and the upper echelons of staff and administration, and the KKK was determined to keep the university segregated—and, if they had their way, for whites only. In an eerie echo of Little Rock, on June 11, 1963, George Wallace, the governor of Alabama, stood at the door of the Foster Auditorium to block two black students, Vivian Malone and James Hood, from enrolling—an incident that would become known as the "Stand in the Schoolhouse Door."

Wallace had campaigned for the governorship by promising to maintain segregation—his inaugural address included a guarantee of "segregation now, segregation tomorrow, segregation forever"—and his "Stand in the Schoolhouse Door" was George Wallace's wanting to be seen putting his promises into action. Nationally, however, with the aftershock of Emmett Till's murder still resonating, politics had moved on, and President Kennedy issued the sort of decree that President Eisenhower had failed to produce during the Little Rock crisis. The head of the Alabama National Guard, General Henry Graham, was dispatched to the university to deliver this line: "Sir, it is my sad duty to ask you to step aside under the orders of the president of the United States." The two students were able to enroll, and Wallace and the KKK had been defeated that day— which amplified their resentment and determination to make their point.

The Brubeck Quartet's concert at the university, on March 12, 1964, became a focal point of KKK frustration. The Klan was outraged that the group contained a black player and that Brubeck insisted that the audience be integrated, and it threatened violence and disruption. The jazz pianist David Vest, then living in Birmingham, Alabama, attended the concert and remembered the KKK and the White Citizens' Council picketing the entrance to the hall, and Brubeck's calm amid the storm: "The performers and the audience were in open defiance of the KKK. . . . Dave Brubeck—and to its everlasting credit, the University of Alabama—had decided not to let terrorists, thugs and bigots call the shots."[8]

Vest also remembered the quartet playing a piece in 13/4 time, which would almost certainly have been "World's Fair" from the quartet's 1963 album *Time Changes*. "I wanted to know how he 'thought' in 13/4 while he was playing it, and how on earth his band managed to swing in such unconventional meter," he said. After the concert, Brubeck stayed on in the auditorium to answer questions from his audience, and Vest noticed how he "effortlessly integrated the student questioners by inviting black students to 'come up here where I can hear the question.'" Vest asked his question; Brubeck willingly answered it. The intricacies of music theory prevailed over the commotion outside.

On December 10, 1966, Brubeck was on a flight to New York when a fellow passenger introduced himself. Wilbur Rowand was head of the Department of Music at the University of Alabama and wanted Brubeck to know what a difference his concert two years earlier had made. Later, he followed up by letter. "That . . . Sunday afternoon program presented by you and your musicians was the first time that the box office at our main auditorium had been integrated. We had a number of colored people at the program in spite of the fact that there was considerable threat on the outside by representatives of the KKK. I am pleased to report to you that we have had no unpleasant

---

8. Ben Windham, "Brubeck Walked the Walk on Race and All the Jazz," *Tuscaloosa News*, July 7, 2013, www.tuscaloosanews.com/opinion/20130707 /southern-lights-brubeck-walked-the-walk-on-race-and-all-the-jazz.

incidents since that day and all of our concerts, lectures and public attractions have been integrated."[9]

What does Eugene Wright remember of that day in Alabama, fifty-three years earlier? In response to my question, he starts to sing what sounds like a gravelly blues. "Dave wrote me this bass solo, which Iola always loved. Damn, what's it called?" He sings some more, and I identify it as "King for a Day" from *The Real Ambassadors*. "We did this thing Dave had written for Louis Armstrong. Jon Hendricks was there! At Monterey! We never did it again because Joe Glaser, you know, got nervous. But, man, what a night . . . "

*The Real Ambassadors*—the "musical play to star Louis Armstrong," music by Dave and lyrics by Iola—that Iola mentioned in a letter to Krzysztof Komeda—had been gestating since the quartet had begun to work with Wright, and the timing of their brush with racism at East Carolina College in 1958, the day before they were due to leave on a government-sponsored tour to promote the benefits of American democracy, clicked the concept firmly into place. Brubeck, rightly so, regarded *The Real Ambassadors* as one of the pinnacles of his career. Its first performance, at the Monterey Jazz Festival in 1962, was both eagerly discussed and widely praised in the jazz press; Brubeck's sharing a stage with Armstrong and Carmen McRae, combined with the emotional punch of his score, proved irresistible and won over even the usually agnostic Ralph Gleason.

But Brubeck made one unfortunate miscalculation. With so much music and so many musicians to coordinate, how to document the performance clean slipped his mind. For $750—to be paid in cash up front—a television crew on location to film other festival performances would have happily obliged; but

9. Wilbur Rowland to Dave Brubeck, February 27, 1967, Personal Correspondence, Brubeck Collection.

Brubeck wasn't in the habit of carrying around today's equivalent of $7,500 in cash. So the performance was not filmed. In retrospect, Columbia's failure to make even an audio recording feels like a clumsy oversight. The company was motivated by selling records, not documenting jazz history, and having already recorded a studio version of *The Real Ambassadors* over two sessions in September and December 1961 for release the following year, to tie in with the Monterey performance, they felt their duty was done.

After the Monterey performance, and despite all the favorable press coverage—more than could be said for *Time Out*— *The Real Ambassadors* sank without trace. Joe Glaser's stubborn refusal to commit Brubeck and Armstrong to a run of live performances, on Broadway or anywhere else, when they could have been on the road playing lucrative live concerts, which benefited him financially, was an extraordinary display of self-interested chutzpah from the same man who had suggested replacing Wright with Norman Bates for twenty-three concerts, not because he was a racist, but because the dollars came first. Glaser could have synchronized schedules and made sure *The Real Ambassadors* happened, but he chose not to. This cut the piece off in its prime and dealt it a fatal blow, and another factor contributing to its neglect was that the album Columbia released in 1962 told only part of the story. The score was diced and spliced. Iola's narration, which she would deliver herself in Monterey, was removed in its entirety, which left listeners with only some of the music and none of the connecting narrative.

When a vocal score was published in 1973,[10] Iola's narration was reinstated, woven around the musical numbers. *The Real Ambassadors*, somewhere between jazz opera and Broadway musical, could also be thought of as a latter-day singspiel— opera interspersed with dialogue, like Mozart's *The Magic Flute*

10. Dave Brubeck, *Deluxe Piano Album Number Two* (New York: Charles Hansen Music and Books, 1973).

and Kurt Weill's *Mahagonny-Songspiel*—around which a debate rolls on about how best to document such works on record. Extended passages of dialogue, which flow naturally between musical numbers on stage, helping build dramatic impetus, don't necessarily work well delivered "cold" on record—a pressure which no doubt preyed on Macero's mind as *The Real Ambassadors* came together in the studio. The best way to appreciate *The Real Ambassadors* today, to get a sense of what it could ideally be, is to merge a reading of the vocal score with the 1961 recording, especially in its 1994 reissue, which restores tracks cut from the original release. Then the piece feels truly like a "work"—something grander than an attractive collection of Brubeck tunes sung by Louis Armstrong and Carmen McRae, with vocal harmony provided by Lambert, Hendricks & Ross.

*The Real Ambassadors* proposes that segregation perverts any form of decency to such a degree that the only feasible way to grapple with something so abhorrently unjust and inhumane in art is to transform reality into a pretend fantasy, which, as Jonathan Swift and Voltaire had already demonstrated in *Gulliver's Travels* and *Candide*, then becomes ripe for satire. Louis Armstrong portrays a character called "the Hero," who could never be mistaken for anybody other than Louis Armstrong—except that the "Louis Armstrong" portrayed by Louis Armstrong in *The Real Ambassadors* is a fictionalized Louis Armstrong; fantasy bends reality.

And as we meet the Hero, he is wrestling with a moral quandary. The Hero, we know, because he is portrayed by Louis Armstrong, is a jazz trumpeter and singer of considerable renown. So famous and respected is he that his government— which you might think bears a striking similarity to the US government—wishes to send him on a "goodwill" diplomatic tour to Africa. Our Hero is feeling compromised. While such a tour would undoubtedly be an honor and an opportunity to take his art to a new audience, he is afraid of the inevitable criticism of hypocrisy—because how can he promote goodwill abroad while his own government is demonstrating such a lack of good-will toward his own people at home? The refrain—"Though he [the Hero] represents the government, the government doesn't represent him," or indeed the millions of other black Americans living under segregation—haunts the memory, in the manner of *Candide*'s "best of all possible worlds."

Multiple levels of reality embedded into *The Real Ambassadors* by Iola's narration and lyrics help give the piece dramatic thrust while shaping Dave's music. Elements of the real world exist within the fantasy world of *The Real Ambassadors*, which proves that fact could be stranger than fiction. On stage, this warped timeline was symbolized by two jazz groups, one traditional and one modern, which faced each other from opposite ends of the stage. Louis Armstrong's All-Stars—Joe Darensbourg (clarinet), Trummy Young (trombone), Billy Kyle (piano), Billy Kronk (bass), and Danny Barcelona (drums)—faced Brubeck, Wright, and Morello (Paul Desmond was not involved). The man who in 1923 had made, with Joe "King" Oliver, what many consider to be the first proper jazz records, and who invented the whole idea of the jazz solo two years later in his own Hot Five recordings, faced the pianist whose hot 5/4 had become such a striking modern jazz phenomenon.

Whether by intelligent design or simply because Brubeck was pressed for time, *The Real Ambassadors*, already immersed in jazz history, also draws liberally on Brubeck's own musical history, which ends up fitting nicely into a piece all about taking new perspectives on old histories, about the distance between now and then, about fantasy versus reality. The opening number, "Everybody's Comin'," transforms *Time Out*'s "Everybody's Jumpin'" into a curtain-raising, bursting-into-song overture. As the vocal trio announces "Everybody's Comin'," around which Armstrong inserts the spoken refrain "Yeah, yeah!" the cast enters—as Iola's stage directions note—"one by one, as their names are sung." Her lyric—"Louis Armstrong will appear / Carmen's promised she will sing / Brubeck's combo gonna swing"—beckons these very real people and dropped them into this picaresque fantasy. A vocal version of "Nomad," from *Jazz Impressions of Eurasia,* leads to three vocal reworkings of pieces that originally appeared on Brubeck's 1957 solo album *Brubeck Plays Brubeck*—"Two-Part Contention" becomes "In the Lurch," "The Duke" morphs into "You Swing Baby," while "One Moment Worth Years" retains its name as Iola's lyric riffs off the sentiment of the title.

The second and third numbers, "Cultural Exchange" and "Good Reviews"—newly composed—begin to plot the story while establishing how *The Real Ambassadors* will spin real history into its world of fantasy. Carmen McRae was cast as Rhonda, the new "girl singer" in the Hero's band, a respectful nod, perhaps, to Velma Middleton, Armstrong's actual singer, whose tragic death in Sierra Leone had cast such a sad shadow over the All-Stars' 1961 State Department tour. Picking up the thread from the Narrator, the Hero reports on Dizzy Gillespie's tour to Greece in 1956 as a way of clarifying the concept behind "Cultural Exchange." "When Diz blew, the riots were routed / People danced and they cheered and shouted," Louis sings, his natural bonhomie matching perfectly the wisecracking tone of Iola's lyric. "And when our neighbors called us vermin, we sent them Woody Herman," he continues, before unleashing some similar punnery around the names Leonard Bernstein and Martha Graham.

Then Iola's narration states, in blunt terms, an uncomfortable paradox. The State Department wants to send the Hero on tour because his unprecedented success as an *un*official ambassador of jazz speaks for itself, but that success, in the minds of government officials, is predicated on a certain sense of decorum: he knows when to keep his opinions about the real world to himself and to "observe in silence." If he starts to speak his mind—and if he is asked on tour about the treatment of his own people, how can he not—that saintly image could too easily become tarnished. In "Good Reviews," Rhonda uses the trauma of a bad review as a conduit for explaining how artists can deflect criticism and why they must not take it seriously. It's a witty song—and you can't help but feel that Brubeck was taking the opportunity to offload some of his own frustration about his treatment at the hands of Ira Gitler, Ralph Gleason, et al.

With the premise fully up and running, the drama picks up pace. Having overcome his natural reticence and agreed to undertake the tour, the Hero is given an officious briefing by the State Department in "Remember Who You Are"— "Always be a credit to your government / No matter what you say what you do, the eyes of the world are watching you." Now on the road, the Hero and Rhonda flirt romantically, a subplot that gives Brubeck reason to include two heartfelt love songs, not normally a genre in which he dabbled. Rhonda sings "My One Bad Habit Is Falling in Love"—a ballad that implores the Hero to reciprocate her love, removing her from further, painful temptation.[11] But in "Summer Song," the Hero, in the summer of his years and more experienced in affairs of the heart, lets her down gently and kindly: "Love to me is like a summer day / Silent 'cause there's just too much to say."

Rhonda's romantic awakening coincides with a wider awareness of world affairs. Their minds are being broadened by travel, and they become intrigued by Talgalla, a small African state (of Iola's invention) where, once a year, the government selects an ordinary person to rule during a celebratory day of carnival. "King for a Day" imagines the joy and liberation of such a day if that enlightened policy could be enacted at home, and the song reinforces Brubeck's message that jazz is a unifier of people—"I'd go form a swingin' band with all the leaders from ev'ry land." When the troupe arrives in Talgalla, we discover the meaning behind the title *The Real Ambassadors*.

---

11. This title came from a backstage encounter with Ella Fitzgerald, who at the time was going through a painful breakup. She told Dave and Iola, "My one bad habit is falling in love."

Armstrong is asked if he is the American ambassador and his response—"That's what they call me, Ambassador Satch"—is deliberately vague: he may not be *the* official ambassador, but he is reveling in his role as *an* ambassador, especially when the Talgallans carry him into town on their shoulders, chanting, "Blow, Satchmo."

And who should show up in Talgalla but the actual—the *real*—ambassador from the US. Fearing they have been duped, the townsfolk turn on Armstrong, but their perfectly reasonable question "Who is the real ambassador?" elicits an unexpected response. The ambassador's role, it is explained, is to "represent American society, noted for its etiquette, its manners and sobriety / We have followed protocol with absolute propriety / We're Yankees to the core." Armstrong argues in response, "I wasn't sent by the government to take your place / All I do is play the blues and meet the people face to face. . . . Certain facts we can't ignore / In my humble way I'm the USA."

"I represent the human race and don't pretend no more," Armstrong continues. And the real ambassador agrees: "In his humble way, he does represent the USA."

By 1962 the criticism that Armstrong, the real Armstrong, had driven his All-Stars into a creative cul-de-sac—the same set list every night, improvised choruses reduced to stock responses— was widespread: the master improviser who had once changed everything with his Hot Five and Hot Seven recordings was now touring a carefully rehearsed show. An unexpected by-product of *The Real Ambassadors* was the sheer thrill of hearing Armstrong taken out of his comfort zone as he dealt with material he hadn't played before. Stylistic turnarounds—as when the All-Stars suddenly took the lead on "Cultural Exchange" and pumped it full of funk—were thrilling, and Louis Armstrong's playing "Nomad" single-handedly demolished any idea that Brubeck's compositions lacked real jazz content. That sound, that phrasing, harked back to the source of everything, and you marvel at Armstrong's innate knack of transforming something you would imagine was so alien to his own instincts—that Paul Desmond had caramelized with sweetness—into something so wholly his own.

Of course deciding to write a musical featuring Louis Armstrong and persuading Louis Armstrong to take part were not the same thing. "When we put the idea to Louis for *The Real Ambassadors*," Brubeck recalled in 2003, "no one thought he would do a musical at his age.[12]

> We were both managed by Joe Glaser, and he was certainly against it, and there was a certain resistance from Louis's wife. But Louis said, "The Brubecks have written me an opera and I'm going to do it." He asked me to record all the songs on tape, which he listened to in his dressing room when he was on tour. But he just had this way of never being wrong. Louis wasn't a great sight-reader, but he didn't miss a thing—his mind was too sharp for that.
>
> I tracked Louis down to his hotel room in Chicago and told him about *The Real Ambassadors*, and asked if he'd do it. It had been a struggle to see him. When I tried to call up from the lobby, one of his entourage picked up and, I felt, by habit, he turned down everything; Louis was just too busy touring to take on anything else. Somehow I found out the number of Louis's room and went up there and sat outside his door. Eventually a waiter turned up with a tray of food, and when Louis opened and saw me there, he gave me a big smile and told the waiter that Mr. Brubeck would be having the same as him—so one more steak, please.
>
> I told him, as we ate, about the project, and to my amazement, he said he was interested. When I thought about his career, it was a dream that he had agreed to learn my music.

---

12. Armstrong was sixty-two.

After we finished the steaks, he asked me to come downstairs, where his band were waiting to play, and I could sit in if I liked. When Louis announced to the crowd that I was coming up to play with him, I burst with pride. We played a couple of standards, and the crowd loved it. But I had one reason to feel embarrassed. Louis's piano player was Billy Kyle, who had been one of my first influences. Man, I loved his playing. And as I walked on, he generously winked as we passed each other, like [he was] saying, "Dave, enjoy it."

The joy Brubeck and Armstrong took in each other's company shines through both the Columbia recording and photographs taken during the Monterey performance. "The only argument we had throughout the entire show was just before we went on stage," Brubeck said. "I'd asked Louis to wear a top hat and carry a briefcase as he walked out, to look the part of a real ambassador, and he didn't want to do it. I went out and started playing, then I look over and there's Louis walking out in the hat and carrying the case. He came straight over to the piano, and said, 'Am I hamming it up enough for you, Pops?'"

Compositionally *The Real Ambassadors* was, because it had to be, completely unlike anything else Brubeck had written, but one fundamental truth held firm: Brubeck created a structure in which an improvising jazzman could be himself, even if in this case that sense of self was given a fictional dusting. To write the sleeve notes for the Columbia recording of *The Real Ambassadors*, Brubeck called up Gilbert Millstein, who had ghost-written "The Beat Heard 'Round the World" article for the *New York Times Magazine* in 1958. Millstein slightly glossed over the subtleties of plot—Talgalla became an "unspecified African country newly arrived at independence"—but his opening statement about the piece was spot on: "*The Real Ambassadors* grew out of the desire of Dave Brubeck and his wife, Iola, a writer, to accomplish two things: in the first place, to crystallize in music, lyrics and book the humanity of jazz and the musicians who make it; and in the second, to offer the creation as a tribute to Louis Armstrong as the principal exemplar of their sentiments."

A week after the Brubeck Quartet completed *Time Out* in August 1959, Lambert, Hendricks & Ross were recording a sequel to their classic 1957 album *Sing a Song of Basie*, a collaboration with Basie himself they called *Sing Along with Basie*. The trio specialized in vocalese, which, in its purest form, added lyrics to a famous improvised jazz solo. The singer Eddie Jefferson had invented the technique in 1952 when, from deep inside Coleman Hawkins's famous 1939 record of "Body and Soul," he imagined a set of lyrics. In *The Real Ambassadors*, the role of Lambert, Hendricks & Ross was, Iola wrote in the vocal score, "to comment on the proceedings in the manner of a Greek chorus." They told the audience in the first number that "Everybody's Comin'," relayed with the sped-up urgency of newsreel the story of Dizzy Gillespie's tour of Greece in "Cultural Exchange," and in the title number, "The Real Ambassadors," they delivered the words of the actual US ambassador with speedy, ambassadorial neatness and precision.

The trio was signed to Columbia in 1959, and their first album for the label, released the following year, proclaimed them *The Hottest New Group in Jazz*. Their hipster, beatnik presence gave Brubeck a contrasting sound color with which to work as he juxtaposed them against the rough-diamond beauty of Armstrong's All-Stars. Lambert, Hendricks & Ross specialized in the rapid-fire delivery of lyrics with a light-touch agility that seemed to defy gravity. The carefully drilled unity of their sound, which could at times feel synthetic in the way of neon light, was cleverly offset by the playful sexiness of their close-knit harmonies, and their distinctive sound world sparked Brubeck's sonic imagination. "The Real Ambassadors" required them, following a gear-changing Morello drum break, to double up on an already recklessly fast tempo, which they managed without breaking a sweat. Brubeck also took full advantage of Annie Ross's facility with high notes. "Everybody's Comin'" ends with Ross leaping up to the E-flat above high C, and throughout the piece, her voice flies majestically high above the rest of the ensemble, cutting through the ozone layer like Duke Ellington's high-note trumpet expert Cat Anderson. The one thing Brubeck did not ask to hear is vocalese.

As the good people of Talgalla carry Armstrong on their shoulders, Lambert, Hendricks & Ross tear lustily into "Blow Satchmo," which, only forty-four seconds long, comes loaded with an extraordinary concentration of musical detail. A piece that strikes up the band with a sunny carnival atmosphere and the uncontained joy of the vocal trio riffing "What are you waiting for? / What are you waiting for? / Blow, Satchmo! / Blow, Satchmo!" is suddenly flooded with gospel harmonies as the lyric digs deep into biblical imagery: "Take us by the hand / Lead us to that promised . . . land."

Now Iola pulls together plot and subplot. The Hero and Rhonda work out their feelings for each other as "In the Lurch" leads to their duet "One Moment Worth Years," in which the Hero recognizes that love might be possible. And, as Iola wrote in her synopsis, "if love on the human level can make the world seem to hold more promise, what could the certainty of divine love reveal?" What came next would have far-reaching consequences for Brubeck's development as a composer. As the Hero is pondering this key question about the nature of love, he becomes entranced by the devotional chanting of priests from the local church, and, in "They Say I Look like God," sings an antiphonal blues response to their biblical text. The overlay of one music against another, familiar from "Blue Rondo à la Turk" and "Three to Get Ready," now journeys into the realm of the spiritual, and the large-scale devotional pieces Brubeck would create during the late 1960s and early 1970s—*The Light in the Wilderness, The Gates of Justice* and

*Truth Is Fallen*—are grand musical, philosophical, and theological extensions of this moment where cultures come together in *The Real Ambassadors*.

Brubeck's exquisite compositional craft and the alchemy of polytonality ensure that the overlay of the blues against biblical chant in "They Say I Look like God" is more elevated than a crude juxtaposition of two opposing sides. Louis's blues and Lambert, Hendricks & Ross's chant rotate around each other: two floating harmonic poles that are brought into each other's orbit. In the middle section, Brubeck, as in "Blow Satchmo," gives the harmony a gospel feel as Armstrong sings "Oh, Lord please hear my plea! / Oh, give me eyes to see that our creation was meant to be an act of God to set Man free." But it was another line that, forty years later, still made Brubeck emotional at the memory of how Armstrong delivered it.

"There were perhaps four thousand people in the audience at Monterey that night," Brubeck remembered, "and *The Real Ambassadors* was, don't forget, supposed to be a satirical show: through laughing at such a sad situation as segregation, we bring it down.

> Then [in "They Say I Look like God"], Louis sang his line "They say I look like God / Could God be black? My God! / If both are made in the image of thee / Could thou perchance a zebra be?" which was supposed to get a laugh. But I looked over to Louis and he wasn't laughing at all—there were tears flowing down his cheeks, and I could feel how moved the audience, who were completely still and quiet, were by how Louis delivered that line. He was serious; he was revealing what was in his soul, I think. After we came offstage, Dizzy Gillespie, who had also played that day, threw his arms around me and Iola. He was crying too.

*The Real Ambassadors* ends with an exuberant shout of joy, with bells ringing out over Talgalla as the finale vaults through a reworked "Blow Satchmo" toward its final affirmation, a heavenly vision of people being taken by the hand on the way toward the promised land. The piece had been inspired directly by Brubeck's 1958 tour and the struggles of touring the US as an integrated group, and it revealed his thoughts about his own State Department tour were more ambivalent and complicated than he had previously admitted in public. A man of Brubeck's age—he was about to turn forty-two—and especially a white, commercially successful jazz musician, would have had reason enough to ponder the injustices and cruelties of racism. But Brubeck's awareness of segregation stretched back far earlier, to a moment during his childhood when an encounter with a former slave shattered his innocence and left the profoundest of impressions.

David Warren Brubeck was born on December 6, 1920, in the small town of Concord, California, twenty-two miles northeast of Oakland. Woodrow Wilson was president of the United States; in movie houses, people were flocking to see Douglas Fairbanks swashbuckle his way through *The Mark of Zorro*; and in Paris, Maurice Ravel was preparing for the premiere of *La valse*, his "*poème chorégraphique pour orchestre*," on December 12. And in Concord, Howard (known as "Pete") and Elizabeth Ivey (known as "Bessie") Brubeck had just welcomed their third son, who was born at home in an elegant townhouse on Colfax Street, a block from Todo Santos Plaza, the focal-point square where the local townspeople met and made merry and bought fresh produce from the farmers market.

Brubeck was a twinkle in his parents' eyes when the Original Dixieland Jazz Band made what are nominally considered the first jazz recordings in 1919, and a toddler of three when Joe "King" Oliver—who would be name-checked in "King for a Day" in *The Real Ambassadors*—took his Creole Jazz Band into a Chicago studio and committed to shellac the first, game-changing recorded statements by black jazz musicians. As young Dave grew, jazz too was sprouting at an alarming rate. Louis Armstrong was taking the art of the jazz solo to new places with his Hot Five and Hot Seven recordings, while Ferdinand LaMothe was perfecting his persona as Jelly Roll Morton, a wisecracking and hip New Orleans piano-playing cardsharp who, in his Red Hot Peppers records, was finding ways of notating the true spirit and "heat" of jazz; Armstrong was jazz's first truly great improviser and Morton its first significant composer.

Brubeck would later find himself drawing on both their examples, not that any of this jazz activity was impinging upon his childhood. As Charlie Parker was stalking his idols from Count Basie's band around the clubs and dives of Kansas City, and Miles Davis was being mentored by trumpet star Clark Terry in St. Louis, and Thelonious Monk was discovering the delights of Harlem stride piano from the likes of James P. Johnson and Willie "the Lion" Smith in New York City, Brubeck grew up surrounded by the wide-open spaces of the Diablo mountain range, itself overlooked by the Sierra Nevadas. In Concord, the near-four-thousand-feet peak of Mount Diablo dominated every view. This was a mythic American landscape that wouldn't feel out of place in a John Huston movie with a score by Aaron Copland. As a teenager, Brubeck spent many hours weaving his way through the Sierras, his gangly frame riding a horse bareback.

Bessie had inherited what would become her marital home on Colfax Street in 1911 from her father, Henry Ivey, who owned a thriving livery stable business—horses for hire—in Concord. Pete had arrived in Concord from Lassen County, with his own father and a trail of cattle and horses: he was about to go into the ranching business, and had bought a ranch in the Ignacio Valley and rented land for pasture not far from Todo Santos Plaza. In 1975, the city decided to build an open-air amphitheater on the same plot of land that Pete had rented, and when the Dave Brubeck Quartet recorded their album *Back Home*[13] at the Concord Pavilion in August 1979, Brubeck wrote in the booklet notes about the thrill of playing on a piano embossed with a plaque dedicated to the memory of his mother, surrounded by childhood friends on the very same land where he had learned to drive a car and his father had once grazed his cattle.

A lot of living, both joyous and painful, was done inside that house on Colfax Street. Dave's eldest brother, Henry, was one when Pete and Bessie took up residence, and the middle brother, Howard, was born at home in 1916. But the house also witnessed a numbingly sad family tragedy. In 1907, Bessie's mother, Johannah, drowned in the backyard of the house during a heavy storm, which had caused a nearby stream to flood. Johannah, who was forty-one, had run into the yard to rescue the chickens that the family kept there, but she slipped on the wet ground and knocked herself out. Bessie was twenty-two, and the heartbreak and horror haunted her for the rest of her life. She was reading indoors and completely unaware of the plight of her mother, who drowned in a shallow puddle of rainwater.

Pete and Bessie met in the house. Bessie's father, Henry, had encountered Pete hanging out around the cattle enclosures and had been impressed enough by his good character to invite him to Colfax Street for dinner, perhaps thinking he might make a suitor for his daughter. To all those who would later look in from the outside, the success of the Brubecks' marriage felt improbable. Bessie was as immersed in culture— music and literature in particular—as Pete was in the great outdoors. Her overriding ambition was to be a concert pianist. She loved Bach, Mozart, Chopin, and Beethoven, and she regularly made the trip by train and ferry to San Francisco for symphony

---

13. Concord, 1979 (CJ-103).

orchestra and chamber music concerts. She also attended summer classes in San Francisco with the experimental composer Henry Cowell, whose ideas about dissonant harmony and experimentation with utilizing the inside of a piano would have such an impact on John Cage and Lou Harrison. "I recently discovered one of his theory books that he had signed for my mother," Brubeck said in 2007. "I remember driving her from the ranch down to San Francisco and her getting up very early to go to class; I used to stay overnight [and] then leave very early to get back to the ranch. In San Francisco she also heard Rachmaninoff perform and Paderewski play. She became so obsessed with Paderewski that she said her friends used to tease her, calling her 'Madame Paderewski.'"[14]

While incubating her ambition to be a concert pianist, Bessie set herself up as a piano teacher at the Colfax Street house— and in grand style. She drew up plans to transform the existing second story of the house into a music studio that, through sliding doors, would open out into a second room, large enough to accommodate a sizable audience for recitals. And as his wife immersed herself in music and took herself to San Francisco for concerts and to learn with Henry Cowell, Pete Brubeck, happiest roaming the prairies, looked after cattle by day and by evening became one of the country's top rodeo competitors, winning roping events at the Salinas Rodeo, the most prestigious rodeo event in the US; when Brubeck evoked a Yankee Rodeo in "Unsquare Dance" on *Time Further Out*, he wrote of what he knew.

The ambitions that Pete and Bess had for their three sons became a fault line in their marriage. Pete wanted at least one of his sons to follow him into the ranching business and become a cowboy, and he viewed Dave as his last chance. Bessie's charms had worked on both Henry, who had taken up violin and drums, and Howard, who was proving very proficient on

---

14. Email interview with the author, May 10, 2007.

piano and pipe organ. Dave, meanwhile, had taken up piano and also flirted with the cello for a while; and there was a constant tug-of-love war between rope and ivory, between Pete's teaching him the rudiments of roping and Bessie's desire to protect Dave's hands from rope burns and from being slashed by the sharp incisions of coarse cattleman's rope.

Bessie, her determination fueled by stubbornness, won the day, and all three of her sons would become musicians. In 1926 she demonstrated her single-mindedness, and no doubt provoked something of a crisis in her marriage, when she traveled to London to enroll as a piano student of the great piano pedagogues Dame Myra Hess and Tobias Matthay. Any West Coast American in the mid-1920s traveling to London for piano tuition showed matchless devotion to the cause; but for a woman with three young children, whose husband at home rode the ranch, Bessie's story must be unique. Hess and Matthay were among the cornerstones of London musical life. Hess was a renowned specialist in Beethoven, Schumann, and Mozart and made a solo transcription of Bach's *Jesu, Joy of Man's Desiring* that became much loved among British concertgoers. Matthay—Hess's onetime professor—lived in Hampstead and ran the Tobias Matthay Piano School from premises on Wigmore Street, a few blocks from London's chamber music concert hall of choice, the Wigmore Hall. Matthay—whose other pupils included Clifford Curzon and Moura Lympany—was considered the most innovative teacher of his day; he analyzed piano touch and focused on infinitesimal subtleties of touch between hands and the keyboard. Into this rigorous and no doubt somewhat stuffy environment came Bessie, but it was Myra Hess who put an end to her ambitions.

"My mother had trained at the King Conservatory in San Jose, California," Brubeck recalled, "and I have a wonderful recommendation the dean of King Conservatory wrote for her, encouraging her to continue with her studies after graduation. She was a remarkably determined woman. She'd had three sons and *then* went to London. She'd always dreamed of becoming a concert pianist, but Hess had other ideas. One day during a lesson my mother was looking out of the window at some children playing and Hess told her, 'Bessie, go home to your children.' Hess told her how hard the life of a concert pianist could be— but this might have been her way of explaining to my mother that she didn't have enough to make it."[15]

Bessie's solution was simple. She returned to Concord, deciding that if the world was not prepared to hear her play, she would bring a world of music into the house on Colfax Street, and the Brubeck home became a hub for music—a place where youngsters learned to play and regular recitals, performed by Bessie and her friends, fulfilled a need for high-quality performances of high-quality music. But in the constant battle between cattle and Chopin that defined the Brubeck marriage, Pete was about to deliver a shock.

He had been hired to manage a ranch owned by cattleman W. H. Moffat—forty-five thousand acres—in Ione in Amador County, about eighty-five miles from Concord. Ione had played an important role in the California Gold Rush, when its geographical position made it an important stop on the route farther into Northern California. But in 1933, when the Brubecks relocated there, its population was tiny, its streets often deserted, and Bessie found living in a small, isolated rural community tough going. She had left Concord with great fanfare by staging a farewell concert on Colfax Street, at which she invited her former students to perform. The concert ended with a hearty rendition of "Stars and Stripes Forever" with Bessie, Henry, Howard, and Dave performing eight hands over two pianos.

From Concord she transported three pianos—an upright on which to teach local pupils and two grand pianos—planning to continue her teaching and concert-giving in Ione. And

---

15. Email interview with the author, May 10, 2007.

continue she did, but on a much smaller scale, and without the regular cultural nourishment that came from trips to San Francisco—Ione was simply too isolated for visiting her favorite city with any regularity. In his unpublished journal, Brubeck doesn't elaborate about the effect on his mother's mental and physical health, but the heartrending extracts he copied into his memoir from her diary tell their own story.

Upon leaving Colfax Street, Bessie wrote, "My home, my ideal dream house where all my ambitions lie buried deep along with my real self." After six years in Ione, Bessie, writing in 1939, complained, "I work and play my part, but I am glad that each day brings me nearer the end of my disappointing life. It seems I never smile anymore, am never happy." Later she noted, "Some day those boys will know what a slave their mother made of herself for them. Why not? My life is done; my dream is over." In May 1939 she was struck by an undisclosed illness, and she spent June and July in and out of hospital.

After the dream that studying in London might have spun her life in a new direction, the remoteness and seclusion of Ione had clearly turned her existence into a nightmare. Her aspirations, she felt, had been stolen, and she lived her ambitions through her three sons. ("Hope Dave gives me the joy they [Howard and Henry] do," she wrote in her diary. "I really think he will turn out alright.") Shortly after the family moved to Ione, Henry and Howard moved away to attend college, and Bessie intensified her concentration on Dave's musical studies, giving him piano lessons and his first taste of how to harmonize Bach chorales, the process through which every musician learns the building blocks of harmony.

She ran the local choir and took Dave along to rehearsals, but otherwise the radio became a welcome source of musical sustenance, and hearing a broadcast of the Mormon Tabernacle Choir singing Handel's *Messiah* made a formative impact on Brubeck. "After we moved to Ione," he remembered, "and my mother didn't have access to the symphony orchestra

concerts she'd attended in San Francisco, she listened reli-
giously to broadcasts of the New York Philharmonic, the NBC
Orchestra, and the Metropolitan Opera Orchestra, and, naturally, she paid particular attention to piano virtuosos. But my
mother wouldn't allow us to listen to the radio much. If you
wanted music, she said, you had to make it yourself. But I did
listen to Benny Goodman, and all of the bands broadcasting
from locations across the country—Ellington, Basie, Harry
James."[16]

On Colfax Street, Dave had received a first taste of music
that wasn't by Bach or Chopin as his mother, very reluctantly,
agreed that his brother Henry could rehearse his band in her
music room. And now in Ione, as glimpses of jazz spilled out
through the family radio, opening his ears to a world outside
rural California, Brubeck began to piece together these different slivers of information.

"Henry's band—which he ran when he was in high school—
rehearsed in our house," he remembered.

Later Del Courtney, a band leader from Oakland, California,
decided to take the band over because he had a better name
as a band leader, and the kind of music they played, the first
jazz I heard, was popular dance music. Henry played drums,
and also sang with the band. I remember so well him singing
"Goofus,"[17] and he also did a lot of Cab Calloway tunes like
"Minnie the Moocher" and Ted Lewis–style songs, "Is Everybody Happy," that kind of thing. Henry was one of the few
in the area who could read anything that was put in front of
him. He had a very fancy kit with a painted gondola on the
bass drum, and was a swing style drummer with a very solid
beat; later he became head of music for Santa Barbara Schools

---

16. Email interview with the author, May 10, 2007.
17. Pop song by Wayne King that dates back to 1930 and was made famous by
the Carpenters in 1976.

but continued to play jazz drums with dance bands up to the 1950s. He'd been in Gil Evans's first band that came out of Stockton. But when Gil went on the road, Henry was a student at the College of the Pacific and couldn't go because he had to stay at school.

Benny Goodman's *Camel Caravan* program, which was broadcast live from New York and was crammed with good music and not a little hokum, would have been typical of the sort of program Brubeck heard in Ione. It was predicated around "Professor" Goodman's attempts to teach America to swing, as he benevolently led his own "Swing Academy." Goodman singer Martha Tilton and songwriter and vocalist Johnny Mercer, a regular guest star, engaged the notoriously prickly clarinetist in comedy routines that suggested Goodman's sense of humor was no laughing matter. But as the Goodman orchestra ripped through their most popular arrangements, including "King Porter Stomp," "Roll 'Em," "Blue Skies," and "Sing, Sing, Sing," Brubeck got a weekly fix of state-of-the-art big-band music. Goodman also featured his small groups—which included musicians like Lionel Hampton (vibraphone) and Teddy Wilson (piano)—playing brightly optimistic music, improvisation rebounding off composed, arranged beginnings, that anticipated the spirit and fleet ensemble interplay of Dave's own quartet.

Teddy Wilson was famed for his gossamer-light keyboard touch and a sense of swing that was as fluid as it was effortless, and, suitably dazzled, Brubeck found his interest in other pianists mushroomed. He listened for Billy Kyle, whom he would work with on *The Real Ambassadors*, then a member of bassist John Kirby's so-called Biggest Little Band, with its trademark shuffle rhythm, and for Milt Buckner, Lionel Hampton's pianist, who had evolved a technique known as "locked-hand" playing, in which his hands were locked into a fixed position, which produced variants on the same chord as he moved up and down the keyboard (also a major influence on George Shearing). Brubeck also admired the British pianist Alec Templeton, who had given Benny Goodman a modest hit in 1939 with his prototype jazzed-up Bach composition "Bach Goes to Town"; it's no surprise that the future composer of "Two-Part Contention" and "Brandenburg Gate" would find this fugue-with-a-swing so appealing.

However, no pianist impressed Dave more than Thomas "Fats" Waller. Appearing on Marian McPartland's *Piano Jazz* radio program in 1981,[18] Brubeck spoke enthusiastically about the first 78 rpm record he bought: Waller's "There's Honey on the Moon Tonight," with "Let's Be Fair and Square in Love" on the B side. Although declining McPartland's invitation to sing the songs—"That would be the worst thing," Brubeck groaned— he launched into note-perfect imitations of both records on the piano. Waller was seriously entertaining and took entertainment seriously, and that moment demonstrated how deeply ingrained Waller was in Brubeck's subconscious. Waller's roots in stride piano and his fiercely intelligent compositional sensibility turned solo piano compositions like "Handful of Keys" and "Alligator Crawl" into perfectly constructed miniatures.

The picture that emerges of the young Dave, holed up on the ranch in Ione, anxiously cupping his ears to the radio in the hope of catching a morsel of Benny Goodman or Count Basie on the radio, is of a dreamer—a teenager lost in music. To that extent he was his mother's son, and Bessie tried to instill in him a well-read, rigorous musicality that she could recognize and respect. For the first time, though, Brubeck's determination to do things his own way came to the fore. Despite Bessie's best efforts to teach Dave written notation, he much preferred to eavesdrop as Bessie taught her other students, then regurgitate what he had heard by ear. Dave's reluctance to engage with notation began with a childhood diagnosis of strabismus,

---

18. Released on CD in 2003; The Jazz Alliance (TJA 12043-2).

which left him wearing glasses at an early age and made reading music a near impossibility. It took Bessie a while to cotton
on to the fact that she was being hoodwinked—a situation that
she came to accept.

Could Dave's aural development and perception—his acute,
bat-sharp ears—have been heightened by his visual impair-
ment? Not that Brubeck knew it, but there was an intriguing
precedent for a pianist with sight problems but all-hearing ears.
Art Tatum, 90 percent blind from birth, was born in Toledo,
Ohio, ten years before Brubeck. Making his formative steps as a
pianist, he replicated the 78 rpm records that littered the Tatum
home to the best of his ability, his aural imagination and burgeoning technique finding workable solutions to the problem
of how to copy what he was hearing. Only subsequently did he
realize he had been listening to four-hand boogie-woogie performances by Pete Johnson and Albert Ammons and had negotiated a way of rendering their performances with two hands.
As Tatum continued to practice, broadcasts of master pianists
like Fats Waller, James P. Johnson, and Earl Hines mulched
with the classical music he heard—Horowitz and Godowsky
playing Liszt, Chopin, Schumann, and American light classical music by Victor Herbert and Edward MacDowell. Through
the imagination of his inner ear, Tatum instinctively blended
the figurations and gestures of early jazz and stride piano into
the elaborate ornamentation he'd heard—but *not* read—in
classical music.

It was the experience of hearing Tatum that eventually persuaded Bessie, who had proved fiercely resistant to music outside the classical mainstream, to the virtues of jazz. "I was driving
her somewhere, this would have been during the late thirties,
and Tatum came on the radio. Perhaps had he been playing
'Avalon,' or some jazz standard, it wouldn't have connected
with her, but he started playing [Dvořák's] 'Humoresque'[19] and

---

19. Tatum's version was released in 1940 (Decca 18049).

I could see from her face how impressed she was: his technique was something else, and then he improvised on it!"[20]

Music gave Brubeck and his mother a unique bond, but he was also extremely close to Pete. If from Bessie Dave inherited a craving to contemplate and dream, from Pete came a rugged practicality—an ability to carry an arduous task through to completion, whether working the ranch or, later, carrying out a three-month tour on behalf of the State Department. When Pete was in charge of the Moffat property, such was the scale of the operation—the ranch sprawled over the Sierras from the road that led from Stockton to Sacramento up to the Mokelumne River—that the simplest repair job might encompass a whole day's round trip. And the teenage Dave chanced upon an ingenious way of passing the time that allowed him to dream while taking care of ranch business.

"My fascination with rhythm began when I was a young boy," he wrote, "and my father would send me on a job to fix the fence or pump water into the tanks so that the cattle could drink. I spent much time in my youth getting water sometimes in a truck, or more often on horseback, which would mean hours of nothing to do except contemplate the surroundings. I would start thinking about rhythm against the gait of the horse, which was the beginning of my polyrhythmic approach."[21] As he rode the Sierras, counting ornate measures of rhythm against the steady plod of his horse, his mind would drift back toward music. He would imagine the Benny Goodman band bus driving through the Sierras on the way to their next gig. They'd want to get past his cattle, and Brubeck decided that, if such an event ever occurred, he wouldn't grant the King of Swing safe passage without first securing a guarantee to join his band. Dream on, Dave. Benny never obliged, but the image

---

20. Email interview with the author, May 10, 2007.

21. Dave Brubeck, handwritten journal, undated entry, Brubeck Collection (uncataloged).

of Brubeck isolated, riding ever deeper into the West Coast's pioneer territory, is ripe with symbolism. Jazz, meanwhile, was developing without him.

That moment when the innocence of Brubeck's childhood shattered, when for the first time the reality of America's division along racial lines became clear to him, was earth-shaking. It spoke of a big untruth that scarred American society while also testifying to Pete's moral compass. Until 2001, when he was interviewed by the filmmaker Ken Burns for his television documentary series *Jazz*, Brubeck had kept this story largely to himself. Telling it in public, he was overwhelmed by emotion and broke down in front of the camera. Here, suddenly, was a missing piece of the puzzle. The battles Brubeck had fought at East Carolina College and at the University of Alabama, and the emotional thrust that led to *The Real Ambassadors*—the urgency that this battle must be without compromise—was partly Brubeck living up to the example of his father.

"The first black man I saw, my dad took me to see him on the Sacramento River in California and he said to his friend,[22] 'Open your shirt for Dave.'" As his eyes filled with tears, Brubeck continued. "There was a brand on his chest, and my dad said, 'These things can't happen.'" And, remembering his time in the army battling fascism in Europe during World War II, Brubeck added, "That's why I fought for what I fought for."[23]

Stepping off the plane at Oakland International Airport in 2017, the day after my encounter with Eugene Wright in Los Angeles, with the jagged mountainous terrain filling the horizon, the scene of so much of Brubeck's formative history,

---

22. Although Brubeck doesn't mention his name onscreen, his father's friend was called Shine.

23. *Jazz*, "Dedicated to Chaos: 1940–1945," directed by Ken Burns, aired January 23, 2001, on PBS.

there is another lesson to be learned. Until the Brubecks moved to the East Coast in 1960, to Wilton, Connecticut, his life was played out over a relatively limited locale. Born in Concord and raised in Ione, Brubeck attended the College of the Pacific in Stockton and, after he returned from the army, Mills College in Oakland. The Burma Lounge, where the Dave Brubeck Trio, with Cal Tjader and Ron Crotty, played their first big-league gigs, was also in Oakland. Dave and Iola spent their early years as a married couple on the other side of the bay, in various rentals in San Francisco, including on Eighteenth Street in Eureka Valley, where Paul Desmond, tail between his legs, turned up that day with his proposal to turn the Dave Brubeck Trio into a quartet.

The dream had always been for the Brubecks to own a place of their own, and shortly after the war they used a $1,000 war bond gifted by Pete to invest in a plot of land on Heartwood Drive, nestled high up in the Oakland Hills, with enviable views over San Francisco Bay. In 1949 they commissioned the innovative modernist architect Beverley David Thorne to draw up plans—and the signing of Brubeck's Columbia contract in 1954 finally provided the funds that turned the virtual plans into reality.

By the time Brubeck moved into Heartwood Drive, he was no longer playing at the Burma Lounge, but the venue was a short drive from his new home—weaving down through the hills, via Colton Boulevard, past Montclair Elementary School, where the Brubecks sent their children, toward downtown Oakland. Standing outside the Burma Lounge today, with its draped frontage, you wish the walls could reveal something of the music that once vibrated against them. I feel compelled to open the small, compact front door—through which Tjader once wheeled his vibraphone and Paul Desmond walked, hoping to sit in—but find it locked, and I wonder if the small hexagonal window to the right of the door is where patrons would have paid their entrance fee before walking into the club.

The car journey to Heartwood Drive refers me back to the conversation I had yesterday with Eugene Wright. The long, winding road up toward number 6630 is the same route Wright would have taken in 1958 in a car borrowed from Paul Desmond, there being no other way to transport a double bass up the steep incline. In a 1958 article published under the title "Dave Brubeck and His 'Tree House,'" the unnamed author went to great lengths to connect Brubeck's music with what was described as an "architectural triumph." "Like his music," the author wrote, "Brubeck's home is imaginative, bold in concept. Moreover, it answers the functional requirements of the owners, and the problems of a perplexing site."[24] As the article went on to explain, the land might have been visually striking, but any conventional architect would have struggled to conceive of how to build a structure on such a narrow plot, surrounded by trees and monolithic slabs of rock.

When the Brubecks met Beverley David Thorne he was still studying architecture at Berkeley, but his keen eyes quickly came up with a keen solution. By fixing five steel fingers into a central slab of rock, Thorne created a cantilevered surface upon which the structure could rest. When the build itself started, Thorne was employed by the architect Roger Lee, and the success of the project gave him confidence to strike out on his own. The building was L-shaped and, given the height of the rock, seemed to propel itself up into the air: a building that grew organically out of its setting. Thorne's cantilevered structure borrowed elements of classic pieces of modernist architecture like Frank Lloyd Wright's Fallingwater and Mies van der Rohe's Farnsworth House, and yet was filled with personal touches. Brubeck's music room was constructed around the rock, which jutted dramatically into the room. Thorne hollowed out a space in the rock into which he inserted a large, solid pane of glass, which became Brubeck's desk. The Brubecks and Thorne

---

24. "Dave Brubeck and His 'Tree House,'" *Business Week*, May 24, 1958.

became firm friends (Thorne even lived in the house during the summer of 1954, while Brubeck was on tour), but building a house for such a famous client also brought problems. Thorne's mission to build houses for everyday folk was derailed by the Brubeck project, after which he was pursued by the rich and well-to-do, which led him to melt into the background, changing his professional name from David to Beverley, until the 1980s, when he founded a new practice in Hawaii.

That music room built around a rock was where Brubeck recorded his two early solo piano albums, *Brubeck Plays Brubeck* in 1956 and, a year later, *Dave Brubeck Plays and Plays and Plays*; it was where, in 1958, Brubeck played with Eugene Wright for the first time, the two men working through "Brother, Can You Spare a Dime?"; and where, in 1959, Paul Desmond reluctantly brought two melodic fragments in 5/4 along, from which Brubeck made "Take Five." So special and unique was 6630 Heartwood Drive that a one-off edition of *The Ed Sullivan Show* was broadcast from there on October 16, 1960. After mutual joshing about Sullivan's alleged "squareness," the quartet performed "In a Dancing Mood," the piece Brubeck always played to introduce the uninitiated to his work. Sadly, this site of such historic significance feels rather dilapidated six decades later. Reckoning there's nobody home, I creep around the side of the building and figure out where the photographer who took pictures of the Brubeck family to accompany the "Dave Brubeck and His 'Tree House'" article stood.

Paint is peeling off the external surfaces and the windows are boarded up at the back of house, but at least the building is still standing. That same afternoon, now in Concord, I stand on Colfax Street looking for the site of Pete and Bessie's house, Dave's childhood home. The house itself, I know, was demolished in 1945, but I'm looking for what I suspect is a wall-mounted plaque that marks the spot. I look, but nothing. I walk into the Presbyterian church that now occupies the site, and I'm told it is in the near vicinity, definitely, and to keep looking, have a nice day. Stepping outside again, I try to match an image of the plaque on my iPad with my surroundings. Then I glance down at the ground: for the last ten minutes I've been standing on top of the thing I've been looking for.

The pavement-mounted plaque, presented by the Concord Historical Society, is simple and dignified. "Brubeck House, 1911–1945. Site of the Elizabeth Ivey Brubeck and H. P. Brubeck home in which they raised three musician sons, Henry, Howard, and Dave. Dave became an internationally acclaimed musician and recipient of many national and international awards. The home had a unique two story music room with a balcony where people gathered for music recitals. Mrs. Brubeck taught music to many of Concord's children. She was the daughter of Henry Ivey, who ran a livery stable in Concord in the horse and buggy days."

I'm standing where it all started.

In Ione, when it was time for college, the decision was made to send the seventeen-year-old Brubeck to the College of the Pacific in Stockton, halfway between Concord and Ione. Pete had, apparently, won: Dave enrolled in the Department of Zoology to study veterinary medicine. The life of a cowboy suited him, and he planned, after graduation, to return to the ranch and devote the rest of his life to livestock and living off the land.

Dr. John Arnold—then the head of zoology at the College of the Pacific, and something of an unsung hero in the Brubeck story—changed everything. His words, delivered to Dave during his second year as a kindly piece of advice—"Brubeck, your mind is not here. It's across the lawn in the [music] conservatory. Please go there. Stop wasting my time and yours"—were both a wake-up call and told Brubeck what he already knew. Brubeck was eager to enter the music department, so eager he hid an important fact—he couldn't read a note of music.

Arriving at what is now the University of the Pacific, I walk to the music conservatory and look across the lawn to where the zoology department had once stood, and take in the same view Brubeck would have seen as, during lessons in microbiology, he looked longingly toward the music school. With its grand staircase and polished wooden panels—like everyone's fantasy of an English boarding school—the conservatory impresses upon everybody who enters the augustness of the Western classical tradition. I overhear one student playing Ravel's *Gaspard de la nuit*, while in another practice room another pianist is working up Chick Corea's "Spain," patiently looping its phrases until it sits comfortably under their fingers.

The wonder is that, in this atmosphere of intense learning, Dave got away with his secret for so long. Pete and Bessie were supportive of his swap, but Dave lived in grave fear of anybody finding out that he couldn't read music. As during his childhood lessons with Bessie, Dave used his finely attuned ears to conceal his deficiency at reading. He even managed to fool Dr. J. Russell Bodley, a conservatory professor, who became amazed at Dave's aptitude for analyzing the most complex chord progressions using his ears alone. Brubeck even managed to fake his program's requirement to learn either a wind or string instrument by remembering the scales and arpeggios he'd learned on the cello as a child. He thought his luck would never run out.

And then it did. Nearing the end of his program, Brubeck was required to take a keyboard instrument, and his piano teacher realized immediately that his ears might have been good, but he couldn't read. Dave was hauled in front of the dean and stripped of his right to graduate. J. Russell Bodley leaped to his defense, arguing that Brubeck had real talent and unbelievable ears; another teacher, Horace Brown, who had taught Brubeck counterpoint, also weighed in and told the dean that his student had written some of the most proficient counterpoint he had seen. The dean relented and allowed Brubeck to graduate—under the condition that he didn't embarrass the department's good name by ever trying to teach.

Truth is, Brubeck didn't need to teach. All through his time at the College of the Pacific, he had been playing gigs to quench his insatiable thirst for music and to help pay his way. He accompanied dance classes, played in big bands, and eventually organized his own Stan Kenton–style big band, which performed in Stockton and featured on tenor saxophone Stockton local Darrell Cutler, who would eventually play with Dave and Norman Bates in the Three Ds. Brubeck also met Dave Van Kriedt for the first time through the local big-band scene and recognized him immediately as a kindred spirit: a musician interested in jazz and techniques of contemporary composition. Van Kriedt moved into Brubeck's rented student dive—a cellar space near campus affectionately nicknamed "the bomb shelter"—and decided to enroll with J. Russell Bodley.

Before living in "the bomb shelter," Brubeck had lived slightly off-campus in a more comfortable but expensive room on Tuxedo Avenue. On the same street lived Charles and Myrtle Whitlock and their daughter Iola, and they were about to change each other's lives for good.

Iola was born on August 14, 1923, in Corning, California, north of Sacramento. Her family background was not dissimilar to her future husband's. Iola's father worked in forestry and her mother's family were ranchers of many decades' experience. Like Dave, Iola was nurturing a creative passion that had nothing to do with the great outdoors. In school she'd become interested in drama and writing, and she enrolled at the College of the Pacific as a speech major, eventually specializing in radio. In college, Dave and Iola were both involved in a weekly on-campus radio show, *Friday Frolics*, Dave helping with the music alongside his friend Harold Meeske, who played guitar.

Dave and Iola had met for the first time in the university's Faye Spanos Concert Hall in 1941, and, a year later, when Dave was looking for a date to take along to a fraternity ball,

Meeske reminded him about Iola. They were both good-looking, highly intelligent young people, and they fell in love immediately.[25] A few hours after they met—hours spent talking incessantly—they decided to marry, much to Meeske's astonishment. A notice published in the *Pacific Weekly* on September 25, 1942, headlined "Iola Whitlock Marries Dave Brubeck," reported, "Sorority sisters of Iola Whitlock were surprised Tuesday night by the receiving of the following telegram: 'Dave and I met in April, Engaged in May, Romanced all summer, Been married one day, You'll get your chocolates when I'm there to have some too.'" Brubeck was identified as being "prominent on campus as a player of boogie woogie."[26]

Dave and Iola had married four days earlier, on September 21, in Carson City, Nevada, while Brubeck was on a three-day pass from the army. Having graduated, he had enlisted earlier in 1942 but was not sent overseas until 1944. As Iola finished her course at the College of the Pacific, Dave was assigned to play in the army band stationed at Camp Haan in Riverside, California. Eventually Iola moved to be with him, and one advantage of being in Riverside was that the city allowed easy access to Los Angeles.

In a sign of Brubeck's unshakable self-confidence, the same strength of character that allowed Brubeck to haggle over his Columbia contract until he got exactly the conditions he required, he used the opportunity of being near Los Angeles to approach two giants of modern music: Stan Kenton and Arnold Schoenberg.

Kenton was about to be signed to Capitol Records and was on the cusp of turning his local success in California into national fame when Brubeck came knocking. "I'd written this

---

25. Chris Brubeck, in a conversation with the author (January 2018), reported that Brubeck had an earlier, short-lived relationship before he met Iola.

26. "Iola Whitlock Marries Dave Brubeck," *Pacific Weekly*, September 25, 1942.

very complex piece for the band in Camp Haan which I called 'Prayer of the Conquered,'" Brubeck remembered.[27]

> Nearly everybody in the band hated it, but one of my friends, Ernie Farmer, liked it and suggested I show it to Kenton, who we all adored. So I walked to Kenton's house. I knocked on the door and when he answered, I knew I'd woken him up from a sleep. But he invited me in and looked at my score. He asked me to play and said he found my voicings very advanced. The next day, his band would be rehearsing for *The Bob Hope Show*, and he asked me to come along, with the music, and said he'd run it down. Sounded wild! And then, when he'd finished, he said, "Bring it back in ten years."

Brubeck's letter to Schoenberg, requesting a consultation, led to an appointment in his office at UCLA:

> We had an interview first and then he said, "Well, okay, if you're sure come back next week with something you've written." I didn't have much to show him, so I wrote a simple piece for piano. The next week, he looked at it and said he liked the harmony, but started questioning me about why I'd written this note and that one. I answered, "Because I like how they sound," which wasn't good enough for Schoenberg—"You *must* have a reason to write a note." He started telling me about his theories and approach to writing music, and I thought, fine, but what does that have to do with me? He then got cross and started showing me Mozart and Beethoven scores and telling me that he knew more about music than anybody else living, and that's why he could tell me how to write. I got out of there fast.

The piece Brubeck wrote for Schoenberg—six bars that start in E minor and make liberal use of chromaticism and end

---

27. Interview with the author, May 1, 2003.

with some block chords—has survived, with a later note from Brubeck explaining that Schoenberg told him he needed "a better background" before attempting anything so ambitious.[28] What that "better background" might entail was put on hold until 1944, when Brubeck was finally sent overseas. But an article he had read, pinned to a notice board at the College of the Pacific, gave him an idea. Its author was Darius Milhaud, who explained about working with different keys simultaneously. And Brubeck liked the sound of that.

Brubeck might have graduated from the College of the Pacific under something of a cloud, but the institution later keenly embraced Brubeck as their most famous son. Until the end of 2019, the university housed the Brubeck Archive and Brubeck Institute, which, established in 2000, provided training for some of America's leading jazz musicians. My week there plundering the wealth of information and documents in the archive coming to an end, I walk along to the Faye Spanos Concert Hall and stand by the door where Dave and Iola met nearly eighty years earlier. Looking toward the stage where, in 1953, a few months after the quartet toured with Charlie Parker, they recorded *Jazz at the College of the Pacific*, I open YouTube on my iPhone and search for the album. As I listen to "All the Things You Are" in the space in which it was recorded, the dry acoustic of the recording and building become one again. I look up to see Dave and Paul smiling back at me—in the same way Brubeck had his visions of Benny Goodman on those long journeys around the Sierras.

---

28. Secular music scores, DB Manuscripts, Secular Works, Box 18, Brubeck Collection.

*Chapter Nine*

# PLAYER PIANO

"I want to stand as close to the edge as I can without going over. Out on the edge you see all kinds of things you can't see from the center."

KURT VONNEGUT, *Player Piano*, 1952

In a practice room up the stairs from the Faye Spanos Concert Hall, Dave Brubeck made his first recordings as a solo pianist in 1942 as a twenty-one-year-old music student whose fingers luxuriated in arpeggiating ripples of pastoral harmony— and then, suddenly, shapes shifted and blurred, moving with remarkable speed, like the revolving spin on a bicycle wheel. "These Foolish Things," "Body and Soul," "I've Found a New Baby," and "On the Alamo" were recorded on a reel-to-reel tape machine the year of his graduation, a selection of tunes entirely befitting a fledging jazzman in the process of moving from old jazz ways toward discovering something new.

325

"On the Alamo" had been a hit record for the Isham Jones Orchestra in 1922; "I've Found a New Baby" was, by 1942, another relic from history, a song that had become famous in 1926 thanks to a novelty record by clarinetist Ted Lewis, with its comedic wah-wahs and flatulent brass bass grunts.[1] But "Body and Soul" was a song that every progressive jazz thinker was making it their business to investigate following the improvisational nuances of tenor saxophonist Coleman Hawkins's famous 1939 recording,[2] which proposed taking a deeper dive inside the structure of a song by improvising around the DNA of its chord sequence, rather than offering variations on its melody. "Body and Soul" would feature again in a 1950 recording by the Dave Brubeck Trio, while "On the Alamo" was given the full quartet treatment on *Jazz at Storyville* in 1954. This would prove his last word on both tunes, on record at least, but the intricate harmonic tracery of "These Foolish Things" would continue to command Brubeck's attention through each incarnation of his quartet and, latterly, as a set-piece duet whenever he put in a guest appearance with Wynton Marsalis.

In 2002, when the prospect of issuing a second volume of *Jazz at the College of the Pacific*[3] was raised—restoring material that failed to make the cut when Fantasy released the original record in 1954—Brubeck decided to add "I've Found a New Baby" as a bonus track. The running time of a CD would have allowed him scope to release all four pieces, but there was a very particular point to be made by releasing this one track. The stylistic imprints of Fats Waller, Earl Hines, and Art Tatum were explicit in all four tunes, but "I've Found a New Baby" pushed matters further. Beyond the Dixieland hokum of Ted Lewis, Brubeck used the song to send a love letter directly to the show-pony keyboard gymnastics of Tatum, who, had he ever

1. Matrix/Runout 141665.
2. Bluebird 30-0825.
3. Fantasy OJCCD 1076-2.

heard it, might have concluded that there was little he could have done differently himself.

The record lay around the Brubeck home in Wilton, his pride at the technical chops on display obvious whenever it was played; and Brubeck was definitely of the opinion that "people who say I can't swing, or I'm heavy-handed—they *need* to listen to this."[4] But a notable number of reviewers failed to reference this historical bonbon in their reviews, missing the point that in 1942 Brubeck was a prodigiously fluent proponent of the language that soon he would be distilling to find his own art.

To have released "Body and Soul" in 2002 would have been to hand over a rawer version of the Brubeck we already know: the harmonic smudges, the right hand gravitating toward out-lying keys and slipping away from the harmonic anchor in the bass, all familiar. Coleman Hawkins's faraway atmospherics had obviously rubbed off on Brubeck as he approached the piece from the distant horizon, hints of Johnny Green's melody peeking through inquisitive chords. Hawkins's feel for the blues was absent from Brubeck's performance at first—a folksy, Aaron Copland–like quality predominated—but then rhythmic impetus built around trotting stride piano steps and Brubeck migrated from Copland to Earl Hines.

"These Foolish Things" followed the same trajectory: sweet, wide-open-prairie harmonizations moving toward invigorating stride piano that Brubeck embellished with ornaments on loan from Tatum. "On the Alamo," far from the "tender light" that shines on the "summer night" suggested by its lyric, was weathered by barrelhouse piano and a deeply illegal harmonic crunch, and by Brubeck co-opting that famously out-there chord from Billy Strayhorn's "Take the 'A' Train" (the chord that underscores the word *train* in the lyric), which he threaded through the melody line. His playing was interrupted midphrase as the door of his practice room bursts open and we

---

4. Interview with the author, June 10, 2006.

hear Brubeck suddenly say, "Hello?"—Iola, perhaps, ready to go on a date.

Polytonality had yet to be figured out as a fully functioning system that could be reliably deployed to overhaul the innards of a tune, although "On the Alamo" and "Body and Soul" came close to playing multiple keys together before Brubeck knew that the term *polytonality*, or Darius Milhaud, existed. But from its opening moments "I've Found a New Baby" felt satisfyingly fully formed and sure of itself, Brubeck's right hand alive to the transformative powers of jazz improvisation as his left provided a muscular, stride piano motor.

Brubeck had intuited a fundamental truth about musical architecture from Tatum: give too much away at the beginning and there will be nowhere left to go. Decorative chromatic asides flooded the space with a torrent of quicksilver, Tatum-infused melodic runs. Brubeck's second chorus began with chiming chords, which were shoved out of the way by a spill-age of twisting passagework that bumped into quarrelling trills and plunging descents down the keyboard. Then gamey block chords headed for the harmonic margins, and Brubeck's gasps and moans suggested that he, too, couldn't quite believe his ferocious buildup of steam as he was about to reach the end. In the final chorus notes chased their own tails—until energy levels hit burnout.

Even at this formative stage, Brubeck had pegged this improvisation to *dis*continuity, with lines dancing against slabs of harmony. His piano rumbled and roared, pianistic polite-ness way down his list of priorities. The language was Tatum's; the imagination and technical brilliance were Brubeck's, which was why he opted to include it on *Jazz at the College of the Pacific, Volume Two*.

♭𝄞

The relationship between a musician and his piano has been at the very core of this book, and 1942 is a good starting point from which to retrace our steps forward through time, because the history of Brubeck's solo piano recordings throw illuminating, and in some cases unlikely, light on the fabric and inner workings of his playing.

Partly it's the *absence* of any solo albums for nearly forty years that is so very intriguing. *Brubeck Plays Brubeck*, his first solo album, was released in 1956 on Columbia, between the quartet records *Jazz: Red Hot and Cool* and *Jazz Impressions of the USA*. Its follow-up, *Dave Brubeck Plays and Plays and Plays*, was rejected by Columbia and all but disappeared off the radar when it was issued on Fantasy in 1957. The occasional solo track (such as "Home at Last" from *Jazz Impressions of the USA*) dropped into a quartet album aside, it would be thirty-seven years before Brubeck sat down, in 1994, in the studio of the Performing Arts Center at the State University of New York, Purchase, to record *Just You, Just Me*, a solo album that begat a chain of sequels: *One Alone* (2000), *Private Brubeck Remembers* (2004), *Indian Summer* (2006)—and the stocking-filling *A Dave Brubeck Christmas* (1996). Often reflective and contemplative in mood, stalked by undercurrents of melancholic rumination (par for the course for a pianist in his seventies and eighties), this is Brubeck leading us directly inside the quiddity of his art, allowing us to judge how far his music had evolved since those bold steps recorded in a student practice room.

Brubeck, aware of the historical echoes, binds his albums together across the decades. "Weep No More," the ballad he wrote in 1945, opens the B side of *Brubeck Plays Brubeck* and is revived on *One Alone*, and again on the World War II–themed *Private Brubeck Remembers*. Victor Herbert's "Indian Summer," which featured on *Plays and Plays and Plays*, gives the eighty-seven-year-old Brubeck the title track of his 2007 album; and Cole Porter's "You'd Be So Nice to Come Home To," also featured on *Dave Brubeck Plays and Plays and Plays*, becomes the emotional hub of *Private Brubeck Remembers*.

The relentless, youthful optimism that pervades both 1950s solo records contrasts sharply with the later records, and *Brubeck Plays Brubeck* (a program of original compositions) and *Dave Brubeck Plays and Plays and Plays* (largely standards) feel like a complementary pair, but history's favoring one over the other has obscured the full picture. The earlier album had the advantage of being pushed by the Columbia publicity department, and its cause was aided and abetted by Miles Davis's cherry-picking two tracks to record. "In Your Own Sweet Way" appeared on the Miles Davis Quintet album *Workin'* later in 1956, while Gil Evans would dress "The Duke" in sumptuous orchestral colors on *Miles Ahead* in 1957 (during which Dave reminisced with Gil about his first drummer, Henry Brubeck).

Both in 1956 and in the 1990s and 2000s, Brubeck saw his solo albums as an opportunity to speak very directly to his audience, a mood that *Brubeck Plays Brubeck* established from the very beginning. The album was recorded at home, on Brubeck's own piano on Heartwood Drive, Oakland, on an Ampex tape recorder that he operated himself. He also communicated directly with the audience, in place of a conventional liner note, a professorial think piece that spoke with candor about his approach to improvisation and his belief that instrumental technique in jazz cannot, and must not, be divorced from the processes of improvisation—pre-echoing thoughts about the emotional immediacy of improvisation that fed into "The Beat Heard 'Round the World," the article published under his name in the *New York Times Magazine* in the aftermath of his 1958 State Department tour.

Brubeck outlined "three basic categories or levels of creativity in jazz." An ideal state of improvisational grace is reached when an "effortless flow of new material" springs from the subconscious—"the performer at this level has neither desire nor need for a preconceived pattern because he knows that the music comes from a source of infinite imagination and limitless variety." But when that blissful state of creation hovers stubbornly out of reach, improvising musicians might hope to produce "an imaginative performance interspersed with 'quotes' (either personal or derivative) which intrude like the human ego into the flow of creative ideas"—and when even that spark of inspiration refuses to rise to the occasion, jazz musicians typically fall back on "backlog repertoire, in which runs and patterns, cadences and progressions are worked out to meet each situation."

The jazz musician who relies on that safety net of pre-learned patterns might, Brubeck considered, achieve technical perfection and swing relentlessly, but their playing "will lack vital involvement with the moment of creation." But harness that moment of creation properly and a soloist can "out-swing, out-create, out-perform any of the other categories." As Charles Mingus so insightfully recognized during his exchange with Miles Davis in the *DownBeat* magazine letters page, Brubeck's concept of swing was intimately tied to the exuberance of any moment: never a ready-made rhythmic reflex. Brubeck was up-front about the rationale behind *Brubeck Plays Brubeck*: "I have tried to maintain the standards of creative experience contained in category 1," he said, before asking listeners to judge whether he needed to default to categories two or three.

Brubeck affirmed a clear and mutually reinforcing relationship between improvisation, piano technique, and emotion. "I believe the true lover of jazz would prefer to experience the same emotions as the artist when an idea is first discovered," he wrote, later adding, "Improvisation, to me, is the core of jazz. Because I believe this, my style of piano is one shaped primarily by the material, or ideas which I am attempting to express—not by a system or a search for an identifying 'sound.'" A telling example of how Brubeck's style of piano was shaped by material is found in his relationship with stride piano and boogie-woogie. Putting the thing itself—and "I've Found a New Baby" demonstrated how hardwired 1920s and '30s piano styles were in Brubeck—up against ripples of bitonal brawn created something new, the need to discover fresh material overriding any desire to simply replicate the style.

His knack of upending the predominant mood music of a solo by abruptly asserting the precise opposite character, mood, texture, or flow of energy, was also about the unfolding of his material dictating the shape of an improvisation, rather than relying on dependable narrative arcs. Two apparently incompatible or unrelated types of material spontaneously colliding could not usually be expressed through an off-the-rack technique, and Brubeck's ideas about improvisation, closely allied to his compositional mind-set, did not always lead to a place where "swing" was a clear-cut concept. "I am aware that I have become a controversial figure in jazz," he noted, as he listed some entirely contradictory critiques of his playing from recent reviews—critics variously described his work as "cerebral" and "emotional"; suggested that he played with the machismo intensity of a "pile driver" while also creating "delicate well-constructed lines"; he was an important "contributor" to jazz who had also "defiled" the music—and Brubeck was happy to embrace all these descriptors "at specific moments, in specific tunes, on a specific night of performance."

Brubeck's essay articulated, as a matter of faith, the moral responsibility that jazz musicians had to nurture the tradition of improvisation—the attitude a jazz musician took toward improvisation defined their art beyond style or technique. When Jelly Roll Morton, the New Orleans huckster and composer of genius and self-proclaimed "inventor of jazz," told the pioneering ethnomusicologist and field recordist Alan Lomax that "ragtime is a certain type of syncopation and only certain tunes can be played in that idea [but] jazz is a style that can be applied to any type of tune,"[5] he was explaining that ragtime had a formal structure and not playing "that certain type of

---

5. Alan Lomax, *Mister Jelly Roll* (Berkeley: University of California Press, 2001), 62.

syncopation" meant that you were not playing authentic rag-time. But jazz was free to draw upon, and fuse with, any avail-able material, including ragtime—and the blues, and opera, and marching band music—that could be developed compo-sitionally and through improvisation. Jazz was a verb, a doing word, something you *did* to musical material.

Brubeck went on to offer a neat summary of the distinc-tion between composition and improvisation that Igor Stravin-sky outlined in his book *Poetics of Music.* Stravinsky's idea was that composition equaled "selective improvisation" and "my freedom will be so much the greater and more meaningful the more narrowly I limit my field of action and the more I sur-round myself with obstacles [because] whatever diminishes constraint diminishes strength [and] the more constraints one imposes, the more one frees one's self of the chains that shackle the spirit."[6] From this Brubeck concluded that "selec-tive improvisation" accords "the element of contemplation, a higher degree of selectivity, and consequently an organically more intricate, and . . . distilled form of musical expression." The pieces on *Brubeck Plays Brubeck* are sketches, he said—"a skeletal framework upon which to improvise, to express a mood or emotion or stimulate musical ideas." While not autonomous compositions as Stravinsky would have understood the term, they were more compositionally integrated than the model of "a new melody superimposed over the old 'easy-to-jam-on' chord changes."

But having built Stravinsky's ideas up, Brubeck added an insistent jazzman's caveat. "However, I wish to emphasize there are moments of creation when all the contemplative time in his-tory could not alter or refine the initial idea to make it any more eloquent or meaningful. In improvisation these rare moments are shared with the listener at the time of their inception. The

---

6. Igor Stravinsky, *Poetics of Music: In the Form of Six Lessons* (Cambridge, MA: Harvard University Press, 1970), 65.

idea, the creation, and the reception occur in one inspired moment of direct communication." Jazz has drawn liberally on classical music, but equally "jazz has revived the almost lost art of improvisation and has acted as a revitalizing force in classical music because of its spontaneity and closeness to basic human emotions."

Expressing confidence that *Brubeck Plays Brubeck*—and by extension *Dave Brubeck Plays and Plays and Plays*—would be "considered and understood" by his jazz colleagues in this shared spirit of creativity and innovation, Brubeck returned to the thorny subject of spontaneous creativity trumping flawless technical precision. Ideals of musical "perfection" and instrumental mastery run deep. So why couldn't Brubeck be technically faultless *and* creative? "None of us is the complete jazz musician," Brubeck stated. The musicians he admired most had powerful individual creative identities, and those he respected would "differ with my opinions. I know this because they are as outspoken in their beliefs as I am in mine." And with that, *Brubeck Plays Brubeck* readied itself to make its place in a world in which many eager young jazz pianists had already changed jazz indelibly, or were about to, with ideas often expressed in their most pure form on solo piano albums.

Lennie Tristano, the blind Chicago-born pianist who moved to New York City in 1946, finished recording his eponymous debut album in 1955, the summer before Brubeck recorded *Brubeck Plays Brubeck*. Tristano was a master of illusion who, in *Lennie Tristano* and its 1962 follow-up *The New Tristano*, used studio techniques such as overdubbing and manipulating tape speed to realize sonic feats that would have been unachievable acoustically. "Turkish Mambo" deployed multitracking to resourceful effect as independent melodic lines turned and switched direction like the colors on a Rubik's cube. Preparing the ground for "East Thirty-Second," bassist Peter Ind and

drummer Jeff Morton pre-recorded rhythm tracks over which
Tristano grafted a ribbon of melody later, the sped-up tape
lending the music an objectified, mechanistic precision.
"Requiem," a memorial piece for Charlie Parker, opened with
disembodied bitonal chords before Tristano changed gear into
a heartfelt, venerating blues.

Tristano's studio craft was widely criticized at the time for
compromising the spontaneity of the moment, and *The New
Tristano* came with a disclaimer: "No use is made of multitracking, overdubbing or tape-speeding on any selection." He
needed everyone to know that he did not need studio techniques to produce the dazzling velocity and effortless, deadpan touch on pieces like "Deliberation," "Love Lines," and
"G Minor Complex." In contrast to Brubeck, Tristano never felt
compelled to thrust harmony toward points of climax, and the
riddle inside the mystery of Tristano's music was how often it
ran as fast as it could just to stay in place. Lines raced forward as
the underlying harmony evolved far more gradually.

Running wild with, and elongating, line was Tristano's
response to the aftermath of bebop, but Thelonious Monk's
sharp-cornered fingers aimed to fragment that same continuity.
Monk is often perceived as the exemplary bebop pianist, and
while he wore the bebop uniform of goatee beard and beret
with aplomb, the sound of his playing betrayed a more complex set of impulses. His great friend Bud Powell, with his even-
ness of touch, translated the instrumental prolixity of Parker's
saxophone and Gillespie's trumpet into liquid pianism, leaving
Monk to reconfigure the molecules of his instrument as conventional wisdom about technique and how pianos "ought" to
sound lay in ruins.

His three solo records made during the 1950s—*Solo 1954,
Thelonious Himself* (1957), and *Alone in San Francisco* (1959)—
have become so thoroughly sucked inside mainstream jazz
thinking that their striking radicalism can be easily overlooked.
The moment that "(I Don't Stand) A Ghost of a Chance (with

You)," on *Thelonious Himself,* threatened to settle into a free-flowing groove was the exact moment that Monk torpedoed rhythmic regularity with rhythmic hiccups. Playing "I Should Care," Monk erected a brittle carapace around Sammy Cahn's tune. A whacked bass note triggered, as though by reflex, a shell-shocked, smashed cluster that resonated over the bar line, as naked sound overwhelmed the structure of the song.

Tristano used harmony to facilitate flow, Monk to suffocate progress. The fast-changing, obstacle-course harmonic complexity of bebop stirred up a rethink of jazz piano technique. Bop pianists like Dodo Marmarosa and Duke Jordan, playing with Parker, worked toward a method ideally suited to the demands of the music: the left hand outlined the rapidly unfolding harmonic patterns, a secure grounding over which the right hand launched busy, athletic lines. Los Angeles–born Hampton Hawes made his debut record in June 1955, four months after Parker's death, and the Pennsylvanian Eddie Costa (who worked extensively with Joe Morello directly before he joined Brubeck) would begin recording a year later, and they both played a fast, furious second-generation bebop that had no place for old-school jazz techniques such as stride piano, boogie-woogie, and walking bass.

Thelonious Monk begged to differ. His work was rooted in gospel music—during his teens he had toured with a Church of God in Christ preacher—and in the joy he had taken observing finger-busting Harlem "ticklers" James P. Johnson and Willie "the Lion" Smith, who had turned stride piano into a high art. Monk was never that close personally to either Parker or Gillespie and had correspondingly little interest in playing stylistically pure bebop.[7] Some of his most radical compositions recalled earlier styles. "Epistrophy" was perched above a rollicking, lopsided boogie-woogie figuration; "Misterioso"

7. Robin D. G. Kelley, *Thelonious Monk: The Life and Times of an American Original* (New York: Free Press, 2009), 121.

inched around a cyclic twelve-bar blues-like stride piano in slow motion; and "Hackensack" contained within its structure the topsy-turvy flow of history between earlier forms of jazz and bop. The riff around which Monk wrote "Hackensack" was recorded by Coleman Hawkins for the first time as "Rifftide" in 1945, a record that was lifted straight out of bebop house style. But Monk embedded a jocose boogie-woogie pattern into his version, calmly slipped under the song's middle section, which would have felt entirely out of place on a Charlie Parker record.

Monk's hunch that the tradition of stride piano was a fundamental jazz truth was not his alone. In *The New Tristano*, by throwing lines between his hands, Tristano had reintegrated an active, functional role for the left hand into music that was not bebop but that would not have been possible without bop. Mary Lou Williams, coming from a slightly earlier generation than Monk and Tristano, began her career as a pianist and arranger for saxophonist Andy Kirk's group Twelve Clouds of Joy, and in 1937 wrote the boogie-woogie-based "Roll 'Em" for the Benny Goodman Orchestra. Only a few years later she was contributing arrangements to Dizzy Gillespie's big band and rechanneling her distinctive compositional voice through the vocabulary and phraseology of bebop. Her knack for keeping pace reached an unlikely apogee in 1977 when she played with Cecil Taylor at Carnegie Hall, a problematic and uneven experience in many ways, but one that proved the ecstatic energy uncorked by stride piano and the elation of free jazz were intimate bedfellows.

For much of the 1960s, Jaki Byard was Charles Mingus's pianist of choice, and the giddy range of his pianism, which ranged from ripe Romanticism to clustered atonality via gospel and stride, made a perfect match for Mingus's bricolage compositions. Most evenings during the Mingus Quintet's European tour of 1964, Byard opened the second set with an unaccompanied solo piece he called "AT-FW-YOU." Mingus would proudly announce the piece as a celebration of "the original traditions of jazz—Art Tatum, Fats Waller, and Jelly Roll Morton," and it unfolded as a mind map of authentic 1920s and '30s stride, boogie-woogie knocked off-center, and churchy swells. His solo piano album, *Blues for Smoke*, recorded in 1960, was driven by similar compulsions: the polite classicism of "Excerpts from European Episode" and the finger-twisting stride piano of "Pete and Thomas (Tribute to the Ticklers)," with "Jaki's Blues Next" joining up the historical dots.

Phineas Newborn Jr., originally from Memphis, began recording as a leader in 1956, the year of *Brubeck Plays Brubeck*, and his prodigious technical capabilities gave him an access-all-areas pass to the piano, although impressing through sheer technical virtuosity alone was never his aim. Newborn's roots lay more audibly in bebop than either Monk's or Byard's, although bop as an ongoing debate rather than a dealt-with piece of history. His version of Charlie Parker's "Cheryl" from his 1961 album *A World of Piano!* (a trio session with Miles Davis's former rhythm section, bassist Paul Chambers and drummer Philly Joe Jones) opened with Parker's line headbutting the lower register of the piano before a spectacularly grand gesture kick-started his improvisation. Against a staccato outline of Parker's harmony punched out in the bass, Newborn's right hand rose eagle-like from the midriff of the keyboard with an immaculately executed chromatic ascent that soared free of those insistently reiterated left-hand harmonies. Then his line flew off the top of the keyboard, leaving our ears to become accustomed to the looming, cavernous drop between right and left hands—not at all a conventional bebop laying-on of hands, sticking to the middle octaves of the piano.

Tristano, Monk, Byard, Williams, and Newborn flexed the piano whole, instincts that Brubeck shared. Criticisms that Brubeck played a pretty commercial or "pop" jazz—with the added sting that at least George Shearing managed to do so without pretension—failed to factor in the collateral impact that resulted from unexpected collisions of incompatible material worked into the improvisational process. Shearing, Jacques Loussier, and the Modern Jazz Quartet's John Lewis were more guarded improvisers, while the technical loquacity of Oscar Peterson, who could carpet any tune with a perfectly formulated improvisational response—and at any tempo you liked—had little in common with Brubeck's willingness to embrace chaos.

Nor did Brubeck's brand of pianism have much in common with Bill Evans, although a connection has sometimes been sought. For a short while, the two men led something of parallel lives. The piano on which Evans recorded his contributions to Miles Davis's *Kind of Blue* at Columbia's 30th Street Studio was the same instrument on which Brubeck recorded *Time Out* later that same summer. The Glenn Gould chic of the two men's beanpole physiques and their black-rimmed spectacles and neatly tailored suits created a certain visual assonance, but their approaches to the art of improvisation diverged significantly.

Recorded in December 1958, four months prior to *Kind of Blue, Everybody Digs Bill Evans* showcased Evans in a trio setting with Sam Jones (bass) and Philly Joe Jones (drums). When they came to record "Some Other Time" from Leonard Bernstein's musical *On the Town*, Evan's imagination became fixated on the pair of oscillating chords with which Bernstein introduced his tune. At the end of the session, alone in the studio, he began to rock those two chords backward and forward like a pendulum. The trio's version of "Some Other Time" was left off the final album (although it would be restored in reissued versions) in favor of these post-session afterthoughts—a track Evans would call "Peace Piece."

Evans's musical intelligence was dazzling. It's impossible not to be reminded of the piano music of Olivier Messiaen as Bernstein's base harmonic alchemy is transformed into a scrollwork of tonalities overlapping and accents crisscrossing. Polytonality did have an important role to play in "Peace Piece," but it functioned very differently from how Brubeck understood, and applied, the term. The piece stretched over seven minutes but only *became* polytonal once Evans had introduced that most illegal "black note" of all—a tritone—which gainsaid the "white note" patterns he had established, becoming a tipping point toward saturating the harmony in deepening polytonal colors. Brubeck's music rarely became polytonal in that same way—for Brubeck, polytonality was a state of mind, a permanent fixture, and the harmonic language through which he conversed.

The bass player in Evans's first great trio, Scott LaFaro, changed the pianist's view of his instrument. LaFaro's experiments with displacing the fundamental note of a chord—the B-flat of B-flat major, or the A of A minor—by shunting it toward an obscure beat within a bar, where the strong harmony note would melt against a weak beat, or by thinly disguising the root in the clothes of a closely related chord, yanked open the territory. Evans spoke later of his disdain for the idea that the bass player's role should be reduced to that of a "time machine" slavishly outlining the root and the fifth. "I wanted to make room for the bass and try to leave some fundamental roles empty so that the bass could pick them up," he said,[8] and "making room for the bass" pushed Evans up the keyboard, where, in the middle octaves of the piano, he was free to create a seamless slipstream of interlocking harmonies.

Evans used polytonality to smooth over the harmonic pathways, to mesh harmonic colors together, continuity always his watchword. But for Brubeck polytonality was all about rupture and disjointed structures, from shading subtle enough to give a common chord an air of unfamiliar mystery to contrary chords slammed together with the intention of disrupting the smooth passage of a chord sequence.

8. Interview with Brian Hennessy, available via www.billevans.nl/Brian.htm (accessed 16 September 2017).

If polytonality was Brubeck's answer, bebop wasn't necessarily the question. Neither *Brubeck Plays Brubeck* nor *Dave Brubeck Plays and Plays and Plays* had anything to say about the technical apparatus or the expressive milieu of bebop. The 1953 package tour he shared with Charlie Parker had given Brubeck a ringside seat, bebop every night, blowing through the guru's own horn. He understood the music intellectually and his soul could be stirred by its emotional message, but bebop could not produce the note combinations and rhythms with which he himself wanted to work.

*Brubeck Plays Brubeck* was the first record devoted to original Brubeck compositions, and his aim was to flesh out those sketchy "skeletal frameworks," as he called them in the liner note, as fully functioning and internally consistent pieces, nurtured by improvisational urges. Without the reliable feedback loop of audience appreciation, working alone at home on a piano that slipped conspicuously, if not entirely unattractively, out of tune in the upper octaves, Brubeck thought through how to play Brubeck.

The turbulent harmonic waters of landmark solos like "These Foolish Things" from *Jazz at Oberlin* and *Jazz: Red Hot and Cool*'s "Little Girl Blue," with their tonality-straining clusters, would have no part in an album that took its stylistic bearings from Bach, Fats Waller, Duke Ellington, Milhaud, and Romantic balladry. "In Your Own Sweet Way," "Walkin' Line," and "Two-Part Contention" forged a living, breathing connection between J. S. Bach's weaves of line and the jazz tradition of walking bass. The balladry of "Weep No More" opened the B side, which then continued with a pair of waltz-based compositions, "When I Was Young" and "The Waltz" (neither of which Brubeck would play again), arranged around two pieces that became fixtures of the quartet repertoire. "One Moment Worth Years" was an appreciative nod toward Fats Waller, and the stately and harmonically palatial "The Duke" would prove more than worthy of its dedicatee. *Dave Brubeck Plays and Plays and Plays* would present a sequence of nine unconnected tracks, but *Brubeck Plays Brubeck* feels internally integrated, like a neoclassical suite of piano pieces, and a faithful, note-for-note transcribed version of the album would work as a stand-alone concert item.

Before "In Your Own Sweet Way," "Swing Bells" served as what Brubeck called a "mood-setting introduction," an overture in all but name. When the tune was revived on the 1987 quartet album *Blue Rondo*, Bill Smith's frolicsome clarinet and Chris Brubeck's tailgating trombone, with Brubeck's rolling left hand adding an underbelly of funk, lent the piece a Dixieland strut that echoed Brubeck's repurposing of his song for the finale of *The Real Ambassadors*. But in 1956 "Swing Bells" was fleeting and elusive, doing more than merely setting the mood.

"Swing Bells" was a descriptive title that rang true. Over a chiming note from the cavernous depths of Brubeck's piano, chords pealed like a hammer striking the dome of a bell, serving notice that *Brubeck Plays Brubeck* would be an essay in kneading harmonic color around the keyboard. Unlike in Bill Evans's "Peace Piece," where the tritone suddenly established a fresh harmonic plateau, in "Swing Bells" the tritone was a fully functional part of the harmony that refused to let the harmony drop anchor. And Brubeck listened in carefully, his hands hovering over notes that rhymed, or clashed, against that unchanging bass note.

"Often when I do not have a clear cut idea as to how I will improvise on a tune, I'll begin by experimenting with many chord changes played against a pedal[9] or bass in the left hand," Brubeck tells us in the essay he wrote for *Brubeck Plays Brubeck*. "Out of diverse approaches to ['Swing Bells'], the searching quality of this version seemed to be the most stimulating." And "searching" was an apt choice of words. Brubeck saturated "Swing Bells" in so many harmonic layers that the theme we hear

9. A repeated bass note.

in full on *The Real Ambassadors* or the 1987 *Blue Rondo* album was kept at a distance, as a texture built on chords blocked out the melodic light. Brubeck wanted to make "Swing Bells" function as idiomatic piano music, a process that ended with him devouring his original song. The moment Brubeck might be about to reveal the whole thing was the same moment the melody was tugged unobtrusively back into the texture. During the second chorus, fragile threads of melody were left dangling as block chords leaped out of the texture. Heading toward the last chorus, the harmony was slipped up a whole step, without Brubeck's preparing the ear with any transition or gear change.

This devouring of melody using harmony obliged listeners to paste those veiled melodic threads together to create their own idea of what "Swing Bells" might be—far from the bebopper's preferred mode of melodic improvisation, where maintaining line was all-important. Parker wasn't much interested in making instrumental color integral to any musical argument; focusing on timbre would have been an invitation to stand back from the unfolding high-speed melodic argument to admire the passing view. Brubeck's approach to transforming a song was closer to the Thelonious Monk of "I Should Care," where harmony was placed in tension against the piano's innate capacity to sustain sound. There were also irresistible echoes of the late-nineteenth-century principle of piano transcription, as composers like Liszt and Busoni reshaped vocal pieces by Schubert, Mozart, and Verdi to make virtuosic piano showpieces.

When the Miles Davis Quintet—with John Coltrane (tenor saxophone), Red Garland (piano), Paul Chambers (bass), and Philly Joe Jones (drums)—recorded their version of "In Your Own Sweet Way," only a month after Brubeck's solo reading, they subtly repositioned the piece as a jazz ballad, which helps gauge where *Brubeck Plays Brubeck* stands in relation to jazz and classical music. Coltrane sculpted a solo of granite beauty from the chord changes, which he investigated from all perspectives, like an architect envisaging how a structure might look in the round. With his trademark mute in place, Davis stretched the melody line, delaying structurally vital notes until the last possible moment, which obliged him to run lesser passing notes together. Miles also messed with Brubeck's harmonic scheme. Brubeck temporarily parked his composition on a fifth in the middle of its first phrase, but Davis's decision to lip down the fifth created a flattened fifth, which was Davis adding his signature to Brubeck's composition.

Brubeck's challenging Davis about why he chose to play a flattened fifth was met with the response, "Because you wrote that motherfuckin' note."[10] Brubeck laughed uneasily when Marian McPartland asked him about the circumstances during his appearance on her radio program *Piano Jazz* in 1984. She demonstrated the offending note on the piano and concluded that this was a definitive "Miles-ism"—as Brubeck kept mum.

But Brubeck's account of events is exonerated by the original lead sheet, written in his own hand and entitled simply "Sweet Way"[11]—with no flattened fifth. That Davis consulted this primary source, had it lying next to him on a music stand as he recorded, is almost certain. Before mailing it back to Brubeck, he wrote "Thank you—Miles" at the top of the page. Dave and Miles weren't going to let a single note—an E natural—spoil their friendship, and Brubeck was happy to bask in the reflected glory of having Miles record his piece: on the facing page, as an aide-mémoire, he noted, "Save—Miles Davis signature."

This working copy of his lead sheet offers other revealing insights into Brubeck's compositional thinking. Below an initial draft of the melody line (in pen), he outlined a basic harmonic skeleton (in pencil) that was finessed on the go; as he

---

10. Retold in an email from Darius Brubeck, November 10, 2017.
11. "Sweet Way," undated, Scores: Secular Music, Brubeck Collection.

sized up a range of alternatives, chord symbols were scribbled at the bottom of the page. But approaching the ending, his certainty about "In Your Own Sweet Way" appeared to evaporate. On a second page, his sketching disintegrated into vigorously crossed-out fragments. A diversion toward the minor was quickly stamped on, but we see the seed of an idea that eventually evolved into the coda we know.

An instruction scrawled at the bottom of the second page— "write ending with Paul, play out then go D"—told his musicians to play the head and then jump to rehearsal letter D to move the piece toward its conclusion; clear enough, apart from Brubeck's neglecting to write a letter D on his score. Cooking up an ending "with Paul" tells us that Brubeck needed to hear his composition unfolding in real time before he could settle on a convincing ending. In the lead-up to *Brubeck Plays Brubeck*, "In Your Own Sweet Way" would feature regularly in the quartet's set list, and a live radio recording from Basin Street East in February 1956[12] finds Brubeck working hard to integrate the composition with his improvisation; at the climax of his solo, the theme reappears as block chords riding a sea of arpeggios. But the grandeur of his theme requires a correspondingly elaborate ending, and the piece finishes with a resolute coda, granite block chords bringing the curtain down before a flourish delivers us back safely to the home key. Miles Davis also felt the need for a coda, and a little arranged interlude that Miles inserted before each solo in his version was looped to provide an ending (an earlier Davis dummy run, with Sonny Rollins on tenor saxophone, unreleased at the time, had no interlude and was weaker for it).

It's little surprise that, as a composer playing his own piece, Brubeck accentuates compositional architecture in his solo version. Whereas Miles stretched Brubeck's theme, massaging it

---

12. The Dave Brubeck Quartet, *On the Radio: Live 1956–57* (Acrobat Music ACMCD4324).

into a shape he found pleasing, Brubeck respects the full rhythmic values of each phrase. He deviates from the lead sheet: Where the first bar opens with a group of three notes, followed by a group of two, Brubeck tucks in an unobtrusive passing note to maintain the rhythmic symmetry. Miles played a group of three notes followed by two; Brubeck accentuates two groups of three notes.

Even through the tart recorded sound, Brubeck's piano shimmers with the grace of an orchestral celesta, an antidote to all that critical sweat about unseemly weight and bombast. Low block chords supported by full-bodied bass notes warm the middle section of the piece, and the reappearance of the opening theme is bolstered by a rich reharmonization. As soon as Brubeck begins his improvisation, the keyboard texture thins. Two rhythmically skipping, limping lines weave together, bunched within the same octave, the left hand shadowing the right. This clipped precision and dry tone provides a slate-wiping contrast to the sumptuous harmonic palette hitherto served up—from celesta to Romantic piano to textures that resemble a harpsichord.

Percolating through *Brubeck Plays Brubeck* like a unifying itch, the long note–short note limp with which Brubeck begins his improvisation on "In Your Own Sweet Way" reappears during "Walkin' Line," "The Duke," and "Two-Part Contention." Its clean-cut rigidity, articulated with mechanical clarity, innocent enough on its own terms, struck some as dangerously antithetical to the true spirit of swing. Louis Armstrong, Lester Young, and Coleman Hawkins did not skip. They *glided* from the long note into the short note, the longer first note giving leverage to sway into the short note; and the music, literally, *swung*.

Heavily dotted, rhythmic hops, a feature of French music since the baroque period, had seeped into the language of French neoclassicism, almost to the point of mannerisms, and always were going to feature in an album that related so explicitly to Darius Milhaud. But Brubeck is experimenting quite consciously with rhythmic feel and weight. "When I Was Young" throws skipping rhythms into relief against passages of gliding swing, while "Two-Part Contention," which might reasonably have been expected to root itself in stately baroque rhythms, is dispatched with a lilting swing. (That Brubeck considered this tune to be a swinger all along is confirmed by its treatment on his 1979 quartet album *Back Home*, where Jerry Bergonzi's tenor saxophone and Chris Brubeck's trombone bind the interweaving strands of the melody line together like a Classic jazz front line, as Butch Miles claws the space open with a sequence of splashy drum breaks.)

The British jazz critic Charles Fox ended his review of *Brubeck Plays Brubeck* for the January 1957 issue of *Gramophone* magazine with a startling and prescient comparison with Thelonious Monk: "Both have difficulty in articulating their ideas, both convey a striking sense of urgency," Fox wrote, his objection based on his discomfort with the fact that neither pianist conformed to the fluid rhythmic flow of bebop.[13] Fox could not bring himself to love the record, that much is clear, but he managed to say something meaningful about the Brubeckian aesthetic nevertheless, making connections many of his colleagues missed. He regretted that so many tracks were "out of or only just in tempo"—beginning with "Swing Bells"—and contended that "people who think jazz has to swing to be any good will hate this record. Dave Brubeck's playing never raises the temperature." But he recognized the "formally ingenious" constructs of "Walkin' Line" and "Two-Part Contention," and that "Brubeck thinks within the jazz idiom, even if his work exploits devices from other musical fields."

Would Fox have changed his mind had he also reviewed, a year later, *Dave Brubeck Plays and Plays and Plays?* The opening track, a four-minute spectacle of rawboned stride piano and

---

13. Jazz and swing reviews, *Gramophone*, January 1957.

blues harmony, torpedoes any generalities about his playing proposed by *Brubeck Plays Brubeck*; "Sweet Cleo Brown," dedicated to an early mentor, gets funkier by the chorus. Cleo Brown was famed from her prowess as a boogie-woogie and stride player, but her career floundered when she acquired a drug habit. She apparently took a shine to Brubeck when she came to Stockton in an attempt to escape her demons and checked into a hospital. Her doctors thought it would be a good idea if she gradually eased herself back into work, and Brubeck was charged with picking her up, taking her to a job, and ensuring she returned home safely. Brubeck also played intermission piano for her shows, and Brown advised Brubeck against his habit of beating time with his feet as he played—the sound, she said, had to come through his fingers.[14] Paying tribute all these years later, Brubeck gnaws on a phrase in the second chorus that pre-echoes *Time Further Out*'s "It's a Raggy Waltz," and his striding gets busier and more raucous as it works back toward his theme—and a long way from the perfumed classicism of *Brubeck Plays Brubeck*.

Brubeck's introduction retraces the stock intro with which Cleo Brown introduced her boogie-woogie performances, and the sleeve note, by Russ Wilson, picks up the history of "Sweet Cleo Brown": the tune's opening melodic strains are "reminiscent of a tune that David Van Kriedt and Paul Desmond used to play," Wilson writes, and a single piece of manuscript paper headed "Paul & Dave's Tune—van Kriedt" joins the historical dots. Underneath three elegantly drawn staves of music in his own hand, Van Kriedt has written: "To whom it may concern: I recognize the right of Dave Brubeck to write a song which resembles this song (Paul & Dave's Tune) in any way for agreements already decided upon." Dated November 24, 1957, Van Kriedt added: "For the above right Dave Brubeck paid me

---

14. Dave Brubeck, handwritten journal, undated entry, Brubeck Collection.

$150.00."[15] Brubeck was helping out a close associate in financial need by buying his music, melodic material that looked, on the page, more suited to baroque-based counterpoint than the blues.

Brubeck's decision to locate the tune explicitly inside jazz tradition was out of deference to Cleo Brown, but perhaps also, having made his big statement with *Brubeck Plays Brubeck*, he felt able, as his title implies, to simply play and play and play. Retaining his $150 worth of melodic contour, he drops in a tangy blue note and pulls notes around the bar to make the rhythmic footfall less predictable. George Gershwin's "Our Love Is Here to Stay" and Cole Porter's "You'd Be So Nice to Come Home To" are also power swingers, punched out with strutting block chords, and even when Victor Herbert's "Indian Summer" encourages Brubeck's classical sensibilities, Rachmaninoff-like plunges and waves of arpeggios swing rather than skip. Brubeck's own composition, "In Search of a Theme," pairs a finger-snapping walking bass line against a theme that comes to rest on a single repeated note, leaving his left hand free to further the interest with thematically enabled block chords, reversing the usual roles of the two hands. The track also includes the first appearance of the Brubeck children on record, who are yelling in the background as the track winds to a close.

Screaming children—even if they might one day turn into sidemen—highlight the perils of recording at home, although this second time around the recorded sound was superior to *Brubeck Plays Brubeck* and the piano was impeccably in tune. Many criticisms aimed at the earlier album are answered by its sequel, which demand to be heard as a pair, even if history has favored *Brubeck Plays Brubeck*. As regards the supposed division between classicism and swing, Brubeck was sending out

---

15. "Paul & Dave's Tune," Biographies, Interviews, Itineraries, Writings, Notes Inventory, Papers, Box 15, Brubeck Collection.

the message, "I can do both." And four decades later, when he returned to the studio to make a solo album of standards interspersed with the occasional original, the layout of *Dave Brubeck Plays and Plays and Plays* was the blueprint he followed, not the overt classicism of *Brubeck Plays Brubeck*.

Sandwiched between two live albums recorded at the Blue Note in New York—*Late Night Brubeck* and *Nightshift*—and his seventy-fifth-birthday album, *Young Lions & Old Tigers, Just You, Just Me* was released during an especially prolific period. "Telarc wants me to record solo," Brubeck said, hinting at behind-the-scenes discussions with his record label. "My solo albums outsell the quartet albums." So why did Brubeck wait so long to return to the studio on his own? "No one asked me to! Plus I was too busy writing music and working with the quartet."[16] But this late outpouring of solo material meant much more to him than vigorous sales figures. Now in his midseventies, fifty-two years after those four student tryouts were recorded at the College of the Pacific, this was Brubeck consolidating everything he had learned about the piano—while still pushing himself.

Although subtle shifts of time and rhythm cast their usual spell, advancing his exploration of asymmetrical time signatures was not normally on the agenda when he played solo; but Brubeck's commitment to polytonality was unswerving. The dichotomy implanted into his head by Igor Stravinsky, originally discussed in his *Brubeck Plays Brubeck* essay, between improvisation and what, in 1956, Brubeck had termed "a higher degree of selectivity" was still on his mind while on the road in 2003, but now a degree of doubt had crept in. "Stravinsky said you can't use your analytical and creative mind at the same time—you're either working analytically or you're letting it flow creatively,"

16. Email interview with the author, May 10, 2007.

Brubeck said. "I've heard other people say that he was wrong; there's this phrase contemporary players use called 'getting into the zone,' and when you are in the zone, you're not really aware. You're just playing and the concentration is so intense you [can] move beyond your normal capabilities and your body."[17]

Being a man of a certain age, Brubeck was more concerned about journeying beyond normal corporeal capabilities as an improviser who was searching an "effortless flow of new material" than when he was in his thirties. The physical muscle that powered him through *Just You, Just Me* and *One Alone*, in his seventies, had weakened perceptibly by the time of *Private Brubeck Remembers* in 2004. The circumstances around *Indian Summer*, recorded three years later, in his eighty-sixth year, were uniquely trying: in a Texas hotel room, Brubeck misjudged the distance between his mattress and the bed frame and wound up in a painful heap on the floor. So the album was recorded a few days before Brubeck underwent surgery to deal with his ankle injury, and integral to the story of these later records is how he compensated musically for the physical limitations imposed by creeping old age.

The polished swing of *Just You, Just Me*'s title track picks up the baton directly from *Dave Brubeck Plays and Plays and Plays* thirty-seven years earlier. Brubeck's booklet notes tell us that "Just You, Just Me" was the only piece fully formed in his head as an arrangement before he arrived at the studio. A welcome revival of the inexplicably neglected "Strange Meadow Lark," on record for only the second time since it sat between "Blue Rondo à la Turk" and "Take Five" on *Time Out*, followed; and then the standard "It's the Talk of the Town," for which Brubeck had worked out an eight-bar polytonal introduction—the rest being "free improvisation on the classic tune"—led to the album's main talking point.

---

17. Ibid.

"Variations on 'Brother, Can You Spare a Dime?'" is a Herculean eight-minute performance as Brubeck takes a stream-of-consciousness ride around various approaches he had pursued with Jay Gorney's standard since his quartet had begun playing the tune in the early 1950s. Acknowledging the formal maze—an improvisation that fans out as a set of continuous variations with overlaps of different musical styles—it was Russell Gloyd's idea to prefix the song title with the tag "Variations," and Brubeck's intention of producing something more complex than the predictable chain of episodes, one flowing neatly into the next, that often denotes variation form is clear. Polytonal chords cross the opening clean-cut textures (memories of "Two-Part Contention") like a questioning blemish, and the music suddenly starts switching direction—from two-part counterpoint into a jazz ballad; then from big-boned harmonies shadowing the contours of Bach's organ masterwork Toccata and Fugue in D Minor into a passage of straight-ahead jazz time, which leads to an open-ended cadence, and you wonder where the music might head next.

By way of an answer, Brubeck digs back to the very earliest days of his quartet. The sprightly line he introduces is the same arranged line that launched the quartet's 1954 recording on *Brubeck Time*, which Eugene Wright played to audition for the Dave Brubeck Quartet in 1958 and which anchored the version the 1980 edition of the group recorded on their album *Tritonis*. Whereas in the original 1954 quartet version Brubeck, Desmond, and Bob Bates introduced the line as a canon, Desmond leading their staggered entries, now Brubeck's extremely nimble fingers carry all the entries himself. But he doesn't allow the structure to settle. A window of quiet introspection is ripped into as a fugal texture picks up on those earlier traces of Bach's Toccata and Fugue in D Minor, which itself is overwhelmed by a funky riff over which Brubeck begins the process of pulling all these various strands together.

But why would a jazzman who regularly proclaimed improvisation as a virtue next to godliness indulge in this display of self-referential borrowing? The formal sweep of "Variations on 'Brother, Can You Spare a Dime?'" stems from the classicism of *Brubeck Plays Brubeck*, and like that album, "Variations on 'Brother, Can You Spare a Dime?'" is a career exception. With his advancing age, and without any expectation that *Just You, Just Me* would herald a chain of sequels, the likelihood of Brubeck's recording another solo version of "Brother, Can You Spare a Dime?" was slim. "Growing up in the Depression, this song was one of the first pieces I knew from beginning to end, complete with words," he wrote in his booklet note to *Tritonis*, and he wanted to review this song that had meant so much to him—the roughness in the construct an honest reflection of the jagged joins resulting from bringing together different periods and styles.

"Bye Bye Blues" on *One Alone* fulfills a similar role to "Variations on 'Brother, Can You Spare a Dime?'" on *Just You, Just Me*. By the time "Bye Bye Blues" appears as the penultimate track, two pieces of classic Ellingtonia, "Just Squeeze Me" and "Things Ain't What They Used to Be," have already been overhauled by Brubeck's granitic, hulking stride piano, but "Bye Bye Blues" goes further. Originally a Cab Calloway record and revived by Les Paul, this is another song grabbed from Brubeck's memory.

In 1980, when he recorded a television special for the BBC in Birmingham, Annie Ross guested with her trio, and we see Dave beaming broadly in the background as she sings "Bye Bye Blues." Two decades later, Brubeck keeps his solo version hanging off a rhythmic precipice as he follows where the sounds he is unleashing lead him. The performance lumbers toward a midpoint climax, where the structure completely buckles, leaving Brubeck to catch the falling pieces. B-flat is layered against G to begin, then the increasing harmonic motion of so many harmonic centers in play at once denies a neat point landing and Brubeck wedges in another beat into a bar of 4/4 to accommodate clashing tonalities. When Brubeck started, did he have this point in mind? The way it spills out of the material you suspect not, although the exploratory context he sets up enables that magical moment to happen—the true improviser spirit.

Despite the discomfort and mobility problems concomitant with Brubeck's ankle injury, the seventy-two minutes' worth of solo music released as *Indian Summer* were completed during two afternoon studio sessions. Russell Gloyd's booklet note talks of "this CD as a documentary of Dave in a recording studio, and consequently [I] have decided to keep the tunes in the same sequence as they were recorded." *Indian Summer* and *Private Brubeck Remembers* lack the variety of programming that made *Just You, Just Me* and *One Alone* sessions into CDs that flow beautifully between tracks. But, with the flesh weak, that spirit of free association keeps the music intellectually alive. "You'll Never Know," from *Indian Summer*, sets up a relaxing groove supported by well-behaved harmony, but suddenly a chromatic wanderer upsets expectations—and Brubeck resolves it, but not in any textbook way.

Brubeck's solo albums were warmly praised after his death, but it was disheartening to read opinions, hooked around the vaguest recall of his history on record, being reported as fact as late as 2012, the year of Brubeck's death. "On all of the odd-metered tunes, he soloed in four," Fred Hersch breezily informed his fellow jazz pianist Ethan Iverson during an extended interview on the latter's blog, Do the Math, demonstrating curious ignorance of Brubeck's music.[18] "He's been making records for sixty years, and has sold however many bazillion records," Hersch continued, "and I don't know anybody he's influenced." Iverson threw back the thought that he did influence Keith Jarrett and Cecil Taylor—"but only as

18. Ethan Iverson, "Interview with Fred Hersch," Do the Math, n.d., https://ethaniverson.com/interviews/interview-with-fred-hersch/.

a gateway." And all this based on Hersch's hazy assertion that he once owned a copy of *Time Further Out*—but, given his dismissive and sniffy tone, you wonder if he might after all mean *Time Out*.

The questions that matter about Brubeck's lineage and DNA as a pianist and his popularity cannot be answered through such selective listening. The Brubeck who recorded that fingertip-sensitive introduction to "Strange Meadow Lark" in 1959 during the *Time Out* sessions was, as unlikely as it may seem, the same man who, twenty-three years later, created an audacious, obstreperous solo on "Truth," from *We're All Together Again for the First Time*, which summoned up the ghosts of progressive American piano music, from Charles Ives's *Concord* Sonata to the free jazz of Cecil Taylor and Don Pullen. The Brubeck who was playing graceful, intimate chamber music with Paul Desmond on their album *1975: The Duets* was, at the same time, unleashing handfuls of clusters and churning left-hand funk in response to his sons' rock grooves during Two Generations of Brubeck gigs—sounds that musicians who sold records in the "bazillions" ought never to make. With hindsight, *Brubeck Plays Brubeck* and *Dave Brubeck Plays and Plays and Plays* do not feel like two separate ways of maneuvering—more like windows on a spectrum of possibilities that Brubeck would continue to chase, a spectrum forever widening and altering its perspective.

*Chapter Ten*

# AMERICAN PASTORAL

"I was a biography in constant motion, memory to
the marrow of my bones."

PHILIP ROTH, *American Pastoral*, 1997

By the time Telarc came to release his late-period solo albums,
beginning with *Just You, Just Me* in 1994, Brubeck was caught in
a paradox. He was leading a fine quartet—with Bobby Militello
(alto saxophone, flute), Jack Six (bass), and Randy Jones
(drums)—but the quartet associated with his name, and still
talked up as quintessential Brubeck, the "classic" Dave Brubeck
Quartet, hadn't existed since 1967. There had been other
groups in the interim. A quartet with Gerry Mulligan, founded
in 1968, toured widely around the US and Europe, keeping
the acoustic faith through the plugged-in age of electric
Miles, Weather Report, Return to Forever, and Headhunters.
Riding high among the reasons why Brubeck's relationship

with Columbia had fizzled out by 1971 was his reluctance to embrace electric keyboards and synthesizers.

But almost as soon as he left Columbia, Brubeck went electric in Two Generations of Brubeck, the group he shared with his sons Darius (keyboards), Chris (electric bass), and Danny (drums)—and the musicians with whom the younger Brubecks had associated in their own ensembles, involved variously in different, and sometimes overlapping, shades of free improvisation, rock fusion, and electric blues. He released music with Gerry Mulligan and with Two Generations of Brubeck on Atlantic Records, the home of Coltrane, Ornette Coleman, and Charles Mingus during the 1950s, and a label by the early 1970s more associated with the Velvet Underground, Sister Sledge, Aretha Franklin, Led Zeppelin, and Roberta Flack. A slimmed-down adaptation of Two Generations toured as the New Brubeck Quartet (Dave, Darius, Chris, Danny), and when the time came in 1979 to re-form as an acoustic quartet, Brubeck's approach to the piano had been changed by these encounters and had metamorphosed into something chewier, harder-edged, and funkier, charged with an inner volatility.

Those qualities had long been part of the mix, but no longer leading a quartet with such a long history, and around which so many people had hung their expectations and affection, was liberating. This new edition of the quartet at first featured the tenor saxophonist Jerry Bergonzi, whose approach to his instrument, rooted in John Coltrane and Sonny Rollins, contrasted sharply with Paul Desmond's style and—at last—brought Brubeck's music into direct contact with saxophone playing rooted in bebop. Bergonzi came into the quartet via Two Generations of Brubeck, and when he left after a three-year tenure, Brubeck looked back to the very beginning of his career.

Extending an invitation to Bill Smith to join the quartet was no exercise in nostalgia. Brubeck was in essence asking Smith to rejoin a quartet of which he had never been a permanent member; he had been the "classic" quartet's fifth Beatle. The set of albums he recorded with the quartet in the 1960s, replacing Paul Desmond—*The Riddle, Near Myth, Brubeck à la Mode,* and the unreleased *Witches Brew*—were never any match for the commercial clout of *Dave Digs Disney, Time Out,* or *Time Further Out,* but they established another way of working that Brubeck and Smith would pursue two decades later. Smith and Desmond had sat side by side in the Brubeck Octet, but they exhibited very different personalities as improvisers. Whereas Desmond basked in his opulent, sensuous saxophone sound, Smith's clarinet tone was matter-of-fact and dispassionate, with no trace of the swing-era sweetness of Artie Shaw or Benny Goodman. Desmond's sound had a magnetism that drew people into the fascination of his notes, but the neutrality and objectivity of Smith's sound, paradoxically, had the same result. There was nothing to listen to in Smith's playing apart from his relentlessly inventive notes, projected with an attractively shrill tone, as if he were dispatching urgent news.

For avowed Brubeck fans who had found reassurance in the settled personnel and established musical language of the classic quartet, suddenly there was a lot of new information to process. The prospect of a new quartet with Gerry Mulligan— which, for contractual reasons and to avoid confusion with the classic group, was billed as "the Dave Brubeck Trio featuring Gerry Mulligan"—made convincing musical sense. Brubeck and Mulligan had a friendship that stretched back to the early 1950s. Mulligan had been signed to Fantasy Records under Brubeck's recommendation and had been part of the 1954 package tour that featured the Brubeck Quartet and Stan Getz with Duke Ellington's orchestra; he had also on occasion deputized for Paul Desmond in the classic quartet. But, as Brubeck delivered a solo that demolished the changes of "Things Ain't What They Used to Be" on the group's 1968 album *Blues Roots,* and the improvisational chemistry between saxophone and piano crackled with a bellicose friction wholly absent from the classic quartet, anyone expecting quartet business as usual was destined to be disappointed.

And the shocks kept coming. The Dave Brubeck Trio featuring Gerry Mulligan had presented as something recognizable to those who had appreciated the old group: an acoustic group of acknowledged, seasoned jazz masters playing acoustic jazz. But Two Generations of Brubeck was a protean leap into all sorts of unknowns. The two records the group recorded for Atlantic—*Two Generations of Brubeck* and *Brother, the Great Spirit Made Us All*—were rough diamonds indeed as reworked versions of "Blue Rondo à la Turk," "Three to Get Ready," "It's a Raggy Waltz," and "Unsquare Dance" (but not "Take Five") slammed into freshly composed pieces like "Circadian Dysrhythmia," "Knives," and "Tin Sink" without anyone appearing to care whether the material coalesced or blended into a satisfying whole.

Which is precisely why they were such powerful statements. "Circadian Dysrhythmia" crackled with funky, glitter-ball electricity, as though Brubeck had been possessed by the spirit of Ornette Coleman's electro-funk band Prime Time, while "Tin Sink," composed by Darius Brubeck, revealed that the young Brubecks had been lapping up an array of contemporary jazz influences: Chick Corea's acoustic quintet album *Tones for Joan's Bones* (which Dave had gifted to Darius for his birthday: "Dave wanted me to hear there was still a future in acoustic jazz"[1]) and Herbie Hancock's funky fusion album *Mwandishi* included. The cross-generational concept behind the group dug deeper into shared histories. Corea and Hancock both testified in interviews about how Brubeck's early quartet music had influenced their own early development ("Ostinato" from

1. Email from Darius Brubeck to the author, July 9, 2019.

*Mwandishi* was in 15/8)[2]—and now, twenty years on, Brubeck was being handed back a version of that influence, utterly transformed by his sons, upon which to work.

There was continuity in the forms of Paul Desmond and Gerry Mulligan, who made guest appearances at Two Generations concerts, but, mirroring that meeting of disparate minds at Mills College in 1946 that led to the formation of the octet, Brubeck found himself surrounded by an entirely new pool of inquiring musicians in 1973. In the regular front line, Bergonzi's leathery, full-throttle tenor saxophone sound was paired with Perry Robinson's clarinet. If Bergonzi's presence was helping Brubeck's music step into a whole world of John Coltrane, Robinson injected the restless vitality of free jazz into the group. Before Brubeck, Robinson had worked with Albert Ayler, Archie Shepp, Henry Grimes, and Charlie Haden's Liberation Music Orchestra (which included Don Cherry, Dewey Redman, and Andrew Cyrille), which is a sentence worth mulling over. This pianist, regularly accused of playing the whitest of white lounge jazz, was now playing with "fire music"—a term, borrowed from the title of a 1965 Archie Shepp album, that had come into popular use to describe the heat and form-seeking chaos of free jazz. Robinson's raspy, choleric clarinet extracted a squalling, free-form call-and-response from the rest of the ensemble in his piece "Call of the Wild," which was planted into the middle of *Two Generations of Brubeck.* Dave—on electric piano—scattered notes over the instrumental texture like swarms of tuned insects. To anyone beholden to the wit and whimsy of Paul Desmond, this was like a bomb going off.

Other musicians who became associated with Two Generations included the harmonica virtuoso Peter "Madcat" Ruth and violinist Stephan Dudash, who brought along their

2. John Novello, *The Contemporary Keyboardist* (New York: Hal Leonard Corporation, 2000).

backgrounds in blues and post–Stéphane Grappelli/Django Reinhardt gypsy swing; also appearing on the Two Generations debut album were the rock guitarist David Mason[3] and rock/fusion drummer Richie Morales. But the most significant musical relationship Brubeck nurtured during this era—which would sustain him until the end of his life—was that with his musician sons. Dan, Chris, and Darius, then in their late teens and early twenties, were already highly accomplished musicians and creative thinkers. Chris made the transition from Two Generations to full-time quartet bassist when Brubeck re-formed it as a quartet in 1979, and the musical journey Brubeck took with his sons would travel through various iterations, from the grand excesses of the 1970s to, beginning in 1990, a series of concerts with the London Symphony Orchestra that marked those big round-numbered birthdays—seventieth, seventy-fifth, eightieth, and eighty-fifth. The youngest Brubeck son, Matthew, who plays cello, too young for Two Generations, began to take his rightful part in family concerts during the 1980s.

If the direction of travel now seems obvious—that the tension that had long existed in Brubeck's music between compositional control and improvisational freedom was now being smashed to pieces by the turbulent 1970s and the input of his sons—life, in fact, was about to get more complicated. There was unfinished business with Paul Desmond and the classic quartet. Following *Brother, the Great Spirit Made Us All* in 1974, the next item in the Brubeck discography was *1975: The Duets*, a delectable album of Brubeck-meets-Desmond duets featuring their current thoughts on dependable standbys like "Alice in Wonderland," "Stardust," and "Balcony Rock"; and a year later the classic quartet would prove their enduring popularity with a reunion tour. And for his embrace of new freedoms in the quartet with Gerry Mulligan and in Two Generations, Brubeck

---

3. The American rock guitarist, not the British guitarist Dave Mason, from Traffic and Fleetwood Mac.

was also devoting much of his time to carefully constructing extended compositions for choirs and orchestras, every note and harmonic sequence considered and weighed with due diligence. Multiple Dave Brubecks were now in operation. It was harder than ever to pin him down.

𝄞

Most obviously, there was, in the 1970s, a pronounced mismatch between Brubeck's records and the live experience. *Two Generations of Brubeck* and *Brother, the Great Spirit Made Us All* did their job of bottling the basic energy and sound of the group, but failing to release a live Two Generations album—with Desmond or Mulligan guesting, perhaps—was a major oversight. The New Brubeck Quartet fared better with a *Live at Montreux* album, recorded in the summer of 1977 and issued on the Tomato label, but the relatively obscure, Nashville-based Direct-Disk Labs released the group's only studio album, *A Cut Above*, as a limited edition. Musically, the album had much to recommend it. An Ellington medley led into long rethinks of "Unsquare Dance," "Blue Rondo à la Turk," "Three to Get Ready," and "Take Five," and the package was accompanied by a thoughtful, extended essay by John Plummer. But Direct-Disk messed up the cover art: commissioning a cartoon of Dave, Darius, Chris, and Dan dressed in space suits running through the grooves of a vinyl LP can only have seemed like a good idea at the time. But the very existence of this two-LP set, released through a small independent label, highlights the fact that Brubeck's recording career lacked stability.

This situation wasn't properly ironed out until 1979, when the newly reborn Dave Brubeck Quartet—featuring Jerry Bergonzi—signed to Concord, where they stayed for eight years, releasing one album a year, beginning with *Back Home*. It's tempting to trace the beginnings of Brubeck's problems with recording back to the final years of his Columbia contract, when he worried, with some justification, that the company was failing to put its promotional weight behind his new records with Gerry Mulligan, *Compadres* and *Blues Roots*. The final Brubeck/Mulligan release for Columbia, *Live at the Berlin Philharmonie*, looked like an inviting prospect on paper: a double album of live material from November 1970, a worthy companion piece, with any luck, to one of the classic quartet's greatest moments on record, 1963's *At Carnegie Hall*. But Columbia's determination to snatch sorry defeat from the jaws of certain victory seemed willful. The two-hour concert was brutally edited: two hours cut to around forty-five minutes. The European release contained six tracks; American listeners had to make do with five. Little thought was given to the recorded sound, which was tinny and clumsily balanced—and Columbia sat on the material for two years before releasing it in 1972. Only in 1995, when the tapes were responsibly remastered and issued in full, was the concert revealed as a jewel in Brubeck's crown.

Brubeck was upset when, as he was making *Compadres* and *Blues Roots*, Columbia declined to issue his extended choral and orchestral pieces *The Light in the Wilderness* and *The Gates of Justice*. He took the projects to Decca instead (which also released *Brubeck/Mulligan/Cincinnati*—Brubeck and Mulligan with the Cincinnati Symphony Orchestra and its conductor, Erich Kunzel), an early public sign that not all was well between Brubeck and his label. When he had signed to Columbia in 1954, much was made of the mystique that this pianist, who had studied with Milhaud and Schoenberg (even if the latter didn't amount to much), was also a happening jazzman. But now that Brubeck was interested in pursuing his career as a composer, he felt Columbia had let him down: *The Light in the Wilderness* and *The Gates of Justice* were resource-hungry projects that, it reckoned, were highly unlikely to recoup their expenses.[4]

---

4. But the ever-faithful Darius Milhaud responded positively when Brubeck sent him the LPs of *The Light in the Wilderness*. "It is a powerful work of very great sincerity," he wrote. (Darius Milhaud to Dave Brubeck, June 12, 1968, Personal Correspondence, Brubeck Collection.)

In truth, *Compadres, Blues Roots,* and *Live at the Berlin Philhar-monie* dragged into the open problems that had been brewing for many years, and revisiting the albums released by the classic quartet in the afterglow of *Time Out*—from *Southern Scene, Brubeck and Rushing,* and *Bernstein Plays Brubeck Plays Bernstein* in 1960–1961 to their valedictory album in 1967, *The Last Time We Saw Paris*—the tick of the time bomb grows ever more insistent. While Teo Macero helped Miles Davis steer a course through a post–*Kind of Blue* future that led to a clear path of musical and aesthetic development from *Sketches of Spain* to *Bitches Brew,* via such landmark moments as *E.S.P., Miles in the Sky,* and *Filles de Kilimanjaro,* the Brubeck discography throughout this same period feels rudderless. The popularity of *Time Out,* especially after the single of "Take Five" was released in 1961, meant an already-crammed schedule was packed with more concerts, and the kind of time Brubeck had lavished on preparing *Jazz Impressions of the USA, Dave Digs Disney,* and *Jazz Impressions of Eurasia* was becoming harder to find. But an obvious answer to that problem was overlooked.

Left to his own devices, Brubeck would have always preferred to record live. Studios made him nervous: as Dan Brubeck put it, quoted in the sleeve notes to *Trio Brubeck,* an album with Dave, Chris, and Dan recorded in 1988, "My dad assumes that if you're in a studio everything is being recorded—like Watergate." Special one-off projects aside, like *The Real Ambassadors* and *Bernstein Plays Brubeck Plays Bernstein,* too many quartet albums were recorded the wrong way 'round. *Countdown—Time in Outer Space* and *Bossa Nova USA* would have benefited from allowing the quartet to discover the dimensions and improvisational potential of Brubeck's new compositions in live performance before bringing them to the studio; but Columbia's preferred business model was that groups recorded first and then toured their new album.

Proof positive of the wisdom of a "tour first and record later, preferably live" policy is the quartet's live performance in New

York on February 21, 1963, rush released as *At Carnegie Hall* and available in record stores by the end of May. The album is arguably Brubeck's greatest-ever record, and a high point of recorded jazz of the 1960s. The quartet's performance that night was a summation of everything the group had achieved. Opening with "St. Louis Blues," as had so many Brubeck concerts, and climaxing with supremely confident, high-tempo, creatively inspired versions of "Blue Rondo à la Turk" and "Take Five," which were taken to a whole other plane with digressive, exploratory solos that clawed open their structures, *At Carnegie Hall* clearly documented an exceptional night and demonstrated an incontestable truth. One solution to making great Dave Brubeck records: have Columbia follow the quartet around with their mobile recording unit.

As early as 1955, in a letter to Steve Race, who would go on to write the sleeve note for *Time Out*, Brubeck worried that his message could be lost in the studio. Race had initially dismissed the Brubeck group after hearing their earliest studio recording—"a thousand miles away from the music I was actually playing nightly on club dates," Brubeck wrote. "I don't think there has ever been an artist whose own studio recordings misrepresented his actual potential as much as mine. Now you have heard some live performances recorded in concert or in a night club you understand our basic aim. . . . My approach to jazz was and is that of the improviser, and come hell or high water I was determined to improvise."[5]

It's a pity, therefore, that Columbia didn't follow the model established by the Carnegie Hall album and issue more live performances, complete and unedited. With the "Take Five" single's robust sales in 1961 came *Take Five Live*, the quartet captured live at Basin Street East with guest vocalist Carmen McRae. The album presented an attractive selection of

5. Dave Brubeck to Steve Race, June 17, 1955, Personal Correspondence, Brubeck Collection.

Brubeck classics—"In Your Own Sweet Way," "Ode to a Cowboy," "There'll Be No Tomorrow" ("Dziekuje" with lyrics), and "It's a Raggy Waltz." But Paul Desmond reportedly loathed the idea of adding lyrics to quartet pieces, and he skulked in the shadows throughout, appearing only to doodle uninterestedly around McRae's vocals when the time came to play "Take Five." *Dave Brubeck in Berlin,* four tracks from a quartet concert recorded by WDR Cologne at the Berlin Philharmonie in September 1964 (not to be confused with *Live at the Berlin Philharmonie*), was released only in Germany.

When Columbia issued the tepid *Jackpot* in 1966, recorded during a club engagement in Las Vegas, Brubeck allowed his frustration to spill over into his sleeve note. He chided Macero, "our rich producer, who blew in from New York and insisted on producing the album from the vantage point of a nearby gambling table," and offered an explanation for the woeful state of his instrument. Piano tuners were apparently not easy to come by in Vegas: "I don't mind telling you, my instrument was slipping badly. I was getting desperate, so the Baldwin Piano Company flew in an itinerant tuner from Santa Barbara (but he couldn't do much under the circumstances, as you'll hear later.)"

*The Last Time We Saw Paris* was recorded live in the French capital, at the Salle Pleyel, on November 13, 1967, and was released in May 1968, overlapping with the new Brubeck/Mulligan albums *Compadres* and *Blues Roots* in the "new releases" section of record stores. This time the piano was impeccably in tune, as one would expect at one of Paris's leading concert venues, but the recorded sound might as well have been produced from a gambling table in Vegas: little attempt was made to achieve balance between the instruments, and the general ambience was remote and woolly. This marked the quartet's last appearance on Columbia,[6] and anyone hoping for a fitting farewell—a

---

6. That is, the quartet's last appearance on Columbia Records while they still technically existed. The company would continue to plunder its archives for releases such as *Brubeck in Amsterdam,* issued in 1969.

complete concert, a souvenir of the quartet's unique spirit and creativity—would have been disappointed. This program of bits and pieces—"Swanee River," "These Foolish Things," "Forty Days," "One Moment Worth Years," "La Paloma Azul"—failed to hang together when pulled out of context from the rest of the concert, which was left on the cutting-room floor. The album ended with "Three to Get Ready," a curious end-point perhaps until you remember the special place the song had in French hearts thanks to Claude Nougaro. Twelve years after George Avakian, who had poured so much devoted care and thought into *Brubeck Time* and *Jazz: Red Hot and Cool,* had signed Brubeck, *The Last Time We Saw Paris* was a sad indictment of Brubeck's relationship with Columbia.

At the end of 1961, as Columbia was preparing to release *Time Further Out,* energy and activity buzzed around this long-awaited sequel to *Time Out.* The sell sheet issued to accompany the album—a promotional document sent to media and record stores—gave the hard sell. "Since 'Take Five' was released several months ago, it has sold close to A QUARTER OF A MILLION COPIES," the document began, then went on to reveal more impressive statistics; *Time Out,* caught up in all the intoxicating enthusiasm, had been fast-tracked to the number two position in the Billboard album charts (number one albums that year included Frank Sinatra's *Nice 'n' Easy* and Judy Garland's *Judy at Carnegie Hall*). As a result, the sell sheet bragged, "demand has increased for the entire Brubeck album catalog," and the Columbia marketing team was keen to stress that their "best selling jazz artist is becoming [an] out-and-out hit artist." They added: "This is the start of something big."

*Time Further Out* was released on November 1, 1961, alongside a single that paired "It's a Raggy Waltz" with "Unsquare Dance," which Columbia hoped might equal, even surpass, the success of "Take Five." No objections were raised this time about original cover art, original compositions, or unorthodox time signatures; in fact, all three were positively encouraged, and a conscious link was forged between Brubeck's music and his chosen cover painting by the Spanish artist Joan Miró. The nondescriptive title of Miró's 1925 painting—*Painting*—was his attempt to focus attention on the painterly *material* of the work, rather than any outside associations. Brubeck had hoped to use the same painting for the cover of *Time Out*, but Miró had failed to respond in time to his letter requesting permission.

Enter Xenia Cage, who, in a coincidence resembling one of those strokes of implausibly good fortune from the plot of *The Real Ambassadors*, had happened to float back into the Brubecks' lives. Xenia, the ex-wife of the composer John Cage, had been part of the social circle surrounding George Avakian, his violinist wife Anahid Ajemian, and her pianist sister Maro in Berkeley in the early 1950s; she had even brought John to hear the quartet. In 1960, when the Brubecks decided to relocate to the East Coast and rent out the Heartwood Drive house in Oakland, they took a sublet on a house in Wilton, Connecticut, where the Columbia record producer Irving Townsend, who had produced Brubeck's *Newport 1958* album and Miles Davis's *Kind of Blue*, and who was about to take a job heading up Columbia's West Coast operation, had been living. Xenia was living in the same complex of houses and had a direct line to Miró via her connections at the Pierre Matisse Gallery in New York. She intervened on Brubeck's behalf, and permission was quickly granted.

S. Neil Fujita's cover painting has become so synonymous with *Time Out*—its shapes and gestures seeming to dance in time with "Blue Rondo à la Turk," "Three to Get Ready," and "Take Five"—that any other image feels unthinkable. But *Painting* would have worked equally well, and for many of the reasons Brubeck set out in his *Time Further Out* sleeve note, the image also suited this new selection of music, to which he'd added the subtitle "Miró Reflections." Bunched together in the bottom left-hand corner of Miró's painting were four abstracted figures, the most recognizably human of which, coincidently, had a decidedly Brubeckian nose. And Brubeck's pupils no doubt dilated when he saw what Miró had drawn in the top right-hand corner: a list of numbers, counting up from three to nine (zero at the end), with an extra three and four dropped next to the seven and eight, suggestive of time signatures and polyrhythms.

In his sleeve note, Brubeck pointed out the "obvious" link between Miró's numbers and time signatures, and suggested that the abstract figures moved "in a visual rhythm which *could* be interpreted as a jazz quartet." But beyond the specifics of the imagery, Brubeck felt a deeper affinity: "[Miró] has expressed in visual terms my own approach to music—that is, a search for something new within old forms, an unexpected perspective, a surprising order and inner balance that belies the spontaneity of composition."

*Time Further Out* did not try to match the flawless design of *Time Out*; instead, each track slotted into an assortment of different delights. "It's a Raggy Waltz"—which ten years later would become a regular part of the Two Generations of Brubeck set lists—indulged in a simple but effective game of rhythmic deception. As waltzes must, it had its basic pulse in 3. But accents dropped in irregularly cut the melody line up into asymmetrical patterns of three and four notes, which defied the regularity of the bar line and, as Brubeck pointed out, gave "a syncopated quality reminiscent of the old time rag." The delight ragtime composers had taken in messing with perceptions of 3 and 4 by dragging melodic lines over bar lines was nothing new, he explained. Mozart and Haydn had, two centuries earlier, sexed up the triple-meter minuet with notes grouped in twos and fours. To that extent, "It's a Raggy Waltz" was a close cousin of the minuet—like "Three to Get Ready," although Brubeck regretted that his tune required such a pedantic explanation. Beyond the theory, it was, he said, "such a natural theme," and it coaxed forthright, gospel-tinged solos from both Desmond and Brubeck.

That mood spilled over into "Charles Matthew Hallelujah," written earlier that year to celebrate the birth of the Brubecks' sixth child (who would become known as Matthew), with Desmond biting hard into Brubeck's theme. *Time Out* had been allowed time to find its identity in the studio because, having failed to prevent Brubeck from recording this material, Columbia had left him alone during the sessions. But *Time Further Out* was a record that was designed to sell well from the beginning. The single culled from the *Time Out* sessions—the wrong take of "Take Five" paired with a "Blue Rondo à la Turk" edited to the point that it made little musical sense—was the result of unpreparedness, and Columbia was not about to repeat that mistake. The meltingly soft, Chopinesque "Bluette" and crepuscular colors of the closing piece "Blue Shadows in the Street" allowed Desmond and Brubeck the capacity to explore the harmonic implications of the themes at length. But "Unsquare Dance" and "Bru's Boogie Woogie"—which Desmond sat out—were clearly calculated with radio play and the time limitations of the 45 rpm single in mind.

Which didn't mean they weren't effective. If the jazz intelligentsia would likely rate "The Duke" or "In Your Own Sweet Way" as the picks of Brubeck's compositions, "Unsquare Dance" appealed more broadly. This two-minute piece, the very definition of an instrumental novelty, albeit one in 7/4 time, was perfect for jukebox consumption, another sort of nongeneric drum feature, like "Take Five." Brubeck's theme evoked an old cowboy square dance mashed into a hoedown, with the expected rhythmic squareness tripping over the 4+3 of the 7/4 time. As handclaps picked out the off beats—"one, TWO, three, FOUR, five, SIX, SEVEN"—Joe Morello's sticks nipped at the rims of his drums like a woodpecker chipping away at a tree.

Taking his cue from Brubeck's theme, which nodded affectionately toward 1920s stride piano, Morello built his solo in its entirety from the rhythmic dance of drumsticks against wood—a feature of 1920s classic jazz drumming that had all but fallen out of use by the 1960s. Closely miked, Morello's playing has a clean, mechanistic precision on the record, and the studio was also used to hint subliminally at a feature of the traditional square dance—four couples facing each other, one couple at each point of a square—as his busy rhythms bounced between the left and right of the stereo. This was unlike anything Brubeck had previously recorded. Ranging far from the spirit of extended improvisations captured on *Jazz at Oberlin* or *Jazz at the College of the Pacific*, "Unsquare Dance," as constituted on *Time Further Out*, was a reality only in the studio and could not be achieved onstage—which is why the piece never became part of Brubeck's live set list until it was reconceived, with a funk backbeat, by Two Generations of Brubeck ten years later.

"Bru's Boogie Woogie" was also unlikely to be replicated live, but for the opposite reason. This eight-to-the-bar skiffle shuffle was off the cuff and compressed everything Brubeck knew about boogie-woogie into just over two minutes. It also brought into the open his background in stride piano and boogie-woogie, and the depth of his understanding might have come as a surprise to those accustomed to Brubeck and his modernist ways. This deftly structured performance opened with Brubeck, Wright, and Morello already riding the crest of a rhythmic wave without needing a surfboard and Brubeck's chording gradually thickened as a climax, marked with fiery drum fills, approached.

"Maori Blues," inspired by the quartet's March 1960 tour of New Zealand, also spotlighted Brubeck the improviser. When Brubeck arrived at Whenuapai Airport in Auckland on March 27, en route back to the US after an Australian tour, he told a press conference that he was hoping New Zealand folk idioms might provide him with some fresh compositional source material. Among the local musicians on the ground to greet the quartet was Kahu Pineaha, celebrated in New Zealand as a cabaret star and popular singer. Brubeck received a crash course in Maori folklore when the two men met socially, and the stylization of the traditional waiata and haka ritual dances that Pineaha sang for him bled into "Maori Blues." The curt precision of the theme—in 6/4 time—and percussive stampede of piano block chords colliding with Morello's hefty accents was suggestive of the action of Maori dance, while the seamless fusion of rhythmic and harmonic momentum with which he worked, building tension by superimposing 4 over 6 and flirting with double time, was pure Brubeck.

The tantalizing tightrope *Time Further Out* walked between spontaneous revelry and the commercial expectations of following up *Time Out* and "Take Five" was encapsulated by Joe Morello's breaking through the fourth wall at the end of "Unsquare Dance" with a guffaw of relief: the group had made it through an obstacle course of cross-rhythms and up-tempo stride piano in 7/4 time. There was no repeat of the gnashing of teeth that, on July 25, 1959, had accompanied the quartet's attempts to record the piece then known as "5/4." By the time they recorded "Far More Blues" and "Far More Drums"—*Time Further Out*'s 5/4 feature numbers—subdividing the brain into 3+2 was second nature.

In an ideal world, Columbia would have recognized *Time Out*'s unique qualities and *Time Further Out* would have followed quickly, thereby satisfying an audience thirsty for more. *Southern Scene* had many merits, from a deeply felt, tenderly executed rendering of Louis Armstrong's theme song "When It's Sleepy Time Down South," an arrangement notable for the unusual sound of Desmond playing a harmony part in the low register of his saxophone, to the rascally joy of piano and alto scampering around swing pianist Joe Sullivan's "Little Rock Getaway" and bouncing off sudden shifts of key. The album followed the model established by *Gone with the Wind*, but nothing quite matched the emotional depth of the earlier record's "Lonesome Road" or "Georgia on My Mind." After *Time Out*, *Southern*

*Scene* felt like Jackson Pollack reverting to still lifes of fruit after dribbling paint everywhere.

The pride Brubeck felt for *Brubeck and Rushing* and *Bernstein Plays Brubeck Plays Bernstein* was twofold: about the music itself and about the fact he'd managed to pull off the unlikely coup of recording with Jimmy Rushing one day and Leonard Bernstein the next. Brubeck and Rushing had cooked up their plan to collaborate on an album during a train journey to what Dave described in his journal as "some Midland city" during a Newport Jazz Festival package tour to the UK in September 1959, which also included Dizzy Gillespie's quintet and the Buck Clayton All-Stars.[7] Although Rushing's proposition, coming from "the top blues singer in jazz," was "one of greatest surprises of my mus(ical) life," Brubeck feared critics might have "negative feelings" about the album before hearing a single note. Also, what would happen if the two friends couldn't agree on what the album should be once they reached the studio? "I was fending off his proposal as a way of self protection," Brubeck wrote. "I knew we would be compared to the Basie band."

But the die had been cast. Brubeck was always ready for a fresh musical challenge and, in reality, was never likely to turn Rushing down: the prospect proved irresistible. Once in the studio, "there was an immediate marriage," and Desmond relished working with Rushing in a way he did not with Carmen McRae. The lightness of Desmond's touch tickled the lusty bulk of Rushing's vocal style, leaving Brubeck to negotiate between the two. "Evenin'," "Blues in the Dark," and "Am I Blue?" were all tunes associated with Basie, and in their distinctive way, the quartet, with their own bass player rooted in the lessons of former Basie bassist Walter Page, played with tremendous swing, delicately applied. "There'll Be Some Changes Made" pushed

---

7. Later in the tour, Brubeck found himself involved in a drugs bust when the police searched the bus as it was about to cross the border into Scotland. Gillespie's saxophonist, Leo Wright, hid his flute, which contained drugs, up his sleeve as Brubeck looked on nervously.

harder, with Brubeck's solo digging deep into resources of swing, while the kindly "You Can Depend on Me" immediately found a relaxed groove that brought out the most tender side of Rushing.

A day later, on January 30, 1960, the quartet was back in the studio—now surrounded by Leonard Bernstein and the New York Philharmonic. For Columbia, putting two of their highest-selling artists together on the front of an album represented something of a dream.[8] Bernstein, two years older than Brubeck, was then two years into his eleven-year stint as music director of the Philharmonic and was still basking in the success of his 1957 musical *West Side Story*, soon to be refashioned into a movie. *Bernstein Plays Brubeck Plays Bernstein* was a title that encapsulated a complex tangle of histories and relationships. The "Brubeck" of the title was not Dave but his brother Howard, whose "Dialogues for Jazz Combo and Orchestra" was given its New York premiere[9] by his brother's quartet and Bernstein on December 10, 1959, at Carnegie Hall, with repeat performances on the 11th and 12th. The concert—"the fourth program in a series devoted to 'The Concerto'" the program book stated—opened with Bernstein leading the orchestra in Bach's Brandenburg Concerto No 4, Mozart's Concerto for Two Pianos and Orchestra, K. 365, and a Concerto for Viola, Strings and Percussion by Robert Starer, then professor of composition at the Juilliard School of Music. The quartet were also in residence at Basin Street, and they needed to finish their club set in time to take a taxi to Carnegie Hall and change from lounge suits into tuxedos, before joining Bernstein and the Philharmonic onstage.

---

8. Although nobody, apparently, thought to photograph the quartet with Bernstein for the front cover; a headshot of Bernstein was crudely dropped in over Joe Morello's left shoulder.

9. An earlier version of the work was premiered in July 1956 by the San Diego Symphony Orchestra; a subsequent revised version was performed by the Cleveland and Oakland Symphony Orchestras during their 1958 seasons.

Beyond his obvious star appeal, Bernstein's own musical background and sympathies made him the perfect conductor for Howard Brubeck's project. Howard had been Darius Milhaud's first pupil at Mills College and stayed on as his assistant after he graduated. By 1960, Bernstein already had two recordings of Milhaud's evergreen *La création du monde* under his belt, made in 1945 and '51, and the depth of his understanding of jazz was woven through *West Side Story*, with its specific references to swing, bebop, and Latin rhythms: he knew better than to reduce jazz down to generic stereotypes.

By 1960, ideas of what might constitute orchestral jazz were stepping up a gear. Columbia had already released the Miles Davis/Gil Evans collaborations *Miles Ahead* and *Porgy and Bess* (and *Sketches of Spain* was soon to follow), and although nobody would claim it as an agenda-setting record of the caliber of *Miles Ahead*, "Dialogues" initiated Brubeck's interest in placing his quartet at the mercy of a symphony orchestra—a lifelong interest that would reach its zenith in those late-career birthday concerts with the London Symphony Orchestra. In the meantime, "Dialogues" like Schoenberg's Five Orchestral Pieces had crashed into Gershwin's Concerto in F—a tapestry of Bach, Broadway, big-band swing, twelve-tone technique, and Chopin, with the quartet stitching the pieces together through improvisation. Howard lacked his brother's talent for generating structural tension by making contrasting styles of music *overlap* rather than merely coexist on the same canvas. But, following the hectic, blustery fanfare-like orchestral prologue, as Wright and Morello lock into a groove, the exhilaration of the group is palpable. Desmond's melodically transformational introductory solo snuggles into the Philharmonic strings, and throughout, the quartet proves remarkably sensitive to the harmonic and timbral palette shifts in the orchestra.

Two highly unlikely figures attended the first New York performance—Ornette Coleman, recently befriended by Bernstein, who was reportedly bored by the whole experience, and

Edgard Varèse. Teo Macero was Varèse's producer at Columbia and persuaded him to attend. "Mr. Varèse and I met with Dave and Howard on the street [after the performance], as it was impossible to get backstage to see them," Macero wrote.[10] "Mr. Varèse proceeded to embrace both Dave and Howard Brubeck, telling them both that it was not only a great performance but an excellent composition as well." Somebody else who enjoyed what he heard was the ever-faithful Bill Smith, who wrote to Brubeck in the summer of 1960 to explain: "Saw Teo today to get some copies of *The Riddle*. Came in on the last movement of the Dialogues on [the] stereo . . . Even the Philharmonic seemed to swing and you guys sounded great."[11]

One final journey home to London, and it's time to start drawing the loose ends together. It's 10:30 p.m. and Brubeck is visibly tiring. Iola would rather he nap than talk, but Dave nods at my tape recorder, and those hands that have just played a magical concert wobble gently as he pours fizzy water into a plastic cup; the sound of effervescent bubbles crackling in the night is the first thing I hear when I play the cassette all these years later.

For no better reason than there's no particular place to start, I ask Brubeck about the set he's just played, which included a solo version of "Dziekuje" and the Jimmy Van Heusen standard "It Could Happen to You," a regular feature of New Brubeck Quartet concerts during the mid-1970s. Why, after so many years, did Brubeck choose it tonight?

---

10. Teo Macero, unpublished and undated note "Brubeck-Bernstein Dialogues for Jazz Combo & Orchestra." Teo Macero Collection, Box 6, Music Division, New York Public Library.

11. Bill Smith to Dave Brubeck, dated "Summer" 1960, Personal Correspondence, Brubeck Collection.

Ha! Well, as we were driving to this theater earlier, I saw an advert on the roadside—"It Could Be You"[12]—and that reminded me of the tune. Simple as that. When I had the quartet with the kids, we'd play it all the time as a drum feature for Dan, and Darius also played rhythms on his [electric] keyboard. I always loved Jimmy Van Heusen. "Like Someone in Love." "Here's That Rainy Day." Played those a lot. George Wein once put on an evening at Newport,[13] lots of jazz musicians—Earl Hines, John Lewis—playing tunes by their favorite song composers. I chose Jimmy and worked the tunes into a suite, and they work well together, I have to say.

Another piece played that night was the slow movement of Howard's "Dialogues for Jazz Combo and Orchestra," which, when performed by the quartet alone, is titled after Howard's wife: "Theme for June." The quartet's 1960 recording with Bernstein was such a highpoint of Brubeck's career that I wonder aloud why he never choose to play the whole four-movement piece again. Was he ever tempted to call up Bernstein and suggest a rematch? His 1980s quartet, with Bill Smith, would surely have the relished the challenge.

It was suggested a few times, but I never had time to learn all the notes again. Would have been great to play it again because the night we worked with Bernstein was one of the most exciting of my life. Before the first performance, I dreamed that myself and Howard were flying an airplane high above New York and arguing because neither of us knew how to fly. Bernstein was very supportive, and I remember him working hard to try to balance the quartet with the orchestra; he had a long conversation with Joe about the problem of balancing jazz drums in an orchestra—"a perpetual mystery," he called it. I'd

---

12. Then the advertising slogan for the British National Lottery.
13. Newport Jazz Festival, July 3, 1973: "A Salute to American Song."

put some money into the recording session, and Bernstein was ten minutes late. Orchestras are expensive to record, and I'm sitting there looking at my watch, thinking "Jeez, Bernstein, you're costing me a fortune." Then he swept into the studio, turned to the orchestra, and said "Gentlemen, this session started with a ten-minute break."

We all know, I say, about that most inglorious end to Brubeck's student career: being hauled up in front of the dean following the revelation that he couldn't read music. At some point Brubeck must have taught himself to read music . . . ? Or how could he have written his own compositions down? "People have often been confused by this. I can *write* music, but I am not a good reader. I got used to using my ears from such an early age, through listening to records [and] then trying to work out what I'd heard by going to the piano, and listening in to the piano lessons my mother gave, that reading kind of passed me by. But my mother did teach me the basics of notating music on paper and harmony, so by the time I went to College of Pacific I had enough to go on. But I could never, even now, play a piece of Beethoven or Milhaud from the sheet music."

Had Brubeck mastered the rules of notation, how would this have changed his perception of improvisation?

Many years ago a pastor[14] contacted me about a paper he was proposing to write about sources of inspiration. He asked me about improvisation, about how ideas come to jazz musicians in the moment. I told him about the notes I'd written for my solo record [*Brubeck Plays Brubeck*] that explained the different levels at which jazz musicians improvise, from relying on learned phrases when you don't know what else to do, to improvising at a point where the inspiration does seem divine:

14. Likely to be Pastor Luverne Jacobson. Brubeck's reply to his letter (March 16, 1989) is filed under "personal correspondence" in the Brubeck Collection.

there are no barriers between your body and the instrument; you just *know* how to reach over and touch the audience. I told him I thought this was similar to how a pastor reached out to his congregation.

I mention the hymnlike quality of "Dziekuje" and Brubeck's habit of recasting pieces from his sacred works for the quartet, like "Forty Days" from *The Light in the Wilderness* and "Truth" from *Truth Is Fallen.* Is there deeper thinking behind including these pieces in quartet concerts than merely giving his musicians fresh material to play? Does improvising on sacred material draw on different impulses than improvising on, say, "Take Five" or a standard like "It Could Happen to You"? "That's an interesting question," Brubeck says, and then his face saddens.

My nephew, Howard's son [Philip], died from a brain tumor when he was sixteen. The pain for the whole family was shattering, and thinking of my brother's pain, and to offer him comfort, because he was a religious man, I wrote a setting of "Let not your heart be troubled," from the book of John, which was the first religious piece I wrote. When Ernie Farmer, who was president of Shawnee Press, saw that piece, he told me that I had a feel for sacred music and encouraged me to write a whole oratorio, and I put that same setting into *The Light in the Wilderness.*

But you have to remember that when I was working on *The Light in the Wilderness* and *The Gates of Justice,* I hadn't written that kind of music before. I had to do simple things like look up the ranges of the different voices, and then I'd find out that not all singers, especially in choirs, can sing at the extremes of the ranges: you read in a book that sopranos can get top Cs, but the reality can be quite different. I realized soon, though, that writing my ideas down quickly kept them fresh; sometimes the more you develop or change an idea, the weaker it gets. I'd think back to Milhaud, who would write directly into ink and never change a thing. I'm not that good. I'll write and check things on the piano, but it's important to keep material on the boil. When I wrote *Beloved Son,* my Easter oratorio [in 1978]— which is forty minutes of music—the whole thing was finished in about three weeks. I hardly slept. I was completely inspired to finish this piece and nothing got in my way. My most recent choral piece is *The Commandments.* It's based around the Ten Commandments, and I got the idea when I was a soldier during the Second World War. We were all Christian nations involved in that war, but I couldn't imagine that anyone who took his religion seriously could be involved. In my mind, I'd already begun composing a piece around "thou shalt not kill." It's taken me sixty years to write it down.

It took me a while to get used to the idea that I had to step back a little when one of these pieces was being performed. During one of the early performances of *Light in the Wilderness,* I had been sitting silently for a long time onstage behind the piano and was feeling uncomfortable. So I responded to something I heard in the orchestra with a huge, unexpected chord—which made the conductor [Erich Kunzel] jump and lose his place.

At Columbia Records, where all the commercial direction of travel was toward jazz/rock fusion, Brubeck's new compositional direction was proving equally disconcerting. Teo Macero, in a memo dated October 1, 1968, which was circulated widely among the company's executives, held nothing back. "It would seem that Dave Brubeck is not even on the label anymore for the amount of promotion and advertising he is receiving from Columbia and Dave is very upset," he began. "Decca is at the moment doing more that we are in this area. I have been after Columbia to promote our jazz artists for years, but it seems like a lost cause. Brubeck complains to me and I am complaining to you. We have some of the greatest jazz artists in the world on our label, i.e. Miles Davis, Thelonious Monk, Dave Brubeck,

Charlie Byrd, in case you have forgotten. Other [labels] like Blue Note, A&M, Verve etc. can promote their artists and become successful at it. . . . I find my memos go unanswered."[15]

Brubeck's entrée into Decca had been through Erich Kunzel, then music director of the Cincinnati Pops Orchestra, which had released a number of albums on the label. Kunzel visited Brubeck at home to invite him to play with the orchestra, and he was impressed with the sketches for *The Light in the Wilderness* he saw spilling around Brubeck's piano. He agreed to perform the piece, and a recording was the next logical step. But, in an echo of the trade-offs between Fantasy and Columbia that marked Brubeck's earliest days on the label, now there were tensions between Columbia and Decca. Robert L. Young, from Decca, wrote to Brubeck's lawyer, Michael Maloney, on November 14, 1968, concerning Decca's exclusive rights to material from *The Light in the Wilderness*, including "Forty Days," which had become a regular item in Brubeck's jazz concerts. "Under our agreement," Young wrote, "Dave was *not to perform* any of these selections for anyone other than Decca for the purpose of making sound records for a period of five years following the expiration of his agreement with us." Brubeck had performed "Forty Days" and other related material in Mexico with Gerry Mulligan earlier that year, and therefore "in this sense, Dave has already breached our agreement of March 18, 1968." Young refused Columbia's request to use these recordings: "We have carefully considered your request. . . . It is our opinion that the inclusion of more than one selection from THE LIGHT IN THE WILDERNESS in any single competitive album performed by Dave will adversely affect our album in the market place."[16]

---

15. Teo Macero, memo, October 1 1968, General Correspondence, Teo Macero Collection, Music Division, New York Public Library.

16. Robert L. Young to Michael J. Maloney, November 14, 1968, General Correspondence, Teo Macero Collection, Music Division, New York Public Library.

Columbia had inadvertently created a vacuum that Decca was all too happy to fill, and the writing was on the wall for Brubeck's continuing relationship with his long-standing record company. The quartet's final years with Columbia included three albums of American Songbook material: *Angel Eyes, My Favorite Things,* and *Anything Goes: The Dave Brubeck Quartet Plays Cole Porter,* which were characteristically slick and creative, but which ultimately failed to make the case *why* Brubeck, at this stage in his career, with so many compositional ideas of his own, needed to default to pop material—did nobody think of recording "Anything Goes" in 5/4 or constructing a fugue from Matt Dennis tunes?

*Time In,* recorded in October 1965 and released the following June, was a worthy and hugely enjoyable attempt to recapture something of the magic of *Time Out* and *Time Further Out.* "Frankie and Johnnie" reworked in 5/4 and called "He Done Her Wrong" was a humorous aside to the serious business of new compositions like "Lost Waltz"—a waltz that flirted with 4/4—and the uncharacteristically bop-flavored "Cassandra." But correspondence reveals that, after so many years together, a certain weariness had set in, and some old cracks were starting to reemerge. "For future reference," Iola wrote to Macero shortly before the release of *Time In,* "[and] to avoid internal difficulties with the Quartet, Joe Morello should be listed in the billing following Paul Desmond. . . . It has appeared in the improper order on some record jackets and Joe gets quite disturbed."[17]

A year later, Iola felt so disturbed about Desmond's increasingly erratic behavior that she felt compelled to issue a warning to Doug Tobutt, the agent at Harold Davison Limited in London who was overseeing the quartet's forthcoming visit to Europe. "All of us are deeply concerned over Paul," she wrote.

17. Iola Brubeck to Teo Macero, February 2, 1966, Business Correspondence, Brubeck Collection.

"His drinking is getting out of hand and we were seriously considering hiring someone to travel with him, but he scoffs at the idea and on the present tour [to] the West Coast he managed to make the gig [but] last week he missed two engagements. . . . I think he hadn't sobered up enough to know what day it was. . . . The concert before that he was too stoned to play TAKE FIVE, so I'm not exaggerating. He has to be watched. He has to be made to eat. Dave is trying to straighten him out in the next two weeks . . . and then comes your turn."[18] Iola, rather presciently, ended with, "Gerry Mulligan flew out to Indiana to play with Dave when Paul couldn't make it. The audience thought they were a great team."

That 1967 European tour would be the quartet's last, before the quartet returned to the US and played their official farewell concert in Pittsburgh on December 26, 1967.[19] In a letter to Jack Higgins at Harold Davidson, Brubeck drew a line under the quartet while looking ahead to the future:

It appears that the Quartet will finally dissolve at the end of this year. Paul and I have tentatively agreed to terminate at the end of 1967. No word of this has leaked to anyone, so please confine this thought to your own office. Do you think a "farewell" tour of Britain and the Continent is advisable? If so, we are still available in October. . . . The next question is, should the public know that it is a "farewell tour"? Not one word should get out—either to the press or to the "underground" until we have decided that psychologically it is right both for my men and for the general public—and also, until I know it is very definite [sic] fact!![20]

---

18. Iola Brubeck to Doug Tobutt, October 4, 1967, Business Correspondence, Brubeck Collection.

19. Issued officially as *Their Last Time Out* in 2012.

20. Dave Brubeck to Jack Higgins, March 3, 1967, Business Correspondence, Brubeck Collection.

Higgins had been talking to the London Philharmonic Orchestra—about to be taken over by the distinguished Dutch conductor Bernard Haitink—about a possible Brubeck concert. Duke Ellington, Tony Bennett, and Danny Kaye had performed with the orchestra in fund-raising galas; but Brubeck's idea to bring *The Light in the Wilderness* is perhaps why the concert never happened—the orchestra clearly wanted "Unsquare Dance" and "Take Five." Brubeck set out his plans to continue his career as a solo performer, "playing concerts of my own compositions with symphony orchestras and cathedral or university choirs," but warned that his new piece was "not a jazz mass. It is not similar to Duke Ellington's service I am told by people who have heard his. It is more of a 'composed, integrated' work in the traditional manner with the improvising laced through as filigree."

There were legal and contractual reasons, Brubeck said, why "the Dave Brubeck Quartet" needed to be dissolved with due diligence; the name could not be used in the immediate aftermath by any other group of four musicians he might lead. Following up on his March 2 letter to Jack Higgins a few weeks later, by which point some tour dates had been booked, Brubeck stressed the sensitivities: "It may work out, if Paul is willing, that we will re-organize from time to time for special events, but we do know for sure that 1967 is the end of our fulltime Quartet activities. Jack Green and others at ABC (including Joe Glaser) do not know this yet, because I want everything worked between Paul and me before their influence comes to bear. Also, it would be very bad for me as far as my relations with Columbia Records is concerned if they thought the breakup of the group was immanent [*sic*]."[21]

By May 1967, Brubeck had broken the news to Glaser, and one of the last letters addressed to Glaser has the ring of finality

---

21. Dave Brubeck to Jack Higgins, March 22, 1967, Business Correspondence, Brubeck Collection.

about it. "Since we have reached the desired goal of one hundred concerts for this year, I wish to accept no further bookings. . . . In 1968, I want no bookings for January, February or March."[22] His assertive tone was in stark contrast to some of his more timid approaches to Glaser in the 1950s. Glaser had, some years earlier, come to Brubeck in a state of panic when Larry Bennett threatened to set up his own agency and poach many of ABC's clients. But Glaser, forever the survivor, endured this crisis and, by the late 1970s, was acting on behalf of Barbra Streisand, B. B. King, and T. Rex—and the boxer Ernie Terrell. There was no longer the same money to be made from jazz, and Macero faded from the Brubeck story. He died in 1969 following a severe stroke.

As things worked out, the fact that the 1967 tour was the quartet's last was neither denied nor especially pushed. But the tour was not a happy experience. The quartet was scheduled to play fifteen concerts, beginning in the UK and traveling through Holland, Germany, and Austria before ending in Paris on November 13—the concert released as *The Last Time We Saw Paris*. On a two-day stopover in Hamburg, after dinner with the saxophonist Herb Geller, Desmond headed to the Reeperbahn, the city's red-light district—where he vanished. The next day the quartet was due to fly to Vienna to play two concerts, a matinee and an evening performance, and the Brubecks raised the alarm when Desmond failed to show at the airport. Herb Geller was asked to search for his friend as Brubeck, Wright, and Morello flew to Vienna to perform as the Dave Brubeck Trio, not knowing whether Desmond was dead or alive. Geller informed the police, checked the bars around the Reeperbahn, and even visited the local morgue. As he headed back to his car, Geller noticed Desmond leaning

---

22. Dave Brubeck to Joe Glaser, May 27, 1967, Business Correspondence, Brubeck Collection.

inelegantly against a bar. Getting him to Vienna in time for the evening concert was a lost cause, but Desmond was put on a flight to Paris the next morning. To explain his behavior, Paul told Brubeck he'd been engaged in research for a book called *Sin Cities of the World*.

Dave and Iola had been genuinely fearful that Paul had been murdered in a brothel or bar, and the experience so tainted the tour that Brubeck refused to grant permission for *The Last Time We Saw Paris* to be reissued during his lifetime. No loss perhaps. The album, with its edits and mushy sound, failed to convey the excitement of a Brubeck performance, and a bootleg recording, *Live at the Kurhaus, 1967*, issued in 2017 on the Fondamenta label, demonstrates how far below acceptable standards Columbia had fallen.

The concert opens with "Three to Get Ready," and a barometer reading of where the quartet is at emerges during the preliminary relay-race exchanges as Paul Desmond fumbles his notes. During "Take Five," Desmond serves up a compendium of phrases and harmonic bon mots familiar from earlier "Take Five" solos, spontaneously reordered into a satisfying whole, but it's Brubeck who is prepared to take risks. As he manhandles Benny Goodman's "Sing, Sing, Sing" into his solo on "Someday My Prince Will Come," crashing its familiar strains into erratic left-hand stabs—an unpredictable gambit that finds a resolution of sorts as he motors toward funky stride piano—this audience hears a performance like no other. Wright and Morello coast joyfully throughout, and the structural ambition and timbral imagination of Morello's sixteen-minute drum feature is worthy to sit alongside his signature 1963 Carnegie Hall solo. Desmond puts on a predictably good show, but some of his responses feel routine; he's clearly ready to kick back with a whiskey at Bradley's.

The Dave Brubeck Quartet's final concert, on December 26, 1967, in Pittsburgh, ended—inevitably—with an orgiastic, up-tempo "Take Five" and recalled some earlier regular pieces from the quartet's book, including "These Foolish Things," "I'm in a Dancing Mood," and "You Go to My Head"; in his journal, Brubeck recorded the "absolute disbelief" of the members of the quartet at the reception afterward.[23] But with the end of the classic quartet, the pressure and expectations of being a "classic" group dispersed, and Brubeck was free to express himself anew. There are clues to what was coming next on the very last recordings of the classic quartet. "Koto Song," released on a 1966 compilation, *Summit Sessions*, finds Brubeck ignoring the pentatonic harmonies of his theme and instead exploring sustained bitonal harmonies that melt into disembodied clusters that leave the rhythm section far behind. On "Forty Days" from *The Last Time We Saw Paris*, released in 1967, Brubeck's solo slaps the keyboard, perhaps in frustration.

Time now for something new.

---

23. Dave Brubeck, handwritten journal, undated entry, Brubeck Collection.

*Coda*

# THE IDEA OF THE
# DAVE BRUBECK QUARTET

On a bitingly cold November evening in New York City in 2010, my wife Olivia and I are killing time in Greenwich Village. We're going to the Blue Note jazz club on West Third Street to see the Dave Brubeck Quartet play the second of their two sets of the evening, and have arrived early. After taking sanctuary from the subzero temperature and cutting wind in Bleecker Street Records, we head to the club a little prematurely. Russell Gloyd catches our eye and, despite the protests of the door staff, motions us toward the bar. The quartet is midway through "Take Five"—the final item of their first set—and the audience is lapping it up.

The quartet is the same lineup as during the 2003 tour of the UK—Bobby Militello, Michael Moore, Randy Jones—and, as Russell takes us up to the greenroom, Jones is pushing his drum solo toward its climax. Iola is waiting for Dave to finish his set and is trying to find a reliable WiFi network so that she can send email. When Dave returns, I notice that he has aged considerably in the twelve months since I last saw him; but his warmth is unmistakable. We talk about the New York free jazz pianist Matthew Shipp, whom I'd seen perform a few days earlier; we also talk about my idea to write what would become this book. A waitress brings Dave a bowl of soup and then quickly disappears. The soup is as cold as the night, and Olivia disappears down the corridor toward the kitchen, carrying the tray and asking for "warm soup for Mr. Brubeck."

As Iola, now logged in to a secure WiFi connection, deals with her email, Dave holds out his hands. The fourth finger of his left hand is swollen; his right hand shakes. He asks Olivia to pass him his finger ointment from his bag on the other side of the room, and she holds his left hand steady as he rubs in his cream and then applies protective Band-Aids to the end of his fingers; at his age, a few days from his ninetieth birthday, his skin is delicate and fragile. Then he hobbles out the door, turns, smiles, and says "Enjoy," before heading back to the bandstand to fill people with joy. This is the last time I will see Dave Brubeck.

With his fourth finger compromised, Brubeck has to accommodate his technique and simply can't muster the same physical strength he did even a year previously, during an earlier Blue Note residency. The quartet plays a medley of Ellington tunes and dependable favorites like "Someday My Prince Will Come," "Unsquare Dance," and "Theme for June," and Brubeck deploys his harmonic lateral thinking to compensate for his frailties. The audience is appreciative and alert; they know there won't be many more opportunities to see the Dave Brubeck Quartet in action.

The Dave Brubeck Quartet had been part of American culture since 1951, sixty years of active service, and when the "Dave Brubeck Quartet" didn't exist between 1967 and 1979, audiences projected their love for the group onto the Dave Brubeck Trio with Gerry Mulligan, Two Generations of Brubeck, and the New Brubeck Quartet.

If it bothered Brubeck that everything was compared with his 1950s/'60s groups, he wore his frustration lightly, while anything he recorded felt effortlessly contemporary. Each new group felt cohesive, an honest reflection of its current members, who were never inclined to look over their shoulders at the history. After the classic quartet folded, Brubeck built a tradition of renewal into his career as the Dave Brubeck Trio with Gerry Mulligan—with Jack Six (bass) and Alan Dawson (drums)—determined to do things its own way. On *Blues Roots*, from 1968, Brubeck's playing feels transformed and reenergized, and the first track, "Limehouse Blues," announces that we're in a different musical world to the classic quartet's. The old quartet had thrived on the contrast between Desmond's whimsy and Brubeck's down-to-earth playing. Gerry Mulligan's approach is earthier, and this new group jettisons the friendly chatter of the old quartet for something far more cutting and aggressive. Had Brubeck put the stabbing chords that he puts under Mulligan in "Limehouse Blues" under a Desmond solo, he would have swamped the saxophonist, who would have likely responded angrily with a quote from "Don't Fence Me In." In the middle of Mulligan's improvisation, Brubeck interrupts with his own solo, and Mulligan enjoys the challenge, bows to the inevitable, and lets Brubeck take over.

On "Things Ain't What They Used to Be," Brubeck's exposition of the theme is raw and undistilled, torn straight from a rhythm-and-blues record. His solo begins with a savage flourish that growls from the lower end of the piano and leaves the tonality of the piece far behind. As he begins to manipulate this phrase, he splices in blues-derived chords that do indeed relate to the tonality, and his solo develops by working out the dialogue he has created.

Recording at the Newport Jazz Festival in 1971—a performance subsequently released as *The Last Set at Newport*—Brubeck was afraid that his acoustic quartet might be rendered impotent by following the dynamic and heavily amplified jazz-rock group led by trumpeter Bill Chase. So he kicks off "Blues for Newport" in the most forthright and strutting way he can, something almost theatrical in his deliberate and puckish presentation of the theme. His thirteen-chorus solo is masterfully designed, and, like "Things Ain't What They Used to Be," contrasts gestures we might expect from the blues with ideas that interrupt the flow. After two choruses of strident blues piano, Brubeck introduces a lolloping figure in his left hand that rubs against the tonality of the piece, and the tension ruptures the music, and so he tightens the reins again. As the solo progresses and the same niggling figure is reintroduced and eventually overtakes the solo, so many keys are in operation that mere harmony gives way to a throbbing, rolling piano texture.

A year later Paul Desmond joined the Brubeck-Mulligan-Six-Dawson group, and his playing retained all its trademark liquidity and lyricism—which highlighted how much Brubeck's playing had evolved. "Truth," which opens *We're All Together Again for the First Time*, the album released after the tour, starts with a relentlessly angry and intense atonal riff that Brubeck pounds out in the bass, given momentum by Dawson and Six. Its fierceness is overwhelming, and you wonder how exactly Desmond is going to cope with something so far outside his normal sphere. In the event, he rides the tumultuous sound with his typical grace, albeit with a slightly rougher sound than usual, even as it's clear that this setting is not entirely comfortable for him. By contrast, Brubeck relishes the intensity of the groove and enters like he's surfing the waves. After two choruses of choppy, angular playing, all hell breaks loose. His right hand parts company with his left, creating an illusion of two different tempi. As the left hand gets slower, the right purposefully pushes against the rhythm section. Dawson realizes the game is up and improvises freely, as Brubeck sends hammered clusters and spiky counterpoint everywhere, interrupted by sudden silences through which Dawson rises to the surface. As Brubeck begins to fade away, Dawson reinstates the original tempo with a brief solo, allowing Six to fizzle over the top in the high register of his bass. You could be listening to European free improvisation, waiting for Derek Bailey or Evan Parker to enter.

One saxophonist who recorded with Bailey and Brubeck in the same year—1974—understood the connection between the formative quartet records of the 1950s and where Brubeck was in the early 1970s. Anthony Braxton, a radical from Chicago who had involved himself with the Association for the Advancement of Creative Musicians and produced an unaccompanied double album, *For Alto*, that drew on ideas from European composed music and jazz, was a passionate Brubeckian who leaped at the offer to record with Brubeck. *All the Things We Are* also featured Lee Konitz (and side two was devoted to the Brubeck trio's Jimmy Van Heusen medley, as performed at Newport), but the standout track was Braxton and Brubeck together on "In Your Own Sweet Way," which became putty in their hands, as Brubeck's solo played free-associative cat and mouse with the changes, the same sort of daring he had shown on "Little Girl Blue" on *Jazz: Red Hot and Cool* clearly resonating with Braxton.

Where these projects from the 1970s still related to a meeting of chamber music precision with an improviser spirit, *Two Generations of Brubeck* (1973) and *Brother, the Great Spirit Made Us All* (1974), resembled unruly workshop performances, but for good reason. As Darius Brubeck reflected:

> Two Generations was how we youngsters were going to maintain a jazz-identity but move away from standards—what was hip about playing "Frank Sinatra covers" in the early '70s?—and discreetly bring on da funk. I emulated Mwandishi and

later Headhunters, but also In a Silent Way on the fusion side; Chick [Corea] for jazz ideas that didn't sound like standard AABA and changes, and sounded great on Fender Rhodes and keyboards, but still had strong structure. Chick also showed that expansion into non-jazz approaches to improv like Indian music and Flamenco was a way back from the precipice of "free jazz" that still avoided bebop II-V clichés. So, Chris, Dan and I were looking for different kinds of musical settings where Dave wouldn't feel alien or constrained, because we knew he always was the best improviser, but we wanted our sound to be as unlike the classic quartet as we could make it. Needless to say, classic Dave holds up a lot better over time but, well, we were young! Speaking for myself in all humility, if I had played straight-ahead in those days, Two Generations would not have had much to say. It was a great platform for learning and experimentation with the security of knowing that we could always end with Take 5 and get a standing ovation for Dan's amazing drum solos.[1]

Brubeck senior enjoyed the paradox of making his "hip" charges play on such material as the Swing era piece "Christopher Columbus," and his playing, infused with references to Fats Waller and Ellington, anchored the group and gave it a sense of historical perspective. Meanwhile, his new compositions, like "Circadian Dysrhythmia" and "Knives," were state-of-the-art pieces that, in this context, related obviously to the younger Brubecks' love of Chick Corea and the Brecker Brothers. These pieces contrasted with new versions of classics like "Blue Rondo à la Turk," "Three to Get Ready," "Unsquare Dance," and "It's a Raggy Waltz."

It was Russell Gloyd's idea to hook the rebirth of the Dave Brubeck Quartet around a star drummer, mirroring the rela-

---

1. Darius Brubeck, email to the author, July 10, 2019.

tionship between Brubeck and Morello in the classic quartet. Butch Miles had played with the Count Basie Orchestra, and the hookup with Brubeck was filled with promise. With Jerry Bergonzi playing tenor saxophone, the turbulence of a 1970s piece like "Truth" was replaced with joyful exuberance. Their album *Back Home* moved from the attractively tart dissonance of "Hometown Blues," cheekily quoting Barry Manilow, to a version of "Caravan" played at a crazy tempo.

But the combination of Bergonzi's Coltrane-toned tenor saxophone and Miles's swing drumming never quite added up; something had to give, and in 1982 Bergonzi left and was replaced by Bill Smith. Their 1984 album *For Iola* captures the group with Chris Brubeck and Randy Jones, one of Brubeck's best recordings. It opens with the Brubeck composition "Polly," which in its first bar hits a level of breathless intensity that most jazz performances end with. Smith's clarinet is shrill and piercing and makes Brubeck's devilishly clever, witty theme float over the bouncy rhythm section. The leader's piano is a perfect example of his later style. It begins with a strong hint of stride piano before typically Brubeckian, irregularly placed block chords appear and he builds a dialogue between them and the regularity of the stride material, pulling the listener two ways at once. Brubeck resolves this by means of a roaring tremolo figure that pervades the performance, leaving any feeling of time behind. As this figure takes hold, he reintroduces the stride piano ideas, and the result is a perfectly conceived and satisfying musical journey that plays on the structure of the tune and superimposes other ideas.

Bobby Militello's tenure in the group—he first appeared on a Brubeck album in 1991—coincided with a critical reassessment of Brubeck's playing: and given that, Militello could, if required, conjure up the ghost of Paul Desmond to perfection (a good example is "Waltzing" from the quartet's 1998 album *So What's*

*New?*), while also playing funky, fat blues or diving headfirst into abstraction, as Brubeck approached the end, Militello was the ideal saxophonist. His bluster and energy could take some of the weight off the ailing Brubeck's shoulders. In the months after Brubeck's Blue Note residency he continued to tour, and then, when his health ruled it out, he quietly slipped from view, without ceremony or fuss.

Brubeck had received America's top arts award, the Kennedy Center Honors, on December 6, 2009, which happened to coincide with his eighty-ninth birthday. Sitting alongside his fellow honorees—Mel Brooks, Grace Bumbry, Robert De Niro, and Bruce Springsteen—Brubeck listened to President Obama's citation, which included the memorable line, "You can't understand America without understanding jazz, and you can't understand jazz without understanding Dave Brubeck."

Brubeck had spent sixty years trying to make America understand jazz, and understand the importance of improvisation and that, paradoxically, great improvisation often came out of great composition. Musicians understood, or not, the very particular view he took of harmony and rhythm; music fans often found the sound of his music irresistible whether or not jazz was their thing; and America had watched as Brubeck had defied the evils of segregation. The idea of the Dave Brubeck Quartet encapsulated so much of what America was, its contradictions and problems. After Brubeck slipped quietly from public view, he continued to practice at home, and his days were cheered by visits from Militello, Moore, and Jones; they would eat, they would talk, they would play music. No one listened now, apart from themselves—that fifth member of the quartet, the audience, was no longer invited.

And when playing became too much and Brubeck entered his final months, he still derived immense pleasure from sharing meals with his family and friends. Herbie Hancock visited; Wynton Marsalis followed with a suggestion that his Jazz at Lincoln Center Orchestra mount a whole evening devoted to Brubeck's music. When Brubeck died on the morning of December 5, 2012, on his way to a cardiology appointment, numbing sadness was soon replaced by a peculiar feeling of celebration. Radio stations pumped out his music; YouTube was suddenly flooded with archival material as every television station in the US, apparently, dug out their interview with Brubeck, during which he patiently answered questions about "Take Five," *Time Out*, and 5/4 time. Because he had made such a difference to so many lives, Brubeck lived another day— his music set to endure for all time.

# ACKNOWLEDGMENTS

Writing a book, I've learnt, is a lonely business—my gratitude to all those people who managed to keep me sane and offered their unflinching support throughout the long process of bringing this project to fruition is boundless.

My agents, Cathryn Summerhayes in London and Daniel Kirschen in New York—hereafter known as Team Dan/Cath—were unwavering in their encouragement and enthusiasm. Cathryn started the process rolling by responding with near-indecent haste to my email asking for her help; Dan then weighed in with zeal and tenacity. Thank you both. At Da Capo Press, I'm grateful to my editor, Ben Schafer, for picking the project up, for his attention to detail and his considerable patience as I was finishing up the manuscript. Senior Project Editor Fred Francis is also a detail man, for whom nothing proves too much trouble. My copyeditor, Erin Granville, can spot a dangling modifier at a thousand paces and did an extraordinary job in helping to shepherd the book toward its final form—rescuing me from many embarrassing mistakes in the process.

At the University of the Pacific, deep in the bowels of the Holt-Atherton Collection, where the Brubeck archive was held until December 2019, Assistant Professor and Head of the Collections Michael Wurtz went out of his way to make me feel welcome—and was gracious enough to answer my many emails once I'd returned home. Nicole Grady, Special Collections Librarian, was also generous with her time and helped make my stay enjoyable and comfortable. Also at UoP, I'd like to thank Dean of Faculty Peter Witte and Program Director for Jazz Studies Patrick Langham for extending the warmest of welcomes. I was also very grateful to receive the 2017 Brubeck Collection Research Travel Grant, which helped facilitate my visit to California.

While in California, the afternoon I spent with Eugene Wright was a privilege. I would like to thank his friend Caroline Howard for graciously organizing my visit—and to Eugene himself for his wisdom and deep memories.

Writing this book meant removing myself from music journalism for two years, but almost every magazine and newspaper editor I've worked for has played their part by either commissioning a Brubeck article or caring enough about the book to keep in touch during my exile. *The Wire*'s Tony Herrington, Rob Young, Derek Walmsley, and Chris Bohn have been great friends. At *Gramophone*, Martin Cullingford, Andrew Mellor, Sarah Kirkup, David Threasher, James Inverne, and James McCarthy all let me write about Brubeck in their magazine; ditto John Evans and Emma Baker at *Classic FM* magazine, and Mike Flynn and Spencer Grady at *Jazzwise*. Imogen Tilden at *The Guardian* commissioned an RIP appreciation of Brubeck, and the sad duty of writing that piece helped clarify thoughts that ended up in this book. Thanks, too, to Neil Evans, then editor of *Classic CD* magazine, who commissioned me to interview Brubeck back in 1999—my first journalistic assignment. And also to Julian Haylock and Maggie Williams, who both commissioned Brubeck articles for *International Piano* magazine.

Chloe Cutts, a former editor at *International Piano*, read through some early versions of the opening chapters and offered many insightful comments. Louis Barfe, whom I've never met, was generous enough to appear in my DMs on Twitter one day with the enticing offer of archival footage of Brubeck from his own collection, which, little did he know, helped me resolve a particularly tricky research question. Thanks, also, to Jacob Slattery, who generously gave up a Sunday afternoon to photograph documents from the Teo Macero Papers at New York Public Library. John Bolger, who runs the davebrubeckjazz.com website, was also generous with his time and photographs. Olivia Horsfall Turner and William Whyte kindly offered up expertise about architectural history.

Other friends whose ideas and thoughts about jazz, and about the art of playing the piano, and about music in general, have bled into this book include Ian Pace, Dominic Alldis, Alexander Hawkins, Steve Beresford, Michael Finnissy, Robert Carter, Ben Watson, Mike and Kate Westbrook, Eddie Prévost, Steven Joerg, Christopher Fox, Karissa Krenz, Seymour Wright, Philip Thomas, Matthew Shipp, Neil Thomson, Jonathan Gee, Tony Kofi, Jean Martin, Elaine Mitchener, Tom Hall, Richard Steinitz, John Tilbury, and Alex Ward. Alexandra Coghlan was kind enough to respond to my email inquiry about singspiel as I was writing about *The Real Ambassadors.*

I would like to pay special tribute to the jazz writer and editor of the now-defunct *Jazz Review* magazine, Richard Cook, whose untimely death in 2007 robbed British music journalism of one of its sharpest minds. Richard was my journalistic mentor, and I still treasure his advice about the ethics of journalism and the art of writing, often delivered in laconic tones—"Phil, if you use 'pleasant' once more, you'll by reviewing Kenny G for the rest of the year." Although this book is far removed from the project I discussed with Richard all those years ago, his sense of what a Brubeck biography should encompass remains in these pages—I couldn't have written it without him. At the launch party for *Jazz Review*, in 1999, I met the music writer Andy Hamilton, whose good humor and salient counsel have been constants throughout my journalistic career. Andy was relentlessly encouraging as I wrote, always at the end of an email when I had a question—or needed a boost.

Thanks also to Jack Kerouac, E. L. Doctorow, Wallace Stevens, John Dos Passos, Don DeLillo, James Baldwin, Kurt Vonnegut, Ralph Ellison, and Philip Roth for being the go-to guys for chapter titles.

There are many Brubecks to thank. Darius Brubeck and his wife, Cathy, have been tireless in their support and patient to a fault as I squeezed them for information. Chris and Tish Brubeck, likewise, eagerly embraced the book and were happy to share their memories and information; Tish led me to William O. Smith, who, at ninety-two, responded immediately to my email and was happy to talk over the phone. An interview with Dan Brubeck helped as I thought about the latter half of Dave's career. Dave's drummer Randy Jones responded warmly to my email request for an interview but sadly died before we were able to meet. Thanks also to Russell Gloyd, Dave's manager, who has helped in many ways over the years, and to Dave's lawyer, Richard Jeweler, who helped track down information about missing tapes and initiated my meeting with Eugene Wright—and picked me up from Oakland Airport at an ungodly hour and drove me to the Brubecks' former house in the Oakland Hills and then to Concord.

Special thanks must, of course, be extended to Dave and Iola Brubeck, who responded with enthusiasm to the idea of a book and then indulged my constant requests for information—I regret they are not able to see the results. My life in music began with Brubeck's work, and his importance to my life has been incalculable.

One of the great lessons of Brubeck's career is the importance of family, and last but certainly not least, I must extend warm thanks and hugs to my own family. My mother, Eileen, who died in 2015, would have liked nothing better than to have held this book in her hands. She would have badgered all her friends to buy it and organized numerous celebratory dinners. Not a day goes by that I don't feel her loss keenly; love you forever, Mum. My father, Tony, started this whole thing off by playing *Time Out* constantly during my childhood and taking me to my first jazz concerts during my early teens. From him I learnt the discipline of creative work—get up early and keep on going; love always too—and to my sister, Louise, and niece, Darcy.

To my in-laws, Siamon and Lyndall Gordon, I owe a debt of gratitude that can never be repaid; it helped to have such a distinguished biographer as a mother-in-law, and Lyndall's guidance was invaluable. What can I say about my extraordinarily lovely wife, Olivia? She has kept the house going while writing a book of her own as I've been in my study sweating over the minutiae of harmonic sequences, release dates of albums, and obscure details of American history. Her resourcefulness, sage-like wisdom, and generosity of spirit are sources of constant inspiration. Our wonderful children, Humphrey and Lovell, have put up with their dad disappearing for hours at a time to write. Humph, the story about Dave and the rattlesnake—that's for you. Lovell made her father very proud when, during a café visit, she asked whether the background music was "Dave Brubeck music." Everybody in the room put their cups down in amazement. It was actually Miles's *Kind of Blue*—but nobody dared question the wisdom of a five-year-old. I love you all.

# DISCOGRAPHY

An exhaustive discography, listing every track Dave Brubeck recorded between 1946 and 2011, would fill a book at least twice the size of this one, but buy everything here and you'll have a complete collection of official releases with the occasional widely available bootleg, included here when the historical importance of the material makes it essential. This list does not include "best of" or "greatest hits" compilations; nor does it include the occasional "private" record issued by universities or other institutions as fund-raisers, with Brubeck's permission, normally after a quartet performance. A complete list of such Brubeck ephemera is available via www.davebrubeckjazz.com.

Generally records are listed with their original catalog number followed by the most desirable recent version on CD. Brubeck's Fantasy catalog represents a challenge for any discographer. The Weiss brothers reused album titles like *The Dave Brubeck Quartet* frequently, didn't keep a proper record of recording dates or venues, and mixed and matched live and studio recordings. So for Fantasy releases, I've noted the catalog numbers of CD reissues only. Brubeck's 1980s work for Concord coincided with CDs becoming the predominant format for recorded music; from the 1980s on I've included only the original CD catalog numbers.

## The Dave Brubeck Octet

*Dave Brubeck Octet* (Original Jazz Classics OJC 101)

## The Dave Brubeck Trio

*The Dave Brubeck Trio—Complete Recordings* (American Jazz Classics AJC 146919)

## Early Quartet and Solo Albums

*The Complete Storyville Broadcasts* [contains *Jazz at Storyville* with previously unreleased radio broadcasts] (Essential Jazz Classics EJC55654)
*Dave Brubeck / Paul Desmond* [contains material originally issued as *The Dave Brubeck Quartet* and *Jazz at Blackhawk*] (Fantasy FCD-24727-2)
*Jazz at Oberlin* (Original Jazz Classics 7231 9912)
*Brubeck & Desmond at Wilshire-Ebell* (Fresh Sound Records FSR-CD 426)
*Jazz at the College of the Pacific* (Original Jazz Classics OJC20 047-2)
*Jazz at the College of the Pacific Volume 2* (Fantasy OJCCD 1076 2)
*Dave Brubeck at Storyville: 1954* (Fresh Sound Records FSR-CD 414)
*At the Sunset Center, Carmel 1955* (Solar Records 4569973)
*At Pennsylvania State University 1955* (Solar Records 4569948)
*Jazz Goes to College* (Columbia CL 566 / Columbia Legacy 45149)
*Brubeck Time* (Columbia CL 622 / Columbia Legacy 750195)
*Jazz: Red Hot and Cool* (Columbia CL 699 / Columbia Legacy 61468)
*Brubeck Plays Brubeck* (Columbia CL 878 / Columbia Legacy 65722)
*Dave Brubeck and Jay & Kai at Newport* (Columbia CL 932; no CD reissue)
*Jazz Impressions of the USA* (Columbia CL 984 / Gambit Records 69308)
*Dave Brubeck Plays and Plays and Plays* (Fantasy 3259 / Original Jazz Classics OJCCD 716)
*Reunion* (Fantasy 3268 / Original Jazz Classics OJCCD 1502)
*Jazz Goes to Junior College* (Columbia CL 1034 / Essential Jazz Classics 55516)

## Classic Quartet Era

*Dave Digs Disney* (Columbia CL 1059 / Columbia Legacy 48820)
*The Dave Brubeck Quartet in Europe* (Columbia CL 1168 / Columbia Legacy 9529)
*Newport 1958* (Columbia CL 1249 / Gambit 69322)
*Jazz Impressions of Eurasia* (Columbia CS 8058 / Columbia Legacy 48531)
*Gone with the Wind* (Columbia CS 8156 / Columbia Legacy 40627)

*Time Out* (Columbia CS 8192 / Columbia Legacy 739852)

*Southern Scene* (Columbia CS 8239 / Sony 9363)

*The Riddle* [with Bill Smith] (Columbia CL 1454 / CD reissued paired with *Southern Scene* Solar Records 4569872)

*Brubeck and Rushing* (Columbia CL 1553 / Columbia Legacy 65727)

*Bernstein Plays Brubeck Plays Bernstein* (Columbia CS 8257 / Essential Jazz Classics EJC55487)

*Brubeck à la Mode* [with Bill Smith] (Fantasy 3301 / Original Jazz Classics 200 2)

*Tonight Only!* [with Carmen McRae] (Columbia CS 8409 / American Jazz Classics 99027)

*Near Myth* [with Bill Smith] (Fantasy 3319 / Original Jazz Classics 236)

*Witches Brew* [with Bill Smith] (unreleased)

*Time Further Out* (Columbia CS 8490 / Columbia Legacy 64668)

*Brandenburg Gate: Revisited* (Columbia CS 8763 / Columbia Legacy 65725)

*The White House Sessions, Live 1962* [with Tony Bennett] (Columbia Legacy 88883718042)

*Take Five Live* [with Carmen McRae] (Columbia CS 9116 / Sony 9370)

*The Real Ambassadors* [with Louis Armstrong, Carmen McRae, and Lambert, Hendricks & Ross] (Columbia OL 5850 / Columbia Legacy 57663)

*Countdown—Time in Outer Space* (Columbia CS 8575 / Columbia Legacy 86405)

*Bossa Nova USA* (Columbia 8789 / Sony 9364)

*Brubeck in Amsterdam* (Columbia CS 9897 / Sony 5027677)

*At Carnegie Hall* (Columbia C2S 826 / Columbia Legacy 61455)

*Time Changes* (Columbia CS 8927 / Columbia Legacy 7843452)

*Jazz Impressions of Japan* (Columbia CS 9012 / Columbia Legacy 65726)

*Jazz Impressions of New York* (Columbia CS 9075 / Sony 723813)

*Dave Brubeck in Berlin* (CBS 62578 / Columbia 9530)

*Angel Eyes* (Columbia CS 9148 / Sony 9368)

*My Favorite Things* (Columbia CS 9237 / Sony 9369)

*Time In* (Columbia CS 9312 / Sony 4746352)

*Anything Goes: The Dave Brubeck Quartet Plays Cole Porter* (Columbia CS 9402 / Sony 1011)

*Jackpot!* (Columbia CS 9512 / Sony 5027625)

*Bravo! Brubeck!* (Columbia CS 9495 / Columbia Legacy 65723)

*Buried Treasures* (Columbia CK65777)

*The Last Time We Saw Paris* (Columbia CS 9672)

*Live at the Kurhaus 1967* (Fondamenta 1704025)
*Their Last Time Out: The Unreleased Live Concert, December 26, 1967*
(Columbia / Legacy 88697 81562 2)

## The Dave Brubeck Trio featuring Gerry Mulligan

*Compadres* (Columbia CS 9704 / no CD reissue)
*Blues Roots* (Columbia CS 9749 / Sony SICP 4256)
*Brubeck/Mulligan/Cincinnati* (Decca DL 710181 / MCA Classics MCAD-42347)
*Live at the Berlin Philharmonie* (CBS S 67261 / Columbia Legacy KC32143)
*The Last Set at Newport* (Atlantic SD 1607)
*We're All Together Again for the First Time* [with Paul Desmond] (Atlantic 1641-2)

## Sacred Works (Late 1960s / Early 1970s)

*The Light in the Wilderness* (Decca DXSA 7202)
*The Gates of Justice* [1969 performance] (Decca 710175)
*The Gates of Justice* [2004 performance] (Naxos 8.559414)
*Truth Is Fallen* (Atlantic ATL 40 367 / Atlantic 7567 80761 2)
*La Fiesta de la Posada* (CBS IM 36662 / Columbia Legacy CK 64669)

## Other 1970s

*Two Generations of Brubeck* (Atlantic SD 1645 / Wounded Bird Records 1645)
*All the Things We Are* (Atlantic SD 1684 / Atlantic 7567 81399 2)
*Two Generations of Brubeck: Brother, the Great Spirit Made Us All* (Atlantic SD 1660 / CD reissue paired with *Truth Has Fallen* Collectables 6403)
*Two Generations of Brubeck: Live at the Apollo Theater, NY, 1973* (Hi Hat 3091—mislabelled as being by Two Generations and the Dave Brubeck Quartet)
*1975: The Duets* [with Paul Desmond] (A&M SP 703 / Horizon 828 394 915-2)
*The Dave Brubeck Quartet: 25th Anniversary Reunion* (A&M SP-714 / A&M 396 998-2)
*The New Brubeck Quartet: Live at Montreux* (Tomato 7018 / Tomato 2029)
*The New Brubeck Quartet: A Cut Above* (Direct-Disk 106 / no CD reissue)

## The Concord Records Era

*Back Home* (Concord 4103)

*Tritonis* (Concord 4129)
*Paper Moon* (Concord 4178)
*Concord on a Summer Night* (Concord 4198)
*Aurex Jazz Festival 1982* (Somethin' Else 8021)
*For Iola* (Concord 4259)
*Reflections* (Concord 4299)
*Blue Rondo* (Concord 4317)
*Moscow Night* (Concord 4353)
*Marian McPartland's Piano Jazz with Guest Dave Brubeck* (Jazz Alliance 12001)
*Dave Brubeck in Moscow* (Melodiya 60 00700)

## The MusicMasters Era

*New Wine* [with Montreal International Jazz Festival Orchestra and Russell Gloyd] (Limelight 820 830 2)
*Quiet as the Moon* (MusicMasters Jazz 01612 65067 2)
*Once When I Was Very Young* (Limelight 844 298 2)
*Trio Brubeck* (Limelight 844 337 2)
*Luminescene—Kool Jazz at Midem* [with B. B. King] (TKO Magum CDMT 503)

## The Telarc Era

*Late Night Brubeck: Live from the Blue Note* (Telarc 83345)
*Nightshift: Live from the Blue Note* (Telarc 83351)
*Just You, Just Me* (Telarc 83363)
*In Their Own Sweet Way* (Telarc 83355)
*Young Lions & Old Tigers* (Telarc 83349)
*To Hope! A Celebration* [with vocal soloists / Cathedral Choral Society Chorus and Orchestra / Gloyd] (Telarc 80430)
*A Dave Brubeck Christmas* (Telarc 83410)
*So What's New?* (Telarc 83434)
*Double Live from the USA & UK* (Telarc 83400)
*The 40th Anniversary Tour of the UK* (Telarc 83440)
*80th Birthday Concert: Live with the LSO* [with London Symphony Orchestra / Gloyd] (LSO Live LSO0011)
*One Alone* (Telarc 83510)
*The Crossing* (Telarc 83520)
*Brubeck in Chattanooga* (Choral Arts Society of Chattanooga 150)
*Park Avenue South* (Telarc 83570)

*Classical Brubeck* [with vocal soloists / London Symphony Orchestra / Gloyd] (Telarc 80621)
*Private Brubeck Remembers* (Telarc 83605)
*London Flat, London Sharp* (Telarc 83625)
*Brubeck Meets Bach* [with Bach Collegium Munich / Gloyd] (Sony Classical 88697060322)
*Songs* [with John De Haan, tenor, and Jan Giering-DeHaan, soprano] (Naxos 8.559220)
*Indian Summer* (Telarc 83670)
*Triple Play: Live at Zankel Music Center* [Dave Brubeck guesting with Chris Brubeck's group] (Blue Forest Records BFR-TP 11003)

## Compilations

*Summit Sessions* (Columbia C 30522): Released in 1971, as Brubeck's relationship with Columbia was coming to an end, this compilation mixes previously available material (with Leonard Bernstein, Carmen McRae, Jimmy Rushing, and Louis Armstrong) with unheard material by the "classic" quartet, the Dave Brubeck Trio with Gerry Mulligan, Tony Bennett, Palghat Raghu, Bill Crofut and Steve Addiss, Thelonious Monk, Darius Brubeck, Peter Paul, & Mary, and Charles Mingus.

*50 Years of Dave Brubeck: Live at the Monterey Jazz Festival 1958–2007* (Monterey Jazz Festival Records MUFR 30680): Beginning with the "classic" quartet in 1958 and moving through the group with Gerry Mulligan and the later quartets with Bill Smith and Bobby Militello, this album documents Brubeck's relationship with Monterey, one of his favorite places to play. Contains a guest appearance by bassist Christian McBride.

# BIBLIOGRAPHY

The most primary of all primary sources documenting the career, music, and thinking of Dave Brubeck is the vast archive of letters, writings, newspaper and magazine articles/reviews, sheet music, photographs, and recordings known as "the Brubeck Collection." From 1999 to December 2019 the Collection was held at the University of the Pacific as part of the Holt-Atherton Special Collection. At the time of writing, the collection has been taken in-house by the Brubeck family and announcements concerning its future will be made via www.brubecklivinglegacy .com. I also drew on letters and other material from the Teo Macero Collection held at New York Public Library. Darius and Chris Brubeck also responded to many questions by email, footnoted as appropriate.

Alkyer, Frank (editor). *The Miles Davis Reader.* New York: Hal Leonard Books, 2007.

Biss, Eula. *Notes From No Man's Land.* London: Fitzcarraldo Editions, 2017.

Bryant, Clora/Collette, Buddy/Green, Willian (editors). *Central Avenue Sounds: Jazz in Los Angeles.* Oakland: University of California Press, 1999.

Carr, Ian. *Keith Jarrett: The Man and His Music.* Boston: Da Capo Press, 1992.

Churchwell, Sarah. *Behold, America: A History of America First and the American Dream.* London: Bloomsbury, 2018.

Collier, James Lincoln. *Louis Armstrong: An American Genius.* New York: Oxford University Press, 1985.

Cook, Richard. *Richard Cook's Jazz Encyclopedia.* London: Penguin Books, 2005.

Crouch, Stanley. *Kansas City Lightning: The Rise and Times of Charlie Parker.* New York: Harper Collins, 2013.

Crow, Bill. *From Birdland to Broadway: Scenes from a Jazz Life.* New York: Oxford University Press, 1992.

Daniels, Douglas H. *Lester Leaps In: The Life and Times of Lester Young.* Boston: Beacon Press, 2003.

DeVeaux, Scott. *The Birth of Bebop: A Social and Musical History.* London: Picador, 2000.

Firestone, Ross. *Swing, Swing, Swing: The Life Times of Benny Goodman.* New York: W. W. Norton, 1993.

Gavin, James. *Deep in a Dream: The Long Night of Chet Baker.* New York: Welcome Rain Publishers, 2002.

Hall, Fred M. *It's About Time: The Dave Brubeck Story.* Fayetteville: University of Arkansas Press, 1996.

Hamilton, Andy. *Lee Konitz: Conversations on the Improviser's Art.* Ann Arbor: University of Michigan Press, 2007.

Harrison, Max/Thacker, Eric/Nicholson, Stuart. *The Essential Jazz Records: Modernism to Post Modernism.* London: Mansell Publishing Limited, 2000.

Horricks, Raymond (editor). *These Jazzmen of our Time.* London: Victor Gollancz, 1960.

Howland, John. *Ellington Uptown: Duke Ellington, James P. Johnson and the Birth of Concert Jazz.* Ann Arbor: University of Michigan Press, 2009.

Jack, Gordon. *Fifties Jazz Talk: An Oral Retrospective.* Lanham, Maryland: Scarecrow Press, 2004.

Jost, Ekkehard. *Free Jazz.* Boston: Da Capo Press, 1994.

Kaplan, Fred. *1959: The Year That Changed Everything.* Hoboken, New Jersey: John Wiley & Sons, 2009.

Kelley, Robin D. G. *Thelonious Monk: The Life and Times of an American Original.* New York: Free Press, 2009.

Lester, James. *Too Marvelous for Words: The Life & Genius of Art Tatum.* New York: Oxford University Press, 1994.

Litweiler, John. *Ornette Coleman: A Harmolodic Life.* Boston: Da Capo Press, 1994.

Lock, Graham. *Forces in Motion: The Music and Thoughts of Anthony Braxton.* Boston: Da Capo Press, 1989.

Lomax, Alan. *Mister Jelly Roll.* Berkeley: University of California Press, 2001.

McPartland, Marian. *All in Good Time.* Champaign, Illinois: University of Illinois Press, 2005.

Milhaud, Darius (translated by Donald Evans, George Hall and Christopher Palmer). *My Happy Life.* London: Marion Boyars, 1995.

Novello, John. *The Contemporary Keyboardist.* New York: Hal Leonard Corporation, 2000.

Pavlić, Ed. *Who Can Afford to Improvise? James Baldwin and Black Music, the Lyric and the Listeners.* New York: Fordham University Press, 2015.

Pettinger, Peter. *Bill Evans: How My Heart Sings.* New Haven, Connecticut: Yale University Press, 1998.

Pleasants, Henry. *Serious Music and All That Jazz.* New York: Simon & Schuster, 1971.

Porter, Lewis. *John Coltrane: His Life and Music.* Ann Arbor: University of Michigan Press, 2000.

Ramsey, Doug. *Take Five: The Public and Private Lives of Paul Desmond.* Seattle, Washington: Parkside Publications, 2005.

Rattenbury, Ken. *Duke Ellington, Jazz Composer.* New Haven, Connecticut: Yale University Press, 1990.

Reich, Howard/Gaines, William M. *Jelly's Blues: The Life, Music, and Redemption of Jelly Roll Morton.* Boston: Da Capo Press, 1996.

Reilly, Jack. *The Harmony of Dave Brubeck.* Milwaukee, Wisconsin: Hal Leonard Books, 2013.

Robinson, Perry (with Wetzel, Florence F). *The Traveler.* San Jose: Writers Club Press, 2002.

Russell, George. *The Lydian Chromatic Concept of Tonal Organization for Improvisation.* New York: Concept Publishing, 1959.

Russell, Ross. *Bird Lives! The High Life and Hard Times of Charlie (Yardbird) Parker.* Boston: Da Capo Press, 1996.

Sachs, Joel. *Henry Cowell: A Man Made of Music.* New York: Oxford University Press, 2012.

Santoro, Gene. *Myself When I Am Real: The Life and Music of Charles Mingus.* New York: Oxford University Press, 2000.

Saul, Scott. *Freedom Is, Freedom Ain't: Jazz and the Making of the Sixties.* Boston: Harvard University Press, 2005.

Shapiro, Nat/Hentoff, Nat. *Hear Me Talkin' to Ya.* New York: Dover Publications, 1966.

Shearing, George (with Shipton, Alyn). *Lullaby of Birdland.* London, Continuum Press, 2005.

Shim, Eunmi. *Lennie Tristano: His Life in Music.* Ann Arbor, Michigan: University of Michigan Press, 2007.

Sinclair, Iain. *American Smoke: Journeys to the End of the Light.* London: Hamish Hamilton, 2013.

Storb, Ilse/Fischer, Klaus G. *Dave Brubeck, Improvisations and Compositions: The Idea of Cultural Exchange.* Oxford: Peter Lang Inc, 1994.

Stravinsky, Igor. *An Autobiography.* New York: Simon & Schuster, 1936.

Stravinsky, Igor. *Poetics of Music: In the Form of Six Lessons.* Cambridge, Massachusetts: Harvard University Press, 1970.

Szwed, John. *So What: The Life of Miles Davis.* London: Arrow Books, 2002.

Teachout, Terry. *Pops: A Life of Louis Armstrong.* Boston: Houghton Mifflin Harcourt, 2009.

Tyson, Timothy B. *The Blood of Emmett Till.* New York: Simon & Schuster, 2017.

Walsh, Stephen. *Stravinsky: The Second Exile; France and America 1934-1971.* London: Jonathan Cape, 2006.

Watson, Ben. *Derek Bailey and the Story of Free Improvisation.* London: Verso, 2004.

# INDEX

# Index